Engendering the Fall

Engendering the Fall

John Milton and Seventeenth-Century Women Writers

SHANNON MILLER

PENN

University of Pennsylvania Press

Philadelphia

Published by
University of Pennsylvania Press
Philadelphia, Pennsylvania 19104-4112

Printed in the United States of America on acid-free paper

10 9 8 7 6 5 4 3 2 1

A Cataloging-in-Publication record is available from the Library of Congress

ISBN 978-0-8122-4086-3

To Richard Helgerson
An inspiring scholar, a wonderful mentor, a valued friend

Contents

Introduction: Rethinking the Practices of Influence, Intertextuality, and (Modern) Subjectivities

On February 24, 2004, at the height of the debate over gay marriage, President George W. Bush described marriage, for him necessarily between a man and woman, as "the most fundamental institution of civilization." In identifying this individual relationship as the foundational cornerstone for culture, Bush recalls the language of both John Locke and the most representative proponent of monarchy in the seventeenth century, Sir Robert Filmer: both men positioned marriage as a primary element in understanding and modeling social organization. In Locke's *Second Treatise of Government*, the "first society" is defined as "between Man and Wife," while Filmer identifies the "original grant of government" as the moment when Adam acquired the right "to rule over his wife" (*Limited or Mixed Monarchy*, 138). This continuity stretching from the mid-seventeenth to the twenty-first century underscores the broader point argued by Carole Pateman in her *Sexual Contract*: the domestic relationship between men and women remains the basis for governmental organization, as well as—according to Bush—"civilization" itself. Western "political theory" as a category of thought could be said to emerge in the seventeenth century, that moment when thinkers were focusing on the terms of political organization, its association with property ownership, and individuals' involvement in the formation of the state, usually through the language of contract.[1] Yet its "beginnings" are not achieved through a distancing from this biblical narrative; instead, the cornerstone for discussing the "first society" and the act of marriage constituting that society is the tale of Adam and Eve, whether in the thinking of Filmer, the writings of Locke, or the worldview of George W. Bush.

The language of the "first" domestic "society" and the beginnings of a more recognizably "political" or public one are unified through contract theory, in particular the substantive parallels—but also the important distinctions—between the marriage and the political contract. The shared and distinct traits of these two forms of contract are central to understanding Locke's views on legitimate government, and they have received sustained attention from Locke scholars, feminist critics of the liberal subject and of social contract theory, and literary critics.[2] For, a major debate raged throughout seventeenth-century England over the terms upon which one could claim political legitimacy. Theorists who supported monarchy, a body of thought often called "patriarchalist," turned explicitly to the foundational narratives of the Garden of Eden and the relationship between Adam and Eve to justify governmental authority: thus for Robert Filmer, the "original grant of government" is modeled by, because an extension of, the right of a husband to rule over his wife.[3] In what has often been presented as an alternative narrative of the organization of the state—in the hands of Hobbes perhaps an areligious narrative, in the hands of Locke a burgeoningly secular one—major seventeenth-century political theorists modified the metaphors that described governmental organization, drawing upon states of "war" or states of "nature" to construct an originary moment at which the contract between subject and sovereign was created.

Yet, whether supporting monarchy or a republican-style government, the grounding narrative of the Garden of Eden infused seventeenth-century thought through to the end of the century. Engaging this "foundational" relationship between gendered interpersonal and governmental organization, *Engendering the Fall* engages a body of texts produced in England during the century that all (re)plot the story of the Garden. The book sets culturally significant texts on political organization in dialogue with a series of writings by women and the period's most important poetic rendering of the Fall, John Milton's *Paradise Lost*: my goal is to illustrate how significant gender was within accounts of social and political organization, and how the Garden narrative plots gender's importance in that organization. This multidirectional and multilayered "conversation" between numerous seventeenth-century women and Milton's Genesis epic thus crystallizes the interplay between the narrative of the Fall, the organization of political structures, and the extent to which both are shaped by cultural debates over women.

The category of gender thus frames this debate while women in this project become active interlocutors of the relationship between governmental organization and gendered roles. On either side of Milton's epic, women are authoring texts that are influencing or are influenced by *Paradise Lost*. Early and mid-seventeenth century texts authored by women, I argue, influenced Milton's portrait of Eve, Milton's account of the gendered spheres of activity open to Adam and Eve, and the character of Milton's epic voice. In later seventeenth-century texts that return to and revise Milton's portrait of the Garden and the Fall, these female-authored texts explore the same matrix of governmental organization and of gender at the core of the political thought of Robert Filmer, Thomas Hobbes, and John Locke. My intersection of these literary acts of retelling Genesis with the political theory of Filmer and Locke suggests that the Garden narrative offered compensation to, and for, the political and psychic unconscious of the later seventeenth century: having experienced the decimation of English political and social culture as a result of the Civil War, many late seventeenth-century writers might well have found the story of all human origins a comforting opportunity through which to re-imagine and reconstruct a political and social world wrenched apart by violence. Additionally, by building domestic and political order from the originary story of Genesis, these narratives are formulating the very ground of what we have come to call "modern" political theory. Further, as the opening of the introduction suggests, these ideas become embedded into the notion of the family as the core institution still shaping our thinking today.

In addition to locating women writers within debates about gender's role in governmental theories, this project simultaneously reconsiders issues of canonicity while rethinking the methodology of literary influence. This project analyzes exchanges between Milton and such writers as Aemilia Lanyer, Rachel Speght, Lucy Hutchinson, Margaret Cavendish, Aphra Behn, and Mary Astell. Building in part on the rich "recovery" projects of women-authored texts undertaken over the past two decades, *Engendering the Fall* draws published writings of women back into a literary canon from which they became gradually expelled. Yet the light cast onto these writers has, in too many studies, considered them in isolation from the major male writers of the period.[4] With a few exceptions, the attempts to offer access to these writers has conjectured a literary tradition, one at times shaped by an ideology of an anachronistic notion of sisterhood. This furtive effort to articulate a distinct female tradition of writing, one emblematized by the deployment of Virginia Woolf's Judith Shakespeare mythology, tended to mute, rather than explore, the sustained intertextuality of male and female writers throughout the Renaissance.[5] Resistant, understandably, to appear to classify women writers as only dim shadows of major canonical figures, explorations of influence have tended not to characterize the growing body of secondary work on Renaissance women writers.[6] And with very few exceptions, there has been little suggestion that these women would have been an influence on the major male figures who, through much of the twentieth century, came to define the literary canon. Placing male and female writers within a dialogue, what I am calling a "conversation," also has the advantage of integrating women and male writers into a richer map of early modern literary traditions.

This book is in part an attempt to address these shortcomings in the secondary material, but simultaneously to allow a rethinking of the methodology of "influence." Taking my cue from Joseph Wittreich's *Feminist Milton*, in which he argues that women in the eighteenth century saw Milton as much more sympathetic to their intellectual concerns than twentieth-century readers might imagine, I have juxtaposed Milton, in particular his *Paradise Lost*, with seventeenth-century women poets, polemicists, and (proto) novelists. The oft-cited influence of Milton's divorce tracts on Mistress Attaway, the Civil War-era Fifth Monarchist who saw Milton's justifications for divorce as freeing her from the marital bond, positions her as one of a large number of seventeenth-century women who engaged Milton's writings.[7] Wittreich concluded, in light of the reception of *Paradise Lost* in the eighteenth century, that Milton was "of Eve's party and knows it full well" (98); the revisionary view of literary history provided by *Feminist Milton* argues that "Milton's early female readership [were] rising up against the patriarchal tradition of Scripture," and saw "Milton himself as an ally in, not antagonist to, such an enterprise" (7). As does John Shawcross, whose discussion of late seventeenth- and early eighteenth-century women writers complements Wittreich's longer project, both critics tend to see the responses of women in the hundred years after the publication of *Paradise Lost* as countering recent feminist readings of Milton. In recent articles, Wittreich has even conjectured that Milton "is at the forefront of an English tradition of male feminism" ("John," 24).

My conclusion about this "conversation" between the multiple texts in *Engendering the Fall* is perhaps less monologic than the conclusions in Wittreich's and Shawcross's projects. I have differently constituted the map of influence, allowing for both influences onto as well as influences exerted by Milton. In that exchange, we see some writers highlighting Milton's conservative views of women, while other writers employ *Paradise Lost* to engage, in Wittreich's term, "conflicts with" as well as revisions to patriarchy ("John," 24). I accomplish this by revising the traditional narrative of influence, in which a canonical figure is either appropriated by later major figures (the Bloomian configuration of influence) or effects an unshakable pressure onto later writers. Instead, by positioning Milton's *Paradise Lost* at the center of a variety of texts, this "influence" study reconsiders the directions in which fluid cultural and literary influences can flow, the forms in which intertextuality can become refracted through a major text like *Paradise Lost*, and the constitutive effects of such a methodology. I am arguing that the influence of Milton onto women writers needs to be considered in concert with the influences that women writers of the seventeenth century exerted onto Milton and *Paradise Lost*. The consequence is a much more multifaceted view of *Paradise Lost* as embedded in gender debates of the seventeenth century; those debates exert—through the influence of early seventeenth-century texts by women—pressure onto Milton that continues to resonate through Milton's major poem in the final decades of the seventeenth century.

I am thus suggesting that *Paradise Lost*, whose influence on late seventeenth-century women writers such as Lucy Hutchinson, Mary Chudleigh, Aphra Behn, and Mary Astell can be well supported, was also internalizing aspects of debates over gendered culpability, the portrait of Eve, and the narrative of the Fall recorded in early seventeenth century texts. The intellectual and methodological lines of this project—the role of influence and intertextuality, the multiplicity of interpretations opened up by redefining the "directions" of a traditional "influence" study, and the intersection between gender and governance—emerge in seven chapters and a conclusion that follows these issues into Locke's *Two Treatises of Government*. I have organized the book into three sections that allow such variegated forms of influence to emerge. The sections of the book are arranged chronologically. Part I, Pretexts, examines *Paradise Lost* in relation to texts produced in the 1610s. Part II, Contexts, considers mid-century texts, including those produced by female prophets in the 1640s and 1650s, Lucy Hutchinson's *Order and Disorder*, which was produced in close temporal proximity to *Paradise Lost*, and Margaret Cavendish's *Blazing World*, published essentially simultaneously to Milton's poem. Part III, Influences, discusses texts—by Aphra Behn, Mary Chudleigh, and Mary Astell—produced in the 1680s and 1690s.

These categories do not indicate a slavish commitment to chronology: these groupings of texts reflect distinct social conflicts and gender's role in these conflicts throughout the seventeenth century. Part I considers how texts produced out of an anti-feminist tradition in the early seventeenth century—the moment when women became interlocutors in this debate—reframed elements of the story of the Fall to which Milton needed to respond. Part II considers texts—whether by Civil War female sectarians, the defeated Republican Lucy Hutchinson, or the Royalist supporter Margaret Cavendish—engaged with the events in or the aftermath of the English Civil War. Part III considers texts produced after the Exclusion Crisis, with most produced after the "Glorious Revolution": the issue of authority in marriage came to the forefront of political discussions at this historical moment because of Queen Mary's complex relation to both the throne of England and her husband. This wide range of literary and cultural texts that exert influence on *Paradise Lost* or engage Milton's epic are thus simultaneously laying the foundation for discussions about familial and political modes of organization, illustrating how an analogy such as that of the family and the state became encoded into retellings of the Garden story.[8]

The chapters in *Engendering the Fall* thus consider how traces of gender debates in the early seventeenth century, encoded within *Paradise Lost*, become revived in alternate forms in the last years of the decade. A central reconfiguration of the practices of influence, then, is that of the generative power of traces in one text that will resonate in a second text. What Shawcross calls metalepsis or transumption, the echo in an earlier writer's work that appears, possibly unconsciously, within a later writer's work, can span multiple, not just a pair of, texts. Driven by ideological ruptures, *Paradise Lost* could encode early seventeenth-century negotiations of gendered representations of Edenic events, only to have these parallel—if now modified—concerns refracted into late seventeenth-century texts. The representations of Eve in responses to Joseph Swetnam's anti-feminist tract become internalized into Milton's portrait of Eve, later drawing Astell toward the image of the solitary Eve that becomes so prominent in her late seventeenth-century political and philosophical writings. Aemilia Lanyer's mystical view of the crucifixion and the surveying position offered to her female patron draw Milton's attention; he considers the dangers of, and the complex gendering of, perspective, voyeurism, and the gaze in *Paradise Lost*.

This emphasis on visual perspective becomes a central component of *Paradise Lost* that Mary Chudleigh engages; she rewrites central aspects of gender within her re-imagination of the Fall narrative, one heavily influenced by Milton's epic. This process of interpretive recursiveness, in which the traces of earlier negotiations by *Paradise Lost* draw significant, if divergent, responses from later writers, imagines influence as an ever-widening circle, not a singularly directed flow. The multilayered intertextuality that occurs between and through these texts charts for us ebbs and flows, redirected currents, mini-whirlpools, and consequent unpredictability. Unlike the dominant line of influence usually constructed, charting a single directional flow of one text that imprints onto another, this narrative and dynamic process of influence needs to be seen instead like that of a tapestry, many strands of individual thread producing a pattern only observable from a distance.

This complex intellectual process called influence also forces a reconsideration of many of the central tenets that have marked literary criticism, including notions of authorial "intent," the agency of literary producers, and the resulting balance between the ideological "influences" shaping writers and the mechanisms for creating literary texts.

One reason that influence studies has become a part of an older and largely devalued style of literary criticism is the seeming necessity to assert instrumentality when engaging a source text. While the psychoanalytic model shaping Harold Bloom's anxiety of influence theory presumes an agonistic relationship with a former—often Miltonic!—source, one shaped by the unconscious oedipal narrative, the haunted author is also offered some agency in the choice of the intertextual encounter. Since the methodological explanation for such textual engagements presumes a fully conscious or at least a semiconscious use of a source text, it is hard to imagine any sustained theory of influence denying that an author engages another text or body of texts without any awareness of its shaping effect. That level of presumed conscious engagement has the effect of revitalizing the very "author" so effectively laid to rest by Michael Foucault and much poststructuralist criticism.[9] Furthermore, such a conscious or semiconscious engagement of texts implies the kind of control over the sources of literary production that theories about the cultural production of texts consider highly suspect. The process of being shaped by ideological forces, a critical truism of most major critical movements of the last two decades, necessitated that the (cultural) text or body of texts that interpolated a writer imprint upon him or her without any conscious awareness of that writer.

What influence studies after poststructuralist theory must do is complicate the matrix of what we have identified as the "author" in theoretical approaches deployed before and after postmodern criticism. A more sustained consideration of influence can grant to writers their choice to engage a particular set of texts or a singular poem, as in the case of *Paradise Lost*. Yet it can intersect such "choices" with cultural impulses that still help to shape, if they do not overdetermine, the terms of and the engagement with influencing texts. Rather than lay "the author" to rest, then, we need instead to more fully interrogate, blurring while also crossing, the lines that demarcate "conscious" and "unconscious" engagements with texts.

In pursuit of a new methodology of influence, *Engendering the Fall* offers a range or continuum of levels of conscious manipulation of a "source" text which will take different forms with different authors and texts. In Chapter 4, Lucy Hutchinson's engagement with *Paradise Lost*, one in which she seeks to correct what she perceives as problems in Milton's Genesis epic, occurs largely on the conscious level. Simultaneously, though, her and Milton's interpolations of Genesis are directed by the cultural forces of gender ideology. Additionally, Hutchinson is negotiating the implications of her own previous translation of a classical, if atheistic, text, through her knowledge of discourses of political theory in the period; such knowledge of texts and anxiety about her own involvement in translation operate both within and without her artistic control. Such an intertextual examination of a text balances moments of overt control or authorial choice with aspects of ideological overdetermination.

I would position the material in Chapter 3, "Milton Among the Prophets," as narrating the process in reverse: an un- or subconscious engagement with texts allows Milton to establish a particular kind of voice at a time of intense political danger. Milton's knowledge of female prophets in the period, negotiated by his "cultural subconscious," provides him an opportunity to produce an encoded, post-Restoration critique of kingship. Mary Chudleigh traverses between conscious and unconscious engagements with and manipulation(s) of her source text. Chudleigh actively and consistently gestures to Milton in prose and verse as she integrates *Paradise Lost* into her own poetry as a "source." Yet Chudleigh's reconfiguration of the Fall, a complex negotiation of the language of gazing that allowed her to resist certain cultural assertions about marriage and gender roles, overtly rewrites *Paradise Lost* while simultaneously adopting, largely unconsciously, the late seventeenth-century characterization of Milton as a political rebel.

Consequently, revisiting the methodology of "influence" in concert with the dominant critical paradigm of new historicism or cultural studies exposes the interdependence between conscious authorial control and culturally determined theories of literary and cultural production.[10] Influence studies, then, allows us, even prompts us, to return to a discussion of the many mechanisms of artistic creation. It forces us to unpack the assumptions about where instrumentality ends and when ideological and cultural discourses frame, even comprise, aspects of literary texts. Further, it necessitates that we identify the limits to such framing ideological forces. Into this critical morass any influence study must enter.

Both in terms of material and methodology, *Engendering the Fall* has a similar project in mind: the integration of and "conversation" between the writings by men and women in conjunction with a productive revision of approaches to their texts. This is particularly true of interpretations of gender in *Paradise Lost* and the range of seventeenth-century texts in this project. By positioning Milton's poetic text in the company of noncanonical women writers, alternative representations of Eve, the Fall, and the implications for social and political order can emerge. The result of placing a myriad of alternative texts in conversation with Milton's Genesis epic, intersecting the noncanonical and the canonical, consequently creates a productive frisson of interpretive options. Differently framing Milton's poem, then, is a major goal of this book, which sets out to expand that frame to include texts proceeding and following the publication of *Paradise Lost*. Much as Joseph Wittreich attempted to reposition certain "truisms" of Milton by contextualizing the poem amid its early reception, I too see the active interplay between *Paradise Lost* and the poetry and prose of various writers shifting the terms of debates about Milton. The most significant act of critical reframing within this project is my argument that certain female writers, or bodies of texts authored by or marked as by women, influenced Milton's poetry. Following from but extending the suggestive connections noted by critics like Kari McBride, John Ulreich, and Desma Polydorou, these first three chapters in *Engendering the Fall* consequently reposition the terms of Milton's connection to and engagement with both women and the categories of gender.

While I differently frame *Paradise Lost* amid seventeenth-century women's voices, my project is explicitly framed by methodological issues in and approaches from feminist criticism. Obviously, this has shaped my choices of noncanonical works set into conversation with Milton. Setting Milton amid these women writers, and thus instigating an alternative set of perspectives onto Milton's views of women and gender, has allowed me to intervene into the body of Milton criticism engaged with the question of gender since the 1970s. The debate over gender in the secondary material on Milton has been shaped by critics such as Barbara Lewalski, Diane McColley, and James Turner on one side, arguing for the progressive treatment of Eve and of marriage, and critics such as Mary Nyquist and Christine Froula, who emphasize the conservative, even misogynistic, representation of gender in the poem.

What multiple contexts for considering the problem of gender in Milton and these many writers do is highlight how *Paradise Lost* refuses to answer this question repeatedly posed within the criticism: is Milton conservative or progressive over issues of gender? Importantly, the consequence of considering Milton amid this series of less canonical writers resists answering this question. The structure of this study thus highlights the richness, the multiplicity, and ultimately the inconclusivity of *Paradise Lost* when viewed through an alternate lens. In this way, I see this book as in keeping with the indeterminacy in what Peter Herman has called the "New Milton Criticism"[11]; the very structure of *Engendering the Fall* can thus map what Joseph Wittreich has elsewhere described as the "dialogic rather than monologic" nature of the poem which can serve as a "repository for overlapping, incongruent discourses" ("Inspir'd with Contradiction," 135).

The multilayered influences shaping this project, in which certain ideas are received into the text of *Paradise Lost* that later writers then engage in their representations of the Garden, Eve, and the Fall, underscore the impossibility of a stable or consistent interpretation of Milton's views toward women and representations of gender.[12] Chapter 1, for example, suggests that Milton purposely places the birth of the antifeminist tradition into Adam's mouth after the Fall. Yet in illustrating the tradition's cultural power, its very ability to restore a gendered hierarchy fundamentally disrupted by the event(s) of the Fall, Milton's poem simultaneously exposes the constructed nature of this tradition: instead of becoming naturalized, the antifeminist tradition is exposed as a social construct serving a particular purpose. Milton's treatment of gender is thus multifaceted, at times illustrating while also undermining certain claims about gender. The ability of *Paradise Lost* to endorse the power of instituted gender hierarchy while exposing the very strictures of this power characterizes the alternate positions on gender that Milton and his poem simultaneously occupy. In Chapter 2, I suggest that Milton does explicitly divide the "spheres" in *Paradise Lost*, positioning Eve amid a much more constrained protodomestic space. While the poem endorses this, it also illustrates the slipperiness, even the impossibility, of Eve's sustained containment within a domesticated sphere.

Domestic spaces may be constructed by Milton, but they are frequently and in multiple forms breached: Chapter 3 considers Milton's engagement with, and internalization of, the female prophetic voice, a voice present when a traditional division of spheres was experiencing significant pressure at midcentury. Thus, Milton engages the female prophetic voice to gain cultural capital, much as Mistress Attaway had invoked Milton's divorce tracts to license her behavior during the Interregnum: we can observe the voice of Mistress Attaway turned inside out, if you will, as Milton nostalgically engages Interregnum discourses produced during a period of greater political and religious license. And while *Paradise Lost* might (unsuccessfully) work to solidify gender ideology at certain points, we observe a late seventeenth-century writer, Mary Chudleigh, un-writing gender as the overdetermining category for understanding eternal souls. The multiplicity that marks Milton's treatment of gender, the variety of responses or refractions of these views in the later seventeenth century, speaks not only to Milton's position on gender. It speaks as well to a methodology of artistic control. Multivalent possibilities in the text are a function of the matrix of authorial agency, culturally determining narratives, and the generative possibilities of intertextuality. The doubleness of the poem's engagement with and reproduction of gender ideology makes *Paradise Lost* Janus-like. Looking in two directions at once, to the past from which it interpolates narratives of gender, and forward where it prompts divergent meditations on women's character and position in marriage, this project consequently resists a conclusive stance on Milton's views of gender in his writings.

While *Paradise Lost*'s location at the center of this project bridges the earlier ideas of and writings of women in the century with writings at the century's end, it is Janus-like in another way. *Paradise Lost* has often been viewed as marking a break between early modernity and the modern age. Nancy Armstrong and Leonard Tennenhouse are not alone in equating Milton with the first "author," a concept equated with modernity for them (1). Similarly, Matthew Jordan's *Milton and Modernity: Politics, Masculinity and* Paradise Lost locates Milton amid a "political modernity" (41). Often described as a text that ushers in modernity, *Paradise Lost* contains for Catherine Belsey "recognizably modern" elements (*John Milton*, 32). I would like to suggest instead that the poem does not mark the break between the early and late seventeenth century, the ushering in of "modernity," but rather shows us that what we call "modern" can still be powerfully inflected by, or layered with, traits that invoke "premodern" ideas.

The most significant of these in *Engendering the Fall* are the dominant metaphors provided by the Western biblical tradition, specifically the pattern for gendered order articulated in the Garden narrative. Hans Blumenburg in *The Legitimacy of the Modern Age* has helpfully broken down the view of the distinctness of a "theological" and a "secular" age, offering instead a model of the interpenetration between the two "ages."[13] One age does not conceptually shape the next. Rather, conceptual gaps which are opened up within and between two ages pose intellectual problems or questions that can only be answered with reference to the mental framework of the previous age. The theological age does not exactly imprint on a later secular age. Instead, any emerging age recursively, and necessarily, looks for answers posed by as yet unanswered questions that have remained open through the events of transition.[14] This does not necessarily model a profound turning or breaking point, or even a "watershed" moment, between ages. Instead, distinct ages are more interdependent, weaving aspects of the "ages" together rather than cleanly dividing then. Following Blumenburg, I would argue that there are many principles we might identify as "secular" that are nonetheless faced with "vacancy": that open question or vacant place which would contain an "answer" necessitates an engagement with an earlier age. Interestingly, this "recourse to the traditional stock of means of expression," necessary when constructing a "secular terminology," is most evident, according to Blumenberg, in the "new political theory" of the age (78).

The discourses of proto- and full-blown "political theory" at the heart of *Engendering the Fall*, from Speght to Milton to Astell to John Locke, highlight how these discourses have numerous "residual needs" which prompt a conceptual engagement with, even a "reoccupation" of, a "traditional stock" of expression (78). These writers thus effect a significant reconsideration of the relationship between religious and secular modes of interpreting the world. This interpenetration between models for understanding the world forces a rethinking of implications of (foundational) biblical thinking down to the twenty-first century. Nowhere is this clearer than in Locke's *Two Treatises of Government*, frequently considered the initiation of "modern" "liberal" political theory. Both Armstrong/Tennenhouse and Jordan position Locke in these very terms, ones which they see as supporting the "watershed" character they assign to Milton's epic poem. At the core of their assertions is the view that the break (in)to modernity occurs as assumptions of religious practice are pushed aside, making way for the rationality of modernity. Jordan, for example, sees Locke's demolishing of Robert Filmer's use of Genesis in the *First Treatise* as evidence of Locke's dismissal, rather than dependence upon, the formative role of Genesis in his own political thought. In *Imaginary Puritan*, Armstrong and Tennenhouse argue that in the "Essay on Understanding" John Locke "is clearly intent on working his way out of the opposition between spiritual and secular definitions of 'soul'. . . . He wants to situate himself within a purely secular definition of consciousness and argue on behalf of reason" (183).

And yet, Locke's *Second Treatise on Government* does not leave behind the site of the Garden of Eden. Rather, discussed extensively throughout the *First Treatise* and implicit in as well as generating meaning in the *Second*, the Garden remains that site of recursivity, a way to answer the questions still posed by late seventeenth-century England that resolutely are not solved by a turn to the secular. The *Second Treatise*, then, emerges from Locke's engagement with the site and narrative of the Garden of Eden. As much recent Locke scholarship has suggested, the formative, even structural nature of theological systems of thought cannot be dismissed by our desire, in the twenty-first century, to draw Locke effortlessly into a modern definition of liberalism unthinkingly linked with notions of secularism.[15]

Julia Reinhard Lupton's *Citizen-Saints: Shakespeare and Political Theology* shares this interest in challenging the "break" of modernity that Armstrong and Tennenhouse, among others, have postulated. The central figure in her book, the citizen-saint, bridges rather than validates the presumed rupture between the saint and the citizen. Usually represented as "fac[ing] each other across an unbridgeable historical divide," Lupton effects a conversation between the "nostalgic afterimage" of the saint with the "modern" subject (1). Like Lupton, this project considers the gaps, the "vacancies" (Blumenburg, 67) which must be revised through engaging previous historical epochs. One of those vacancies is the pattern of gender relations revised as a result of replotting the story of

Genesis. The thinking that these seventeenth-century women writers do through the biblical text of, and Milton's major poem about, Genesis and Creation suggests an integration rather than rupture at the boundaries of what we call "modern" political theory. The return to this primal, and primarily gendered, Garden scene from the writings of Speght to those of Locke forces a reconsideration of visions of a "rupture" between the grounds of "modern" "secular" thought, and instead directs us to the recursive questioning of a previous epoch.

And because of the fundamentally gendered import of the story of the Garden, this imagined "break" of modernity needs to consider how this recursive process of experiencing and returning to such "vacancies" differentially treats men and women. The third section of *The Legitimacy of the Modern Age* traces the development of curiosity: considered a vice in the premodern age, Blumenburg argues that it is reconfigured into a "problematic of theoretical curiosity" (403) for various philosophers in the Renaissance, while transformed into a virtue in the modern epoch since it produces knowledge. And yet, as the recursive engagement with the "primal" story of the Garden of Eden in the seventeenth century illustrates, "curiosity" remains culturally gendered. Barbara Benedict helpfully historicizes this moment of the Enlightenment. While the "curious personality appears as the triumph of modernity itself," the terms shift when one directs the lens toward gender: "female curiosity attracts a passionate new derogation" in the eighteenth century (72, 118): "The 'curious maid' emblematizes self-distortion; the curious man symbolizes self-realization" (72). The "transition" from one age to another is shown to be a recursive revisiting of premises embedded into the earlier age. I would suggest more generally that the association of Eve's act of taking the forbidden fruit with the instigation of man's Fall is never fully distilled out of the evocative concept of curiosity, even in a full-blown "modern" age. As will be clear throughout the chapters of this book, seventeenth-century English women writers are constantly negotiating this problematic of Eve's curiosity.

This deep cultural concern, also a repeated motif in Milton's analogs, continues to shape women's access to knowledge and education. This latency of biblical thinking within what Blumenberg views as a successfully achieved transition—that of curiosity—from a premodern to a modern epoch serves as an example of a gendered division that remains within modern subjectivity. Just as curiosity carries within it a gendered set of associations, ones that gesture back to motifs of Pandora but more foundationally to Eve, so too does the emerging discourse of "political theory" reengage the Garden narrative. Through these acts of retelling, and returning to, the story of the Fall, a gendered construction of modern subjectivity is exposed. Here I have clearly been influenced by Catherine Belsey's work on the gendering of the humanist subject. In *The Subject of Tragedy*, Belsey suggested that female subjectivity in the Renaissance was necessarily divided; women were unable to access the unitary vision of the male subject, largely as a result of the dictum that divided them from themselves: as mothers, they were provided with authority over their children, but were denied such authority in their seemingly contradictory position as subservient wife.

A distinction between the form of subjectivity accorded to men and to women also emerges in the uses of the Creation story in seventeenth-century theoretical reflections on gendered and governmental order. The narratives of the Garden, the Fall, and of Adam and Eve become, in the seventeenth-century female-authored texts discussed in *Engendering the Fall*, a laboratory for considering the relationship between governmental organization and female subjectivity or, more accurately, the limitations placed around female subjectivity. As these writers consider women's engagement with the social or political sphere, they consistently characterize women as figures for Eve. They consequently highlight what I call "biblical subjectivity": a constraint upon a notion of individual identity for women which is generated by the subsumption of individual women into the category of "woman" represented in and by the figure of Eve. This categorical treatment of women, in which they lack an individualized notion of a "self," is the result of becoming inextricably associated with the first mother and the narrative of culpability that she has come to represent.

The texts explored in *Engendering the Fall* model the sustained cultural power of the figure Eve in the seventeenth century and beyond; the category and consequences of gender become one of those "vacant" spaces or questions which necessitate a modern or "secular" age's turn to "traditional" discourses from the earlier period. Locke's *First Treatise* offers us one example: though defined as a "formative" "modern" text, I will show in the conclusion that it aligns women more closely with the characteristics of Eve than it aligns men to Adam. This text models a contemporary alignment of women—as a category—with the (overdetermining) traits of Eve. Similarly, consider the opening to the popular television show *Desperate Housewives*: the visual prologue to this narrative of four often dissatisfied (and usually seductive) housewives immediately associates them with an image of Eve taking the apple from the Tree of Knowledge. The sequence closes with the four main characters explicitly fused with Eve as they all acquire, and sumptuously offer to the audience, these apples of (biblical) disobedience. All "housewives," then, are associated with Eve's traits of sin and seduction in this (comedic) twenty-first-century show. This example from a popular television show coincides with Mieke Bal's exploration of biblical hermeneutics in *Lethal Love*. Unpacking the first three chapters of Genesis in order to illustrate the process by which Eve is granted a name and takes on the traits of a "character," Bal describes the iconic rather than individualized elements of Eve's character as "she" comes to represent a series of traits. Eve is "imprisoned in motherhood" at the point in the text where she is offered a name (128). The category of woman, subsumed into this portrayal of Eve, consequently becomes overdetermined by this synecdoche of the first woman: Eve becomes a repository of a series of meanings that then issue to all women. Not a character, but a category of and for all women, Eve stands in conceptually for women as a group, who are consequently denied an individualized status.

If modern subjectivity could be described as according individuality to each person, then biblical subjectivity works the opposite way, erasing the individual to a category of group identification. *Engendering the Fall* thus maps how difficult it is for "women" as a category to escape this association with a group identity, one embodied in and emblematized by Eve. In the seventeenth-century discourses I discuss, biblical and modern subjectivity are shown to be marked not by a break with, but instead a layering of and a coexistence with, "premodern" gendered notions of identity. Thus, to answer the problem or question of female subjectivity requires "reoccupying" the "traditional stock" or space available through older narratives, which highlight Eve's narrative. As women writers attempt to understand their own relation to, and position in, discourses of political theory, they—from Locke to the writers of *Desperate Housewives*—reoccupy the narrative of Genesis to negotiate this void.

This question of the individualized treatment of Eve, the ability to treat her as a "character," as an individual rather than as a series of meanings attached to women in general, is the very problem that *Engendering the Fall* traces. In early seventeenth-century tracts produced in the anti-feminist tradition, defenses of, as well as attacks on, women subsume "woman" to the figure of Eve, a stand-in for all women. While writings from the early seventeenth century locate women more explicitly within the biblical framework of the Garden—quite literally as we will see in the case of Speght—a doubledness emerges in the writings at the end of the century. In the writings of Rachel Speght or Aemilia Lanyer, Eve is an iconic character, not an individual: they attempt to improve the representation of Eve and thus to improve the condition of women as a category. At the end of the century, Behn plays with the subjectivity of her protagonist Silvia while Astell offers a biblical, and specifically Miltonic, narrative of female identity that engages the issue of female interiority. Astell thus models a doubled representation of women's identity: while women are more easily reclaimed by the biblical narrative, Astell nonetheless attempts to articulate an individual identity for women—the kind of individuality usually associated with modern subjectivity. Astell's political and educational tracts illustrate an individualized figure who also figures or alludes to Eve. Simultaneously imagined as a person while subsumed back into the narrative of the Garden, Astell illustrates how coexistent "modern" and "biblical" representations of women's subjectivity are.

Positioned, in multiple ways, at the narrative and theoretical center of this project, Milton's *Paradise Lost* models this same recursive deployment of gendered biblical narratives. Shaped by, among other narratives, the antifeminist tradition, Milton's Eve is an overdetermined trope. Yet she is also a character: Milton's unique application of available Fall analogues results in an individualized "Eve" or character who is the sine qua non of the categories of "woman's" behavior. Further, the poem positions Eve as like all women while simultaneously depicting her uniqueness. In this doubledness, we observe the simultaneity of a "modern" and a "biblical" subjectivity, one that coexists for women to the end of the seventeenth century and, I would argue, beyond. The emergence of female subjectivity occurs through the conflicts in and debates over gender and governmental organization in the seventeenth century. Consequently, by reasserting gender into this discussion of the formative nature of biblically inflected subjectivities, we can offer a more dynamic and much fuller understanding of the "origins" of "modern" political theory. Further, I would argue that this layering of modes of subjectivity into our understanding of gender and its relationship to governance is still present today. The "foundational" nature of marriage rests on the biblical story, the Western origin—as we hear in George W. Bush, Robert Filmer, and John Locke—of familial and governmental organization. The seventeenth-century narratives of *Engendering the Fall*, all engaging Genesis, gender hierarchy, and governmental organization, thus return to many of the insights made by Pateman in *The Sexual Contract* where she detailed the "sexual contract" that precedes the social contract of liberalism. Yet my project restores female voices and the issue of female subjectivity to the debate over the genesis, if you will, of liberalism. These women's very engagement with the narrative of the Fall, and the manner in which they—as Milton and Locke—understood women through biblical categories, allows us to see how modern political organization is negotiated through a distinct form of female subjectivity, one in which the individualized promise of modern subjectivity is often skirted.

As a result, readers might anticipate that I would make similar objections to the liberal tradition as thinkers such as Pateman, Chris Nyland, and Lorenne Clark.[16] Because of my emphasis on the involvement of women in this "conversation" about governmental organization and gender's role in that organization, my project is closer to Katherine Gillespie's *Domesticity and Dissent in the Seventeenth Century*; Gillespie locates a number of English female sectarians in a teleological intellectual line that she sees leading to Locke's main premises in the *Two Treatises*. Her work follows upon the efforts of scholars such as Hilda Smith and Patricia Springborg; they have placed women thinkers and writers back into this dynamic late seventeenth-century moment, as did Smith's 1998 collection, *Women Writers and the Early Modern British Political Tradition*. It restored women, historically and theoretically, into scholarly discussions about state organization and the development of political theory. The need to reintroduce women's voices and issues of gender into late seventeenth-century narratives of political thought forms an intriguing parallel to the treatment of these issues in Milton studies. Despite some very influential articles that highlight these issues, such as Mary Nyquist's "The Genesis of Gendered Subjectivity" and John Guillory's work on gender, governance, and astronomy, Milton studies has been somewhat resistant to consider these issues in unison. Quite revealing was the program of the 2005 International Milton Congress. The explicitly political theme of the conference, Rights and Liberties ("Droit(s) et Liberté(s)"), contained very few sessions focusing on gender; the structure of the program thus appeared to reify an inherently "male" identification of the political subject—who is both the subject of politics and the subject imagined as an agent within politics. *Engendering the Fall* can explicitly extend and reformulate this discussion by illuminating how women entered into these debates about social and political organization. And in so doing, these writers provided divergent models for (gendered) subjectivity produced through such debates.

One central argument of *Engendering the Fall*, then, is the involvement of female writers and thinkers in what we have come to call "political theory," interventions that occur through a negotiation of the story of Adam and Eve in the Garden. Thus, the conclusion on Locke considers how these reflections on gender and governmental organization by women alter our view of Locke's own engagement of the Garden within his foundational narrative of "modern" government. Locke's recursive engagement of the Genesis tale exposes for us how the layering of biblical and modern subjectivities, and the differential alignment of these forms of subjectivity with men rather than women, are plotted for us in the writings of Hutchinson, Chudleigh, Behn, Astell, and Locke. Their manner of constructing or reconstructing identities—male and female—highlights the parallels to but also the distinctions between their own theoretical experiments and Locke's own thinking in the *Two Treatises of Government*.

The process charted in *Engendering the Fall* also allows us to observe the continuity of these layered forms of subjectivities down to the present. As with the opening quotation from George W. Bush, the foundational narrative of marriage, and specifically that of the first Edenic marriage, still powerfully inflects the Western mind and Western assumptions about social and cultural organization. The late seventeenth century has traditionally been understood to be the breaking point between a premodern state and a rationalist, secular subjectivity, the very benchmark of modernity. The bridge that *Engendering the Fall* attempts to achieve between John Milton's writings and those of his female contemporaries, between political theory and biblical mythology, is also an attempt to bridge the assumed, but unsupportable, break between biblical narratives that still undergird our assumptions about "modern" modes of understanding the world.

Part I
Pretexts

In 1615, Joseph Swetnam's publication of *The Arraignment of Lewd, Idle, Froward, and unconstant women* reconfigured the long-standing Medieval and Renaissance tradition of the anti-feminist debate, propelling it into a small Jacobean media frenzy. While individual women—Christine de Pizan in the fourteenth century in France and Jane Anger during the late 1590s in England—had made interventions into what had initially been a clerically produced exchange on the status of women, Swetnam's very popular attack prompted a number of women to enter into print: Rachel Speght, Ester Sowernam, Constantia Munda. These defenses by women, or produced under a female pseudonym, asserted and developed the female identities of the writers. Nor was this "debate" the only forum in which a woman offered a defense of her kind. In her 1611 companion poems *Salve Deus Rex Judaeorum* and "A Description of Cookeham," Aemilia Lanyer, as did Speght and Sowernam, reconstructed significant details within the Fall story in order defend Eve and all women. The two chapters that begin *Engendering the Fall* take these female-authored defenses of women as their focus. Posing specific challenges to the gender ideology of the period, these texts would prompt John Milton to engage aspects of this earlier debate in his account of the Fall in *Paradise Lost*.

The exuberance of this "debate" itself would die down; even though Swetnam's tract was printed eleven times between 1615 and 1682, the responses to him were limited to single editions. Yet the broader "debate" lived on, as critics such as Linda Woodbridge, Ann Rosalind Jones, and Diane Purkiss have shown, into the first half of the century. Swetnam himself was arraigned in the play entitled *Swetnam, the Woman Hater* (1620), and in the 1640s another spate of responses appeared, including *The womens sharp revenge*. While individual texts, such as those by Speght, do not go into multiple editions, modes of responding to Swetnam do as the "debate" spawns a range of generic innovation. Further, this flurry of publication around Swetnam suggests, especially when considered in concert with the debate on womanish men and masculine women in the *Haec-Vir/ Hic Mulier* exchange of 1620, a fissure within the gender codes and ideologies less discernable within contemporary conduct books or marriage manuals. Such breaks in the crust of gender stability suggest that these particular texts within the anti-feminist tradition served as a productive site for uncovering cultural assumptions about gender, and the alternatives to this ideology, emergent at the beginning of the seventeenth century. The following chapters consider the broader implications of generic and gendered interventions and innovations within the writings of Rachel Speght, Ester Sowernam, Aemilia Lanyer, and John Milton.

Chapter 1

Serpentine Eve: Plotting Gender in the Seventeenth-Century Garden

Despite the prominence of the English "anti-feminist debate" in the early seventeenth century, which argued for and against the qualities of women, critics have been routinely resistant to set Milton's *Paradise Lost* in conversation with the pamphlet controversy initiated by Joseph Swetnam's *The Arraignment of Lewd, Idle, Froward, and unconstant women.*[1] Mary Nyquist asserts that "Milton could not but have known that questions of priority figure prominently in the Renaissance debate over 'woman'" (107), while Kari McBride and John Ulreich suggest that Milton be read "in the light of early modern treatises on the nature of women and the entire history of the *querelle des femmes*" (109); this publishing tradition realized a particular vogue in England during the late sixteenth century and then in the 1610s with the many texts that followed the publication of Joseph Swetnam's "*Arraignment of . . . women.*"[2] Yet neither Nyquist nor McBride and Ulreich suggest that Milton was an active interlocutor of this tradition. Nonetheless, Milton's poem appears steeped in the terms of this active debate, still popular if reconfigured in the 1650s and 1660s when *Paradise Lost* was being composed. All of these texts similarly interrogate the issues of women's secondariness, Eve's motivations for the Fall, and, of course, the character of women, and have thus prompted my rather bold claim: these seventeenth-century "anti-feminist" debates, particularly the exchange between Joseph Swetnam and three women pamphleteers—Rachel Speght, Ester Sowernam, and Constantia Munda—who respond, result in arguments for and against women's culpability that Milton dramatizes in *Paradise Lost*.

My assertion cannot stand on irrefutable evidence, such as an annotated copy of Rachel Speght's *A Mouzell for Melastomus* in Milton's library. Yet Milton was part of a community of readers, and writers, of similar kinds of tracts: engaged in the Smectymnuus debate in the early 1640s, Milton was an avid reader of a huge range of pamphlets and a participant in print-mediated debates of the period. He was also fully located within what Robert Darnton has called the communication circuit of the "anti-feminist" tracts. Wandering among the booksellers' stalls in the 1630s, he details in a letter to Alexander Gill, Jr., that Gill is to "look for me (God willing) in London on Monday, among the booksellers" (*Familiar Letters*, 12-13). The shop owned by Matthew Simmons, which Sabrina Baron claims Milton would have known well, was located in Aldersgate (225); it was on the other side of Christ's Church from the very "Saracen's Head" where copies of Joseph Swetnam's *Arraignment* were reprinted in both 1634 and 1637.[3] A revolution of printing and of reprinting framed Milton's world, and Milton was fully a member of this world, both as a reader and as a participant.[4]

I am suggesting, then, that Milton had every opportunity to engage and access the world of pamphlet production in the early and mid-century, a world that continued to generate texts imbued with shifting gender ideologies. The representations of women and the use of the narrative of the Garden and the Fall within this tradition are very popular early in the century; these strategies of representation will become redirected through the Civil War and Interregnum years, thus remaining available to readers and producers of pamphlets at mid-century. Swetnam's text is reprinted throughout the period, in 1645, 1660, and again 1667, while another brief "debate" emerges in 1639 and 1640 with the publication of John Taylor's *A Juniper Lecture*, to which Mary Tattle-well and Joan Hit-him-home respond with *The womens sharp revenge*. This redeployment of the earlier debate thus carries within it traces of the gender debates from the 1610s. Milton would not have had to pick up copies of Speght's or Sowernam's responses to Swetnam in order to engage aspects of this tradition. And yet, the unique innovations introduced into the "anti-feminist" debate in the early seventeenth century do appear to shape Milton's choices in *Paradise Lost*. By considering Milton's apparent access to, in conjunction with the history of, this pamphlet tradition, we can broaden the cultural context through which we evaluate Milton's representations of women and of gender in his epic poem.

Because of the centrality of the Genesis tale to defenses of women, both those authored by men and undertaken by the female-pseudonymed responders to Joseph Swetnam, these writings as a Genesis epic such as Milton's *Paradise Lost* will replot the narrative of the Garden. Tracts by Rachel Speght and Ester Sowernam introduce rhetorical and narrative innovations to the story of Genesis which include the association of Eve with the female defender herself.[5] Specific aspects of their writings appear as central elements in Milton's portrait of Eve. But Milton is not simply dramatizing the qualities that are attributed to Adam and to Eve within these debates: he actually enacts these disagreements within conversations between Adam and Eve, Adam and Raphael, and Eve and Satan. *Paradise Lost*, then, is plotted along many of the same lines as the anti-feminist debate, yet chooses to employ this genre in a dramatized form. While Eve will turn at the end of Book 9 to many of the same kinds of arguments and language embedded into the anti-feminist tracts, in Book 10 the poem will offer a seeming reconciliation to this swirling debate from the early seventeenth century as Milton transforms the contested nature of the debate forum into a singular vision of the relationship between the sexes.

And yet, the appearance of a stock, anti-feminist discourse in Book 10 of *Paradise Lost* also highlights the socially created identity—if also the effectiveness—of this form. Dramatically presented as a necessity for Eve to concede to this discourse in Book 10, the poem records the effectiveness of anti-feminist rhetoric while exposing its constructedness. One significant effect of *Paradise Lost*'s use of the anti-feminist "scene" will be the silencing of the female interlocutor who had emerged onto the scene of the anti-feminist debate in the early seventeenth century. But, while Milton may represent the historical necessity of silencing an Eve through the anti-feminist tradition, he embeds into his poem the very defenses for women that had been promulgated by male- and female-authored tracts alike. The very debate form of these tracts that is adapted in *Paradise Lost* results in earlier modes of defending women remaining as traces within the poem. Milton's very attempt to stabilize these discourses results instead in the very doubledness of the poem, a characteristic that has allowed critics to argue entirely contradictory positions about the representation of women in *Paradise Lost*. The poem's polyvocal nature, as I will show, is due in part to its engaging the gender debate recorded in the *querelle des femmes* reconfigured by women's entrance into it.[6]

Although I have been employing the oft-used phrase "anti-feminist debate" to describe the English tradition, this phrase contains a certain historical inaccuracy. As Linda Woodbridge has suggested, the mid- to late sixteenth century *querelle des femmes* in England was actually not structured along the lines of a debate. Conventional arguments for and against women were often employed by the same writer, such as Edward Gosynhill's *Scholehouse of women* and *Mulierum Paean*, the first an attack, the second a defense.[7] Many attacks and defenses, then, staged a (false) debate because they were written by the same author. Only in the seventeenth century does the structure of an actual publishing debate finally emerge. With the 1615 publication of Joseph Swetnam's *Arraignment*, five responses—all defenses—were prompted by this very popular tract. Three of these were published by women or under a female name while the reactive nature of the texts produced by, especially, Rachel Speght and Ester Sowernam gives real validity to the name "debate," which had not previously been a driving force for publication (Woodbridge, 104).[8]

As these shifts in the publishing tradition suggest, when women—as Speght definitely was, and Sowernam could possibly have been—enter into the fray, these responses, though partaking of many conventions from earlier tracts, become quite serious in contradistinction to the playful tone of earlier defenses. Whether produced by "material" women, such as Speght, or by men taking on the pseudonym of a woman, this assumption in print of a female identity shifts the character of these discourses. In some cases, an overt level of sincerity emerges within a tract: Rachel Speght means to offer a defense to the "filthie froth" "foamed" onto "Eves sex" within Swetnam's attack ("A Dreame," 243).

In a complementary fashion, the tropes or forms of argumentation employed by these writers shift as a result of self-identifying as female defenders. While the name Ester Sowernam is almost certainly a pseudonym, the specifics within "her" tract become distinct because of the assertion of a female identity. Thus, such an adoption of a female identity in print, either because it accords with one's sex or not, results in the reconfiguration of certain familiar conventions of the genre. As did tracts previous to 1617, the responses by Speght, Sowernam, and Munda will invoke the Genesis account of the Fall, as well as an extensive range of biblical narratives. Yet now the proportion of their tracts that turns to the story of Adam and Eve becomes significantly higher than either Joseph Swetnam's attack on women (in which four references to Eve appear), or other male-authored defenses of women.[9] In both Speght and Sowernam's tracts, the narrative of the Fall becomes the first line of defense in protecting women from the attacks of Swetnam and others.

And in their hands, a twofold use of the Fall story becomes an alternative form of defense. Defenses, which spend a much higher percentage of time on the narrative of the Fall, utilize an expanded account of "our first disobedience" to restage aspects of the Fall. A particular rhetorical shift is these writers' acknowledgment of a structural challenge embedded within any female-authored defense. Women are described are seducers within the tracts attacking women. Thus, in defenses where women are arguing for themselves (or appear to be doing so), they could be viewed as taking on the identity of a seducing Eve; since Eve's arguments had, of course, seduced Adam to fall, women defenders could be aligned with Eve. Instead, these writers turn this liability to an advantage, appropriating the potential association with the first mother.

Speght and Sowernam, we will see, utilize, even embrace, the identity of Eve within their texts. Their reasons for adopting this role may in fact have been to address the association directly: they could be, disparagingly, viewed as disputing Eves, women attempting to achieve forgiveness for their own sins in order to prompt male acceptance of their acts: the consequence would be to generate sin once again. Yet, by aligning themselves with the figure of the postlapsarian Eve—and not a Mary figure—writers like Speght and Sowernam defend women's characters as well as justify their own entrance into print. Both Speght and Sowernam accomplish this through their portrait of Eve: by entering back into a (prelapsarian) garden space, their Eve-like figure can operate outside of the gender hierarchy uttered after the Fall. Consequently, their version of the defense audibly challenges the social and political implications of gender hierarchy. As I will suggest later in the chapter, it is to this that Milton appears to be responding in *Paradise Lost*.

The tropes within Speght's and Sowernam's defenses of Eve will rehabilitate her by effectively undermining Swetnam's attack: he will be placed amidst the story of the Fall itself. Thus, their counternarrative builds toward a much

larger rejection of the premises of the anti-feminist debate. Speght and Sowernam begin very generally, suggesting that Swetnam's attack violates God's
plan. Yet they ultimately will position him as a tempter as they shift the traditional identity of seducer away from Eve and all women. Their initial response
is to attack Swetnam's religious piety—in fact to insist on his absence of piety.
Their claim that Swetnam's arguments against women are "irreligious" graces
the cover of Speght's defense and occurs within Sowernam's first chapter
(Speght, tp; Sowernam, 2 [B1v]). In essence accusing Swetnam of heresy, both
of their arguments become testimonies to the glories of God's creation. Sowernam "undertooke this enterprise...to set out the glory of Almightie God, in
so blessed a worke of his Creation" (A3r); more than just defending women, "I
am more violently vrged to *defend diuine Maiestie*, in the worke of his Creation"
(1 [B1r]; my emphasis). The project of defending Eve is thus accomplished
through the larger project of justifying God's creation of man and woman.

Once they have established the blasphemy that characterizes Swetnam's argument, female defenders can deploy their more specific strategy for defending and redeeming Eve: distancing her from the popular and longstanding
tradition of aligning Eve with the serpent. Speght and Sowernam begin by reconfiguring the associations with the snake traditionally linked to women in
such tracts. In the hands of Speght and Sowernam, the snake becomes instead
the male pamphleteer, the very seducing force that must be resisted. By redirecting this title onto either men or Swetnam himself, the Eve-like figure of the
female defender can initiate an enactment of the narrative of the Fall. Yet this
time the story will end differently: she will now reject the arguments of the
snake. These tracts consequently combine individual defenses of women with
a narrative reworking of the story of the Fall, one that replots the anti-feminist
conventions upon which these tracts are built. In Speght, the serpent is identified as the male detractor of women. For, only once Eve is distanced from the
epitaph of "earthly Serpent" (Swetnam, 27) can she become a model for all
women. The result? Sowernam and Speght narrate a return to the Garden, offering a vision of a postlapsarian Eve who restages an account of the Fall.

Speght begins to link the misogynist pamphlet writer to the devil himself by
employing the very motifs of the "snake" against Swetnam. Reformulating the
dominant animal image in *A Mouzell for Melastomus* of him as a biting dog, the
imagery clusters establish multiple links between him and a snake. The opening letter implicitly links Swetnam to a snake and a viper in its first reference,
a conceit that Speght employs to justify publishing her defense: "as Historiog-
raphers report the viper to doe, who in the Winter time doth vomit forth her
poyson, and in the spring time sucketh the same up againe" (3), so too will
Swetnam: he has threatened to publish another attack, and "a more deadly
poyson" from this "viper" must be countered with this "Antidote" (3, 4). As
Speght closes the first letter, Swetnam becomes a "fierie and furious Dragon"
(5). Thus Speght establishes a constellation of images—of serpent, viper,

While Speght links Swetnam to serpent imagery and then to the Devil himself, Sowernam distributes the title of serpents more generally. While "The
Serpent at first tempted woman, he dare assault her no more in that shape,
now he imployeth men to supply his part" (25 [E1r]). Instead, "men" have
"turn'd to Serpents" since "The Serpent with men in their workes may agree"
(50 [H1v]). The "contagion of Masculine serpents" stands in for a figure like
Swetnam, though Sowernam does not connect him as explicitly to the serpent
as did Speght (Sowernam, 48 [G4v]). Sowernam ends her text with the chris-
tening of all men as snakes, though we hear the implications for Swetnam. In
her conclusion, she addresses him, asserting that "You haue exceeded in your
furie against Widdowes," and she directs him to "recollect your wits, write out
of deliberation, not out of furie; write out of aduice, not out of idlenesse: for-
beare to charge women with faults which come from the contagion of Masculine serpents." That "contagion," she has shown us, is in fact a disease derived
from pamphleteers like Swetnam (48 [G4v]).

While both texts offer a defense of women by generating a small narrative
in which Swetnam, or all men, becomes a serpent, they complement this with
the development of the figure of the defender of women who is in a position
analogous to Eve. Sowernam pursues this identification most aggressively.
While she defends women, Eve, and God's actions throughout, Sowernam's
narrative actually links herself to the figure of Eve. Sowernam claims that she
has "entred into the Garden of Paradice, and there haue gathered the choysest flowers which that Garden may affoord, and those I offer to you" (A4r).
She thus returns to the story of Eve and Adam in Eden by literally returning
to that site. Her goal? To offer an alternate defense through an alternative narrative of the Garden. Sowernam, in positioning herself as a postlapsarian Eve,
is able to enter this space in order to make her argument. This fusion of herself with Eve also stands as an inversion of the normal use made of Eve, particularly in misogynist tracts. In the tradition of these tracts, and of misogyny
in general, Eve in her act of disobedience, vanity, and pride becomes all
women. That link between Eve and women is what Sowernam seizes on—
since all women are like Eve, she can assume a position like the first of women.
Once that association with Eve allows her access to the Garden, she can then
reconfigure women's identity through her journey back into the Garden.

Sowernam's rehabilitation of Eve has occurred in large part through her extended identification with the first mother. Sowernam actually reenters the
Garden in order to author her defense: "*I have entred into the Garden of Paradice,
and there haue gathered the choysest flowers which that Garden may affoord, and those I offer
to you*" (A4r; emphasis original). In doing so, she paints herself as a pre-fallen
Eve linked with the beauty, even the flowers, of the Garden which Milton will
have her name in *Paradise Lost*. Instead of shying away from an identification
with Eve, Sowernam embraces this link as she develops the "*esse*" of all women
[B3v]; they all become the "*choysest flowers*" (A4r). By embracing an identity

with Eve, both for all women but explicitly here for herself, Sowernam restages the narrative of the Garden as a defense of women. Impersonating a postlapsarian Eve, Sowernam's narrative entrance into this space actually makes her argument.

Sowernam accomplishes this in part by aligning Eve to the Garden through the oft-debated issue of Adam and Eve's birthplace. Sowernam identifies Eve as "*a Paraditian Creature*" (A4r) since she was formed in the Garden. Adam, conversely, was made outside of it, and thus—in one tradition of defenses—is less pure. Sowernam expands upon this issue of the birthplace of Eve, an idea then distributed to all women. As we will see, Sowernam transforms the walled boundaries of the Garden into a permeable membrane. In the process, Sowernam makes fluid the boundaries between womankind and this "*Paraditian Creature*" Eve. This permeable boundary—both of the Garden's wall and the association of Eve and all women—allows for this "*Paraditian*" identity to be transported out of the Garden. Because this "*Paraditian*" trait was within Eve, the women that follow from her carry this trace of the Garden's perfection within them. Further, they bring this essence of perfection into all marriages: "there is no delight more exceeding then to be ioyned in marriage with a Paraditian Creature. Who *as shee commeth out of the Garden*, so shall you finde her a flower of delight, answerable to the Countrey from whence she commeth" (A4r, my emphasis). Eden is located in Eve, and thus within all women. The postlapsarian status of women, then, is not one separated from the positive elements of the prelapsarian Garden of Eden. Further, the departure from the Garden, originally an image of expulsion resulting from Eve's sin, now evokes Eve's original perfection. What Sowernam will call the "esse" or essence of Paradise thus exists within all (postlapsarian) women.

The site of Eve's creation consequently becomes one of Sowernam's central arguments against Swetnam that allows her to rewrite the Fall itself: "So that woman neither can or may degenerate in her disposition from that naturall inclination of the place, in which she was first framed, she is a Paradician, that is, a delightfull creature, borne in so delightfull a country" (B3v). While Sowernam will acknowledge the Fall, the character of Eve is defined—and elevated above Adam—by the Garden: "euery element hath his creatures, euery creature doth corresponde the temper and the inclination of that element wherein it hath and tooke his first and principall *esse* or being" (B3v). Eve becomes defined here by this "esse" of Paradise rather than by the act that results in her and Adam's expulsion from Eden. Instead of a portrait of the Fall as loss, Sowernam's defense playfully reconfigures the notion of women's innate identity to offer a redeemed Eve in this space as well as outside of it in postlapsarian marriages.

The centrality of the story of the Fall, then, not only offers to these women an effective defense, it also becomes a method within their tracts: they turn to the narrative of the Garden because they can produce an alternative one for their purposes. The imagery patterns within Speght's prefatory material re-cast—literally—the players in the Fall: Eve isn't the seducing serpent; the male misogynist pamphleteer is. We will have to wait until 1621 to see Speght restage Eve's actions in her second publication, a volume of poems that operates in concert with her earlier tract. Her publication of "A Dreame," a poem which is "imaginarie in manner" but "*reall in matter*," returns to this same constellation of motifs which invokes the narrative of the Garden and the Fall (tp). Like Sower-nam, Speght will cast herself as a figure for Eve when she identifies herself as the writer of defenses for women. Here, her method—as in Sowernam's earlier text—includes locating herself within a reconfigured version of the Fall and thus aligning herself with a portrait of a redeemed Eve. She accomplishes this through a decisively gendered narrative of the acquisition of knowledge.

While the *Mouzell* has received a fair amount of attention because of recent scholarly interest in the anti-feminist debate and the resulting entrance of women into print, the entire publication in which "A Dreame" appears, *Mortalities Memorandum*, has generated less interest. And yet, in "A Dreame" we see Speght return in significant and complex ways to the issue of female culpabil-ity: the prefatory material to the text even announces a thematic and intertex-tual connection between her earlier 1617 and this 1621 publication. The defense of women that she had produced within *Mouzell* is further strength-ened by her preface to the elegy for which the volume is named. The dream allegory that precedes "Mortalities Memorandum," an elegy for her mother, also continues the defense of women begun in her 1617 tract. Explicitly invok-ing the earlier text that Speght had published, she aligns herself with a recon-figured portrait of a redeemed Eve, now introduced to us within a reconceived Fall narrative detailing the acquisition of knowledge.[10]

In the prefatory material to *Mortalities Memorandum*, Speght uses this intertex-tual opportunity to invoke her earlier publication; thematically, *Mortalities Mem-orandum* could even be considered a sequel to *Mouzell*. In the dedication to her godmother, Speght provides a defense of her earlier authorship: Because of "my *mouzeling Melastomus*, I am now, as by a strong motive induced (for my rights sake) to produce and divulge this off-spring of my indevour, to prove them further futurely who have formerly deprived me of my due, imposing my abortive upon the father of me, but not of it" (45). Her insistence on author-ship is infused with the defense of women to which that earlier tract was com-mitted, both issues underscored through her use of a dream vision. Here, she allegorically (re)stages her textual exchange with Swetnam's *Arraignment*:

But by the way I saw a full fed Beast,
Which roared like some monster, or a Devill,
And on *Eves* sex he foamed filthie froth,
As if that he had had the falling evill;
To whom I went to free them from mishaps,
And with a *Mouzel* sought to binde his chaps. (241–46)

The "Dreame," a metatextual meditation on the act of writing and publishing by a woman, is thus equally a defense of "*Eves* sex" against the "Devill" that is Swetnam.

The conventions that mark defenses consequently grace the body of *A Dreame*, complementing both the form and purpose of her earlier publication. *A Dreame* contains a list of well-educated women, one meant to illustrate the good traits of women.

Cleobulina, and *Demophila*,
with *Telesilla*, as Historians tell,
(Whose fame doth live, though they have long bin dead)
Did all of them in Poetrie excell.
A Roman matron that *Cornelia* hight,
An eloquent and learned style did write. (139–44)

The list continues, as now she turns to female practitioners of "Astronomie," "Rheth'ricke," and other sciences (145, 146). This list, which recalls the structure of Christine de Pizan's *The Book of the City of Ladies*, reconfigures the conventions of a defense into a tribute to women who have successfully acquired knowledge. As we will see, the defense of women's acquisition of knowledge allows the narrator—explicitly linked to Speght through the numerous biographical references—to offer a defense of Eve; Eve, of course, had previously pursued a "plant" of knowledge. As a female defender of women, as I have suggested, Speght runs the risk of becoming identified as an Eve figure. Her poem makes the identification explicit as she offers a defense of women tailored to their pursuit of knowledge.

"A Dreame" consequently offers an elaborate allegorical vision that reimagines the terms of the Fall itself. As both a volume and an individual poem, this 1621 publication counters the "filthie froth" "foamed" "on Eve's sex" by Joseph Swetnam (Speght, "A Dreame," 243). As Barbara Lewalski has suggested, this autobiographically resonant narrative locates the speaker in a garden of learning, rather than a garden of love; the insertion of her narrative of authorship suggests how this poem operates as a meditation on the problem of women's learning and writing (*Writing Women*, 173).

The poem will work to differentiate forms of knowledge, casting the search for one kind of knowledge as laudable. Experience, the opposite of Innocence, guides her, instructing Speght that

The onely medicine for your maladie,
By which, and nothing else your helpe is wrought,
Is *Knowledge*, of the which there is two sorts,
The one is good, the other bad and nought;
The former sort by labour is attain'd,
The latter may without much toyle be gain'd. (91–96)

A distinction is made here, one which may partially offset the problematic resonances to Eve's prelapsarian act to acquire knowledge. Yet the detailed account of her activities in the Garden, including Speght's "desire" to acquire the "plant" of knowledge, inflect her search with echoes of Eve's acquisition of Knowledge.

Such "desire" to acquire knowledge is experienced within an equally pleasurable garden that recalls the original Garden of Genesis. Lush and dominated by sensual attraction, "fragrant flowers of sage and fruitfull plants, / Did send sweete savours up into my head" (189–90). The beauty of the garden recalls the "choysest flowers which that Garden may affoord" in Sowernam's account of her entrance back into the Garden of Eden (A4v). The garden is linked to "pleasure" while the acquisition of "Knowledge" is cast in desirable terms as well:

> If thou didst know the pleasure of the place,
> Where *Knowledge* growes, and where thou mayst it gaine;
> Or rather knew the vertue of the plant,
> Thou would'st not grudge at any cost, or paine,
> Thou canst bestow, to purchase for thy cure
> This plant, by which of helpe thou shalt be sure. (169–74)

The pleasurable pursuit of knowledge, the taking of this "vertue" filled plant, establishes a link to the motivations of Eve at the moment of her fall: in fact, in *Paradise Lost* Eve will detail "The virtue of that Fruit" (9.616). That "pleasure" motivates Speght's acquisition of knowledge is signaled by "desire"'s role in this search: "Desire, / Who did incite me to increase my store, / And told me 'twas a lawfull avarice, / To covet *Knowledge* daily more and more" (229–32). Speght thus employs, and revises, conventions about Eve's character and reasons for taking the fruit: Eve was often described as covetous and filled with desire when eating the forbidden fruit.

Nor is the act of tasting, so intertwined with the consumption of the fruit of the Tree of Knowledge, avoided by Speght in the account. The link between "taste" and "knowledge" is embedded in the Latin root "sapere," and becomes the narrator's inducement to acquire this "plant" of Knowledge. This language begins early in the poem. In the narrator's first attempt to distinguish herself from the animals in the Garden, we are told that "Their seeming science is but customes fruit" (46). As the poem continues, the narrator's goal is to acquire real, not "seeming," science, and thus a different fruit: one from the "plant" of "knowledge" (171, 170). For this she is "hungry," a sensual drive that predicts the tasting to come: "And taste of science appetite did [her] move" (53; 191). Speght thus creates a powerful constellation of images of hunger, appetite, and tasting to invoke the narrative of Eve's eating of the apple. Further, the knowledge of "higher" things, a motivation of Eve's seen so clearly in Milton, is both the goal of, and the method of, "augmenting" the narrator's "*Theorie* of things above" (191–92). While the "plant," which is described as having "vertue" as in Milton, is not cast as a fruit, the language of appetite and taste draw us back to the earlier description of the animals' "customs fruit." The resonances to the first Fall are thick, from the aspiration to knowledge "desired" by this female narrator to the knowledge she imagines distinguishing her from lower beings.

The consequences of rewriting the Garden narrative become clearest when Swetnam bursts into the "Dream." The threat he poses actually justifies this Eve-like acquisition of knowledge's "plant": Speght is now in a position to defend women against this "monster, or a Devill" pamphleteer (242). "[O]n Eves sex he foamed filthie froth, / As if that he had had the falling evill; / To whom I went to free them from mishaps, / And with a *Mouzel* sought to binde his chaps" (243–36); Speght's knowledge can effect the containment—and silencing—of this "Devill" (242). This outcome, which is presented positively—obviously—by the *Mouzel*'s own author, offers a reconfigured narrative of the Garden and of Knowledge. Now, the rhetoric of this "Devill" will not delude her as her knowledge will defeat him. In a reimagination of the context of knowledge and the attack by Satan that results in the Fall, Speght has constructed a postlapsarian narrative of acquiring knowledge to which women can return. As in Sowernam, then, the Garden becomes accessible and able to illustrate women's positive traits. Instead of the story of Eve and the Garden proving women's evilness, these narratives offer a detailed reimagination of women's character and actions through an alignment with Eve. An Eve-like figure now able to defend women against attacks, Speght joins Sowernam in recasting all women in a positive light. The effect in both texts is to offer a defense of women through a narrative retelling of the Garden story that refigures issues of culpability.

The centrality of the Garden narrative in these defenses, in addition to the motifs within these defenses, suggests a productive intertextuality between female-authored defenses and Milton's use of both a narrative account of the Fall and the use of tropes from the anti-feminist tradition in *Paradise Lost*.[11] The innovation of these female writers during the 1610s and 1620s—that in taking up a defense of women, they actually operate in the position of Eve—is one to which Milton appears to respond in his epic poem. True, by mid-century the energy of this earlier and active anti-feminist pamphlet debate appears redirected into other forms of writing. As the English Revolution approached, the voices of women—as Mihoko Suzuki and Katherine Romack have shown—become directed toward a political sphere, often in acts of petitioning the pre- and then post-Revolution government.[12] The disputing Eve elaborated by Speght and Sowernam appears to turn her back on a prelapsarian Garden space as she reorients her female voice toward a much more contemporary political site. Nonetheless, the textual dissemination of this earlier tradition offers a particularly rich context in which to consider the future of the portrait of a "disputing Eve," especially as Swetnam's own tract, and thus the tropes of the anti-feminist debate, remained available down to 1667: the *Arraignment* was reprinted in 1634, 1637, 1645, 1660, and 1667. Milton could well have seen or heard of these tracts, and thus have had exposure to the characteristic language of female attack within this tradition. Access to central tropes within the tradition remained easily accessible even if the unique figure of the disputing Eve, who defended herself in the terms of the Fall while being assaulted by Swetnam-style language, went underground at mid-century.

But she will resurface in *Paradise Lost*. This text, as had Speght and Sowernam earlier, grapples with modes of representing the story of the Garden, the Fall, and its relationship to gender. In *Paradise Lost*, Eve undertakes her own defense after the Fall. Milton thus appears to show an awareness of this development within the anti-feminist genre by casting Eve in the role of a defender. We watch as Milton embeds this tradition into a scene where the very conventions of the anti-feminist tract are created through Adam's response to Eve's fall. While Eve briefly will become a defender of her actions—the consequence of which is to defend all women—Adam momentarily takes on the linguistic characteristics of a misogynist pamphleteer like Joseph Swetnam. A pattern emerges: these traces of earlier defenses in the poem (from Agrippa to Sowernam) threaten the inversion of gender hierarchy. Such traces will then be righted, clarified, even codified by an authorizing voice in the epic. And yet Milton will highlight this very process: calling attention to an older-style "debate" about gender and the resulting hierarchy that he is resurrecting, Milton simultaneously attempts to silence its resonant echoes.

I have suggested above that the centrality of the Genesis story within these early seventeenth-century tracts aligns them to Milton's own account of the Garden and the Fall. Further, Milton's engagement with elements from earlier defenses of women sprinkle the middle books of *Paradise Lost*. We see, for example, Milton place into Adam's mouth the argument for women as the last, and thus best, creation, a position first expressed by Agrippa and argued by many female defenders such as Sowernam[13]: "Women were the last worke and therefore the best, / For what was the end, excelleth the rest" (Sowernam, 50 [H1v]). Milton engages this possible consequence of Eve's creation by having Adam describe her as "Heaven's last best gift" in Book 5, an initially objectifying account of Eve that develops, directly before the Fall, into Adam's claim that she is the "fairest of Creation, last and best / Of all God's Works" (9.896–97). Obviously, this identification takes on an entirely different tone at the Fall, framed in large part by Raphael's Book 8 upbraiding of Adam. I am inclined to agree with Kari Boyd McBride and John C. Ulreich that Adam's error, articulated by Raphael as "attribúting overmuch to things / Less excellent" (8.565–66), is a response to the Agrippan argument found within the *querelle*. More significant, though, appears to be Milton's method throughout the poem: he draws upon the defenses of women to initially open up possible links between these texts over the question of the "esse" of Eve only to return to a more orthodox view of Eve's character and description of expected behavior after the Fall. Though Adam is rebuked by Raphael in Book 8 for describing "Her loveliness [as] so absolute," up until this point in the poem Adam speaks as though he has been reading defenses of women, particularly those authored by women. This will change dramatically after the Fall. Now, Milton will place the language and the arguments of Swetnam, rather than Sowernam, into Adam's mouth. In Book 10, then, Adam will transform Eve into a "fair defect," whose creation second makes her not better, but instead derogatorily "last": Eve was "create[d] at last / This novelty on Earth, this fair defect / Of Nature" (10.890–92).

The issue of priority, which is so central in Sowernam, was often interwoven with, and buttressed by, arguments about the material out of which Eve was made. The "material cause" of Eve, as Rachel Speght will explain the concept, was a "refined mould," since "man was created of the dust of the earth, but woman was made of a part of man, after that he was a living soule" (18). For Speght, this fact leads to an argument for "their authority equall" (18) since Eve was made "from his side, neare his heart, to be his equall" (18). This argument occurs earlier in Jane Anger's "Her Protection for Women," and Sowernam underscores the importance of this argument by repeating it in her own tract: "as the Maide, *in her Muzzle for Melastomus* hath obserued . . . [God] created her out of a subject refined, as out of a Quintissence: For the ribbe is in Substance more solid, in place as most near, so in estimate most dear, to mans heart" (6 [B3v]). The language of the rib, of course, is repeatedly invoked within the anti-feminist debate as in any Genesis retelling. At the Fall, we hear this language explicitly: women "were made of the ribbe of a man, and that their froward nature sheweth; for a ribbe is a crooked thing, good for nothing else, and women are crooked by nature" (Swetnam, 1 [B1r]). But Milton specifies Adam's response to Eve to suggest a connection between the language and concepts in these defenses by women. Now Adam doesn't just gesture to the language of Swetnam: he responds in a manner that explicitly counters Sowernam: "And [I] understood not all was but a *show* / Rather than *solid* virtue, all but a Rib / Crooked by nature, bent, as now appears / More to the part sinister from me drawn" (10.883–86; my emphasis). Eve is neither "solid" nor substance: she is "show."[14] Adam learns here what Eve has already learned in Book 4: her appearance of superiority is false, and it is "manly grace / And wisdom, which alone is truly fair" (4.490–91). This interjection engages the tradition of the anti-feminist debate. But more significantly, it locates Adam's response as in a possible dialogue with Sowernam.

While the argument of Eve's composition derives from the issue of priority in Creation, the larger question is the essential composition of Eve. Speght engages this issue more materially, while Sowernam stresses the metaphysical nature of women's being: there is a "temper and inclination" that defines the "first and principll *esse*, or being" of women's character (6, [B3v]). According to Sowernam, that "naturall inclination" of women is toward the Paradisical (6, [B3v]). Milton's poem, more so than any other analog or source for the story of the Fall, explores what this "principll *esse*" is in Eve by delineating her "inclinations." The protracted experience that Adam and Eve have in the Garden—rather than the almost immediate Fall conventionally represented within the analogs—allowed Milton time to explore Eve's character.[15] In contrast, Grotius's *Adamus Exul* avoids any portrait of Eve prior to the Fall. The generic demands of Grotius's closet drama may explain the absence of any quest for Eve's "esse." Yet Serafino Della Salandra's play, with room for character development, also eschews this: Eve has an almost fetishistic fascination with the apple itself, but any sense of character remains undeveloped.

In Speght, Sowernam, and in Milton, one of these "inclinations" or character traits of Eve is her solitariness. The narrative of entering back into the Garden in Sowernam, where the narrator can discover the "esse" of Eve, offers a solitary image of Eve, a portrait sustained in Speght's redeemed Eve figure searching for knowledge in a garden dreamscape. In fact, the Eve-like narrator in "A Dreame" seems to eschew companionship in a sequence whose parallels to Milton are quite revealing. Adam's search for a helpmate is one of the most dramatically and emotionally significant events in *Paradise Lost*. As we are told in Book 8, he initially looked at the animals as he "nam'd them," but "found not what methought I wanted still" (352, 355). "In solitude," Adam concludes, "What happiness, who can enjoy alone"? (364–65). Yet in Speght's "A Dreame," solitude is never articulated as a problem during her search for knowledge: "My griefe, quoth I, is called *Ignorance*" (43). More significantly, she understands this condition by comparing herself with the animals: it is "*Ignorance*" that "makes me differ little from a brute: / For animals are led by natures lore" (44–45). Eve's meditation on the animals of the Garden clarifies her need to escape ignorance, but it prompts no thoughts about a mate. If Adam, in *Paradise Lost*, asks the question, "how can I be solitary?," the Eve-figure in Speght's poem asks, "how do I differentiate myself from the animals in order to have knowledge?" Companionship is never a component of her goal.

To Adam's dismay, Milton's Eve appears to share this impulse; this trait can even be seen as contributing to Eve's fall. The poem will even establish frequent links between Eve's tendency toward being solitary and Satan's frequent description as "alone." We hear Adam articulate this in his Book 8 account of Eve's superiority: "she seems / And in her self complete" (8.547–48).[16] Yet Adam—and I might suggest the poem itself—fears the Eve-like figures appearing in Speght and Sowernam who do not seem to need an Adam. Eve's creation in Book 4 certainly links her to narcissism, but even once she is taught that the observed image "is thyself," she turns away from Adam when led to him: "yet methought less fair, / Less winning soft, less amiably mild, / Than that smooth wat'ry image" and "back I turn'd" (478–80). Only when her hand is "Seiz'd" does she "yield" to become Adam's "other half" (489, 488). Adam is not really wrong in Book 8 that "she seems / And in her self complete" (547–48); she has illustrated this "esse" since her creation. The doubledness of Eve's identity, meant to be Adam's helpmate and yet maintaining a desire to be "sole," is described accurately, if unknowingly, by Adam. In response to her suggestion in Book 9 that they separate, Adam calls her "Sole Eve, Associate sole" (9.227). A tension thus exists between her leanings toward being "sole" and her identity as another's "sole" partner. "Sole partner and sole part of all these joys" (4.411), Eve is, contradictorily, both: in inclination "sole," at times "alone," she is nonetheless described as Adam's only "Associate."[17]

The language in Eve's dream links her to solitariness as well. Though in the dream she initially responds to a "call" she believes to be Adam's, Eve wanders solitary: "And on, methought, alone I pass'd through ways / That brought me on a sudden to the Tree / Of interdicted Knowledge" (5.50–52). Adam is right to argue to God that he needs a mate: God responds that "I, ere thou spak'st, / Knew it not good for Man to be alone" (8.444–45). Yet Eve's impulse is not to join Adam, and her status "alone" in the dream associates her with, instead, Satan. Sustained references to Satan as "alone" recur throughout the poem: he departs for Earth on "his solitary flight" (2.632); he is "Alone thus wand'ring" (3.667) toward Earth; and he arrives in Eden "alone" (4.129). While a number of other traits could be said to link Satan and Eve, her inclination to lean toward solitude aligns her with the portrait of Eve in Speght and Sowernam while suggesting that Milton may be engaging these particular details in the early seventeenth-century portraits of our first mother.[18]

No where can we see this more clearly than in the aftermath of the Fall in *Paradise Lost*. The link that Speght and Sowernam establish between Eve and the anti-feminist debate becomes, I will suggest, the largest influence on Milton's use of anti-feminist conventions within his text. His portrait of Eve will take on—briefly—the role of a defender of women's position. Departing from analogs for—and possible influences on—*Paradise Lost*, Milton has Eve engage not only in a pre-Fall argument about the reasons to fall, but a post-Fall defense of her actions. While almost all of Milton's early and mid-century analogs offer an immediately repentant Eve, Milton creates an Eve who justifies her fault by recalling the strategies of early seventeenth-century defenses of women. Subsequently in Book 10, Milton's engagement with the anti-feminist tradition becomes clearest in his rant against Eve's actions and then women in general. While, as I will suggest, this passage aligns very closely to the language of, and conventions in, seventeenth-century attacks on women, criticism of Milton has paid much less attention to this sequence. When it is discussed, the imagery is linked to much older traditions—classical, biblical, Hebraic—even though the texts in the anti-feminist tradition are much more contemporary for Milton as well as closer in tone and language.[19]

The scene, which follows God's condemnation of Adam and Eve for their sin, begins when Adam, who has "lamented loud / Through the still Night," is prompted out of this soliloquy by Eve; she "approaching nigh, / Soft words to his fierce passion she assay'd" (10.845–46, 864–65). What follows is a 50-line diatribe that links Eve, and all women, to the stock conventions contained within contemporary anti-feminist attacks.

> Out of my sight, thou Serpent, that name best
> Befits thee with him leagu'd, thyself as false
> And hateful; nothing wants, but that thy shape,
> Like his, and color Serpentine may show
> Thy inward fraud, to warn all Creatures from thee
> Henceforth; lest that too heav'nly form, pretended
> To hellish falsehood, snare them. But for thee
> I had persisted happy, had not thy pride
> And wand'ring vanity, when least was safe,
> Rejected my forewarning, and disdain'd
> Not to be trusted, longing to be seen
> Though by the Devil himself, him overweening
> To over-reach, but with the Serpent meeting
> Fool'd and beguil'd, by him thou, I by thee,
> To trust thee from my side, imagin'd wise,
> Constant, mature, proof against all assaults,
> And understood not all was but a show
> Rather than solid virtue, all but a Rib
> Crooked by nature, bent, as now appears,
> More to the part sinister from me drawn,
> Well if thrown out, as supernumerary
> To my just number found. O why did God,
> Creator wise, that peopl'd highest Heav'n
> With Spirits Masculine, create at last
> This novelty on Earth, this fair defect
> Of Nature, and not fill the World at once
> With Men as Angels without Feminine,
> Or find some other way to generate
> Mankind? this mischief had not then befall'n,
> And more that shall befall, innumerable
> Disturbances on Earth through Female snares,
> And strait conjunction with this Sex: for either
> He never shall find out fit Mate, but such
> As some misfortune brings him, or mistake,
> Or whom he wishes most shall seldom gain
> Through her perverseness, but shall see her gain'd
> By a far worse, or if she love, withheld
> By Parents, or his happiest choice too late
> Shall meet, already linkt and Wedlock-bound
> To a fell Adversary, his hate or shame:
> Which infinite calamity shall cause
> To Human life, and household peace confound. (867–908)

The connection between this speech of Adam's and the conventions of anti-feminist attacks is quite explicit: one of the most damning attacks on women—

which Speght and Sowernam re-author—is the link between Eve and the snake. Adam begins: "Out of my sight, thou Serpent, that name best / Befits thee." Eve is linked to the "Serpent," and though "thy shape" hides this identity, he hopes it will "show / Thy inward fraud" to protect others from her "snaring" possibilities. Swetnam had, of course, characterized women as "these venomous Adders, Serpents, and Snakes" (A4r), and this dramatic moment in *Paradise Lost* identifies women through the same imagery. Adam recursively attacks Eve's internal "shape" as having the same "color Serpentine" as the tempter snake while Swetnam highlights how a woman will "turne to a Serpent" (B1v) whenever she does not get what she wants. The danger that women cause, Adam shouts, is that their external, and beautiful, "heav'nly form" "snares" men, hiding women's internal perversity (872–73).

This language of "snar[ing]" men through beauty comes directly from the anti-feminist tradition, which Swetnam's language highlighted: women are "subtill and dangerous for . . . their faces are lures, their beauties are baytes, their looks are netts" (B2v). Milton will repeat women's capacity to "snare" men at line 897 when their "Female snares" are expanded to describe all of womankind. This attack on all of women, begun in Milton with his attack on Eve and extended to all women in the course of the speech, is characteristic of this tradition and particularly of Swetnam's popular tract. Other conventions infuse this speech by Adam. While both Adam's diatribe and Swetnam's text will attack women's vanity, a general accusation against Eve, they also deploy the very image of the crooked rib. While in Swetnam women are "crooked by nature" since the rib from which she has been fashioned is "a crooked thing good for nothing else," Adam's language appears as if directly drawn from this tract. Women are "a Rib / Crooked by nature," a phrase directly echoing Swetnam's epitaph, while the implications of the "bent" nature of the rib become extended to women's nature in both texts.

The implication that these traits inherently exist within Eve is developed in Adam's elaboration of Eve's origin on the "sinister" or left side of man. The character flaws of women were a mainstay of many of these anti-feminist tracts: Swetnam's very title accuses women of being "Lewde, Idle, Froward, and vnconstant" (tp). Alongside traits of this kind, the theological judgments of Eve's "pride" and "vanity" appear in Adam's condemnation. Further, women's secondary status—both in terms of the order of creation and of their moral composition—is clarified in Adam's claim about Eve's supplemental nature: "Well if thrown out, as supernumerary / To my just number found." [20] Not "just" as is Adam, Eve is shown to be a "defect," an incomplete as well as unnecessary second thought by God.

Most significant is the effect that both Adam's speech and Swetnam's tract wish to achieve. From the beginning of Swetnam's *Arraignment*, his goal is to silence women, to keep them from responding to his attack: "I wish you to conceal it with silence, lest in starting up to find fault, you proue yourselues guilty of these monstrous accusations" (A2v). This will achieve the very silence Swetnam hoped to accomplish: Eve is silent in the face of his diatribe as she kneels "at [Adam's] feet," where she "Fell humble and imbraced them" (911–12). Eve thus enacts the very desire expressed within Swetnam's tract: "downe, downe vpon your knees, you earthly Serpents" (E2r). Thus, not only is the very language in Adam's *Paradise Lost* diatribe parallel to Swetnam's *Arraignment*, the stated goals of this anti-feminist language and tradition echo through Adam's speech.[21]

The passage will continue to align itself with the tracts' conventions in Adam's ensuing lament about men's unhappiness in love, all a result of female character and actions. The sequence is marked, then, by another convention of late sixteenth- and early seventeenth-century anti-feminist tracts: men who publish attacks on women are often dismissed or upbraided as writing because they "surfeit," or overly experience emotion, when in love. Their own romantic failures actually produce their decision to blame all women. Constantia Munda accuses Swetnam of this in her tract, *The Worming of a mad Dogge*: "you, hauing peraduenture had some curst wife that hath giuen you as good as you brought . . . you run a madding vp and downe to make a scrole of female frailties" (8 [C1v]). Adam could be so accused. He laments in the poem that man will always be frustrated in love: man "never shall find out fit Mate, but such / As some misfortune brings him, or mistake" (10: 899–900). Unhappiness in love, then, becomes the closing argument for man's unlucky state: the "innumerable / Disturbances on Earth" that have "befall'n" men "through Female snares" (10: 896–97). Adam's emphasis on men's suffering in love as a result of the Fall again aligns his rant with conventions that dominated anti-feminist tracts.

Yet Milton's deployment of these conventions does not clarify the status that Adam's remarks are supposed to have in the poem. To locate how this sequence is operating in the poem, let us return to the previous instance in which Eve's actions—and the resulting Fall—are described as producing the future character of women, and man's resulting unhappiness. In Book 9, Adam first states that all women's future behavior is determined by the Fall. During a "fruitless" "mutual accusation" that ensues after their sequential eating of the apple, Adam states

> . . . Thus it shall befall
> Him who to worth in Woman overtrusting
> Lets her Will rule; restraint she will not brook,
> And left to herself, if evil thence ensue,
> Shee first his weak indulgence will accuse. (1182–86)

Adam abstracts from this event, consequently passing judgment on how women will be: Eve's sin will pattern all future women's behavior.

The overarching convention of anti-feminist attacks, that women can be classified as a group inherently "crooked," is explicit in Adam's statement, but is further reinforced by the tradition of editing this passage. While the 1667 and 1674 editions of the poem read "Him who to worth in *Women* overtrusting," authoritative modern editors like Merritt Hughes have transformed the word to its singular form "Woman."[22] One of only three uses of "women" in the poem, Adam here is employing a more contemporary descriptor for women as a category, distinct from his and the poem's usual use of "Woman" when describing womankind.[23] Editors seem to be motivated by consistency: the category of "women" is infrequently used in the poem, and so they maintain the biblical style of the poem by changing this word. And yet, the unusual deployment of "women" rather than "woman" here to describe a (gendered) category of persons is the point. As Adam abstracts from his Book 9 experience with Eve, he imagines the many future times that "women" will lead men astray. As a result, he similarly deploys the (future) negative classification of all "women" featured in Swetnam's title: "Lewd, Idle, Froward, and vnconstant *women*" (tp; my emphasis). Modern editions consequently erase, by "correcting" this line, Milton's alignment to anti-feminist conventions, which judge all "women" to be such as a result of the Fall.

Most significant, though, is the exchange between Adam and Eve that prompts Adam's Book 9 summary of the dangers women pose. As we will see, Milton's Eve differs significantly from the female protagonists of other Fall narratives because she offers a defense of herself, an explicit response to Adam's attack in Book 9. Eve, "mov'd with touch of blame," offers a fifteen-line defense in which she accuses Adam of susceptibility to "Fraud in the Serpent" (1143, 1150) and blames him for having allowed her to wander off alone.

Eve's arguments are hardly satisfying, relying as they do on redirected blame and contradictory logic: she had wanted to separate from Adam, which allowed Satan access to her alone, and now she blames Adam for letting her go. Yet the true significance of this passage lies not in the terms of her defense, but in the fact that she defends herself at all. Like Speght and Sowernam, who reconstruct an alternative identity of Eve in their defenses, Eve argues against the conventional language of attack within the anti-feminist debate. And she does so by employing its very language. She even anticipates how the synecdoche of her as a "crooked rib" will be employed, transforming the image in her defense: "Was I to have never parted from thy side? / As good have grown there still a lifeless Rib" (9.1153–54). While the "crooked rib" may have erred, her "lifeless Rib" image asserts that women must have some independent status, or they would have no existence at all.

In explicitly invoking the language of the debate over women in her defense, Eve is offering the "Apology" for her actions that has been alluded to earlier in Book 9. Just after she has taken the apple and decided to share her good fortune with Adam, her approach to him is described in language evocative of the actual anti-feminist debate: "To him she hasted, in her face excuse / Came Prologue, and Apology to prompt, / Which with bland words at will she thus addrest" (9.854–56). By labeling her address to Adam as an "Apology," she explicitly positions her resulting speech in the tradition of defenses of women. "Apology" was a popular title for these texts; three different defenses entitled "Apology for Womankind" appeared in 1605, 1609, and then again in 1620. The phrase is used as well by female defenders of women: the defense of Eve in Aemilia Lanyer's *Salve Deus Rex Judaeorum* is glossed in the margin as "Eves Apologie" (84). Most significantly, here we observe Milton represent Eve as the first defender of women.

When we compare Eve's actions to Milton's other analogs, Eve's choice to defend herself in *Paradise Lost* is unique. Or, perhaps more accurately, the texts by Speght, Sowernam, and Lanyer offer a counter analog for Milton's portrait of Eve—one in which she too will produce an "Apology." In Milton, Eve imagines that she has experienced great fortune by eating the fruit from the Tree of Knowledge: by delaying her recognition of the grievous error, Milton allows Eve time in which to contemplate her action and then produce an "Apology." Alternately, in most of the analog texts, Eve is immediately repentant upon sinning. In Giambattista Andreini's play *L'Adamo*, Eve instantly understands the gravity of her sin upon Adam's tasting of the apple; her response is extreme self-castigation: "I was a sightless mole to all my good, . . . I was a foe to Adam; against God / A rebel; and for daring to exalt / Myself to heaven's gates, I am cast down / Even to the threshold of deep Hell itself" (257); she doesn't offer a defense, but instead a self-authored attack: "I have caused your ruin. . . . A woman, only evil do I merit" (258–59). In Salandra's play *Adamo Caduto*, immediately after the Fall Adam and Eve blame themselves jointly, not each other as in Book 9. Instead of Eve producing an "Apology" for her actions, Adam and Eve become unified in their castigation of their joint fall: "Was [Satan's] example / (Fools that *we* are) no adequate restraint / To hold the hand back from its poisonous act?" (335; my emphasis). Even in Grotius's *Adamus Exul*, which offers a scene that is the closest to Milton's account of the Fall, Eve defends herself against Adam's quick judgment, but she does not engage issues of her culpability. In fact, she has even begun self-castigating before her decision to take the apple: "Woman, what wouldst thou do? Art ready to desert / the Author of all Good, Creator of all things. . . . Chose better counselors" (173).

Book 9, alternately, offers us a debate between Adam and Eve ending in an exchange that recalls the tracts of Swetnam and Speght: Adam begins with critique, Eve responds, and Adam counters. This "vain contést," as Milton describes it in the final line of Book 9, further underscores its identity as a debate. In fact, his inflection of "contést" [with the emphasis on the second syllable] opens the word up to a doubled meaning: the "contest" of skill that had marked the body of sixteenth-century anti-feminist tracts as well as the "contest"-ation or fight in which Adam and Eve engage at this moment.

This event in Book 9 thus provides us a frame for reading the Book 10 tirade produced by Adam. It will end this "contést": Eve, who countered Adam's critique in Book 9, will now become a tableau of utter repentance. Immediately following his speech and his "turn" from her, "Eve, / Not so repulst, with Tears that ceas'd not flowing, / And tresses all disorder'd, at his feet / Fell humble, and imbracing them, besought / His peace" (10.909–13). The "contést" characterizing the close of Book 9 is ended by Adam's generation—not just repetition—of the anti-feminist tradition: following his summary of what will *become* the tradition of attacks on women, Eve announces herself "thy suppliant / I beg, and clasp thy knees" (916–17). She absorbs the fault for the Fall, requesting of Heaven "that all / The sentence from thy head remov'd may light / On me, sole cause to thee of all this woe" (933–35). Eve becomes silenced by the eruption—in fact the creation of—anti-feminist language.

Further, in the course of taking responsibility for the Fall, Eve re-positions herself within the very gender hierarchy that had been disrupted by her sinning and then Adam's choice to follow her: by falling, Adam valued Eve over God, reversing the spiritual hierarchy articulated in Book 4. There, in our first vision of Adam and Eve, the gender and spiritual hierarchy of *Paradise Lost* is explicitly plotted by this line: "Hee for God only, shee for God in him" (4.299).[24] Eve will return to that line following Adam's rebuke, confessing the profundity of her sin as she now echoes the hierarchical language she had previously rejected through her actions. She declares that they "both have sinn'd, but thou / Against god only, I against God and thee" (10.930–31). A close echo to the Book 4 line, it is spoken not by the narrator but by Eve herself. Yet parallels emerge both relationally and metrically. The hierarchical position of God, then Adam, then Eve expressed within Book 4 is now repeated through an almost parallel arrangement of the elements in this phrase. "God" and "only" occupy the same metric position in the line. By compressing "against" into a single syllable, we keep the line to ten feet; the effect of this compression is that the pronouns in the Book 4 and Book 10 lines align perfectly. "Shee" and "I" (both referring to Eve) occupy the fifth foot of the line, "God" is positioned in the same place in both lines, and the line ends with "him" and "thee"—both referring to Adam—in the final foot. These pronoun alignments further underscore that the parallel line, as the same hierarchical relationship between God, Adam and Eve, is now spoken by her: in her acknowledgment of sin, Eve actually mouths the very gendered and spiritual hierarchy the poem had previously asserted. Eve's scripted recasting of the earlier line means that now she will speak the language of proper gender hierarchy.[25] Most significantly, though, her rehearsal of this line directly follows Adam's anti-feminist tirade. His speech has the effect of training Eve to articulate the appropriate spiritually subordinate position for women.

The speech's effectiveness takes us to the heart of the interpretive problem posed by the passage. Adam's speech may work, but it is highly unsatisfying in dramatic and poetic terms. The character of Adam that emerges here is one likely to be rejected by the reader: Merritt Hughes describes Adam in his attack on Eve as "behav[ing] rather badly" and "in danger of losing his laurels as a human being to her" (177)[26]: much of this is attributable to Adam's refusal to assume some responsibility for the Fall. He then transforms this unwillingness into a discourse of misogyny; we watch as Adam takes on the role of the tract-publishing misogynist at this moment, fueled by his anger and stubbornness. Yet the tone within anti-feminist tracts such as Swetnam's was jocular fun—at the expense of women, of course. The pleasure that most readers of the anti-feminist debate would probably have enjoyed seems absent here. In this moment, Adam's words produce instead an acutely serious situation filled with emotional intensity: "Eve . . . with Tears that ceas'd not flowing, / And tresses al disorder'd, at his feet / Fell humble, and imbracing them, besought / His peace, and thus proceeded in her plaint" (10.909–13). The power of Adam's tirade produces a pathos-filled, if compliant, Eve.

I would argue as well that the style of the passage continues to link Milton's verse with the published tradition of attacks on women, a parallel that might explain many readers' dissatisfaction with the language, as with the dramatic experience, of the passage. For, if Adam is at his ugliest as a character here, the verse appears to be some of the ugliest within the poem. Metrically, this speech produces the most concentrated number of extrametrical syllables, a stylistic "lapse" that critics from Sprott to André Verbart have linked to the moral lapse of the Fall.[27] Furthermore, as if attempting to match the run-on rambling style of the anti-feminist tracts, Milton's constant enjambment in these lines—the carrying over of the grammatical structure from one line to the next—produces a reading experience like that of an unstoppable diatribe; this list of woman's ills moves from one to the next to the next with no complexity derived from modifying or qualifying statements. The normal flow of Milton's verse works by placing phrases within and between lines, thus shifting the cadence while complicating the meaning of such phrases. We can observe this practice in an earlier speech by Adam:

Bold deed thou hast presum'd, advent'rous Eve,
And peril great provok't, who thus hath dar'd
Had it been only coveting to Eye
That sacred Fruit, sacred to abstinence,
Much more to taste it under ban to touch. (9.921–25)

Both in sound and in meaning, the interjected phrases, "sacred to abstinence," "Much more to taste it under ban to touch," unveil layers of meaning that add richness to the "Bold deed" and the consequent "peril" she now faces. If that creates an accumulation of meaning, Adam's diatribe becomes a perversion of Milton's usual "or":

for either
He never shall find out fit Mate, but such

As some misfortune brings him, or mistake,
Or whom he wishes most shall seldom gain
Through her perverseness, but shall see her gain'd
By a far worse, or if she love, withheld
By Parents, or his happiest choice too late
Shall meet, already linkt and Wedlock-bound
To a fell Adversary, his hate or shame. (10.897–906)

The "or" here allows for the piling on of the effects of "woeman," each example of man's pain equally shallow and undeveloped; as a result, it com-
prises an unmediated list. Instead of elaborating an idea through his verse,
this unnuanced rhetorical force carries, even hurries, the reader to the end of
the passage. The structure of the anti-feminist diatribe thus replaces Milton's
more subtle unwrapping of meaning: as the reader is carried through to the
end of Adam's speech, she is allowed no rest from the accusations hurled at
us and Eve.

I am suggesting, then, that efficacy and style are purposely set into conflict
in this passage. The speech does work: it forces a particular kind of repentance
on Eve's part, and the terms of her repentance resonate with the text's earlier
account of Adam and Eve. She is now scripted to mouth the text's earlier spiritual location of women. Milton's text, then, exposes the cultural efficacy of
the anti-feminist tradition in silencing women as it makes Adam the father of
anti-feminist discourse. Adam's construction of the tradition within the narrative becomes the manner by which Eve can be re-authored into acknowledg-
ing the very hierarchy she had rejected when imagining the fruit as
"render[ing] me more equal" (9.823).

Looking to the analogs underscores the uniqueness of Adam's effective
scripting of Eve more generally and confirms the purpose of his tirade. Attacks
of this kind on Eve or women more generally are not placed in the mouth of
the first man: In Du Bartas's *Devine Weekes*, Adam and Eve do not even discuss
their fall; Eve is castigated by the narrator, not by Adam. In Salandra's *Adamo
Caduto*, the play employs the allegorical figure of Guile to show that Eve and
Guile are inextricable. Though Eve, and all women, may be interpolated into
the anti-feminist tradition through these powerful critiques of female character, these Eves do not need to be trained. As we see in Giambattista Andreini's
L'Adamo, Eve immediately castigates herself; there is no need for her to be
trained by Adam's anachronistic tirade since Eve has already confessed: "I
have caused your ruin . . . A woman, only evil do I merit" (258–59). With no
narrative consequence to Adam's anger, these analogs paint an already compliant Eve. In *Paradise Lost*, Adam's speech must effect that.

Further, this Book 10 speech, its language, the overt conventionality of the
tropes, even the seeming structuring of the passage to match this anti-feminist
discourse, needs to be viewed as an effective social phenomenon. Milton could
have cast this language of misogyny as authoritative either through the narra-

tor's voice, as does Du Bartas, or have found an external narrative to naturalize this judgment of Eve, as in Salandra. Instead, Milton incorporates the highly artificial language of the anti-feminist tradition into this single, narratively prominent, moment. The very stylistic dissatisfactions of the passage are intended, I believe, to jar us into noticing the speech's status as convention—in fact the birth of the conventional tropes of misogynist argument. As a consequence, Milton's presentation of Adam's speech illustrates the cultural power of anti-feminist language. Milton does highlight how gender hierarchy can be enacted. But in doing so, he illustrates how that hierarchy is accomplished through a cultural rehearsal of tropes.

At this moment, though, we have to ask what has been so disruptive within Eve's attempted defense in Book 9 such that Milton needs to restage this "anti-feminist" exchange. The particular danger to which Adam must respond is Eve's assertion of the need for some female self-determination; she has argued that without this, woman would be a "lifeless Rib." When female self-determination is asserted, though, the status of male authority is challenged; whom do men now have authority over? That is the danger that has been offered by Eve's defense, and by the seventeenth-century defenses offered by Eve-like figures like Speght and Sowernam. Book 10 must work to stabilize this disruption by generating a figure of Eve who can be instructed, literally, to talk the talk of hierarchical gender authority. Adam's tirade will expose its conventional status, but the terms of Eve's defense have made this culturally and socially necessary. Adam's scripting of Eve will restore order between the pair, while laying bare the mechanism that has accomplished it.

The dialogue that I am suggesting exists between Milton's enactment of the anti-feminist tradition in *Paradise Lost* and earlier defenses by women is also part of the larger social conversation in which these pamphlets were engaged. The seventeenth-century pamphlet wars, while reflecting a long tradition of misogyny, are obviously inflected by a political ideology of gender hierarchy, but one that was beginning to experience a series of challenges. A powerful analogy between the state and the family that characterized English political thought through much of the seventeenth century meant that order in the household—and of the relationship between men and women within it—modeled political order.[28] As the work of historians including Anthony Fletcher, Susan Amussen, and Margaret Ezell has illustrated, "Relations between husband and wife are part of the larger questions in the seventeenth century on the nature of political theory and individual liberty" (Ezell, 60). The family/state analogy that dominates until the end of the seventeenth century necessitates order within the family, which supports governmental organization; the analogy, according to Amussen, "helped define order and hierarchy in early modern Europe" (204). As the seventeenth century moved on, this analogy became a central tenet of Royalist thought to which Republican thinkers, such as Milton, would need to respond. While the tradition of classical

Republican thought framed Milton's thinking, the debate over the theoretical grounding of the state necessarily fused these older classical and English traditions of liberty to the political issues of the familial metaphor.[29] We can observe just one of Milton's intersections of these two discourses within his *Doctrine and Discipline of Divorce*. When he says it is "unprofitable and dangerous to the Common-wealth, when the household estate, out of which must flourish forth the vigor and the spirit of all public enterprises, is so ill contented and procu'd at home, and cannot be supported" (247), we hear attempts to support the Republican state through, and to plot the Republican state on, the workings of family itself. Disruption in the "household estate" will destabilize the state.[30] Consequently, notions of political obedience were based on the obedience of a wife to her husband. When Milton engages the narrative of the Garden and these earlier narratives of Eve defending herself within that Garden, he is engaging the core issue of state organization and the Republican possibilities embedded within this.[31]

For, the story of Adam and Eve served as the grounding narrative of familial structure and hierarchy, providing an account of, and pattern for, both gendered and political relationships. The foundations of government and social order were thus derived in the seventeenth century from the gendered implications of the story in Eden and of the Fall. Social and political stability depended upon the maintenance of gender identities, yet the wide-ranging anti-feminist debate—particularly some of the modifications it undergoes in the seventeenth century that stress the events in the Garden—suggests how much pressure these categories were under during the period. The stakes are not, simply, order or "peace" achieved between men and women or, here, between Adam and Eve. "Peace" in marriage—and between Adam and Eve as the model for all future marriages—is a powerfully political issue since it models stability for, or disruption to, the state. All of these texts—the defenses by Sowernam and Speght and the negotiation of the "disputing" Eve figure by Milton—are thus engaging a central political issue within the seventeenth century as they map alternate images of male and female relations. If with different political goals than other writers employing aspects of the family/state analogy, Milton engages such issues directly. He thus had many reasons to consider the distinct reformulations of the Garden story in the writings of Rachel Speght and Ester Sowernam.

A mappable gender hierarchy serves as the underpinning for governmental structure in the seventeenth century, yet that map will become, if not entirely replotted in the course of the period, redrawn as the theories of patriarchal power become placed under increasing pressure. Anthony Fletcher states, "there is good reason to think that many Englishmen felt some unease about the security of their hold upon the gender order" (162). As we have seen, the figure of the disputing Eve threatens, but I would also suggest exposes, the foundation upon which the state was perilously balanced. I have argued here

that Milton turns to this language of the anti-feminist debate—and particularly the more challenging representations offered by the women pamphleteers
in the early seventeenth century—in order to try and stabilize the debate about
gender. Yet, the manner in which he tries to accomplish this, by which he attempts to maintain the old lines of the map, simultaneously exposes how fully
the structure of government depended upon these very pillars of gendered authority. In an attempt to shore the artifice, he, like the disputing Eves before
him, exposes its construction.

Milton's turn to these debates thus offers a historically contingent stabilization of a vision of gendered responsibility for the Fall while simultaneously
containing traces of an alternative vision of women's interlocutory engagement with issues of gendered and political hierarchy. Milton's Adam over-
writes, if you will, Eve's own authorship of a "defense" or "apology." Yet
Adam, like the text of *Paradise Lost*, cannot erase the tropes that composed Milton's complex portrait of Eve. Even though Eve's defense is overridden, and
overwritten, in the course of the poem, the traces of that debate resonate
through the language in the text. Adam, now cast as the "author" of the anti-
feminist debate, can no more silence his disputing Eve than could Swetnam
end debate. Just as Speght and Sowernam's adoption of the identity of Eve
prompts a reconfiguration of the strategies in their defenses, numerous writers
in the seventeenth century continue to explore this very connection between
Eve and the author. Aemilia Lanyer in her contribution to the *querelle des femmes*
will also engage the identity of Eve within her literary text. While the texts by
Speght and Sowernam explore the implications of gender hierarchy for the organization of government, political organization comes to be at the heart of
Lanyer's defense of women. Because of the terms by which Lanyer renarrates
the story of the Fall, as well as generic innovations within *Salve Deus Rex Judaeorum*, Lanyer's poem also offers a suggestive challenge to which—I will argue—
Milton responds.

Gazing, Gender, and the Construction of Governance in Aemilia Lanyer's *Salve Deus Rex Judaeorum* and Milton's *Paradise Lost*

As the previous chapter argues, a convention of "disputing Eves" emerges in seventeenth-century female-authored defenses, to which Milton appears to respond with his apology-offering Eve. The narrator in Aemilia Lanyer's 1611 poem *Salve Deus Rex Judaeorum* could also be located within this tradition of disputing Eves, as could the women depicted in the accompanying country house poem, "The Description of Cookeham." As with other tracts in what I have termed the "disputing Eve" tradition, *Salve Deus* has been appropriately located in the *querelle des femmes* genre, both because of its goal of defending womankind against conventional attacks and for its portrait of a devout community of female worshippers.[1] With the multiple figures for a disputing Eve in *Salve Deus* recalling these aspects of Speght's and Sowernam's texts, it's possible that the generic link to these female-authored 1620s defenses might have offered some reason for Milton to have perused this poem. Yet as this chapter will show, the seventeenth-century *querelle des femmes* offers only one point of connection between Milton's and Lanyer's poetry.

Drawn together by a similar exploration of the problems in, and strategies for, versifying the Passion, both poets explore the relationship between mystical visions, acts of (gendered) gazing, and the implications of structures of governance. This chapter will thus engage what I see as another "conversation" between an early seventeenth-century text by a woman and Milton's *Paradise Lost*, a conversation discernible through generic, theoretical, and linguistic links between Lanyer's writings and Milton's early poetry and late epic. Generic problems posed by the Passion poem work in concert with the politically inflected consequences of gaining visual access to the mystical sight of Christ's body and to the site of the original Garden. Milton, who engages the poetic practices deployed in *Salve Deus Rex Judaeorum* to address the challenges of a Protestant Passion poem, will ultimately rework certain social and political implications which Lanyer's use of the female gaze had allowed her engage. Thus, Lanyer introduces into her country house poem, "A Description of

Cookeham," a series of reflections on the gendered implications of gazing and their relationship to aspects of governance which appear refracted in Milton's own exploration of a parallel matrix in *Paradise Lost*. Their theoretical exploration of the social and political implications of the gaze, then, joins the parallel uses each poet makes of the passion poem. This chapter thus considers the influence of Lanyer's poetry—located at the interstices of the traditions of the *querelle des femmes*—female prophecy, and the Passion poem, on Milton's writings, initially in his own failed 1630 "The Passion" and later in *Paradise Lost*.

In establishing this generic bridge between these two poets' experiments with the Passion poem form, I am specifically aligning Milton's 1630 poem to Lanyer's 1611 text. As such, the circulation of Lanyer's text, and thus accessibility for Milton, becomes tantamount for such a claim. Published only in 1611, *Salve Deus Rex Judaeorum*'s title pages appear to have had two different impressions, and the volume exists today in a number of different forms, almost always as a result of different combinations of extensive dedicatory material.[2] We know that the text circulated among the royal family, court musicians, and the Cumberland family itself: the Countess's own Puritan proclivities, Milton's connection to Henry Lawes, and even the possible performance of Milton's *Comus* at the fourth Earl of Cumberland's Skipton Castle offer possible lines of connection between the author of *Paradise Lost* and Lanyer's volume of poems.[3] More importantly, though, are Milton's own reading practices, routinely considered to be voracious; in considering the interconnections between Milton's and Lanyer's Passion poems, I am thus extending the list of poets from whom Milton could have drawn. Until now, all of the poets whose Passion poems have been compared to and considered as possible models for Milton have been male. This chapter, which will identify a range of connections between Milton's and Lanyer's poetry, thus begins by hazarding the connection between this female and male poet through a suggestive range of stylistic tropes.

Protestant Passions: Possible Models for Milton's Failed 1630 Poem

John Milton's "Passion" poem, composed in 1630, would remain unfinished but nonetheless appear in print in the 1645 *Poems*.[4] Thus, Milton—who describes his youthful experiment as "roving verse"—saw "The Passion" as noteworthy, even impressive, in its failure.[5] Further, the significance of this topic for a poet undertaking religious verse, as well as Milton's placement of it in his collected poems, suggests how seriously Milton considered its composition. Consequently, it seems reasonable that Milton might have consulted some of the approximately eleven Passion poems produced between the 1590s and the 1620s when undertaking his own poem in the genre.[6] Later in the chapter, I will contextualize Lanyer's and Milton's strategies amid contemporaries who attempted to create a Passion poem. As this opening discussion of Lanyer's and Milton's poems will reveal, though, only among these two Passion poems do we find parallel poetic strategies, including the gendering of an inspiring "Patroness," the invocation of the muse, and the thematization of perspective.

As Milton prepares to acquire inspiration for the weighty topic of Christ's crucifixion, Milton positions himself amid the "softer airs" and "softer strings" of the "Lute" or "Viol" (27–28). This elegiac tone prompts his turn to "Night, [the] best Patroness of grief" (29). As such, the poem gestures to a range of feminine associations as it invokes a mystical vision necessary to undertake a poem on Christ's crucifixion. The "softer airs" and Milton's turn to Night as his poetic "Patroness" become integrated with the form of inspiration he can (not) achieve, where "my soul [would] in holy vision sit, / In pensive trance, and anguish, and ecstatic fit" (41–42). The narrator's attempt to acquire the inspiration necessary for a Passion poem progressively aligns him to a more passive, if "pensive," "trance" and "ecstatic fit," even if this positioning of the poetic self cannot achieve needed inspiration. While unable to sustain and succeed at a Passion poem, Milton's account of these "softer" strains and the female "Patroness" intriguingly corresponds to details in Lanyer's own Passion poem. Lanyer interweaves her production of this Passion poem with a portrait of her actual patroness; the Countess of Cumberland serves as a central figure enabling Lanyer's portrait of Christ's death. Yet the very devices Lanyer employs to succeed at this "vexed and perplexing subject for lyric poetry in seventeenth-century England" (Schoenfeldt, 561) interlace her 1611 poem with Milton's 1630 effort. For, on closer inspection, Lanyer's strategies within this "comparatively marginal [poetic] subject" (561) of the Passion poem genre are closer to Milton's poem than any other contemporary poets' strategies.

Able to avoid viewing the event "through squinting eyes amid slumping postures"—how Schoenfeldt describes many of the Protestant negotiations of the visual power inherent in the Crucifixion event (562)—Lanyer will embrace and deploy acts of gazing in this poem; these allow her to establish a perspective onto the event and a stable position as a narrator, while often negotiating these acts of gazing through her "Patroness." Because she is taking on the significant and challenging Passion poem form, Lanyer also draws upon a muse and the language of spiritual, even prophetic, inspiration. Louis Martz's influential *Poetry of Meditation* helps to explain the challenges that this form posed for writers, and thus details how Lanyer's mode of entering the subject of the crucifixion enabled her production of this poem.[7] The first step in any meditative process, in poetry or other genres of mediation, was to find a position from which to narrate the religious event or scene (Martz, 43; 30). While three different strategies exist in meditative handbooks of the period, all three require the individual—and in the case of meditative poetry, the poet—to establish a perspective onto the scene. Lanyer describes this acquisition of perspective, which she achieves through invoking an initially itinerant muse who finally establishes a position from which the narrator can describe the event; the "roving verse" that Milton describes in his poem becomes a specific narrative position for Lanyer in *Salve Deus*. Further, by employing the language of (heavenly) inspiration through a muse, Lanyer can access her subject: the crucifixion narrative and Christ's body at the center of this event.

In the "preamble of the Author before the passion" (beginning at line 265), Lanyer introduces her muse to enable her undertaking of the topic of Christ's "Death and Passion" (271). But that muse almost immediately takes flight. Lanyer's account of poetic inspiration and the consequent ability to write a Passion poem will become negotiated through spatial terms as her muse aspires, soars, and flies until finding a position from which to narrate Christ's crucifixion:

These high deserts invites my lowely Muse
To write of Him, and pardon crave of thee,
For Time so spent, I need make no excuse,
Knowing it doth with thy faire Minde agree
So well, as thou no Labour wilt refuse,
That to thy holy Love may pleasing be:
      His Death and Passion I desire to write,
      And thee to reade, the blessed Soules delight.

But my deare Muse, now wither wouldst thou flie,
Above the pitch of thy appointed straine?
With *Icarus* thou seekest now to trie,
Not waxen wings, but thy poore barren Braine,
Which farre too weake, these siely lines descrie;
Yet cannot this thy forward Mind restraine,
      But thy poore Infant Verse must soare aloft,
      Not fearing threat'ning dangers, happening oft.

Thinke when the eye of Wisdom shall discover
Thy weakling Muse to flie, that scarce could creepe,
And in the Ayre above the Clowdes to hover,
When better 'twere mued up, and fast asleepe;
They'l thinke with *Phaeton*, thou canst ne'r recover,
But helplesse with that poore yong Lad to weepe:
      The little World of thy weake Wit on fire,
      Where thou wilt perish in thine owne desire.

But yet the Weaker thou doest seeme to be
In Sexe, or Sence, the more his Glory shines,
That doth infuze such powrefull Grace in thee,
To shew thy Love in these few humble Lines. . . . (265–92)

This "preamble of the Author before the Passion" serves a conventional purpose of declaring her unworthiness for the great project. This language of aspiration, but also the threat of failure, is equally sustained in her use of the imagery of "Icarus" and later "Phaeton." Meanwhile, the motif of flight and of movement becomes Lanyer's mechanism for negotiating the epic voice. Her "deare Muse" will be able to accomplish this great task by allowing her "poore Infant Verse" to "soare aloft."

Poetic aspiration and its fusion with the language of ascent will initially "soare" or wander, but some 20 lines later the narrative voice has found a location from which to complete the task of describing the crucifixion—the very "roving" from which Milton will not be able to escape. Lanyer's narrator will now "run so swiftly up this mightie Hill"; from this position she "may behold" the story of Christ's Passion "with the eye of Faith" (317–18). If God "please t'illuminate my Spirit," she will receive the "Wisdom from his holy Hill" (321–22) as well as the ability to ascend the hill of spiritual poetry in order to recount the passion. The invocation of the muse combines a poetic convention with a religious one: Lanyer portrays a mystical experience in her account of God's spirit entering her, one which makes her a kind of vessel as "he [will] vouchsafe to guide my Hand and Quill" (324). This literal inspiration, one staged through the figure of the muse, makes possible her narrative: "Then will I tell of that sad blacke fac'd Night, / Whose mourning Mantle covered Heavenly Light" (327–28). The effect of Lanyer's "preamble" is to locate a physical position from which she can apprehend and then describe the Passion, this spatial location allowing her to tell this tale.

Lanyer will further highlight the visual terms of access to the event in providing to her patroness, the Countess of Cumberland, such a "view" onto Christ's crucifixion; resonant with Milton's poem, Lanyer's patroness helps constitute this view of, this perspective onto, the event of the crucifixion. Specifically, both poet and patroness become fused by the access they have onto Christ's body, access that makes the narrative of the Passion possible. Gazing in this text becomes one of Lanyer's most prominent, even solidifying, strategies. The Countess's gaze onto the "perfect picture" (1326) of Christ's body is constantly described in language which underscores the importance of the practices of visuality: she is "see[ing] him as a God in glory" "Whereon thine eyes continually may looke" (1329, 1352). Thus her "Eagles eyes" will behold "the glorious Sunne / Of th'all-creating Providence" (25–26), the stress on the act of seeing Christ's body linked throughout to the experience of redemption in the poem:

This with the eie of Faith thou maist behold,
Deere Spouse of Christ, and more than I can write;
And here both Griefe and Joy thou maist unfold,
To *view thy Love* in this most heavy plight . . . (1169–72; my emphasis)

Lanyer's address "To my Ladie of Cumberland" continues to underscore the doubled spectatorship onto Christ's body and story as "I present (deare Lady) to your view, / Upon the Crosse depriv'd of life or breath" (1265–66). Lanyer achieves the goal of gazing onto Christ's body and his death by acquiring a perspectival position from which to tell the story and then awarding this visual access to her patroness.

Her deployment of visual perspective, in particular deploying the Muse to gain the narrator a specific spatial location, will link Milton's work in the genre closely to Lanyer's poem. Lanyer is singular in her use of the muse in early seventeenth-century Passion poems to establish a perspectival position in her poem. Milton's and Lanyer's Passion poems are thus associated by their parallel attempts to resolve the generic dilemmas—particularly the need to find a position from which to narrate the religious event or scene. When Milton notes in the coda to his unfinished poem that he left this poem "unfinisht" because he was "nothing satisfied" with it, the main problem he appears to struggle with is transporting himself to the scene from which he can visualize the events in "The Passion." While Milton will ultimately be un"satisfied" with his efforts, the moves he attempts in the poem align most closely to Lanyer's own 1611 efforts to establish a perspectival position. After drawing his muse to this story of "saddest woe" in the second stanza, Milton turns in the third stanza to an account of Christ as the "sovereign priest," his body as the "Poor fleshly Tabernacle" onto which the poet gazes. But immediately, Milton expresses his sense of constraint within this narrative: "These later scenes confine my roving verse," he tells us at the beginning of stanza four, "bound"ing his muse to "Phoebus."

This language of limitation illustrates Milton's frustration about this first meditative step of visualizing the event; immediately Milton's narrative voice appears in motion. The "roving" verse cannot be contained as the Chariot of Ezekiel in stanza six begins an ascent that releases the poet from the "bound"ing aspect of the meditative position. "My spirit some transporting *Cherub*, feels, / To bear me where the Towers of *Salem* stood" (38–39). Now, his "soul in holy vision sit[s]," establishing a possible perspective from which "Mine eye" can view and recount the event of the death of Christ.

Yet this move to the top of Jerusalem's towers does not resolve Milton's perspectival position. In the following stanza he wonders, "Or should I thence hurried on viewless wing, / Take up a weeping on the Mountains wild" (50–51). Having attempted first to turn to a description of the "Most perfect Hero" (13) in the second and third stanzas, Milton then tries to gain knowledge through an internal inspiration by following Ezekiel's chariot. Finally, at line 43 he attempts to return to a visual account of the experience of Christ: "Mine eye hath found that sad Sepulchral rock / That was the Casket of Heaven's richest store" (43–44). But in the final stanza, he "hurrie[s]" from here "on viewless wing"; when unable to access, through "Mine eye," the event of the Crucifixion, the poet, now "viewless," must admit defeat (50). These shifts in position through which he attempts to access the Passion illustrate Milton's shortcoming; he cannot locate the stable perspective so important to meditation and meditative poetry, and necessary for completing a Passion poem. While Erin Henriksen considers this "habit" of Milton's to approach and then withdraw from the Crucifixion a poetic strategy rather than the failure signed by Milton, the poet who cannot establish a perspectival position cannot continue with this narrative.

Additionally, these poetic moves—and the physical movement of the narrating voice—closely align to Lanyer's poem. In invoking a muse who can then fuel a self-conscious search for a perspectival position onto the Crucifixion event, Milton appears to pattern on the successful strategies that Lanyer employed in *Salve Deus Rex Judaeorum*. Lanyer (anxiously) ascends through the threatening imagery of Icarus and Phaeton, while in "The Passion" Milton indicates a desire to ascend by titling his muse "Phoebus." Milton's movement is more frenetic, as he begins "with Angels" (4), descends to "latter scenes" (22), reascends to "glorious Towers" (40) and then moves onto "Mountains wild" (51); in both poems, though, the ascent motif dominates, as in Lanyer's "preamble" as she moves "in the Ayre above the Clowdes to hover" (283). So too does Milton's muse (re)ascend, in search of a position from which "my soul in holy vision sit" (41).[8] Yet because Milton "roves" from heightened position to heightened position attempting to discover the perspective from which to "score / my plaining verse" (46–47), he never can descend to, and remain on, earth to tell the story.

Milton's unsuccessful perspective onto the Passion consequently highlights the success that Lanyer is able to achieve within the genre. Lanyer too fuses the problem of poetic ambition in this genre with that of finding a location from which to be able to narrate the story of the Passion. Lanyer will choose to descend back to earth in order to tell her tale, which she accomplishes through her turn to Night: "Then will I tell of that sad blacke fac'd Night, / Whose mourning Mantle covered Heavenly Light" (327–28), a complement to Milton's invocation of his "Patroness" of Night. Just as Milton attempts to imagine the night of Christ's crucifixion, Lanyer uses this setting to begin her story of the Passion: "that very Night our Saviour was betrayed, / Oh night! exceeding all the nights of sorrow, / When our most blessed lord . . . to *Mount Olives* went" (329–31, 333). While Milton's central problem in "The Passion" is locating a spatial position from which to establish a visual perspective, Lanyer moves through the positions by which she could locate herself, settling on the descent to Night in order to tell the story of the Passion. It is this descent that Milton can never locate. He has invoked the Night, "Befriend me Night, best Patroness of grief, / Over the Pole thy thickest mantle throw" (29–30), but instead of entering into the story at this point, he reascends: "See, see the Chariot and those rushing wheels / That whirl'd the Prophet up at *Chebar flood*" (36–37). A possible narrative opportunity to enter the Passion lost, he can never tell the story of the Saviour who undertakes human form.

Aemilia Lanyer's search for, and successful identification of, a perspectival position from which to recount the events may have offered a model for Milton's (ultimately failed) attempts to locate a place from which to tell the story. Authors of other (completed) Passion poems negotiated their entrance into the topic of the Passion in many ways, yet all of them are quite distinct from the strategies of Lanyer and Milton. In positioning Lanyer's and Milton's poems against poems by Robert Southwell, Abraham Fraunce, and Giles Fletcher, we see that only Milton and Lanyer resolve, or attempt to resolve, the narrative problem by gazing upon Christ's body through a visually generated perspective. Further, the invocation of the muse is the very mechanism through which Lanyer and Milton can enter this fraught sight/site of the Crucifixion, again setting these two poets apart from all other early seventeenth-century poets: no other contemporary Passion poems either invoke or engage a muse in the narrative of the poem itself.[9] Only Gervase Markham's *The Lamentation of Saint John* mentions a "harsh and vntuned muse, which being as my talent is, slender and simple" (A2v) in the dedicatory letter "To the Christian Reader." Yet Markham will not invoke that muse within the terms of the poem itself. The trope of the muse as inspiring the poet is not deployed in any other Passion poem published between 1600 and 1620.

Instead, the catalog of strategies for entering into the story of Christ's passion included dramatic perspective, historical narrative, and allegorical abstraction: all of these allowed contemporaries to avoid looking directly onto the body of Christ and thus evade the problem of establishing a visual perspective. Of the eleven passion poems (or verse histories of Christ) that were printed in the twenty years surrounding Lanyer's poem, the majority solve the problem of finding perspective onto the meditative event through dramatic narrative.[10] Five tell the story of the Passion by narrating the event through an apostle or through Mary.[11] Samuel Rowlands's 1598 *The betraying of Christ*, which generically resembles a closet drama, employs substantial soliloquies of Judas and then of Peter to tell the story of Christ. By recounting the events of the Crucifixion through this dramatic structure, Rowlands, like other early seventeenth-century poets of the Passion, easily establishes the ground from which the event will be narrated. It alleviates the poet's need to locate a specific meditative position from which to access, spiritually and visually, the Passion itself.

The other six Passion poems use alternate strategies. One group stresses a historical mode of entry into the events of the Crucifixion, such as Robert Holland's 1594 *The Holie History of Our Lord and Saviour Iesus Christs natiuitie, life, acts, miracles, doctrine, death, passion*. Abraham Fraunce's *Emanuel* offers "the natiuity, passion, buriall, and resurrection of Christ," easily beginning the story of "apoynted fight, that feareful combat" led by that "cursed capten Caiphas" (B3r, lines 6, 7, 10). Even much more focused accounts of the Crucifixion, such as John Bullokar's 1622 *A true description of the passion of our Sauior Iesus Christ*, find their entrance to the story of Christ's death through events in the history of Christ's life: "And when he had full thirty three yeeres space. . . . The time was come" (A3r, lines 7, 11). The historical location of the event thus allows the narrative to be told without the apparatus of an observing, surveying narrative eye.

If history provides a narrative entrance into the event of the Crucifixion for many of these poets, allegorical framing of the event is the strategy employed by poets like Christopher Lever and Giles Fletcher. The conceit of the "court of lawe, and equitie" (B1r) opens and continues to structure Lever's version of the Crucifixion, while Giles Fletcher's 1610 *Christs Victorie, and Triumph in Heaven* will locate many of the events of the Passion within a much more abstracted discussion of Christ's influence on the world. The Crucifixion is positioned among a series of four "victories" or "triumphs" of Christ and embedded into the third section on "Christs Triumph over Death," "personified abstractions" dominating a poem that is largely structured around allegory (Mueller, 108). Again, this generic strategy allows Fletcher to narrate the consequences of Christ's death and suffering in broader terms, thus avoiding having to focus on the wounded body. Only Milton and Lanyer, then, position themselves through spatial narratives of perspectival location. Finally, Lanyer's almost unique invocation of the muse for the purposes of producing this poem establishes extensive parallels between her and Milton's later work within the genre. As a consequence, Lanyer's poem offers suggestive generic and stylistic strategies that appear to be echoed in Milton's poem dated nineteen years later.

As a more extensive discussion of Lanyer's practices of gazing in this poem and her entire volume will show, this female gaze, here making possible the view onto the tactile body of Christ, gestures to broader practices of theorizing acts of looking during the period. In employing a mystic's gaze onto Christ's body, thus staging a "redemptive vision" of Christ that Suzanne Biernoff has discerned in the writings of figures like Julian of Norwich (162), Lanyer positions herself (or her narrator) as a female subject with a perspectivally positioned gaze onto the event of the Crucifixion.[12] For, acts of looking abound within the poem: the Countess's gaze onto the "perfect picture" of Christ's body employs sustained ocular language, including "seeing," "looking," "viewing," and the repeated motif of the Countess's "eyes" (26; 1169). In Lanyer's hands, acts of gazing gesture to larger issues of gender always embedded into acts of gazing. Lanyer's own mystical engagement of the gaze consequently complicates the meaning of looking in this poem; the "spectatorial reciprocity" that Biernoff had identified reconfigures, and redistributes, the mechanisms of psychic and social-political power traditionally associated with a male-gendered gaze. Lanyer's Passion poem at the heart of *Salve Deus Rex Judaeorum* thus begins the process of rewriting sociopolitical acts of gazing in the Renaissance which characterize her country house poem, "A Description of Cookeham," as well.

In this period, gazing onto a mystic site, either that of the Crucifixion or of the Edenic space, was interwoven with political implications. As William Poole has delineated in *Milton and the Idea of the Fall*, writers from Gerrald Winstanley to La Peyrère deployed images of, or accounts of, the Garden to further their political claims. In the seventeenth century, then, the very "visions of" or views onto "redemption" that Biernoff describes earlier female mystics as achieving are as embedded with political as with spiritual power. The cultural, social, and political implications of mystical visions are as inflected with gender as with issues of political import. Mystical acts of viewing can offer spiritual as well as cultural power to women, even though that "gaze" has been transhistorically associated with the male and male power. As Lanyer will explore in the complementary poem, "The Description of Cookeham," Lanyer and her "Patroness" will acquire a spiritual perspective as they did in *Salve Deus*. Yet Lanyer's mystical acts of viewing expose the complex relationship between gazing and being gazed upon while granting to the Countess of Cumberland a politically and culturally over-determined perspective.

From stylistic connections between Lanyer's and Milton's poetry, I will now move to certain thematic implications of Lanyer's own poetic choices, ones which continue to provide significant links between Milton's earlier poetic experiment and his later epic poem, *Paradise Lost*. The generic demands of the Passion poem prompt Lanyer and Milton to interrogate the relationship between mystical access and issues of looking and gazing, ones which expose the political and social implications of such acts.

Gendering the Mystical Gaze: Viewing Eden in Lanyer's "Description of Cookeham"
and Milton's Paradise Lost

Published in 1611 as the final poem in *Salve Deus Rex Judareorum*, Lanyer's "Description of Cookeham" details the Countess of Cumberland's estate while describing the loss that the Countess has experienced because of legal battles between husband and wife over the land and house.[13] Elegiac in tone as well as invoking a prelapsarian Edenic space, the account of this garden resonates intriguingly with the re-written Fall narratives in Rachel Speght's and Ester Sowernam's texts. Yet this view provided onto the site of Cookeham allows us to interrogate Lanyer's interweaving of gazing, gender, and social organization in the poem. Political and social order is mapped by and onto the gazing subject who, throughout Lanyer's poem, is Margaret, the Countess of Cumberland.

Given multiple "goodly Prospects" onto the land that the poem argues should be hers, the persistent gazing eye of Margaret comes to acquire power over the land which was traditionally imagined as male. As decades of criticism on the implications of gazing, and being gazed upon, remind us, acts of seeing and being seen are intimately connected to gendered identities as to the social-political implications of looking. Here, the acts of viewing are explicitly linked to acts of ownership and regnal power. The poem, for example, describes "A Prospect fit to please the eyes of Kings: / And thirteene shires appear'd all in your sight" (72–73). In granting to the Countess visual perspective over these "prospects," she is associated with acts of surveying and the language of gaining visual access to the land that was distinctly gendered male. Landowner; surveyor; monarch: in the early seventeenth century, all of these titles describe a man. Conversely, as Patricia Parker has detailed in "Rhetorics of Property: Exploration, Inventory, Blazon," the feminized body of the land was routinely described as a site for control, control enacted by poetic and geographic discourses.

But Lanyer's invocation of the gaze in her poem revises the conventions of surveying land and the assignment of political power that single perspective could accord to an individual. The language of "A Prospect fit to please the eyes of Kings" records the ultimate form, in 1611, of power: the monarch. Lanyer's description of the Countess's "view" thus gestures toward the King's own specific control of visual power, routinely enacted throughout courtly Stuart masques. There, the single perspective from which all political power derived was simultaneous to the position the King occupied within the audience.[14] Now, the view "all in your sight" that the Countess has over "thirteene shires" reconfigures traditional political and gendered forms of power: she, not her husband or King James, is granted perspective onto, and consequent power over, these "thirteene shires."

The Countess's perspective onto the land provided to her by the poet prompts reflection on the meaning of gendered gazing in the early modern period. Harry Berger, in responding to Patricia Simons's discussion of female portraiture in the Italian Renaissance, suggests that these women might become located as subjects in, rather than objects of, the distribution of property through their acts of gazing within portraits. While Simon positions women as "primarily objects of a male discourse which appropriated a kind of female labor or property" (18), this is explicitly countered in the Lanyer poem. Berger, in revising the notion of the exclusively male-empowering gaze, helps us to understand Lanyer's strategies: paintings also depict women, and their process of looking, as accessing social-political power because female property owners could also serve as "upholders of patrilineal order and patriarchal power" (191). We can see this very process in the well-known Piero della Francesca profile portraits of the Duke and Duchess of Urbino. In both portraits, a viewer would look upon the Duke's and Duchess's profiles as they gaze onto the lands of Urbino—the space that their surveying eye marks as under their political control. True, the Duke's view onto the Duchess could be viewed as a controlling male view, making the Duchess "primarily" an object "of a male discourse" of property. Yet, as the two overlook the lands under (their) ducal control, both benefit from the mechanism of "patrilineal order and patriarchal power" implied by this gaze. The Countess, presented in Lanyer purposely without the complementary male counterpart, exerts the same visual power confirming her political control over these "thirteene shires." As we observe the Countess survey her lands, the mechanisms of the gaze are profoundly redesigned: Lanyer works to appropriate for the Countess the very access to "patriarchal power" implied by gazing over the land.

To gaze and to be gazed upon can thus signify a range of avenues to power, ones that negotiate gender positions in unlikely ways. Just as the gaze accessed by Lanyer and the Countess is aligned with certain traditionally male subject positions—the unified subject who acquires single-point perspective, for example—these sequences illustrate how profoundly entwined the prophetic or spiritual gaze is with a legally or politically empowering gaze. The figure of the Countess, offered a prophetic identity as she "often did . . . walke, / With Christ and his Apostles there to talke" (81–82), gains that spiritual inspiration through her perspective over the land. From one such "Prospect," the Countess's gaze will allow her a mystical union with "Christ and his Apostles," spiritually joining Moses, David, and Joseph through her meditation. Thus, throughout Lanyer's poem, the mystical gaze and the sociopolitical gaze over landscape or property become interwoven.

This connection is further supported through the alignment of the Countess's estate with an Edenic site: this prelapsarian space in the "Description of Cookeham" is identified as *"Paradice"* from the opening of the *Salve Deus Rex Judaeorum* (21). The focus entirely on the garden spaces, with the avoidance of the great house or hall usually central to country house discourses, further reenforces the Edenic garden aspects of Cookeham.[15] Lanyer also offers an alternative version of the Fall in her poem: in "Description of Cookeham," the fault that necessitates the Countess's and her daughter's departure from Eden is not a consequence of their actions. Innocence is explicitly attached to the Countess and her daughter throughout the poem as male legal action—rather than the conventional acquisitiveness, curiosity, or uxoriousness attributed to Eve—forces their eviction from "Paradice." The legal system which ultimately evicts the Countess from Cookeham's garden(s) is to blame, not the sinless woman. None of the traits traditionally associated with Eve and with women are the cause of the loss of this Eden, consequently remapping the narrative of the Fall.

Thus, in portraying this garden, and the manner in which gazing accords power within it, Lanyer highlights the political stakes of representing the Garden. The Garden—access to which space demands mystical visual access—is an inherently political space precisely because it was the originary site of governmental organization in seventeenth-century political thought. The deployment of the Fall narrative carries equal political weight, as distinct sectarian groups would utilize the narrative for their competing goals. Complementing this are the political uses to which prophetic revelation is put throughout the seventeenth century.[16] The identification of the Cookeham site as Edenic thus links the mystical gaze to politically resonant acts of viewing Eden. In the "Description of Cookeham," Milton's biblical epic, and Lanyer's Passion poem, then, we can observe each poet's configuration of gazing, gender, and ultimately governance in portraying the site/sight of the original Garden.

From Passions to Falls: Linguistic Parallels and the Problems of Governance in Salve Deus Rex Judaeorum *and* Paradise Lost

The broader cultural negotiation of the problem of gazing and its relationship to gender, social organization, and governance interweave Milton's and Lanyer's experiments in the Passion poem genre and with the Edenic narrative. As we will see, the conceptual connections between these mystical visionary poems become punctuated by specific linguistic echoes between their poems. Linguistic echoes back to Lanyer's poem—to in fact the most politically disruptive moment in her poem—will serve to cement their negotiation of this cultural matrix.

Our first view of Milton's Eden and then of Adam and Eve offers a highly suggestive link to Lanyer's "Description of Cookeham": as Neil Forsyth has argued in *The Satanic Epic*, the "happy rural seat" of Eden is presented to us much as is the view onto a country house (130). Donald Friedman has even termed this Edenic "rural seat" a "locus and the sign of Adam and Eve's regnal authority" over a country estate (115). Recalling the language of surveying, and the control over these practices signified in the period, "regnal authority" grants a specifically political (and I have argued above, definitely masculine) character to the opening view onto Adam and Eve. If their looking over the land enacts, through vision, a kind of political power, our gazing upon them also marks Adam and Eve as figures infused with political authority. In *Paradise Lost*, the opening vision both we and Satan have of Adam and Eve begins, as many critics have noted, with an account of the two.

> . . . where the Fiend
> Saw undelighted all delight, all kind
> Of living Creatures new to sight and strange:
> Two of far nobler shape erect and tall,
> Godlike erect, with native Honor clad
> In naked Majesty seem'd Lords of all,
> And worthy seem'd, for in thir looks Divine
> The image of thir glorious Maker shone,
> Truth, Wisdom, Sanctitude severe and pure,
> Severe, but in true filial freedom plac't;
> Whence true autority in men: though both
> Not equal, as thir sex not equal seem'd. (4.288–96)

The view onto Adam and Eve accords them the same power over the landscape as is distributed in country house poems or another visual representations of political power, such as Piero della Francesca's portraits of the Duke and Duchess of Urbino. Milton's own manipulation of the vagaries of "gazing" also invokes the Passion poem: the one being gazed upon can be offered power, as is Christ through the visualized account of his death. This insight from Milton's generic experience with the Passion poem genre becomes integrated here with the significant political implications of gazing: the ones being gazed upon are granted, in Friedman's terms, "regnal authority" over this Edenic space which they "seem'd Lords of all" (293). In this scene, to be gazed upon constitutes the awarding of political authority, denuding Satan's act of voyeuristic gazing control.[17] Regina Schwartz has astutely noted that the multiplicity of acts of gazing in *Paradise Lost*, what she calls "the dynamics of specularity," "challenge any conventional understanding of what voyeurism might mean" ("Rethinking Voyeurism," 86). Here, the dynamic nature of the gaze, as we saw in Lanyer's poetry, prompts us to reconsider the position accorded to the object of, versus the subject of, the gaze.[18]

As many critics, especially Mary Nyquist, have noted, Milton's opening view of Adam and Eve describe them, at least initially, in similar, not differentiating, terms. In particular, the beginning lines of this passage make no distinction based on gender as both figures are linked to the language of governance: In their "naked Majesty," Adam and Eve "seem'd Lords of all" (4.290). As Berger notes, placing men and women amid representational enactments of "patrilineal order and patriarchal power"—such as portraits—might well, at least temporarily, mute gender distinctions. This appears to happen here as in the visual analog of the profile portraits of the Duke and Duchess of Urbino. Adam and Eve are granted power because they are the object of the viewer's gaze; the viewer, by looking upon them exerting their politically inflected gaze, awards them (political) control. And that gaze does not differentiate along the lines of a (yet created) category of gender. The structure of human authority described to us here is derived from the "filial freedom" given to them by God. Once this genealogy of authority is provided, though, the text will make a significant turn: on the word "in men," what had been conveyed to us in genderless language suddenly becomes explicitly gendered. Adam now is accorded political authority as he receives the "Absolute Rule" (4.301) of man while Eve embodies the "implied/ Subjection" (4.307–8) of woman. Political authority now is shown to be intimately interwoven with the structures of gendered hierarchy. Yet, what occurs in this sequence suggests that gender emerges—in fact one could claim that it is constituted—by theorizing governance through visual observation.

Milton's focus here on acts of gazing, the mode by which that distributes power, and its relationship to gender intriguingly revises aspects of Lanyer's use of these concepts. In Lanyer, the male scopophilic view is challenged: gazing can accord power to Lanyer's narrator and the Countess in *Salve Deus*, while being gazed upon—as is the body of Christ or King James during his power-consolidating masques—constitutes a form of power as well. Milton takes up this issue, first by granting political authority to those gazed upon, and then by later considering the implications of such power in his treatment of

Eve. In the Book 9 temptation scene, one in which Satan accords power to Eve because she is the site of the gaze, Satan is actually taken over by the power she acquires through being the site/sight of the gaze.

Larger stylistic and theoretical connections between Lanyer's and Milton's poems and their engagement of acts of gazing and power have been my focus up until now. Now, I want to suggest how linguistic parallels between the poems suggest Milton's need to engage Lanyer's earlier representation of gazing, its relation to (political) power, and how these frame the category of, and consequences of, gender in the poem. Just as in the opening view provided of Adam and Eve in Book 4, links between the gaze, governmental authority, and gender are embedded into Satan's temptation of Eve in Book 9. Satan's argument to Eve suggests that the figure gazed upon can be accorded power, even political power, just as we see in masque performances, mystical discourses, and portraiture. We see Milton and Lanyer theoretically linked by their exploration of gazing within mystically inspired texts. Adam and Eve have been granted "naked Majesty" as a result of their position as the object of the gaze, and Satan uses this very argument to link Eve to political authority. Milton stages this connection at the opening of the temptation: "uncall'd before her stood; / But as in gaze admiring" (9.523–24). The poem will subsequently give voice to that "admiring" "gaze"; because of the power she has over those that gaze on her, Satan claims, she deserves the title "sovran Mistress" (9.532). Satan insists that Eve is "sovran" because "Thee all living things gaze on" (9.539). His and all creatures' gazes make her "A Goddess among Gods, ador'd and serv'd / By Angels numberless, thy daily Train" (547–48). Thus, while Satan sustains the language of "worship," the act of gazing is the vehicle—as it was in Book 4—for the acquisition of the language of sovereign, political power: "Mee thus, though importune perhaps, to come / And gaze, and worship thee of right declar'd / Sovran of Creatures, universal Dame" (610–12).

Nor, as we will see in an episode that appears to linguistically engage Lanyer's poem, does this strategy seem aligned solely to Satanic practices. Satan himself will experience the power that the object of the gaze can exert— the very position of Christ in a Passion poem and of Eve, momentarily, in Book 9. The relationship between gazing and sovereignty that the Book 4 narrator proposes resonates with the later visual scene featuring Satan and Eve. As Milton engages this process, he will invoke the specular methods of, as well as linguistic echoes from, Lanyer's *Salve Deus*. Satan, we know, has not always been in control of his gaze onto Eve. His temptation of her, and her subsequent fall, were in fact delayed by this very gaze. Initially, Eve is only "Half spi'd" (9.426) by Satan, but as his view of her becomes complete, she comes to embody beauty and goodness.

She most, and in her look sums all Delight.
Such Pleasure took the Serpent to behold
This Flow'ry Plat, the sweet recess of Eve

Thus early, thus alone; her Heav'nly form
Angelic, but more soft, and Feminine,
Her graceful Innocence, her every Air
Of gesture or least action overaw'd
His Malice, and with rapine sweet bereav'd
His fierceness of the fierce intent it brought:
That space the Evil one abstracted stood
From his own evil, and for the time remain'd
Stupidly good, of enmity disarm'd,
Of guile, of hate, of envy, of revenge. . . . (9.454–66)

In an account of Satan's experience of gazing onto Eve, the simplicity of her goodness and beauty has the effect of stupefying him into a state of goodness, suspending momentarily his "enmity," "guile," "hate," "envy", and desire for revenge. The stupor-like state into which Satan is prompted does not, of course, last long: "the hot hell that always in him burns . . . soon ended his delight, / and tortures him now more . . ." (467–69). Though a transitory moment, this pause nonetheless suggests that it is a trait in Eve effecting this evacuation of Satan's "evil."

At this moment of considering the effect of Eve on Satan, Milton establishes a strong linguistic bridge to Lanyer's earlier poem. Just as *Salve Deus* had provided a mystical view onto Christ's body and a prelapsarian view of the Cookeham garden, Lanyer's poem also provided us a view of Eve at the moment of the Fall. In Lanyer's explicit contribution to the *querelle des femmes*, she depicts Eve's fall such that Eve's culpability is offset by aspects of her goodness, casting Eve as less culpable because of her ignorance. Her "undiscerning Ignorance perceav'd / No guile, or craft that was by him intended" (769–70), and "had she knowne" (771), she never would have taken the fruit. This aspect of Eve's simpleness and her deluded state is repeated numerous times, but stated most explicitly at the opening of this 80-line digression:

Our Mother *Eve*, who tasted of the Tree,
Giving to *Adam* what she held most deare,
Was *simply good*, and had no powre to see,
The after-comming harme. . . . (763–66; my emphasis)

The defense offered is that Eve lacks the capacity to evaluate the consequences of the Fall, implicitly arguing that Eve is too "simple" to resist falling.[19]

Generic links between Lanyer's and Milton's poems, joined as they have been by the theoretical issues of power and specularity within Garden sites, now become a resonant linguistic parallel at the very moment of the Fall. Meditating on culpability within the Fall itself, the poets both describe a form of constrained goodness, Satan's "stupidly good" in *Paradise Lost* and Eve's "simply good" state in *Salve Deus*. The parallel location—at the very moment of the Fall—of this construction is reenforced by the unique status of this adverbial modification, even mortification, of "good" in *Paradise Lost*. "Good" operates in *Paradise Lost* as an absolute, a word whose essence is fully conveyed by the term itself, such as "God" or "love." Rarely modified, "good" can be described in an adverbial or adjectival phrase, but only to reinforce the completeness of the state of "good": "infinitely good" (4.414); "entirely good" (7.549); "solid good" (8.93). Only "household good" in Book 9 (233) offers a branch of goodness, one which qualifies the fullness implied by the concept of "good."[20] "Stupidly good" like "simply good" convey the modification of, but also the limitation of, the concept of "good." Not complete in herself, Eve is good in her simpleness within Lanyer's phrase. Milton's use of the phrase appears to define the good that Satan could experience as one of rapture, of a suspension in time, and most significantly of inaction: "That space the Evil one abstracted stood / From his own evil, and for the time remain'd / Stupidly good" (9.463–65).

The state of goodness as limited by each author precedes each one's account of the Fall; at the moment just preceding the sinning act, both are granted a state of constrained goodness. Eve is guileless in Lanyer's poem, while Satan's—very transitory—state distances him from evil much as does Lanyer's account of Eve. These connections—phrasing, location in the narrative, and effect on the character's state of goodness—argue the link between the poems. Yet this potential transfer by Milton of a state of limited goodness from Eve to Satan is immensely significant. In transferring to Satan the revised epitaph "stupidly good," Milton illustrates the inadequacy of goodness as a state of suspended culpability. Such a state is the primary defense offered by Lanyer in "Eve's Apology." Because Eve is "simply good," she cannot be blamed. Further, Lanyer's less culpable Eve will have "Knowledge" taken from her hand in an implicitly passive act: "Men will boast of Knowledge, which he tooke / From *Eves* faire hand" (807–8). Milton cannot allow the active nature of Eve's thoughts about choosing to fall to be eroded by a passive simplicity. Milton reimagines this phrase such that Eve loses her "simple" goodness in *Paradise Lost*: the choice of knowledge must be conscious for him. By creating this suspended moment of evil's absence, Milton underscores that Satan's rapturous moment of goodness no more excuses him than does the suspension of culpability in a simple Eve. Transferring the notion of "simple" or "stupid" goodness from Eve to Satan actually could be seen as an explicit rebuttal of Lanyer's claim.

Secondarily, this translation of "simply good" to "stupidly good" adds culpability to Eve through the vehicle of her beauty. This unintentional seduction to momentary goodness (passively and unknowingly) achieved by Eve highlights the power of her beauty in *Paradise Lost*, power she will use for the opposite purpose in her subsequent seduction of Adam. Milton, of course, has distanced Eve from the actively seductive figures that mark many accounts of Eve's fall.[21] Yet her seeming absence of consciousness about her beauty's effect does not relieve her of culpability, just as her lack of awareness of the (momentary) goodness wrought in Satan does not grant to her any greater goodness. Milton can both prepare us for Adam's fall caused largely by his uxoriousness while continuing to argue for the necessity of conscious, not "simple," choices.

This linguistic parallel between Lanyer's and Milton's Fall scenes thus grounds the culturally diffused, theoretical practices of gazing, gender, and governance that are embedded into both of their Fall scenes. *Paradise Lost* engages—in terms quite like Lanyer's Passion poem—the assignment of authority through the act of being gazed upon. In the course of his temptation, Satan offers to Eve "sovereign" power, (re)assigning to her power initially granted to Adam and Eve jointly in Book 4. Perverting, and employing for his own purposes, this earlier Book 4 language, Satan effectively redeploys the earlier pregendered offers of "sovereignty" to enact his temptation of Eve. As such, the Book 9 Fall scene in Milton will engage the very categories of gendered authority that Milton and Lanyer have delineated, specifically the differentiation between the terms of power accorded to men and to women.

Yet these distinctions of gender that emerge within the Book 4 vision of Adam and Eve are inverted every bit as much as Lanyer's introduction of Eve's "simple" goodness in her "Apologie" challenged the implications—social, political, as well as gendered—of the Fall. Redefining the terms of gendered authority as a result of the Passion, Lanyer's possible stylistic influence onto Milton's earlier Passion poem combines with her explicitly political account of a mystical view into, first, Christ's authority and, then, the Garden itself. Lanyer's argument plots out, while it ultimately rejects, the very spheres of authority accorded to men and women that unfold in Milton's temptation scene. A theme of political organization—based on gender differentiation—thus continues to weave these two mystical "views" onto the Garden site together.

As we have seen in Chapter 1, and can see throughout political theory throughout the seventeenth century, the issue of culpability for the Fall becomes the foundation for a gendered organization of the state predicated on family structure. Thus, the challenges that Lanyer makes to this organizational structure resonate with Milton's representation of the formative moment of social organization within the Garden. Linguistic and stylistic connections between the two poems become distinct interrogations by each poet about the organization of the household and the state. For culpability explains only part of Milton's revision of the phrase "simply good" to "stupidly good." The scenes that surround the linguistic crux in both Lanyer's and Milton's poems highlight the connection between gender hierarchy and governance. While Lanyer gestures at these issues in "To Cookeham," she explicitly engages them in her defense of Eve. In the "Apologie," Lanyer's act of distancing Eve from culpability has explicit political consequences. The heart of Lanyer's argument is that men bear greater culpability as a result of sacrificing Christ: the "sinne of yours" (both of Pilate and of all men) "surmounts" the sin of Eve (823), whose culpability was limited by her "simple"ness.

Enormous social and political implications follow in *Salve Deus*: because men crucified Christ, women no longer need to submit to men: "This sinne of yours, surmounts them all . . . Then let us have our Libertie againe" (823, 825). As Mihoko Suzuki has noted, this moment "articulates the *political* import of Lanyer's poem" (120), import which was more diffusely, but no less significantly, embedded into mystical accounts of Christ's body and politically overdetermined Garden scenes. *Salve Deus Rex Judaeorum* now explicitly politicizes the implications of the Fall in terms to which Milton must respond; in Lanyer and in Milton, since culpability and choice lead to gender hierarchy (Eve disobeys and her punishment is subjection), these issues are the heart of political order. In this lies, I would argue, another reason that Milton must reconfigure Lanyer's "simply good" Eve—the stabilization of gendered authority, and of resulting social stability, that Lanyer eradicates in the closing stanza of the "Eve's Apology"[22]:

> Then let us have our Libertie againe,
> And challendge to your selves no Sov'raigntie;
> You came not in the world without our paine,
> Make that a barre against your crueltie;
> Your fault beeing greater, why should you disdaine
> Our beeing your equals, free from tyranny?
>> If one weake woman simply did offend,
>> This sinne of yours, hath no excuse, nor end. (825–32)

The political rather than protofeminist implications of this passage are the most significant here, as noted by Suzuki and Achsah Guibbory.[23] Lanyer rejects male "Sov'raigntie" over women because of the events of the Fall and the Passion; the story of the Passion, then, has explicit political implications as Lanyer's rejection of women's need to concede sovereignty to men undermines the very analogy supporting patriarchal theory. The challenge that Lanyer poses to ordered gender hierarchy becomes a theme that Milton's poem will engage throughout his Book 9 account of the Fall.

Divided Spheres, "Household" Goods, and the Formation of the Modern State

Lanyer's attack on the tenets of patriarchal theory in the seventeenth century positions her "Apologie" for Eve among the conventions of the broader *querelle des femmes* debate. This earlier seventeenth-century debate, of which Lanyer was a much more radical participant than Speght and Sowernam, provides us with a context for considering one last mode of exchange between Lanyer's and Milton's poems: the role of household versus "state" or more "public" spheres. In *Paradise Lost*, an outgrowth of Milton's exploration of the modes of constructing governmental organization is his distinction between,

and the gendering of, such spheres. Satan's temptation of Eve, while deploying the gazing to highlight gendered forms of power, also replays many of the
tropes that marked the *querelle des femmes* tradition to which Lanyer contributed.

To summarize a much more detailed tradition, attacks on women consistently located women within more of a household realm, while defenses delineated women's affiliation with the social or political realm. While female
defenders such as Rachel Speght, Ester Sowernam, and Jane Anger all employ language about women that links them to a larger discussion of political
organization, attacks would evade this language. Pursuing an opposite tack,
attacks on women rarely mention Adam's sovereignty over women, but work
to keep women outside of any political activity. The discrepancy between the
defenses and the attacks suggests that defenders of women rely on the analogy between gender relations and political organization. For, the analogy actually illustrates women's central importance to cultural order—even if that
order is subordination. Alternately, attacks offer a much more fundamental
dismissal of women: by not drawing upon the issue of gendered authority,
women's position in relation to men is not represented as a cornerstone of
cultural organization. While patriarchal theory would hardly be considered
liberating, it does in fact make women a vital element in the organization of
the state, even in her submission. These early seventeenth-century defenses
thus illustrate that an engagement with patriarchal theory—via the
family/state analogy—positions women in the political realm, even if they operate, conceptually and literally, as its base. For the state, there must be family;
for male political organization, there must be women in that state as modeled
in the household.[24]

Located within this tradition, Aemilia Lanyer also explores the analogy of
the household to the state. While Lanyer's radical return of "Libertie" to
women will free them from a household-based governmental structure, the
very use of language like "Sov'raigntie" and "Libertie" announces how linked
the family is to larger political structures in Lanyer's thinking. Other defenders
of women do not undermine traditional male authority, as does Lanyer, but
they all engage the relationship between domestic and more political spheres
in their defenses. A significant political theory component thus exists in both
Lanyer's and other (female) defenders in the *querelle des femmes*. Their discourses
are complementary to the developing body of writings on patriarchal theory.

In the final segment of this chapter, I will suggest how the broader context
of these female-authored defenses, as well as specifics from Lanyer's text, become embedded into the temptation in Book 9 of *Paradise Lost*. *Paradise Lost*'s
engagement of the issue of women's position in the political realm is shaped
by anti-feminist discourse, as was Adam's misogynistic rant in Book 10. The
question of women's connection to the political realm is highlighted in both
Book 4 and the Book 9 temptation. Female defenses, such as Lanyer's explicitly political defense of women, consequently continue to provide an important

context for understanding Book 9. Milton's engagement with these issues, especially the pressure placed on the family/state analogy by women writing in the
querelle tradition, is particularly significant because Milton needs to theorize how
to detach the authority within the family, and foundationally between husband
and wife, from the authority of the monarch and even of the state. These questions, about where women are or should be located in relation to state formation, become central to the representation of Adam and Eve within the Garden
and Eve's consequent (if quickly curtailed) engagement of the political sphere.

Milton and *Paradise Lost* are thus located at the juncture of the analogy of
the family and the state—employed by patriarchal theorists such as Sir Robert
Filmer—and the distinct "public" and "private" spheres, which will be codified in Locke's *Two Treatises*. While there is extensive debate over the moment
when a distinct "public" and "private" sphere emerges in the early modern period, as well as the mechanisms by which this distinction emerges, many critics, including David Norbrook, have suggested how *Paradise Lost* anticipates this
later division by delineating and gendering these spheres in the 1667 poem.
Norbrook points to the location of Eve inside of the bower, and Adam outside
of it, at the arrival of Raphael in Book 5 (*English Republic*, 115). This visual
tableau complements the repeated distancing of Eve from conversations of political, historical, or intellectual significance in the poem. I consider the poem
less a harbinger of this private/public divide and more a moment of negotiating the family/state analogy and the widening gap between the domestic
household and the broader cultural or political world outside of the home.[25]
Milton's representation of Adam and Eve illustrates bounds around appropriate gendered activities, which raise the question of women's connection to the
cultural or political sphere.

While Book 9 is the narrative moment when the most significant boundary—
that of the prohibition not to eat from the Tree of Knowledge—is transgressed,
it is also the point in the poem when many new boundaries are established, in
particular woman's engagement with a broader cultural or political sphere. This
is highlighted by Adam's and Satan's distinct modes of representing Eve's position in the world of the Garden and beyond. In what some critics have called
the first fall of Book 9, the argument between Adam and Eve preceding her departure follows the distinctions I have outlined above: female defenders of
women continue to locate women in a more public context, while attacks on
women repeatedly position them within a more domestic space.

The very argument between Eve and Adam records this conflict over the
position of women. Eve's suggestion that they separate is prompted, it appears,
by a characteristic innovation of our first Mother: the concept of the division
of labor.

> Adam, well may we labor still to dress
> This Garden, still to tend Plant, Herb and Flow'r,

Our pleasant task enjoin'd, but till more hands
Aid us, the work under our labor grows,
Luxurious by restraint; what we by day
Lop overgrown, or prune, or prop, or bind,
One night or two with wanton growth derides
Tending to wild. Thou therefore now advise
Or hear what to my mind first thoughts present,
Let us divide our labors . . . (9.205–14)

Here, Eve speculates on the appropriate use of labor, offering a systematic
evaluation about the effectiveness of labor in the Garden. As such, her idea is
about the "economy," a term that emerged in the seventeenth century as a tool
for understanding and organizing the workings of the community. The OED
defines "economy" as "The administration of the concerns and resources of
any community or establishment with a view to orderly conduct and produc-
tiveness" or the "art or science of such administration." Such aspects of the
term "economy" are present, for example, in 1651 in Hobbes's *Leviathan*, which
worked to provide "the oeconomy of a Commonwealth" (5.2.75).

Eve, in her thoughts about the proper administration of the Garden, is speculating on how the system of labor functions in their culture. Eve is clearly
thinking beyond the ordering of a singular domestic space and, instead, attempting a broader cultural rethinking, and reorganization, of the purpose of
labor; Eve thinks beyond the two of them as a couple or even a future family
unit by speculating on the entire Garden world. In suggesting a model for more
effective production, she could be called the first economist. While the composition of the Garden resists simple divisions between "public" and the "private" spheres in many ways, Eve is clearly focusing on the collective nature of
the space that they know, live, and within which they work.

Adam's response to Eve's vision of the "oeconomy of a Commonwealth" establishes boundaries around her idea, ones which distinguish between the domestic sphere and broader cultural or political concerns. He explicitly defines
her thoughts as about only the "household":

Well hast thou motion'd, well thy thoughts imploy'd
How we might best fulfil the work which here
God hath assign'd us, nor of me shalt pass
Unprais'd: for nothing lovelier can be found
In Woman, than to study household good,
And good works in her Husband to promote. (9.229–34)

While the "household" had traditionally described the larger economic practices of a domestic economy within a family or more extended unit, Adam's use
of the term gestures toward a highly significant shift in the language of the *oikos*
(household) in the seventeenth century. David Norbrook defines this reconfiguration of the economic structure in the seventeenth century: "The classical

household was a site of economic production as well as the rearing of children; with the emergence of a market economy the productive and familial sides of the *oikos* moved further apart, and the household came to offer an idealized spiritual centre. Puritan ideology laid special emphasis on the household as an instrument of godly reformation which could do its work even when the public world was corrupt" (117). The "household" comes to be a signal of the domestic sphere as distinct from larger economic or social practices.[26]

Adam's response to Eve enacts this same shift as he transforms her vision of the "economy of a Commonwealth" into a domestically oriented observation. In completing his praise of Eve's well-employed thoughts, Adam ends with a positive description of women who promote good acts in their husbands. In praising she who will, in Adam's vision, "good works in her Husband . . . promote," first Eve's vision of economic value and then her own practices are thoroughly domesticated. As Adam continues, the general applicability of Eve's suggestion for the *oikos* is further telescoped to become solely about domestic relations between him and his spouse. He dismisses Eve's concerns that they do not get enough done during a day because "near [each other] / Looks intervene and smiles" (9.221–22). Intimate pleasures are smiled upon by God, he insists:

Yet not so strictly hath our Lord impos'd
Labor, as to debar us when we need
Refreshment, whether food, or talk between,
Food of the mind, or this sweet intercourse
Of looks and smiles, for smiles from Reason flow,
To brute deni'd, and are of Love the food. . . . (9.235–40)

By highlighting the individual pleasures of love, Adam draws Eve's remarks even closer to a vision of the domesticated, if affection-filled, household.

Adam's epitaph "household good" also has the effect of bounding Eve's goodness, much as she has been bound into the private household. In a very suggestive parallel to Satan's "stupidly good" 200 lines later, Adam has defined Eve with a phrase describing partial goodness, a limiting of the wholeness that marks the usually transcendent nature of "good" in Milton's work. This limiting of the otherwise boundlessness of the concept of "good" or "goodness" is intriguing resonant with Lanyer's mode of limiting culpability in her description of Eve as "simply good." In both Lanyer's and Milton's poems, the effort of limiting "goodness" has social and political consequences. In *Salve Deus*, Eve is free from the political restraint of masculine tyranny since Lanyer stresses women's access to independent political identity: women earn back their "Sov'raigntie" and their "Libertie," both words that position them in a political framework. Adam's generation of a "household" space works toward the opposite goal. As Eve will "good works in her Husband to promote," Adam envisions the wife functioning through her husband (234). Milton limits women's goodness in order to lock women into a privatized space, rather than allow Eve to participate in an "oeconomy of the Commonwealth."

The elements in Eve's temptation scene that follow continue to highlight the issue, or the growing cultural problem, of women's connection to a political realm, the very issues raised by Lanyer's portrait of Eve. Adam attempts to pull Eve away from a more political or social context by domesticating her and her suggestion about a division of labor. But Satan will alternately engage the conventions in female defenses that maintained women's connection to the political realm. What Milton adds to the tradition of Satan's temptation of Eve, then, is the very language of political power that the *querelle* engaged implicitly and Lanyer explicitly articulated. Further, the political language that will mark this scene does not occur in temptation scenes by Du Bartas, Della Salandra, Grotius, or Andreini. More particularly, the political imagery Satan uses in his opening speech to Eve fuses the accounts of control over a domestic economy with the language of political authority. I would go so far as to suggest that Satan's temptation is modeled on an older view of the "oeconomy" that Adam, and Milton, have suppressed to transform Eve's proposed organization of their social practices into simply a domestic activity.

If Adam, then, is attempting to create distinct spheres, Satan's language throughout his temptation of Eve defies this separation of spheres. Satan's opening call to Eve, "Wonder not, sovran Mistress" (9.532), sustains the usual inversion of authority that marks Satan's thought and actions. We will watch as Satan now inverts aspects of the earlier Book 4 vision of Adam and Eve where the poem explored the relationship between gazing, governance, and gender. Satan now perverts the Book 4 sequence through his redeployment of the power implicit in gazing. In the earlier Book 4 sequence, the gaze onto these "Two of far nobler shape" (288) granted governmental authority, but an authority almost immediately specified as masculine when gender—"Not equal, as thir *sex* not equal seem'd" (296)—was introduced into the equation. Now Satan redeploys the power granted to Adam and Eve, offering her the language of political authority: "as in gaze admiring," he calls out to her as his "sovran Mistress." Thus, it is the act of gazing onto Eve that grants power to her. He "gaze[s] / Insatiate" (9.535–36), claiming that "Thee all things living gaze on." As Lanyer's experiments throughout *Salve Deus* illustrate, the experience of the Passion accords power to the object of view while disrupting the gendering of cultural and political power through gazing. We see this occur here as Satan, while appealing to Eve's vanity, exposes the act of being gazed upon as that which grants her the title "sovran." Elevated above her husband, who acquired gendered authority in Book 4, Satan now describes her as "Sovran of Creatures, universal Dame," later awarding her the imperial title "Empress" and "Queen of this Universe" (9.612, 626, 684).

Satan's use of the language of sovereignty when addressing Eve also continues to link governmental organization with the family unit, as had defenses of women from Lanyer to Sowernam. Satan's opening gambit is to fuse Eve's identification of "Mistress" of the "household"—where Adam has positioned her—with the language of "sovereignty." Eve had lost that "true autority" once it became located only "in men" in Book 4 (4.295). Yet Satan will give such power back—much as does Lanyer—to Eve. He invokes Eve's authority through phrases such as "Sovran of Creatures" (9.612) and "sovran Mistress," echoing Lanyer's denial of men's "Sov'raigntie" over women in "Eve's Apology" (826). In a political inversion parallel to the claims made by Lanyer, Satan negates the hierarchy upon which the family/state analogy rests. There, the master would be sovereign over the mistress, a vertical hierarchy that Satan levels by offering both terms to Eve. Yet Satan engages aspects of the early seventeenth-century *querelle des femmes* in another way: he maintains the connection between the political and the domestic spheres. Eve is both mistress of the household AND sovereign over it when these two epithets, "sovran Mistress," are placed side by side. The invocation of Eve as "universal Dame" functions in much the same way: Hughes notes that "Dame" keeps its original Latin connotation of "mistress" (392), consequently extending the space of the "household" that Adam circumscribed in his earlier interaction with Eve. In Satan's temptation, her realm is not the household, but is instead "universal." The temptation continues to offer Eve titles of power that become more wide-reaching, as with "Queen of this Universe," while explicitly offering monarchical and imperial power. Granted a position within the traditional household as "Mistress," she is then offered control in an expanding political realm. Like Lanyer's patroness, then, Eve is accorded power independent of the complementary figure of the Count through the acts of gazing engineered by Satan.

In the course of his temptation, Satan redeploys the very power that Eve can acquire as an object of the gaze. Eve's visual and explicitly political power, illustrated first in Book 4 and then detailed by Adam in Book 8, needs to be controlled within the poem. When Adam later describes looking upon Eve in Book 8, he attributes power to her in the language of political rule: "so *absolute* she seems" (8.547; my emphasis). In response, Raphael instructs Adam in domestic authority: "The more she will acknowledge thee *her* Head" (8.574; my emphasis). Any governmental power attributed to the first couple is now to be distinguished, and delimited, through an assertion of gender. The consequence, in Book 9, becomes the (gendered) hierarchy that Adam tries to create through detaching the family/state analogy. For, as Adam attempts to establish the husband as "Head" of the family, he is distinctly not handed the (patriarchalist) title of monarch of the nation, reigning over her in the domestic sphere only.

Satan's temptation of Eve thus revisits the language of gazing and its relation to governmental authority as he reweaves the domestic and the political spheres that Adam had been instructed to detach. The family/state analogy, conveyed through phrases that recall its use in defenses by women, is thus offered to and accepted by Eve in the Book 9 temptation. Throughout the narrative of the Fall, Milton explicitly engages the role of the family/state analogy in defenses of women. He may even be recording the erasure of the connection between these spheres that dominated attacks on women in the *querelle des femmes*.[27] Raphael's Book 8 reprimand of Adam and Adam's delimiting of Eve's economic reorganization provide a corrected model of governance built upon gendered distinctions. Adam heeded the instructions to detach the analogy, separate the political from the domestic, and distinguish the family from the state. Yet while Raphael and a rebuked Adam work to excise the political implications from the language of familial authority, Satan and then Eve work to restore the analogy. It is Eve who considers the advantages of being "sometime / Superior: for inferior who is free" (9.824–25). Besides echoing Satan's capacity to invert authority, she links the language of domestic hierarchy asserted by Raphael with the language of "freedom." When positioned alongside Lanyer's own generic and Garden-based innovations, such an explicit political term—here voiced by Eve—resonates powerfully with Lanyer's insistence on women's "Libertie."

Many of the political issues that dominate Milton's representation of the Fall in *Paradise Lost*, I have suggested, begin at the Crucifixion. What begins as a generic issue with "The Passion"—how do I access and represent the body of Christ?—becomes overlaid with issues of gender as Milton works through this form: these "softer airs" defied his entrance into the mystical experience. But the possibilities within a form that can invert power through acts of gazing allowed Lanyer to succeed within the genre. By reading Milton's poems in light of Lanyer's *Salve Rex Deus Judaeorum*, we can see how his experimentation with the politically infused form of the Passion poem becomes an engagement with the early seventeenth-century anti-feminist debate. When Milton effects his entrance into the Garden, when he effectively substitutes his "Patroness" of night for the "Celestial Patroness" in Book 9, he rewrites the political implications of the Fall that Lanyer had traced in her Crucifixion poem. As we will see in Chapter 3, the political import of mystical experiences in the mid-century will shape Milton's representation of poetic inspiration. His mode of representing these mystical experiences will, again, allow him to explore the relationship between gender and political organization. For, form quickly leads us to much broader cultural and political issues. The Passion poem format of Lanyer's *Salve Deus Rex Judaeorum* very likely prompted Milton's interest, but Lanyer's portrait of Eve and re-narration of the Fall, "Eve's Apology," required a response.

In Lanyer's defense, the political location of women is maintained by the family/state analogy through which they—in "Eve's Apology"—gain freedom from domestic and political hierarchy. Making explicit the parallels between governmental organization and gendered order, Lanyer's defense bases itself upon the premises of patriarchal theory; like Satan, she inverts the result, but relies upon the same analogic structure. The specifics in Lanyer's text as well as the anti-feminist tradition from which she was writing engaged the family/state analogy. Throughout Book 9 of *Paradise Lost*, Milton struggles with the political implications of the family/state analogy, implications that early seventeenth-century defenses of women explored. Milton—probably because of its ties to patriarchal theory—was unwilling to maintain the analogy of political organization as modeled upon familial authority. Nonetheless, he did not want to lose order within the family that a gendered hierarchy held stable. The poem thus attempts to sever the political from the domestic while locating the connection between women and the political realm in the mouth of Satan and then a fallen Eve.

Milton's republican investment in abandoning this family/state analogy thus shows him experimenting with a separation between "public" and "private" spheres fifteen years before Locke would codify the division between the state and the family in the *Two Treatises of Government*. Located historically and theoretically between women in the *querelle des femmes* tradition deploying this analogy and the increasingly loud debates between contractual and patriarchal theories at mid-century, Milton negotiates a tradition and its future through the figure of Eve. The battle over the family/state analogy is one fought on many fronts in the seventeenth century. While Milton's and other Republicans' rejection of patriarchal theory defines one field of contest, the use that female defenses make of the analogy proves to be another. The defenses by writers such as Lanyer, Speght, and Sowernam constitute a field of contest that Milton appears to have engaged in his account of women's relation to the political realm and its relationship to the Fall. As such, these writers, in what appears to be a significant political conversation with Milton's *Paradise Lost*, help to establish the terms of political organization by which we still operate today.[28]

Part II
Contexts

The mid-seventeenth century in England, experiencing growing conflicts between the monarch and the Parliament, between the established church and ever-multiplying religious sects, and between theorists clashing over the justifications for political organization, provided a rich environment for the entry of a number of women into print. This section considers women writers from the late 1620s down to the early 1670s, a sizable period of time that also incorporates quite distinct writers. On either end of this time spectrum lie aristocratic women: Lady Eleanor Davies, whose first published prophetic text appeared in 1620, while Margaret Cavendish, the Duchess of Newcastle, and Lucy Hutchinson published their works in the 1660s and 1670s. In the middle of the seventeenth century, the women whose voices I argue are instructively framing aspects of Milton's *Paradise Lost* are a substantial group of nongentry women. Inspired by God's voice and often prompted to distribute these thoughts through print, writers like Mary Cary, Anna Trapnel, and Elizabeth Poole produced numerous tracts during the 1640s and 1650s.

Unlike Parts I and III, Part II offers accounts of influence onto Milton, the influence of Milton onto a female writer (Hutchinson), and a parallel reading of *Paradise Lost* and Cavendish's *Blazing World*, published essentially simultaneously between 1666 and 1668. This grouping of chapters is not chronological so much as it is thematic. All three chapters illustrate how quite varied writers negotiated the English Civil War and the consequence of the Stuart Restoration while simultaneously charting distinct flows of influence between writings by women and *Paradise Lost*. The main texts thus expose different aspects of the political imaginary generated through the events of the Civil War, the Interregnum, and then the Restoration. In Chapter 3, Milton's look backward toward the Protectorate period provides him access to a set of discourses through which he negotiates the events of Charles's restoration. In Chapter 4, Lucy Hutchinson and Milton, both republicans, engage the theoretical debates that helped to prompt, but more importantly appeared to justify, the execution of Charles I. In Chapter 5, I consider how Milton and Margaret Cavendish confront Restoration politics through the nexus of knowledge and gender.

The order of the chapters thus resists a slavish commitment to chronology. Lucy Hutchinson's composition of *Order and Disorder* followed that of Milton's 1667 *Paradise Lost* as well as that of Cavendish's *Blazing World*, the text at the heart of Chapter 5. Yet since Hutchinson engages debates over republican government, her text is the product of the Protectorate and its failure. Cavendish's text, while it looks back toward the events of the Interregnum, is much more supportive of and invested in the Restoration government of Charles II. Thus, each chapter has a distinct historical footprint. Chapter 3 engages the Interregnum and then events after 1660, Chapter 4 considers the Restoration in light of Interregnum debates over government, and Chapter 5 embeds itself in Restoration concerns about political stability and the mechanisms necessary to accomplish this.

Milton Among the Prophets: Inspiration and Gendered Discourse in the Mid-Seventeenth Century

As Chapter 2 has suggested, Milton's engagement with the *querelle des femmes* tradition is mediated through his gendering of distinct spheres in the seventeenth century. Given the gendered distinctions that Milton begins to make between these two spaces in *Paradise Lost*, the events of December 1648 and January 1649 provide an ironic context for this separation of a domestic from a political or public sphere. On the eve of deciding the fate of Charles I, Elizabeth Poole was addressing the Army's General Council about justifications for deposing the King while at the same time Milton was likely at home, busily attempting to finish his justification for Charles's deposition and execution: his *Tenure of Kings and Magistrates* entered into print only after the public execution of Charles I.

There are notable parallels between the argument that Poole makes to the General Council and the theoretical grounds Milton elaborates in the *Tenure*.[1] The basis of governmental organization in Poole is the marital unit, but instead of offering traditional patriarchal arguments about the unseverability of either union, she describes justifiable divorce, a dissolution that could occur, and in this case should: "the King is your Father and husband . . . for when he forgot his Subordination to divine Father-hood and headship . . . taking you a wife for his own lusts, there by is the yoke taken from your necks" (A3r).[2] This very severability of marriage Milton had asserted five years earlier in the Divorce tracts. Now he recalls that position, arguing that the people—as husbands—are always able to dissolve that governmental bond: "since the King or Magistrate holds his autoritie of the people, both originally and naturally for their good in the first place, and not his own, then may the people *as oft as they shall judge it for the best,* either choose him or reject him" (Riverside, 1061). The "people" do not, as in Poole's theory, need an extreme situation to justify the ending of a king or magistrate's power; a husband (and possibly a wife) need only experience incompatibility to justify severability as in the Divorce tracts.

Milton and Poole's most easily identifiable disagreement—the fate of

Charles himself—reverses the situation as to who had the ear of the Army Council in December 1648 and January 1649. Since Poole rejected the idea that the king could be executed or physically harmed, she lost the initially enthusiastic attention of the General Council. Milton, famously, went on to argue for and then serve the Protectorate by defending Charles's January 30 execution: "be he King, or Tyrant, or Emperor, the Sword of Justice is above him; in whose hand soever is found sufficient power to avenge the effusion, and so great a deluge of innocent blood" (Riverside, 1059). If the *Tenure* offered a theoretical framework for judging, and punishing, a ruler, *Eikonoclastes* justified the actual deed: "no *mockery of Justice*," Charles's execution was "a most gratefull and well-pleasing Sacrifice" (1094). The public position that Milton would come to occupy as a key propagandist for the Protectorate would become redefined as that of a "regicide" when he came to face possible execution after the Restoration.

This change of circumstance, this reversal of fortune, will again map to distinct or gendered "spheres" of power. While Milton would have been unable to discern any biographical connections between himself and Poole in 1649, Elizabeth Poole's moment with the "Council of War" becomes analogous to Milton's position after the Restoration. By the 1660s, many of the strategies employed by Elizabeth Poole and many other female sectarians and prophetesses would have resonance for a poet who had "fall'n on evil days . . . and evil tongues" (7.25–26). While invested with political and social power that enabled his production of political pamphlets through the 1640s and 1650s, at the Restoration Milton's cultural license to publish had been revoked, and his political views were more than unwelcome: they were treasonous. Labeled heretical, "diabolical," a rebel, many of Milton's political writings were banned. This chapter will argue that Milton's banishment from a position of political power prompted his engagement with the language of prophecy and the complementary discourse of prodigious births that circulated widely in the 1640s and 1650s. Milton thus mines a nostalgic discourse that had allowed female, as well as male, sectaries to call upon the authority of God, enter into print, and speak directly to political issues. Redeploying these strategies in *Paradise Lost* thus served Milton's purposes by the mid-1660s.

While I opened this chapter with Elizabeth Poole, she was only one of many prophets, male and female, whose access to a spiritual "voice" and concomitant traits of receiving this inspiration from God had allowed them to engage the growingly contentious political scene of the mid-century. As in Poole, women prophets were allowed entry into this space in part because of the traditional associations of the female body with the weaker vessel. This image of physical weakness could enable a potential evacuation of self. Both of Poole's tracts, *An Alarum of War* and *A Vision: Wherein is manifested the disease and cure of the Kingdome*, open with an image of "a woman crooked, sick, weak, & imperfect in body" who serves as the figure of the "weak and imperfect state of the Kingdom" (A2r). Yet this ironically debilitated image of the female body makes Poole's entrée into a discussion of the state possible: this language of the nation's weakness, conflated with the weak female body, becomes transformed explicitly into (political) power: "she by the gift of faith upon her, shall be your guide for the cure of her body" (5). This image of physical weakness is also registered structurally within Poole's discussion of marriage. Poole's hierarchical invocation of husband and wife—and her necessary placing of herself at the bottom of this hierarchy—allows her to narrate a distinct model of political authority. Speaking in the position of the wife allows her to spin out her theory of political obligation, yes. But it is a position that begins in cultural disempowerment.[3] The language of prophecy, in which she receives this inspiration from a higher source, reconfigures her "weakness" into validation for her political theory: "I know I appeale by the gift of God upon me" (A3r). Poole fused prophetic subservience to God's instruction and the positioning of herself, and the nation, in the role of the weaker vessel that, during the Civil War, could allow such a female voice to be heard.[4] Marginality, even secondariness, became a position from which one could derive authority and speak.

Female prophecy will become a method, albeit problematic, by which Milton can speak to politically resonant issues at a (later) moment when this "Diabolical Rebel" experienced condemnation for his "impious doctrines" (Jane, tp). After 1660, Milton could be described much as Sue Wiseman describes female prophets: "excluded from the centres of political power and speech" (191). The many voices of prophets throughout the 1640s and 1650s, consequently, provide us a fruitful context for reconsidering the traditional view of Milton as a "vates" poet, one who channeled the epic tradition and rewrote that tradition through his Christian faith.[5] For, Milton also lived through possibly the most disruptive religious, political, and social period of English history. While *Paradise Lost* was not published until 1667, an outpouring of texts by male and female prophets appeared between 1641 and 1660 when regulation of the press was intermittently suspended; the strategies deployed in these texts internalize both the religious nature of inspiration and political implications of these earlier texts. As we see so overtly in Elizabeth Poole's prophecies, prophetic utterances were frequently used for or appropriated to political movements as they promoted the religious beliefs of these prophets and their respective sects.

Milton's mode of poetic inspiration—as expressed in his invocations and the description of his "muse"—thus needs to be contextualized amid the "voices" inspiring prophets from Arise Evans and Abiezer Coppe to Anna Trapnel and Mary Cary. The conventions that marked the spiritual illumination of these prophets become embedded into the invocations of *Paradise Lost*, prompting us to locate Milton's notion of poetic and religious inspiration amid this powerful cultural phenomenon of God's inspiration and the production of texts recording this "voice." Fifth Monarchists, Levellers, Ranters—they all had their prophets whose divergent religious and political goals were offered some protection and authority by their direct inspiration by God. Contextualizing Milton's own prophetic inspiration among such contemporary prophetic discourses allows us to observe how politically, as well as religiously, significant Milton's use of prophecy was in *Paradise Lost*.

Recent work by David Loewenstein, John King, and Elizabeth Sauer has located Milton amid religious sectarians and seventeenth-century religious controversies. Yet even when, as Loewenstein and Sauer do, critics consider women prominent among the contemporary religious and political foment of the period, they are resistant to plot a narrative of influence: Sauer, for example, will insist that she is not undertaking "a study of influence—direct or indirect" in her discussion of female sectarians (Sauer, "Experience," 135).[6] I have argued for more direct forms of influence in earlier chapters. Now, turning from the more conscious negotiations of rhetorical and generic traditions that marked the first two chapters, I will suggest how Milton is shaped by tropes of prophecy so prominent around the Civil War, which he engages at varying stages of awareness. These prophetic and, later, prodigious birth discourses are a strategy for Milton. Yet they are not engagements which he undertakes with full consciousness. The exigencies of Milton's historical situation and the events of the mid-century provide the motivation for him to engage, rework, and reconfigure motifs of prophecy for his own poetic and political purposes. A "historical subconscious" directs Milton's nonetheless strategic manipulations of the language of disempowerment that had allowed prophets from various sectarian groups, and women in particular, to speak. With full historical consciousness of sectarian discourses and his own biographical situation at the Restoration, Milton internalizes these strategies, employing them in his invocations and in the Sin and Death sequence in Book 2.

In the most sustained investigation of prophecy in Milton's works, William Kerrigan details what he calls the "one harmonious person" into which Milton blends the traditions and the conventions of "the classical vates, the Christian poet, [and] the biblical prophet" (139). Kerrigan's work emblematizes the engagement with the issue of prophecy in John Milton's poetry, one which locates the sources of inspiration in the Homeric and Virgilian tradition of the inspiring muse, the European influences of poets such as Du Bartas and Spenser, and religious figures from Moses to Daniel to John.[7] Yet few critics have considered the historical implications of language about the "voice" of God, a "voice" that began speaking to greater and greater numbers of Englishmen and women during the 1640s and 1650s. The prominence of the "voice of God" in the period directly preceding the Restoration and Milton's publication of *Paradise Lost* offers a backdrop that resonates with, even is echoed in, Milton's account of his own poetic inspiration. The Book 3 invocation introduces the "voice" of God as the Holy Spirit, a description of Milton's muse sustained throughout the poem. This description of the "voice/ of God" that creates the Earth also identifies the method through which the epic poet is receiving aid from the "Heavenly Muse." The prominence of such motifs is sustained in the language of the subsequent invocations. As the poem moves on, Milton specifies both the identity and the power of the "voice" directing him. Consequently, we begin to hear the "voice of God" at more and more audible levels in *Paradise Lost*: "that warning voice" which was "heard cry in Heav'n aloud" (4.1,2) continues the stress upon the auditory character of God's inspiration. And by Book 7, Milton invokes "Urania, by that name / If rightly thou art call'd, whose Voice divine" the poet follows (1, 2). That "Voice divine" is then described as "dictat[ing]" to the poet in Book 9. This emphasis in the later invocations upon a "voice" distinct from the author results in a poem that is increasingly directed by that "voice" throughout the second two-thirds of the poem.

The conventions of a divine epic explain some of Milton's extensive, even in fact intensifying, use of the "voice" of God throughout his epic.[8] Yet the historical presence of God's inspiring "voice," visited upon multiple prophets throughout the mid-seventeenth century, offers us another context for evaluating Milton's language choices. The very volume of mid-century prophecy, when considered in conjunction with the similar language employed by prophets and Milton, suggests the need to contextualize Milton's trope of God's voice as "dictat[ing]" to the poet (9.23). These "voices" also spoke to sectarians supporting a wide variety of political and religious opinions during, particularly, the mid-century. Arise Evans, a Welshman critical of Henrietta Maria though a supporter of the monarchy's restoration, described how "then a voice came to me in a dream" (14), "a laudable sharp shrill, hasting voice near mine ear" which he understands to be "the same voice to come from God" (16). The Ranter Abiezer Coppe recounts the voice that accompanies his vision in *A fiery flying roll*: "And at this vision, a most strong, glorious voyce uttered these words the spirits of just men made perfect," words which he then records in his text (A3r).[9] The Digger Gerrand Winstanley describes in the 1650 *Fire in the Bush* how "then one night as I waked out of sleep, the voyce was in my very heart and mouth, ready to come forth," and he "obeyed the voyce" (A3r, A4r). The Fifth Monarchist Anna Trapnel, as Sue Wiseman notes, particularly emphasized voice in her prophesies (186). Trapnel was "as one that heard only the voice of God sounding forth unto me" a motif that expands into an aural image of an echo in her 1654 *Cry of the Stone*: "Oh it is for thy sake, and for thy servants sake, that thy Servant is made a voyce, a sound, it is a voyce within a voyce, another's voyce, even thy voyce through her" (16, 42). The echo, here a voice that seems to resound throughout Trapnel's body, was a popular motif, employed by, among others, Evans in his 1652 *A Echoo to the Voice from Heaven*.

Obviously, receiving the "Word of the Lord" is one of the most significant motifs of Christian theology. And yet the prominence of the "voice" within prophetic texts is recorded in an explosion of works produced by self-appointed prophets visited by such a voice. God appears to have been speaking in unprecedented numbers to prophet/authors such as Arise Evans and John Saltmarch. Upon receiving their initial inspiration dictated by the voice of God, they then relate that experience to a print audience, employing this same title *A Voice from Heaven* for their respective publications as similarly named tracts erupted onto the printing scene. While only one book is published between 1620 and 1640 with reference to the voice of God in the title, "A heavenly voice," 34 such titles occur between 1640 and 1660, their peak reached in 1653 and 1654.[10] And while printing volume grows enormously during this period, the three-fold increase in publication between 1640 and 1660 (compared to the previous twenty years) underscores how significant this 34-fold increase is in tracts that convey the "voice of God."

The frequency and power of the "voice" of God is underscored by the frequent image of mute or "dumb" men and women in prophetic accounts. Receiving this "voice" while unable to speak, prophetic figures become vessels for the spiritual voice, now operating as a form of human megaphone. Elinor Channel, in *A Message from God, [By a Dumb woman]*, "heard an audible voice" (1); "dumb" when she receives God's message, she is to communicate this message, making "audible" the spirit of God "dictated and made plain to her" (7). The dumb and deaf boy, George Carr, who presages Eleanor Davies's acquisition of prophecy, is himself given "a whistling voice" (183); voices, of God's and of Carr's, resonate throughout Davies's "Appeal," preparing the way for the "Voice from Heaven" that she then receives (184). Even the apocalyptic tone of the mini-invocation to Book 4, in which "that warning voice" (1) cries out from Heaven to announce the end of the world, aligns Milton's language of inspirational voices with the prominent apocalyptic character of most prophecy in the period.[11]

While the "vates" position made possible by the muse resonates through the epic tradition, Milton's reception of the "voice/ of God" in *Paradise Lost* nonetheless sets his text apart from his classical predecessors. While Homer and Virgil do request (oral) aid from the muse, the process by which her inspiration—rather than her actual words—is transformed into poetry is not provided. And yet Milton's many invocations, which shift tone as *Paradise Lost* unfold, details this method of inspiration. Further, it matches contemporary accounts of prophetic inspiration. Milton's classical models detail a goddess who "Sing[s]" or "Tell[s] me" (Homer). Virgil asks his muse to "Tell me." Both emphasize the story conveyed to the poet. Milton, instead, emphasizes the power of a disembodied voice heard by the poet. Alternately, Milton's closest major model for epic, Spenser, turns away from the recording of the voice by stressing instead an explicitly literate construction of a record of history: when Spenser invokes the help of the muse, he avoids an auditory trope, asking Clio instead to "Lay forth out of thine everlasting scryne / the antique rolles (FQ 1,

Proem, 2, 3–4): Spenser's emphasis is on viewing the history he will relate to his readers.

When viewed in concert with epic devices of inspiration, the seventeenth-century prominence of the motif of the "voice of God" links Milton to contemporary prophets receiving this "voice." Milton's final Book 9 invocation follows his explicit Book 7 transformation of the female muse Urania into the "Heav'nly born" Holy Spirit. Milton now describes she "who deigns / Her nightly visitations unimplor'd, / And dictates to me slumb'ring, or inspires / Easy my unpremeditated Verse" (9.21–24). The Holy Spirit approaches the (religious) poet, yet not on his request. Transformed into the passive recipient of inspiration, Milton and his "unpremeditated Verse" come to suggest both unplanned as well as uncomposed poetry (9.24). Kerrigan has explored the "paradox of an artless art" throughout Milton's invocations and his narrative(s) of composition, describing Milton as "both author and amanuensis. He has both everything and nothing to do with *Paradise Lost*" (138). Prophets like Coppe and Winstanley provide an alternative context for considering Milton's abdication of control over the poem as a "Voice divine" takes on all forms of agency in Book 9. Milton's "nightly visitations" recall Winstanley who "one night as I waked out of sleep, the voyce was in my very heart and mouth, ready to come forth" (A3r). Elinor Channel explicitly describes her relation to God's word as one of dictation, paralleling the account provided by the narrator of *Paradise Lost*: the matter is "dictated and made plain to her [Elinor Channel] by the Spirit of God" (7). After gesturing to the historically resonant "voice" of prophecy at in the beginning of the poem and embedding that in the invocations that follow, Milton continues to negotiate within *Paradise Lost* the implications of the potential erasure of self that poetic prophecy can signal.

Such an erasure of the self through prophecy could be plotted along a continuum, one observable within *Paradise Lost*. While the Book 1 invocation offers a portrait of a narrator infused with ambition, who "with no middle flight intends to soar" (1.14), the poem's successive invocations drift toward an increasingly negated self. By Book 9, we see the practice of composing poetry and the identity of the poet described through negation. Milton's own poem thus enacts a traditional tension that marks the prophetic tradition. As William Kerrigan's overview of the tradition of pagan and Christian sources illustrates, a significant anxiety characterized descriptions of prophets as simply "instruments" where God operates as a "ventriloquist" (Plutarch). A critic such as E. W. Heaton thus defends the agency of the canonical prophets: they were "not mere tools" in Gods' hands; "their personalities were [not] dissolved" through the process; "commissioned as 'men of God,' they remained *men*—and that is why they can so powerfully mediate [God's message] to human persons" (quoted in Hill, 102). Heaton insists that the agency of the prophet, specified here as male, must retain his masculine identity; their "powerful" act of communicating to others embeds this masculine nature in their very actions: rather than becoming transformed into a passive vessel, this "solid" prophet remains explicitly associated with masculinity. Abraham Heschel's distinction between ecstasy and prophecy sustains this masculine theme of control, and an intact selfhood. Ecstasy denotes a loss of self or identity, but the prophet is a "self-conscious active 'I'" who retains self-possession (357; 366): "The prophet is not a mouthpiece, but a person; not an instrument, but a partner, an associate of God" (25). Heaton and Heschel offer a somewhat outdated, because either explicitly or implicitly ideologically gendered, account of (biblical) prophets. Yet Elizabeth Sauer, in her more recent work with the Quaker Edward Burrough, underscores this same distinction in a more subtle manner. She remarks that "The fluidity of the male identity and experimentation with feminine discourses were not intended to compromise the essential, integral nature of the (male) self" ("Maternity," 139). All three critics thus construct a continuum of prophecy. On one end, the prophet retains agency, which allows for a "powerful," "self-conscious," and intact "selfhood." On the other end of this spectrum, the passive role of the prophet is marked by loss of self, an emptiness where such "personality" would otherwise reside.

Gender also frames these distinctions. As we will see later, male and female prophets will align along this continuum: male prophets generally described their experiences along one end of the continuum, where such active, "powerful" "personality"-filled prophets reside. Alternately, women more frequently turn to more passive representations of a "self" that could diffuse during the prophetic experience. In considering Milton's accounts of his own poetic production, I want first to consider how distinctly gendered tropes of prophecy illustrate Milton's movement along this continuum. Later, I will compare, and contextualize Milton amid, distinct styles deployed male and female prophets. Yet even without turning to the practices actually deployed by women prophets, we can see Milton engaging cultural categories of gender in his negotiation of the "selfhood" of his prophetic voice: passivity was associated more with femininity while agency and activity, in everything from reproductive practices to political rights, were associated with men.

While the audacious claims of the narrator dominate Book 1, with a seemingly undissolving "I" invoking the aid of the muse and "assert[ing] Eternal Providence," even this opening portrait of the epic narrator generates a potentially androgynous identity for the poet, particularly the imagery of impregnation:

> Thou from the first
> Wast present, and with mighty wings outspread
> Dove-like satst brooding on the vast Abyss
> And mad'st it pregnant: What in me is dark
> Illumine, what is low raise and support. (1.19–23)

The sexualizing of Creation, through God's insemination of Chaos, is aligned, as O. B. Hardison has noted, with poetic creation: the spirit and the writer consequently enter into this (sexual) union. Thus any assertions of an "I" become balanced with, or challenged by, the portrait of the narrator as a passive and a feminized vessel. It is androgyny, rather than a clear distinction between male impregnators and female vessels, that comes to dominate the narrator's various encounters with his muse. As Virginia Mollenkott has suggested, the gender of that muse is unstable from Book 1: while impregnating Chaos, the "Dove-like" deity invokes female practices of birth through the word "brooding." Both female and male in Book 1, this impregnating muse maintains an androgynous identity as in the course of the poem, as the muse becomes reassigned from the male "heav'nly Muse" in Book 3 to a female "Celestial Patroness" in Book 9.[12]

Yet a sexualized process of inspiration remains even in the course of such gender reassignment. In the later invocations, Milton allows himself, or at least his narrator, to be visited by a spiritually impregnating entity each night.[13] The androgyny accorded to both the inspiring voice and the receiving prophet/poet amplifies the dislocation of stable gender identities introduced by a feminized practice of prophecy. This pregnancy motif furthers the anxiety the poet could experience in such a position of feminized passivity. The destabilization of tightly defined gendered categories, the androgynous possibilities that allow a male muse to become a female one, a male poet to be impregnated, also deepens the association between the language of Milton's invocations and prophetic discourses.[14] In his work on Abiezer Coppe, Clement Hawes has explored the "fluidity in gender identities" that is represented in Coppe's statement, "Man is the Woman" (69), and Coppe's representation of himself as impregnated: "These base things (I say) words and actions have confounded and plagued to death, the child in the womb that I was so big of" (108).[15] Hawes concludes that "the exchange is ideologically ambivalent: although it does reinforce an equation of passivity with 'femininity,' it also ecstatically surrenders the 'masculine' position of conscious, self-transparent mastery" (51).

If the androgyny that Hawes associates with prophetic writings marks the opening invocation, Milton's language comes to reflect the passive evacuation of self that characterizes the other side of this continuum as he elaborates his method of prophetic inspiration. Though early invocations prepare the reader for this, by Book 9 Milton's poetic voice moves toward a "passive" extreme: the sentence structure, imagery, and the weakening presence of an active "I" convey a narrator contingent upon the agency of his "Celestial Patroness." By introducing his muse with the conditional "If answerable style I can obtain" (9.20), the narrator is suggesting, first, a stylistic dependence upon her. The image of the sleeping poet inspired by a muse who attends him "unimplor'd" also implies a passivity in relation to the project of the poem and the process of receiving it. Registered in a suppression of an "I" more prominent than in earlier invocations, agency thus streams away from the poet in this account: "Since first this Subject for Heroic Song / Pleas'd me long choosing, and beginning late" (25–26). While the narrator operates implicitly as an agent, the verb choices obscure any active role: his own "Subject" for his poem becomes the grammatical subject propelling this sentence forward—"this Subject . . . Pleas'd me." The writing subject, the "me" who is pleased, becomes the direct object of this phase. Even Milton's use of gerunds sustains this obscuring of agency: while "choosing" the topic of the epic and "beginning" to write *Paradise Lost* are actions performed by Milton, the process by which the poem is created remains hidden behind passive language.

This disappearance of active language and of a directing "I" in the invocation combines with a trope of negation that comes to define the poem itself: in describing *Paradise Lost*, the subject of the poem becomes "the better fortitude / Of Patience and Heroic Martyrdom" but is yet "*Unsung*" (31–33; my emphasis). "Unpremeditated"; "Unsung": these become Milton's account of creating the poem. Milton's choice of topic even follows this evasion of agency-oriented phrases:

Not sedulous by Nature to indite
Wars, hitherto the only Argument
Heroic deem'd, chief maistry to dissect
With long and tedious havoc fabl'd Knights
In Battles feign'd; the better fortitude
Of Patience and Heroic Martyrdom
Unsung; or to describe Races and Games,
Or tilting Furniture, emblazon'd Shields,
Impreses quaint, Caparisons and Steeds;
Bases and tinsel Trappings, gorgeous Knights
At Joust and Tournament; then marshall'd Feast
Serv'd up in Hall with Sewers, and Seneschals;
The skill of Artifice or Office mean,
Not that which justly gives Heroic name
To Person or to Poem. (27–41)

In this sequence, we are repeatedly told what *Paradise Lost*, or Milton, is not: "Not sedulous by Nature," "Unsung"; "Not that which justly gives Heroic name." Such a pattern has marked the invocation from the opening: "No more talk where God or Angel Guest / With Man . . . familiar us'd / To sit indulgent" (1–3), Book 9 begins. Though one might see parts of the "Races and Games" ironically portrayed in the hell of Book 2 as the poem's subject, the context makes clear that this is "not" what describes the poem. In describing the "not" of the poem, style and meaning merge: the absence of directing verbs becomes appropriate. Most of these phrases—describing narratives that the poem has rejected—also lack a specific human agent behind them while many of the phrases are simply verbless.

This negating of poetic production appropriately models the new directing power behind the poem: the "Celestial Patroness" who overwhelms an "I" that has been gradually operating as less of an agent in each preceding invocation:

> Mee of these
> Nor skill'd nor studious, higher Argument
> Remains, sufficient of itself to raise
> That name, unless an age too late, or cold
> Climate, or Years damp my intended wing
> Deprest; and much they may, if all be mine,
> Not Hers who brings it nightly to my Ear. (9.41–47)

Even as the narrator is reintroduced into the poem through an indirect pronoun, "Mee," the subject of the first phrase becomes the "higher Argument"
able to "raise / That [his] name." The argument may "raise" the name of the
poet, but he remains passive and acted upon, even grammatically now reduced
to an indirect object. The identity of the poet seems equally obscured by the
phrasing "That name," a pronoun that actually distances "his" name from us.
The sustained language of negation—"Mee of these / Nor skill'd nor stu-
dious" (41–42)—appropriately complements the diffusion of an active poetic
figure. The association between such an image of negation and the erasure of
self continues to the invocation's end. The final lines suggest that only through
the actions of the spiritual muse will the poem occur: "and much they may, if
all be mine, / Not Hers who brings it nightly to my Ear"; the poem is "Hers"
not "mine" as she "brings" it to my "unpremeditated" "Ear." The final phrase
of the final invocation of *Paradise Lost* suspends Milton's active role in versification. This language of negation, of course, works to prepare us for the Fall that
Book 9 will recount; "No more," the book opens, will we experience such
pleasures of the prelapsarian state. At the point where pride will cause the Fall,
Milton's own hubris-filled invocations—"I may assert Eternal Providence /
And justify the ways of God to men"—may need to give way to the erasure of
self characterizing Book 9's invocation.

Yet such narrative explanations of Milton's turn to this form of inspiration,
in which he literally has the poem breathed into his ear, do not provide us with
the complete story. Instead, the rich historical body of prophecy from the mid-
century provides models for Milton. Contemporary prophetic language provided extensive imagery of a (passive) instrument filled spiritually by God's
words. And as I will suggest, this passivity characterized both the feminized
practice of prophecy and the prophetic event as experienced by female
prophets. The voice of the "Celestial Patroness" who whispers into the "un-
premeditative Ear" recalls the mechanism of inspiration detailed by countless
prophets. In Mary Cary's 1651 *The Little Horns Doom & Downfall: or A Scripture-
Prophesie of King James, and King Charles, and of this present Parliament, unfolded*, she
presents herself as a forum through which this message will be presented to others, even positioning herself as an amanuensis as did Milton: "a very weake, and
unworthy instrument," Cary "could doe no more herein . . . of my selfe, then a
pencill, or pen can do, when no hand guide's it" (A8r). An erasure of a self accompanies Cary's transformation into a writing "Instrument" to convey God's

prophetic message, as we saw with Milton; "I am not sufficient to thinke a good thought, but my sufficiency is of God" (A8r).[16] This language of the prophet as God's "instrument" recurs in Anna Trapnel's 1654 *Cry of the Stone*: God communicates to her that "I will make thee an instrument of much more" when she "desired of the Lord to tell me whether I had done that which was of and from himself" (6). Her prophetic performance recounted in the *Strange and Wonderful Newes from White-hall: or, The Mighty Visions* stresses this passive status: "she should be made an instrument of much more" (4). And in a later poem, she will recall her many years as a visionary in language fusing the motif of "instrument" with a suppressed prophetic "I": "O Spirit, poor Instrument hath found / Thee a very constant friend. . . . Poor Instrument hath found thee, Lord / For fourteen years together."[17] Abdicating any formative role in her prophesies, in *Cry of the Stone* she describes how "The Lord put it all in my mouth, and told me what I should say: so that I will have nothing ascribed to me" (14).

While I have led with examples of female prophets, male, as female, prophets would invoke this trope of the instrument. Arise Evans appeals to God to "give me grace, wisdom, and understanding that I may glorifie thee as this Instrument doth now before all the world" (*A Voice from Heaven*, 10). Yet the vacating of a self and a concomitant passivity marks female prophetic speech in this period much more so than male speech. While Evans employs the trope of the prophet as an "instrument," he will reassert some possession of the self in the following lines: "this petition on or desire of mine in this matter was not known to any but God and myself" (10). Both Trapnel and Evans may "desire" God's instruction, but in Evans's hands, it becomes a "petition," a desire that he makes "mine." His use of a first-person pronoun allows his claim of exclusive (with God, of course) knowledge of this "matter." Further, the very language of a "petition," a public "demand," links Evans's prophetic experience to the acquisition of political authority or power conventionally gendered male. Certainly a select number of women, such as Katherine Chidley, did present petitions to the governmental organ of the day. Yet most of the female sectarian prophets positioned their visions, trances, and the resulting (published) texts as produced by God speaking through them. In contrast, Evans retains notable, linguistic possession over this "petition," one not fully ceded to God.

Evans's language choice emblematizes the distinct patterns in male versus female prophetic discourse, patterns that can be plotted along a continuum of prophecy. Hilary Hinds emphasizes the helplessness and passivity embedded in the more frequent use of language like "instrument" by female prophets, distinctions framed by cultural traditions casting women as weak, passive, and portraying the female body as an empty vessel waiting to be filled.[18] Such cultural views framed seventeenth-century prophecy as "a feminine activity, whether or not the actual prophet was a man or woman" (Mack, 24). Possibly as a result of this feminizing of the prophetic experience, large numbers of female prophets emerged between 1640 and 1660—around 300, according to Phyllis Mack. And if we define prophecy, as Patricia Crawford does, as including a visionary or ecstatic experience, female prophets outnumbered men experiencing trances or visions (106): in such events, a "solid" self dissipates in the course of the prophetic event.

In fact, distinctions do emerge between the writings of male and female prophets. I would agree with critics such as Hawes and Rachel Trubowitz that the practices of prophecy allowed for gendered language innovations and experiments. Yet the notable differences between male and female prophetic language produce an important context for Milton's (or his narrator's) prophetic voice. Male prophets generally described their experiences along the end of the continuum characterized by active, "powerful" "personality"-filled prophets. Women more consistently turned to more passive representations of a "self" that could diffuse during the prophetic experience.[19] Even while inserting themselves into, and asserting themselves in, a political arena, women's mode of self-presentation remained the vacating of the self.

Such differences further align Milton's account of his—or his narrator's—experience of inspiration in Books 7 and 9 to the language employed by female prophets. Sarah Wight ends A Wonderful Pleasant and Profitable Letter with a form of signature undermining the very assertion of self that publication would seem to imply: "Sarah Wight /, an empty nothing, whose fulness is all in that Fountain that filleth all and all" (80). Elizabeth Stirredge described herself as unable to "utter a word, but what the Lord giveth into my mouth" (quoted in Hinds, 88). Offering, without question, the most extreme style employed by male or female prophets, Eleanor Davies rhetorically employs an agentless verb construction and the erasure of an "I" in "The Restitution of Prophecy"; here, she introduces her prophetic "babe" with neither the invocation of an "I" pronoun nor a verb construction allowing for the action or agency of the writer: "This Babe, object to their scorn, for speaking the truth, informing of things future, notwithstanding thus difficult to be fathered or licensed. That incision to the quick, hath under gone; without their Benediction, in these plain Swathe-bands, though commended unto thy hands" (344). A comparison between male and female prophetic language thus reveals a much more consistent abdication of the "I" in women, and thus the negation of the agency of the prophet receiving inspiration.

Significantly, this portrait of women's loss of self in prophesy is directly opposed to Nigel Smith's account of Abeizer Coppe as a figure who becomes obsessed with his identity (Perfection Proclaimed, 61). The amazing image dominating Coppe's A fiery flying roll keeps the presence of the prophet's "I" squarely within the story:

And behold I writ, and lo a hand was sent to me, and a roll of a book was therein, which this fleshly hand would have put wings to, before the time. Whereupon it was snatcht out of my hand, & the Roll thrust into my mouth, and I eat it up, and filed my bowels with it, . . . where it was as bitter as worm-wood; and it lay broiling, and burning in my stomack, till I brought it forth in this forme. (A3v).

While he is, in part, acted upon—the "roll" is "snatchet out of my hand" and "thrust into my mouth"—this vision features Coppe prominently. Locating himself amid the actions of the Book of Revelation, Coppe is not the relator of a voice, but an actor in this series of events while the prophecy is accomplished through Coppe's actions. The maintenance of an active and present "I" is equally discernible in Arise Evans's summary of "my calling to this work": "you shall finde Gods special purpose in me, preparing me from my infancy, and also leading me by his special hand . . . declaring his minde unto me, giving me to understand" that "God had appointed me for some great work" (*A Echoo to the Voice from Heaven*, Bb8r). No empty vessel he: Evans, again, may be "lead . . . by his . . . hand" and spoken to by God, but an "I" acknowledged by all around him is never under pressure or in danger of disappearing.

That presence or disappearance of the "I" serves as a general, and yet effective, distinguisher between the bulk of male and female prophets. While Nigel Smith defines a form of agent-ness for prophets, again and again the writings of female prophets are characterized by the frequent evacuation of that self[20]; Milton's representation of his narrator as receiving language "unimplor'd," "unpremeditated," through a disappearing or suppressed "I" in Book 9 thus seems closer to this tradition of female prophetic language than to that emphasized by male prophets. What emerges is a possible "conversation" that Milton could be said to be having with women from the mid-century. These female prophets' representation of receiving God's inspiration becomes embedded in a stylistically gendered set of tropes that Milton deploys in his account of prophetic inspiration.

This portrait of a gendered vision of seventeenth-century prophecy is reinforced in *Paradise Lost* by the alternate representations of Adam and Eve's "prophetic" experiences. Thus, Milton appears to embed not just prophetic language into his text but reflects on the historical characteristics of midcentury prophets. As critics have recently noted, Eve's access to divine information models much more closely to the experiences of postlapsarian prophets. While Kerrigan describes Adam's vision in the final two books as "the true model for divine prophecy" (145), Adam's experiences structurally evade the challenges facing contemporary prophets. The dream-like access to knowledge he is given at his creation is immediately framed by the appearance of the "Presence Divine." Meanwhile, the prophetic spectacle that Michael stages for him in Books 11 and 12 comes complete with angelic commentary to keep Adam from any interpretive errors.

Instead, it is Eve's Satanic dream, which Kerrigan acknowledges as "genuinely prophetic" (144), that embodies this very ambiguity. More in line with postlapsarian prophecy, Eve is presented with dreams but no certainty as to their source. In fact, in her dream Eve first mistakes Satan for Adam and then thinks he is "one of those from Heav'n" (5.55). Her information about the power of the fruit, then, comes from a multiply misidentified source within the dream.[21] With no stable, unquestionable "Presence Divine" or angelic guide to guarantee their visions or voices, prophets could well be accused of receiving their inspiration from the Devil, rather than from God (8.314). Thus, biographical, even hagiographic, narratives published in conjunction with Sarah Wight's and Anna Trapnel's prophecies describe the early temptations by the Devil these prophetesses experienced. And beyond the uncertainty of the source of inspiration, these women could face significant social consequences: prophets, such as Anna Trapnel and Elizabeth Poole, had to defend themselves from claims that they were practicing witchcraft. We hear this cultural problem refracted through Eve's "prophetic" dream, one which threatens to turn into the Satanic experience of "transvection," a flying experience that Satan could produce and was often cited in witchcraft accusations.[22] Eve's dream experience thus seems to offer a more applicable vision of prophecy, including the very ambiguity, even danger, of claiming divine inspiration.

Eve's experience of dreams in Book 12 also aligns her closely with the portrait of prophecy present at mid-century. Rachel Trubowitz calls Eve "oracular" ("Feminizing Vision," 27), "evoking the culturally subversive Civil War figure of the woman prophet in the form of the enlightened post-lapsarian Eve" ("Female Preachers," 128), while Elizabeth Sauer describes the prophetic future described at the end of *Paradise Lost* as feminine ("Maternity," 146). Further, this Book 12 sequence enacts the passivity characterizing feminized prophetic experience: Michael tells Adam that "Her also I with gentle Dreams have calm'd" (595), effecting a "meek submission" in a now much more tractable Eve. Eve, rather than Adam, thus models what many critics have noted as the "feminine" or feminized nature of prophecy in the period.

Additionally, the representation of prophetic, and demonic, dreams within the narrative of *Paradise Lost* positions the experiences of Eve closer to that of the poet. Eve's two dreams both come in sleep, her demonically inspired dream appearing at night just as the "Celestial Patroness" comes "unimplor'd" to Milton. The time for (poetic) inspiration is also the time for seduction by a formally divine source: Satan. Thus, Milton is more like Eve than Adam in his reception of the nightly language of inspiration. The Book 3 account of the inspired "wakeful Bird / [that] Sings darkling, and in shadiest Covert hid / Tunes her nocturnal Note" (3.38–40) is echoed in the Book 5 language of Eve's seduction: the silence of the night "yields / To the night-warbling Bird, that now awake / Tunes sweetest his love-labor'd song" (5.39–41): both dreams are surrounded by the sounds of warbling night birds. We thus hear Satan's temptation of Eve and God's inspiration fused through these similar motifs. Closer to Eve, whose prophetic experiences match the exigencies of female prophets, Milton thus explores the problematics of a feminized identity of prophecy throughout his poem.

This sequence provides a methodological model for Milton's "historical sub-conscious" that I see as directing his deployment of prophetic motifs. Milton's exposure to female prophecy in the mid-century culture occurs consciously; he is aware of the characteristics of such prophecy and its association with the feminine in the culture. These discourses leave behind traces that then affect Milton's poetic production. We can see that process modeled with Eve's Book 5 dream. In the Book 5 dream that Eve experiences, she is aware of the details of the dream she relates to Adam. The influences of the dream upon Eve, though, cannot be dismissed, despite Adam's claims that "Evil into the mind of God or Man / May come and go, so unapprov'd, and leave / No spot or blame behind" (5.117–19). Yet all is not "clear'd" from Eve's mind as she "let fall / From either eye" a "gentle tear" (136, 130–31). The events of the temptation and Fall in Book 9 confirm this: "What in sleep thou didst abhor to dream / Waking," Eve *will* later "consent to do" (5.120, 121). As Eve's dream enters the "private Cell" of Eve's mind (109), these tropes will reappear during her conversation with Satan and prompt her fall. Satan's initial temptation included many inversions of hierarchy. Promoting night over day, Satan then disrupts a spiritual and implicitly political hierarchy: Eve is offered to be "among the Gods / Thyself a Goddess" (109, 73). The language of aspiring to such a "Goddess"-like state, introduced in the dream, then shapes her choice in Book 9: "nor was God-head from her thought" (9.790). The lusciousness of the fruit in the dream, "the pleasant savory smell / [which] So quick'n'd appetite, that I, methought, / Could not but taste" (5.84–86), predicts, perhaps even shapes, the sensuous appeal it offers to Eve in Book 9: in her is "wak'd / An eager appetite, rais'd by the smell / So savory of that Fruit" (9.739–41). This earlier experience, placing into Eve's head a series of tropes, or images, or ideas, models the subconscious: events to which one have been overtly introduced—such as the historical condition of female and feminized prophecy—remain in one's mind, the "private cell" below the surface of consciousness. These tropes then return and affect, perhaps even effect, action, as with Satan's Book 5 temptation and Eve's subsequent drives to taste the fruit.

This model of Milton's own practices allows me to explore the uses to which Milton puts prophetic speech within *Paradise Lost*. Milton deploys the language of prophecy in his epic poem, ambivalently exploring his relationship to discourses of cultural disempowerment. And yet, this language of passivity marking much of prophetic language and moments in Milton's text offered an opportunity to engage the sites of political power. The strategies that these prophets deployed included presenting themselves as physically weak, articulating their role as a (usually subservient) wife, and erasing the "self" as the "voice" of God spoke through them. Yet through this, Poole as Trapnel as Wight find mechanisms to address a wide audience: Poole engages the marital metaphor in ways to appeal to the Army's War Council; Trapnel lapses into visions filled with song, poetry, and prophesies that draw visitors to an inn outside of Whitehall; Wight's extensive trances will be recorded in print. Their use during the 1640s and 1650s of strategies that configure a (culturally) weaker self able to engage larger political issues and debates propels Milton's "subconscious" engagement of these tropes of female prophecy during the Restoration.

Contextualizing Milton among these discourses requires reconsideration of certain biographical assumptions about Milton's involvements with extreme religious groups and practices. David Loewenstein has been able to illustrate Milton's engagement with and potential sympathy for sectarians in *Representing Revolution*. Furthermore, Milton's opposition to the professional preaching class in his companion tracts "A Treatise of Civil Power in Ecclesiastical Causes" and "Means to Remove Hirelings" suggests support for itinerant preachers, a position that men as well as women filled during the Civil War and Interregnum periods.[23] Internalizing aspects of a discourse that allowed women, as well as male sectaries, to call upon the authority of God, enter into print, and speak directly to political issues served Milton's purposes after the Restoration.

Positioning Milton among both these prophetic texts and prodigious birth texts also necessitates that we (re)consider Milton's reading practices—or redefine our understanding of them, as Stephen Dobranski has prompted us to do. As a licenser of, and possibly even a collaborator with Marchamont Nedham on, *Mercurius Politicus*, Milton was professionally positioned as a consumer of politically inflected texts at the beginning of the Protectorate. The threats posed to the newly formed Protectorate by sectarian groups—Fifth Monarchists, Levellers, Quakers—are registered, for example, in Nedham's comments on Anna Trapnel; her prophesizing, and one would suspect the subsequent publication of her trances, "does a world of mischief in London" (CSP, 7 Feb. 1654). If we accept Stephen Dobranski's argument that the bulk of Milton's work in 1649–1650 would have been the "policing" of authors, printers, and booksellers (127), his exposure to texts with potentially damaging political content was likely extensive. Milton's earlier role as a producer and consumer of pamphlets in the early 1640s provides another link to these tracts: the Smectymnuus controversy in which he participated had deployed images of "monstrous geneologies," as Kristen Poole has described them. The images of monstrosity, and its links to religious error, might well have drawn Milton to an adjacent body of prophetic texts at mid-century which spoke to sectarian challenges to the Protectorate.

Milton's analogous use of the "prophetic" revelations embodied in prodigious birth tracts sustains his deployment of mid-century accounts of "prophetic" truth to speak of and speak to power in the Restoration. This adjacent discourse, I will argue in the second half of this chapter, provides Milton's "historical subconscious" with motifs that he could draw upon in order to (re)gain access to public discourse at the Restoration.[24] Popular accounts and interpretations of another form of "prodigious" outpourings from women's bodies, the genre of monstrous births which reached the height of its popularity in the 1640s and 1650s, provide raw material for scenes in *Paradise Lost*. This body of pamphlets offers another explicit connection between Milton's 1667 poem and a rather nostalgic set of texts that had recorded political and religious upheavals during the Civil War and Interregnum. During the mid-1640s and the early 1650s, a large number of tracts recounting "monstrous" births served the purposes of sectarians, royalist supporters, and Parliamentary propagandists alike. As with prophecy—particularly the more female-dominated field of the ecstatic experience—the "prodigious" results of these pregnancies could serve as confirmation of one's religious and political goals. Both such pregnancies and the outpouring of prophecy configured the body as "vessels"—in the case of "monstrous" births these "vessels" or wombs were always female—through which God could convey his message.

While the act of being the vessel—in these cases the unwitting body that brings forth a child with a severe birth defect—might appear fundamentally different from the act of prophesizing, culturally these two acts were closely fused. Prophecy and acts of birth were consistently linked both in the physicalized prodigious births and in the metaphors used by male and female sectaries. Coppe's birth of the "fiery roll," which is the prophecy itself, stands as the most imaginative appropriation of the act of birthing. More frequent were motifs that linked prophecy and pregnancy/birth within women's metaphoric and literal bodies. Birthing imagery characterizes Elizabeth's Poole's entire opening of *A Vision*. As she opens her speech to the "Councel of War," their "labours" take on the imagery of birth which she regenders as female and then assimilates to herself: "the pangs of a travelling woman" are "upon" Poole who will "deliver" her prophetic message to Parliament (A2v; tp). Poole's second prophetic account of England, *An Alarum of War*, explicitly invokes the language of pregnancy. Parliament "can not but groane for deliverance," a delivery that Poole makes possible through her own body with the "delivery" of her prophetic statements (6). Poole's doubled use of the birthing image, then, equates the linguistic act with the physical act.[25]

Just as the body of the female prophet operates as a vessel through which speech—and possibly truth—comes from God, so too does the body of the mother "deliver" these aspects of truth through "prodigious," "monstrous," and meaningful births. Both discourses imagined truth delivered through the vessel, a process made explicit in the 1661 *Strange and True relation of a Wonderful and Terrible Earth-quake*. Here, "prodigious and wonderful Apparitions" prompt women's bodies to deliver or "fall into Travel"; one of these women then brings forth speaking children (tp). Articulate prodigious births thus sustain the link between female bodies producing truths or prophetic judgments and the messages conveyed by "monstrous" deliveries. Julie Crawford has identified other literal and figurative tropes that link such prophetic speaking births and the prophetic female body. The frequency with which sectarian women prophets "delivered" these prophecies from their beds underscores the similarity between birthing practices and the birth of these forms of truth (Crawford, 165). Further, female prophecy and prodigious births are bridged through the claims of divine pregnancies offered by female prophets such as Mary Adams (Crawford, 167).

Nor are the mothers who deliver these prodigious births considered innocent or without any traces of agency. As Julie Crawford has detailed in *Marvelous Protestantism*, these mothers were often judged guilty of an action or speech which then produced this "prodigious" sign.[26] Articulating or enacting questionable, even heretical, religious and/or political positions, these mothers then receive punishment for their speech: that punishment becomes literally inscribed into their bodies. In many instances these women would be positioned as enemies of the state. They represent, if you will, an adjacent line of prophecy. Just as the mothers of these prodigious births were subject to judgment, many female prophets had to fight off accusations of heretical beliefs, even of witchcraft, during their moment in the public spotlight. The very differences between them also expose strong similarities. These mothers are more immediately encircled by cultural discourses that can condemn them as heretical, while female sectarians were often able to remain in control of the cultural discourses that surrounded them longer than mothers of prodigious births. Yet whether "delivering" prophetic truths to an overtly political audience or having one's "prodigious" birth operate as politically inflected propaganda, the bodies of these women—prophets and "vessels" alike—were positioned at the center of political debates at the mid-century.

Milton's use of both sets of ideologically and imagistically rich historical texts becomes another strategy for engaging elements of the political sphere. For Milton's "historical subconscious" will draw upon these accounts of pregnant bodies and births in his construction of the Sin and Death sequence in Book 2. An anxiety about the androgynous portrait of the narrator in Book 1 and the imagery of impregnation may well resonate through these images of prodigious births.[27] I would suggest that the historical material embedded in these accounts of prodigious births, ones that Milton echoes within the Sin and Death scene, resonates textually with the prophetic pregnancy bestowed upon Milton. While in Book 1 he initiated a strategy of feminizing the narrative voice in order to enable his own prophetic abilities, he then strategically deploys these accounts of pregnant bodies and monstrous births. As with his use of a discourse of feminized passivity, Milton's gesture back to the pregnancy motif in Book 1 of *Paradise Lost* allows "subconscious" strategies of disempowerment to generate a politically pointed response to the restored government of Charles II. Questions of governmental authority and of the stability of political meaning thus characterize the Book 2 sequence.

Milton's account of Sin's pregnancy and Death's birth is overly modeled by the language of this particular subgenre of "monstrous" or "prodigious" births. Historical contexts have rarely been used to interpret this sequence, where the criticism has been dominated by allegorical and theological readings: Louis Schwartz's consideration of this scene amid actual practices of childbirth is rare in its approach.[28] Here, I will be shifting the historical lens to observe Milton's strategic deployment of the conventions in these tracts. One convention is the thick detailing of the birth and the deformed "shape" of the subsequent "monstrous" product throughout accounts in the 1640s. The "Monstrous childe" brought forth in the 1646 *A Declaration of a strange and Wonderfull Monster* is "ugly and deformed" (8). The 1645 *Signs and wonders from Heaven* describes how women "bringeth forth ugly and deformed Monsters" (2), specifically in this account a "deformed Monster . . . borne alive" (5). The 1652 *Ranters Monster: Being a true Relation* describes "how she was delivered of the ugliest ill-shapen Monster that ever eyes beheld" (tp). Milton introduces his portrait of the Book 2 "Monster" of Death through parallel language. At line 675, Death proceeds to grow "More dreadful and deform" (706). His children, the "Hell Hounds" that reside within Sin's womb, are "Nor uglier" than the creatures which follow the "Night-Hag," their ugliness confirmed through Milton's simile and mini-narrative of witchcraft practices (654, 662).

The distorted or indiscernible shape of the birth repeats throughout these tracts, dominating, for example, the 1644 London-produced accounts of Anne Hutchinson's monstrous births. Resonating in multiple ways with Milton's narrative, Hutchinson "brought forth not one, (as Mistris Dier did) but (what was more strange to amazement) 30 monstrous births or thereabouts, at once; some of them bigger, some lesser, some of one shape, some of another, few of any perfect shape, none at all of them (as farre as I could every learne) of humane shape" (Winthrop, B3v). The horror of the "shape" of Death in Milton's sequence is confirmed by his very indescribability: "The other shape, / If shape it might be call'd that shape had none / Distinguishable in member, joint, or limb, / Or substance might be call'd that shadow seem'd" (2. 666–69). The multiple monstrous births in the Book 2 sequence also bear a striking similarity to this account of Hutchinson's "30 monstrous births or thereabouts." Following Death's birth, the "forcible and foul / Ingendr'ing" of Sin by her own son produces "These yelling Monsters that with ceaseless cry / Surround me" (793–96). Nor were monstrous births who produced secondary progeny unheard of: the birth of one monster in the 1645 *The most strange and woounderfull apperation of blood in a poole . . . As also the true relation of a miraculous and prodigious birth* produces a second offspring, though in this case from the "one monster" "thence did proceed another birth in the shape of a man child" who is "perfect in every limb" (8). The significance of Spenser's Error scene on the Sin and Death episode should not, of course, be forgotten: Spenser's influence, as Maureen Quilligan has shown us, was immense. But whereas the account of

"A thousand yong ones, which [Error] dayly fed" forms part of the influences on this scene, Milton explicitly separates the "vgly monster" from the half woman/half snake that is commingled in Spenser (I.i.15.5; 14.6). In making the "monster" the progeny of Sin, and not Error herself, Milton distinctly operates within the conventions of these prodigious birth tracts.

While viscerally embodying the theological tradition of Sin producing Death in this scene, Milton follows contemporary discourses that allegorically figured Sin as mothering a monster. Central in accusations against Anne Hutchinson, as well as Mary Dyer, were the doctrinal associations between the generation of such monstrous births and the commission of sin. These "monstrous births" were interpreted by many New Englanders as "manifestations of their mothers' doctrinal errors" (Schutte, 103). The standard assumption within this body of English narratives was that these births were the "products of Hutchinson's own monstrous opinions" (Crawford, 152). Milton thus represents sin's power to generate the physical manifestations of a mother's error common in the English narratives. In the 1647 *Strange news from Scotland*, a "monstrous and ill-shapen" child declares "I am thus disformed for the sinnes of my Parents" (2–3). His mother even acknowledges that sin is the cause of this "disformed" monster. In this account of a monstrous birth, Sin, Death, and serpent imagery are further conflated. During her confession, she describes a nation "pestered with as many serpents," and "Death put an Exit" to the mothers' life (*Strange* news, 4). In *Paradise Lost*, Sin's body is equally encircled by serpent imagery: she "ended foul in many a scaly fold / Voluminous and vast, a Serpent arm'd / With mortal sting" (651–53). This theological matrix of Sin, Death, and the imagery of the serpent, often viewed as the main force determining aspects of Milton's allegory, was equally embedded in this 1647 prodigious birth tract.

Common as well to the "monstrous" birth tracts and Milton's narrative are anxieties about the birthing process and the perversion of the maternal act in witchcraft. In the 1645 *Signs and wonders from Heaven. With a true Relation of a Monster*, the pregnant mother "would often say that she was mightily troubled with what she borne in her womb" (4). And where is the materiality of the deliveries of monstrous births more amplified than in the protracted, horrifying delivery scene in Book 2. It opens, of course, with Sin who "Pensive here I sat / Alone" before her "prodigious motion" and "rueful throes" begin (2.777–78, 780). Such maternal concerns during a "prodigious" birth are often interwoven with anxieties about witchcraft, as in the 1640s tracts. In 1646 Lancashire, the headless monster child born to a "Popish Gentlewoman" emerges, we are told, from amid a den of witches: "No parts in England hath so many Witches" (4). In many of these accounts, physical proximity links witchcraft to the birth of a monster. The 1645 *Signs and wonders from Heaven. With a true Relation of a Monster* begins with the most prodigious sign, the birth of "the strangest mis-shapen Monster that ever they lookt on, or heard tell of" (4), while the title page lists the many acts of witchcraft in the area. Equally, witches could actually prompt misshapen births: after meeting with a witch, a "woman went home, and was delivered of two lumps of flesh" (5). Such associations are woven into the Miltonic sequence. Sin is compared to the "Night-Hag" "Lur'd with the smell of infant blood, to dance / With Lapland Witches" (2.662–65); the mother of this "monster," through both the simile and the account of her as a "Snaky Sorceress" (2.724), is associated with, even identified as, a witch.

While witches frequently appear in tracts, so too does the speaking child. The linguistic skills attributed to many of these monstrous births occur in both the loquacious monster-child Death and the "yelling Monsters" from Sin's womb whose "ceaseless cry" "rung / A hideous Peal" (2.795, 655–66). The speaking child, announcing himself the product of sin in *Strange newes from Scotland*, is joined by other speaking infants: three "male-children, who had all teeth . . . spake as soon as they were born" (*Strange . . . Earth-quake*, tp). The horror of Sin's "yelling Monsters that with "ceaseless cry / Surround me" who "into the womb / That breed them . . . return, and howl and gnaw / My Bowels" combines the sound they produce and their "gnaw"ing "teeth" with this image of the physically internalized consequences of sin (2.795–96, 798–800). The tract *Strange news from Scotland* closes with parallel imagery. Many others, besides this "Sin"ful mother who produced her talking child, have "their in-sides . . . hung round with all sorts of crying sinnes" (5). The products of Sin "cry" out and produce pain internally, invoking the womb-like entrance and torture to which Sin is subjected. These accounts of monstrous births thus appear to serve as raw material for Milton's account of Sin and Death, subconsciously molding Milton's portrait of this "prodigious" birth scene (2.780). Yet these images function strategically for Milton as the Sin and Death scene unfolds.

For, accounts of monstrous births make overt what has been latent in my discussion of prophecy in the 1640s and 1650s: their frequent explicit political significance. As *Marvelous Protestantism*, as well as my more contracted summary here, has illustrated, throughout the 1640s and 1650s, "prodigious" or "monstrous" births were everywhere. More importantly, these accounts were politically all over the map, symbolic weapons used by monarchical and Parliamentary supporters.[29] As in prophecy, which could be used to condemn Cromwell as well as Charles, the political affiliation of these births was unstable. "[P]arents who are sectaries" produce a "monster" in the second part of *Gangreana* (tp), the same year, 1646, that "a Popish Gentlewoman" birthed a child "without a head (after the mother had wished rather to bear a Childe without a head then a Roundhead) and had curst the Parliamnet" (sic) (*A Declaration*, tp). Resistance to the monarchy was probably recorded more frequently than resistance to the Parliament: the 1645 *The most strange and wounderful apperation of blood in a poole* offers the political allegory of a female "monster" as the monarchy, horribly deformed but also "very plump and fat" (8). The secondary prodigious birth seems an image of parliamentary government: the "spare and leane" "man child" that emerges "received its originall and the beginning of its growth from the imperfect ruines of the other" (8). Yet monarchical supporters could and did use the womb for their own political purposes: in the 1649 *Vox Infantis. Or, The propheticall child*, the prophetic child introduced by this text describes the future restoration of the monarchy and of Charles II.

Yet this clearly partisan, if conflicting, imagery of monstrous births became politically unified under the restored monarchy. In the early 1660s, the monstrous birth "genre" undergoes a series of transformations. Crawford has argued that texts such as John Gadbury's 1660 *Natura Prodigiorum: or, A Discourse Touching the Nature of Prodigies* and John Spencer's 1663 *A Discourse Concerning Prodigies* prompt readers to reject sacred meanings present in such prodigies.[30] An analogous Restoration response, which also forsakes the previous multiplicity of prophetic "prodigious" signs, is the transformation of this subgenre into satire. This generic reconfiguration effectively reduces the power of these earlier tracts while reappropriating the imagery for Royalist propaganda. In the "Mistress Rump" satires, Mother Rump's birth of a monstrous child enables the recounting of crimes committed against the monarchy. Milton's Sin and Death sequence, shaped by the mid-century discourses of prophetic inspiration, employs these motifs to strategically engage the reworking of the popular "monstrous birth" pamphlets under Charles II. These historical texts thus provided Milton a tool with which to engage this highly political appropriation of images of birth, ones previously linked to prophetic truths. In the hands of Royalist satirists and propagandists, these motifs were distributed to buttress the restored monarchy. The political purposes to which the monarchy's supporters transformed this tradition required a response by Milton.

The stakes surrounding the appropriation of these motifs were very high. The explicit feminization of "Rebellion" in Charles's procession to his coronation shows these images deployed to promote the new monarchy. In his 1660 coronation progress, Charles was confronted at the first triumphal arch by "a Woman personating REBELLION, mounted on an Hydra . . . Snakes crawling on her Habit, and begirt with Serpents, her Hair snaky" (Ogilby, 13). Announcing herself as "Hell's daughter, Satan's eldest child," this figure, a multiheaded monster between her legs and "Serpents" encircling her midsection, resonates with Milton's "Snaky Sorceress" who "ended foul in many a scaly fold / Voluminous and vast, a Serpent arm'd / With mortal sting" (2.724, 651–53). In his representation of Sin in *Paradise Lost*, Milton engages rewritings of the (failed) republican experiment as a birthing female body. Milton's Book 2 imagery thus employs the very language of prodigious births, with all of their political import, to reject this cooptation—in fact perversion—of earlier forms of revealing "truths" through prophecy.

In the hands of Stuart propagandists, Milton's Revolution became political perversion in the Mistress Rump tracts and gendered perversity in Charles's procession. As critics have noted, the "Mistress Rump" satires draw explicitly on the tropes of monstrous birth tracts from the Civil War years.[31] Experiencing "terrible pangs, bitter teming, hard labour, and lamentable travel," Mistress Rump produces—as a function of her explicit political sins—an "ugly, deformed, ill-shapen, base, begotten Babe" that is explicitly identified as a "Monster of reformation" (*Mris. Rump brought to Bed*, tp). This creature follows the traits of previous "prodigious" births: a "Monster without a head, goggle-ey'd, bloody hands, growing out on both sides of its devouring panch," it recalls the horrible deformities of earlier tracts (*Famous Tragedie*, 6–7). Details that previous tracts presented about monstrous births become redeployed as explicit products of *political* sin. As Julie Crawford's detailed readings of the tracts illustrate, the theological import of prodigious births was always linked to distinct political affiliations during the Civil War and Interregnum period. While the dominant theological import of these earlier tracts is gestured at in the Mistress Rump satires—the child is of course a "Monster of reformation"—earlier religious divides become much more muted in this satire of previous political enemies. When Mistress Rump confesses "instead of Reforming I have deformed" (*Famous Tragedie*, 6), religious issues of the "reformation" that Puritans and sectarians saw themselves as undertaking become instead attacks on political and religious organization during the Interregnum and the Rump Parliament. Further, the heretical sins embodied in such births are redirected into, and codified as, political sins. Thus, Mistress Rump's birthing experience narrates the Stuart version of Charles's (unjustified) execution and the (invalid) Protectorate: "the death of my King . . . causes my pains to encrease, I understand too late he suffered by my Tyranny" (3).

The pro-monarchical solidification of previously fluid images of monstrous births becomes challenged by Milton's manipulation of the very monstrous birth tropes upon which the Mistress Rump pamphlets and the Book 2 Sin and Death scene are built; Milton's episode transforms the very imagery from monstrous birth tracts into a critique of monarchy. Death, the offspring of a laboring Sin, is not a monster who validates monarchy's claims as in the "Mistress Rump" satires. Instead, he is the symbol of monarchy itself: "what seem'd his head / The likeness of a Kingly Crown had on" (2.672–73). The previously shadowy link between Death and monarchical aspirations is confirmed as Death asserts that "I reign King, and to enrage thee more, / Thy King and Lord" (698–99).[32] Milton thus represents Sin as the mother of monarchical authority; if this "Hell's daughter, Satan's eldest child" is the snake-covered figure of "Rebellion" that met Charles II during his procession, she is the rebel of, not against, monarchy. Certainly, Milton is employing the female body for alternative propaganda purposes by maintaining its link to monstrous birthing. And yet, as we have seen, the feminized body of the prophet—even an impregnated body—is a motif with which he aligns himself in his own invocations. We observe, in this engagement of the tropes of prodigious bodies and births,

Milton drawing upon the very political and psychic possibilities and instabilities that such tropes had offered at the mid-century. The effect of this subconscious manipulation of these motifs and possibilities? To provide a counter to monarchical attacks on republican beliefs.

And yet Milton's recycling of "monstrous" birth tropes also speaks more broadly to an issue of political organization literally embodied within these narratives: the metaphor of the body politic and the consequent meaning for the organization of the state. The image of the headless child, a birth defect that appears in tracts describing the monstrous births of Anne Hutchinson, Mary Dyer, Mary Wilmore, and Mrs. Haughton, necessarily invokes the structure of the state and the political implications of a state operating without a monarchical head. These prodigious birth narratives also resonate with the prophetic speech of women, as in Mary Pope's 1649 *Behold, here is a word or, An Answer to the late Remonstrance of the Army*. In this "Word or Message from Heaven," Pope's critique of the Parliament's actions against Charles I underscores the political import of the motif of the headless body (tp). She describes the country as "now instead of having one head to make up the Body with the Members compleat, wee have had a preposterous Body without a Head" (5).

Milton's account of the monstrous birth of Death engages this very trope. Death is not headless, since he speaks. Yet Milton's syntactic structure will do double duty in rejecting the, for him, dangerous metaphor of the body politic. The image of a headless body politic would support the monarchy, as we see Pope insist upon. In Milton's narrative, therefore, he subtly deploys the motifs from the monstrous birth genre to discount any use of the body politic metaphor: "what seem'd his head / The likeness of a Kingly Crown had on" (2.672–73). Death could be interpreted, with the "likeness of a Kingly Crown" on his head, as the king he claims to be, the "one head to make up the Body with the Members compleat," in Pope's words (5). Yet in his representation of Death, Milton has engaged the various tropes in the monstrous birth genre, effecting the rejection of any stable, even identifiable, image of the body politic that would support the monarchy. Milton's language thus draws upon a generic vagueness that derives from these tracts in his description of the "shape," or more appropriately shapelessness, of Death: it "seem'd his head," but this potential symbol of the body politic had nothing "Distinguishable in member, joint, or limb" (668).[33]

This inability to locate a recognizable body politic in the "indistinguishable" shape of Death results from the very instability of monarchical authority that Death and Satan represent. The Sin and Death sequence introduces into the poem the threat posed by a series of claimants to authority. At the beginning of Book 2, we were shown Satan's undisputed claim to the title of "Monarch." Now Satan encounters the (oedipally inflected) counterclaim of his "monstrous" son. Following this destabilization of the signifier "monarch,"

Satan will enter the "Realm" of Chaos, the power of whose "Throne" has been challenged by God's power and sovereignty.

Introducing multiple claimants to the title of king or monarchy becomes only part of the work that Milton performs in this scene. Is Satan a "Monarch"? Or is he, in Death's words, a "Traitor" guilty of "rebellious" acts? It is this "monstrous" birth who thus first articulates the inverted classification of Satan as a "rebellious" "Traitor," rather than as a "Monarch," in the poem. Invoking a cultural discourse that made competing sectarian, even royalist, claims of authority possible, Milton now has that mouthpiece, the "speaking" monstrous birth who often spoke both theological and political truths, articulate the possibility of competing claims to authority. Stuart supporters attempted to unify support for the "rightful" King through their reconfigured satirical portrait of "monstrous" births. Milton's narrative rejects this discourse through the very sources for Royalist satire: in the Book 2 sequence, he offers instead claimants to monarchical power who are transformed into multiple bickering hopefuls to a throne. Further, Milton's method for staging this collapse of undisputed monarchical power is enacted through the very discourses—of prophetic voices and prodigious births—that had allowed competition between political perspectives during the Civil War and the Interregnum. Death, the first to model the sliding signification of a monarchical title in *Paradise Lost*, thus reintroduces the instability of the language that marked prodigious births and prophecy throughout the Civil War and Interregnum periods.

Analogous to prophecy as an embodied form of prophetic speech, the conventions of the monstrous birth genre thus allow Milton to disrupt the politically stabilized representation of the monarchy. The broader prophetic genre thus allows this Book 2 sequence to argue against propaganda for, and validation of, the monarch. Female prophecy comes to be a method for speaking to politically resonant issues at a moment when "the Diabolical Rebel Milton" was condemned for his "impious doctrines" (Jane, tp). His engagement of the Mistress Rump discourses employs the feminized prophetic voice in two seemingly contradictory ways. It emphasizes the female body as a passive vessel capable of revealing truths which Milton can transform into a critique of the monarchy. The very images of weakness and the associations of femininity with prophecy provided Milton a number of opportunities. Recalling prophetic discourses allowed him to engage the topic of state organization, and the possibility of affecting the political sphere. Milton, as seventeenth-century prophets before him, had been able to strategically deploy the trope of God's inspiration to his advantage. Most significantly, this language allowed him access when he had been all but cut off from the political sphere during the Restoration. By undercutting the Stuart association between a republican rebellion and the female body, Milton appears—as in his own use of the feminized, impregnated image of the narrator of *Paradise*

Lost—to draw that body back into a more politically viable, active, and socially efficacious position.

While I have argued in Chapter 2 that Milton works to distance women from a political sphere in his rather direct engagement with Aemilia Lanyer's poem, this chapter offers us a view into the effects of an indirect engagement with female writers. The alignment between Milton and the language and imagery of female prophecy, one that I am arguing operates at a subconscious level, allows Milton to engage the very doubledness that marked the highly disruptive Civil War and Interregnum periods. While Milton's overt response to women's claims to a "political" sphere seem resistant, as echoed in his residual engagement of the family/state analog in the opening of *Doctrine and Discipline of Divorce*, we have also observed in Chapter 1 how the traces of alternative, even nostalgic, narratives about women and Eve swirl through the body of *Paradise Lost*.

That body of contested readings about gender is distinctly employed by Milton as he encounters his isolation from political discourse after the Restoration. The multiplicity of political positions, the lack of stability at the center during the Protectorate, appears reflected as well in Milton's layered, and also multiple, engagements with gendered access to authority in the period. We can also observe psychic doubledness or anxiety in his representation of the prophetic voice. I am not attempting to dismiss the implications of Milton's ambivalent representation of pregnancy and birth that he introduces in Book 1 and enacts, in such a violent way, in the Book 2 scene. A psychoanalytic reading would highlight Milton's anxiety about his alignment with an impregnated female figure, resulting in redirected violence enacted onto the body of Sin. Alternately, these motifs, both in the invocations and then in the Book 2 Sin and Death sequence, allow Milton to explore what an alignment with the feminine prophetic voice and body could accomplish for him politically.[34] During the Restoration, these motifs could accomplish psychic work for the poet.

His text consequently resurrects these mid-century prophets. Embedding these women's voices within *Paradise Lost* also offers an alternative view of women's involvement in political discourses during the later part of the century. Many critics have viewed the end of the 1650s as ending women's opportunity to engage the public sphere, silencing women once the socially and politically turbulent times of the Civil War gave way to "restored" order. Yet the specific political uses to which Milton put these discourses suggest an alternate story: the traces of Poole's, Trapnel's, Wight's, and Davies's engagement with theories of political organization echo through *Paradise Lost*.

This prompts me to revise Katherine Romack's conclusions about the effects of the "Mistress Rump" pamphlets; she sees them as "undermin[ing] women's bid for political entitlement by appropriating the residual language of monstrosity and labor to deflate women's claims to membership in the body politic" (218). In terms of the uses of the discourses by Stuart supporters, her reading seems absolutely correct. Yet the implications of the "Mistress Rump" satires, when refracted through Milton's own "monstrous birth" episode, produce an ironic reinvocation of the prophetic female voice that had "birthed" multiple interpretations in the 1640s and 1650s. The prophetic strategies deployed by these women offered them opportunities to address the political organization of the state: often, they specifically reimagined how the image of the family— a family which included wives and mothers—was central to that (re)organization. Prophets like Mary Cary would use the metaphor to justify Parliament's actions because "that which is given to the head, the wife must partake of: for there is nothing which he possesses, which she hath not a right unto" (54). Ultimately, many of these women's use of the family/state metaphor would not serve Milton's purposes: his discussion of the family unit in *Paradise Lost* largely rejects the monarchically supporting metaphor in his attempts to justify a republic. Yet this role of the family remained prominent in reconfigurations of *Paradise Lost* during the Restoration. As I will argue in Chapter 4, Lucy Hutchinson, a devout Parliamentarian, returns to the Genesis story, explicitly responding to elements in *Paradise Lost* as her biblical epic, *Order and Disorder*, interrogates maternity's role in both matrimony and in state organization.

In this, I see Milton's poem as supporting aspects of Katherine Gillespie's argument; she reads female prophets and writers from Katherine Chidley to Mary Cary as engaging the same issues that Locke would codify in his political theory. Yet this chapter necessarily counters her attempts to trace a teleological predevelopment of Lockean thought in their writings. Their experiments in imagining the role of the family and reconfiguring the organizing motif of the marital unit led, as did the writings of women like Aemilia Lanyer, Lucy Hutchinson, and Margaret Cavendish, in a variety of directions, ones that did not necessarily either prepare for or predict Locke's theories. Such alternative narratives, variously reflected in and reconfigured by *Paradise Lost*, are the heart of this study.

Maternity, Marriage, and Contract: Lucy Hutchinson's Response to Patriarchal Theory in *Order and Disorder*

In 1674, the first five cantos of the biblical epic *Order and Disorder* were published anonymously. The rest of the poem, in its entirety 20 cantos, remained only in manuscript until 2001. The poem thus lacked the exposure, if you will, of the materials I have discussed in previous chapters. But this poem, which David Norbrook has convincingly attributed to Lucy Hutchinson,[1] offers a probable Restoration re-writing of Milton's *Paradise Lost*, an act of rewriting that Lady Mary Chudleigh and to a lesser extent Aphra Behn and Mary Astell will undertake at the end of the century.[2] Like *Paradise Lost*, published in 1667, Hutchinson's poem takes as its subject the narrative of Genesis and thus considers the event and consequences of the Fall. Even the relatively small critical tradition on the published five cantos associates the poem with *Paradise Lost*. C. A. Moore's 1927 essay "Miltoniana (1679–1741)" referred to the then-unattributed published cantos as "an imitation" and "also a veiled rebuke of Milton" (323).[3] In what is overtly a rethinking of Milton's narrative of the Fall, the method of retelling the story of Genesis, and the modes of organizing the family and human society, Hutchinson's poem offers us an opportunity to examine what certain women writers did with Milton's poem.

A complement to my discussions of the uses Milton made of women writers in the first half of the century, this chapter reverses the direction of "influence" that I have been charting in the first three chapters. The central use Hutchinson makes of Milton, the opportunity, if you will, that *Paradise Lost* provided to her, has significant implications for reconsidering contemporary women's responses to the poem. While Joseph Wittreich proposed in *Feminist Milton* that *Paradise Lost* was read by eighteenth-century women intellectuals who considered it to be a pro-woman text, critics like Beth Kowaleski-Wallace have contested this reading, delineating instead the constriction Restoration and eighteenth-century women writers experienced in responding to male authors such as Milton and Locke.[4] More recently, Maria Magro has suggested that Milton's representation of the domestic sphere has significant, if "indirect," "reverberations for women writers in the public sphere" (109). She sees female authorship after the 1640s and 1650s as moving away from a "public and political model" toward an emphasis on "women's special relationship to the world of love, sex and sentiment" (109); she considers this a lasting legacy of Milton's text. *Order and Disorder*, both its very existence and its mode of engaging *Paradise Lost*, contests the argument that Milton's poem limits female responses.[5] *Paradise Lost* provides a rich opportunity for Hutchinson to undertake the issues of biblical exegesis, political organization, and the influence of gender on both topics. While countering many of Milton's gendered representations, Hutchinson also shows that *Paradise Lost* provides a productive space for politically resonant female authorship in the late seventeenth century.

While the interplay of, and audience for, texts is much harder to discern in a manuscript than in published texts,[6] Hutchinson locates her own narrative amid a rich and varied group of texts. *Order and Disorder* explores the intersection of Genesis narrative, theology, political theory, and classical poetry. The texts that are placed into conversation in Hutchinson's poem illuminate her biography as they enumerate her impressive literary production. Like Milton, she was both a Puritan and a Parliamentary supporter; her husband had signed Charles I's death warrant, and his struggle to regain his freedom after the Restoration of the Stuart family forms a significant segment of her *Memoirs of Colonel Hutchinson*, composed during the 1660s.[7] Her extensive corpus also includes a translation of Lucretius's Epicurean poem *De rerum natura*, a work of theology addressed to her daughter, and a series of elegies. This experience in historical and political narrative, poetry, and theology are embedded in her own Genesis epic. The debates between contractual and patriarchal theorists at the heart of seventeenth-century claims about governmental authority were of great concern to a Parliamentarian, and Hutchinson interweaves these debates into her engagement with Milton's poem. Her own literary forays, specifically her translation of Lucretius, equally shape her meditation on Genesis: her subtitle for *Order and Disorder* was "Meditations upon the Creation and the Fall; As it is recorded in the beginning of Genesis" (tp). Thus, while the process of "influence" might first appear to occur within a singular line, Milton's and Hutchinson's poems reveal instead a richly intertextual conversation; her "response" to Milton is configured through a sustained meditation on the role of the maternal in the events of Genesis and attention to the implications of family structure on the formation of government.

Hutchinson's response, as Moore pointed out, is also a "rebuke" of aspects of Milton's narrative strategies and theology. Hutchinson announces in the Preface that "I found I could know nothing but what God taught me, so I resolved never to search after any knowledge of him and his productions, but what he himself hath given forth. Those that will be wise above what is written may hug their philosophical clouds, but let them take heed they find not themselves without God in the world, adoring figments of their own brains, instead of the living and true God" (4). Hutchinson thus sees her poem as a kind of check on Milton's narrative of "things invisible to mortal sight" (3.55); the "figments" of his "own brain" deny him access to the "living and true God," whom she can engage through her closer work with the Bible (4).

This approach accounts for one aspect of what David Norbrook describes as a conservative aspect of this poem, since Hutchinson "rebukes" Milton's innovation in representing the Fall and other events in Genesis. Yet the poem defies the claim of a greater gender conservatism leveled by Joseph Witteich.[8] Hutchinson is explicitly rethinking Milton's representation of a more material topic: the presence of the mother. While critics of Milton's poem have engaged the issue of the elided mother in *Paradise Lost*, I will be establishing here how Milton re- and de-genders the womb while casting female reproduction as dangerous and violent.[9] Hutchinson revises aspects of Genesis and of Milton's poem to suggest how maternal procreation can be used as a counter to seventeenth-century patriarchal theory.[10] Her accounts of the Creation, particularly set against Milton's gendering of such images, highlight the role the maternal figure plays in both biological creation and the establishment of government. Hutchinson's return to the Genesis narrative, then, has significant political implications for accounts of the family, as she suggests—through her interpolations of Genesis—how motherhood becomes part of the political process. In doing so, Hutchinson explicitly responds to patriarchal theory of the period, challenging the theoretical implications of the highly gendered biblical notions of "dominion." While she seeks to counter the bulk of patriarchal theory—best represented by the theories of Sir Robert Filmer—Hutchinson's active engagement with these political issues is shaped by her own literary achievement in translating *De rerum natura*. I am suggesting, then, that Hutchinson's *Order and Disorder* is distinctly more than an engagement with Milton's poem: it is a sophisticated political rethinking of tenets of patriarchal theory that offers an alternative vision of governmental formation in the late seventeenth century.

So, while this chapter will take as its initial focus the response that Hutchinson provides to Milton's Genesis epic, thus reversing the method structuring the previous chapter, many of the same concerns about reproduction and the formation, and validation, of the state remain at the core of Hutchinson's engagement with *Paradise Lost*. Milton turned to accounts of prodigious births and the maternal embodiments of prophecy to engage monarchical claims at the Restoration. Hutchinson reconsiders the role of marriage and of the mother within that institution in her engagement of Milton's representation of reproduction. Hutchinson's response to, perhaps even a "rebuke" of, Milton recalls Christina Froula's argument about the "repressed mother" in the "nativity scenes" of *Paradise Lost*. Certain larger claims in Froula's article, particularly the transformation of Milton's traditionally female muse into a "powerful, self-sufficient male Creator . . . in such a way as to annihilate its female aspect," argue from a modern feminist perspective that would not have accorded with Hutchinson's own religious or ideologically shaped personal views (338); furthermore, I have suggested in the previous chapter that Milton's ambivalent, even anxiety-filled engagement with the "female aspect" of the muse must be viewed in concert with his use of motifs of female prophecy from the period.

Certainly, as the Sin and Death scene highlights, the female body's birthing process exists within a matrix of cultural and gendered anxieties. A review of Milton's devaluing of female generative power by projecting a clean and positive vision of a male God's creativity will highlight the interventions that Hutchinson is making in her Genesis poem. While they share many assumptions about the gendering of divine creation, Hutchinson's accounts of biological reproduction and larger claims about social production become crystallized by comparison with Milton's narrative. And just as the discourse of female prophecy and prodigous births allowed Milton to intervene in the political world from which he was cut off during the Restoration, his poem provides a similar mechanism for Hutchinson to consider the relationship between maternity, marriage, and the foundations of a "modern" state.

In one of *Paradise Lost*'s first references to the imagery of reproduction, an intriguingly male-gendered reference to the "womb," we see modeled Milton's suppression of aspects of female generation. As the fallen angels plan to build their Pandemonium in Hell, they search the ground for materials because "in *his* womb was hid metallic Ore" (1.673; my emphasis). Yet this explicit male-gendering of a womb is perhaps less common than the poem's refusal to gender motifs conventionally seen as female. Even when this space takes on the usually female imagery of penetration as they "digg'd out ribs of Gold" from this "spacious wound," no assignment of the female pronoun acknowledges the gendered inflection of these images (1.690, 689). Milton sustains this practice throughout the description of Chaos, where the imagery of creation and womb-like spaces abounds: Chaos is "the wide womb of uncreated night" (2.150), "the void profound / Of unessential Night" which "receives [Satan] next / Wide gaping, and with utter loss of being / Threatens him." Satan's actions are further detailed as he "plung'd into that abortive gulf" (2.438–41). Yet throughout this materially detailed account, we are denied a female pronoun, though everything in it—the birth imagery of the "womb" and an "abortive gulf"—combines with the previous sexual imagery of the "wide gaping" wound to suggest a woman's opened body and genitalia.

Accounts of Chaos consistently degender the associations of Creation. Initially, Chaos is "The Womb of nature, and perhaps her Grave," a gesture to the traditional feminization of nature (2.911). Yet the account of Creation that follows strips Chaos of the female generative power, returning control to a male God: "But all these in thir pregnant causes mixt / Confus'dly, and which thus must ever fight, / Unless th'Almighty Maker them ordain / His dark materials to create more Worlds" (2.913–16). Confusion and violence mark Creation unless it is directed by a male God. We also begin to see how violent imagery ("mixt Confus'dly" and "ever fight") comes to characterize creativity outside God's own acts of making. Such violent representations characterize the most gendered of scenes, Sin's description of her delivery of her son, Death.

The imagery of birth and creativity becomes gradually more negative as we approach this description of Sin at the heart of Book 2. In Hell, the angels find spaces "Where all life dies, death lives, and Nature breeds, / Perverse, all monstrous, all prodigious things, / Abominable, inutterable, and worse" (2.623–26).[11] "Nature" has a traditional female connotation, here "breed"ing "all monstrous, all prodigious things"; as the imagery of physical creation becomes more negative, we approach the reproductive horror that is Sin's "womb" (2.657). This scene stresses the materiality of female reproduction in a nightmarish account of the consequences of conception and of delivery:

> but long I sat not, till my womb
> Pregnant by thee, and now excessive grown
> Prodigious motion felt and rueful throes.
> At last this odium offspring whom thou seest
> Thine own begotten, breaking violent way
> Tore through my entrails, that with fear and pain
> Distorted, all my nether shape thus grew
> Transform'd . . . (778–85)

The detailing of the pain in delivery is meant, of course, to foreshadow Eve's punishment to bear children in pain: this imagery of violence, rendered bodies, and "distortion" of the female body is thus linked to human women.[12] This negative materiality is pushed even farther by the account that follows of Sin subjected to an incestuous rape by her own offspring. As Michael Lieb remarks in *The Dialectics of Creation*, "The womb becomes a place of defilement and horror" with "language that describes the perverted process of birth" (152).

Milton's two modes of representing maternal creation—evading its feminine identity or casting it as a scene of horror—prepare for his treatment of Eve in the final books. Because of the framing narrative of *Paradise Lost*—which ends as Adam and Eve are evicted from Eden—we never see Eve give birth in pain: the account of Sin is the only account of female reproduction. Eve is, however, the mother of mankind. Hailed repeatedly as "our Mother Eve," "right call'd, Mother of all Mankind / Mother of all things living, since by thee / Man is to live, and all things live for Man" (12.624;11.159–61), her position as genetrix is recorded in the poem.

Yet the pattern of suspended positive images of female creation extends to the final two books of *Paradise Lost*, where repression of the mother and her procreative power is most prominent. While all generation must come through the female body, the emphasis is placed firmly on patriarchal generation in

Books 11 and 12. Eve, of course, is put to sleep during this sequence, and her marginalization in this scene with Michael allows her generative power to be usurped by Adam; he is shown what is "to come / Out of thy loins" (11.454–55), thus suppressing the generative role of Eve. This erasure of the female—here most significantly the mother—is reinforced by phrases that explicitly distance Adam from acts of female reproduction. At line 495, Adam is described as "not of Woman born." This erasure of the mother occurs as well in Michael's account of Adam's future death, the moment when "like ripe Fruit thou drop / Into thy Mother's lap" (11.535–36). This "mother" is God; the description of Adam as "not of Woman born" forty lines earlier has already drawn a strong line associating Adam with the father, and keeping him from being associated with a female, maternal body. The maternal image, then, is employed in order to provide the substitution of the male generative figure; as the image of "thy Mother" is taken on by God, the repression of maternal activity is effected.

The entire reproductive complex in Books 11 and 12 occurs without the presence of a woman, a process transformed in Hutchinson's poem.[13] In *Paradise Lost*, the repopulation of the world occurs, twice in fact, without the presence of either Eve or pregnant women, and it is described in terms again emphasizing male-defined generation. The rebirth of mankind after the Deluge is described as "This second source of Men" (12.13), a phrase repeated in Book 12: "Thus thou has seen one World begin and end; / and Man as from a second stock proceed" (12.6–7). Only at the point that the line to Mary and Christ is established can women's role in the production of humankind be acknowledged in Milton's poem. Halfway through Book 12, the identity of Eve as the mother of mankind is partially restored: "of the Royal Stock / of David (so I name this King) shall rise / A Son, the Woman's Seed to thee foretold" (12.325–27). This acknowledgement of the redemptive role of the woman, and of the female body, at the moment that a political line is created—"David (so I name this King)"—gestures to how enmeshed the language of maternal activity and patriarchal power are in the period. But the establishment of human society and the governments that are being formed through the events of Genesis described in Books 11 and 12 continue to emphasize male lines, and male bodies, producing these lines.

Consequently, Book 12 emphasizes patriarchal lines of authority, both in its accounts of the generative "Stock" of Adam and in the aligned narratives of political organization and obligation. In Milton, accounts of constructing governmental rule are simultaneously narratives of paternal authority: "Long time in peace by Families and Tribes / Under *paternal rule*" (12.23–24; my emphasis). Milton and Hutchinson are both staunch antimonarchists, and they counter patriarchal political theories that justify the formation of monarchy. Where they differ so significantly is in the manner of telling the story of governmental origin. In *Order and Disorder*, reproduction and the production of government are interwoven and explored by both patriarchal theories and contract theories. While Milton appears to erase the mother in his accounts of governmental organization, he had no political sympathies with theories of monarchical origin that relied on erasing the figure of the mother. He simply does not identify the link between maternal representation and the origin of government. Nonetheless, *Paradise Lost*'s treatment of the maternal figure and its antimonarchical sentiment open up possibilities for Hutchinson to explore these connections in her poem.

Hutchinson's narrative, and the role awarded to producing mothers through the biblical language of "dominion," differ significantly from Milton's emphasis on fathers and their begotten sons as the source for biblical human history. While both poems tell the story of Genesis, Hutchinson stays much closer to the events in the Bible; consequently, we hear a great deal from the later books of Genesis, which Milton compresses into Books 11 and 12. Hutchinson's emphasis on the actual generation of mankind continues to suggest how she—like Milton—is exploring the political options for a Republican in telling us the tale of the growth of governmental authority.[14] Her historically located response to images of motherhood aligns her poem to Milton's, but it also allows her to elaborate on the politically significant topic of parental authority. Like Milton, she grants God un- or male-gendered images of creation. But when she represents mothers such as Eve, Sarah, Rebecca, and Rachel, maternal control becomes linked to the expansion of government and empire. Her narrative thus highlights the generative role of women within a biological as well as political process. Though Hutchinson's own location as a devout seventeenth-century Puritan makes it impossible for her to question the patriarchy inherent in Christian narratives of creation, she takes up the secular issues of governmental origin through her representation of female productivity.

In undertaking a narrative of Genesis, Hutchinson may well provide a "rebuke" to Milton, but she also offers one to herself; her poem is simultaneously an intertextual engagement with Milton's poem about Creation and the Fall and her earlier translation of Lucretius's *De rerum natura*. Initially, Hutchinson presents *Order and Disorder* as her rehabilitation for translating Lucretius's atheistic text a decade earlier. Her engagement with the "fountain of Truth" of the Bible will redeem her from her previous literary activities: "the vain curiosity of youth had drawn me to consider to translate the account some old poets and philosophers give of the original of things" (3). Her translation of *De rerum natura* "filled my brain with such foolish fancies, that I found it necessary to have recourse to the fountain of Truth, to wash out all ugly wild impressions, and fortify my mind with a strong antidote" (Preface, 3). *Order and Disorder* will serve as "prevention" against any claim that "the profane Helicon of ancient poets" has affected her thinking (Preface, 4).

The "vindicat[ion]" she seeks "from those heathenish authors I have been conversant in" appears registered in her account of the creation of the universe, and of mankind, that—as we see in Milton's poem—emphasizes God's power over the metaphor of female procreative power (Preface, 4). In language that contrasts sharply with the imagery Hutchinson translates in Lucretius's poem, images of birth and creation in the first canto of *Order and Disorder* highlight the ungendered use of words such as "birth" and "womb." At line 43, "Time had its birth, / In whose *Beginning God made Heaven and Earth*" (bold emphasis mine). Just like Milton, Hutchinson employs words that narrate biological creation, but denies gendering them in her account of the creation: "Thus leading back all ages to the womb / Of vast Eternity from whence *they* come, / And bringing new successions forth until Heaven its last revolutions shall fulfill, / And all things unto *their* first state restore" (1.163–67; my emphasis).

Thus, Hutchinson's emphasis in the first few cantos on nonfeminine images of creation has been shaped by her experience with Lucretius's poem. Her translation of Lucretius had revealed his atheistic philosophy, imagistically illustrated and compounded by his prominent images of the generative creation of the universe.[15] Lucretius's universe lacks a "first eternal Cause," as Hutchinson will describe the Christian God in *Order and Disorder*; this "Cause" is "th'original / Of being, life, and motion, [whom] God we call" (1.77–78). Lucretius's mechanistic universe, in striking contrast, is powered by female-gendered procreative power; in fact, as S. Georgia Nugent remarks, the "generative body" is the dominant image used to portray the female body throughout the poem (183). Following this characteristic of Lucretius's poem, Hutchinson's translation describes "The first productions of the earth" through the imagery of a female earth bearing the products of this world: "earth, / Impregnated with her first various birth, / Exposd her ofspring" (5.818–20). In this, as in many other passages in *De rerum natura*, reference to "th'earths fruitfull womb, who hence the name / Of the greate mother gaind" is repeated (5.833–34), "the human female's reproductive life cycle provid[ing] a model for Lucretius's understanding of the earth's fertility" (Nugent, 185). Only a few lines later, we hear how "Impregnated her womb [is] with humane race, / When the ripe infant births disclosed were" (5.847–48). Birthing imagery is further physicalized in Hutchinson's translation through the prominent imagery of mother's milk, just as a "new deliverd woemens brests, being filld / With sweete milke, food for their young infants yeild" (5.852–54). This language does occur in the original Latin, yet Hutchinson's translation often highlights metaphors of maternal production.

This atheistic text, then, represents creation as a female, biological practice, a portrait of Epicurean mechanistic philosophy that necessarily displaces the control of a (Christian male) God over the organization of the universe.[16] Hutchinson is thus true to her word that in *Order and Disorder* she will "vindicate" herself through the account of Creation. Like Milton, she initially turns away from images of female-gendered creation; many of her opening images recall the process by which Milton transforms a conventionally female image of creation into an image of male procreative power. Parallels between creation accounts in *De rerum natura* and *Order and Disorder* illustrate Hutchinson's practice of degendering imagery in the later poem. She employs the imagery of the womb in these lines from *Order and Disorder*: "Thus leading back all ages to the womb / Of vast Eternity from whence they come" (1.163–64). The couplet rhyme of "womb" and "come" also appeared in her Lucretius translation: "Thus from above doth the maine tempest come / With showers and lightenings in its pregnant womb" (6.276–77). In the Lucretius, the gendering of creation remains consistent ("Earth for her part made by her fruitfull womb / The generall mother" [5.272–73]); in *Order and Disorder* she removes the feminine element. Milton consistently works, in Froula's terms, to repress the mother, "annihilat[ing]" the "female aspect" of creation in order to reinforce a "powerful, self-sufficient male Creator" (338). Initially, this trait marks *Order and Disorder* as well. We observe Lucy Hutchinson reauthoring, if you will, her own Lucretius translation in order to deemphasize the generative role of a female Nature and a female-gendered earth.

In the male-gendered account of Creation in Canto 2 of *Order and Disorder*, Hutchinson emphasizes the sole power of the "First Mover's force" (2.143). She offers the image of the womb, even of a "teeming earth," but renders the procreative power as God's, an association reinforced by an almost complete absence of traditionally gendered female metaphors. The first image, which repeats throughout, is of "those thicker clouds from whose dark womb / Th'imprisoned winds in flame and thunder come" (2.9–10). While productive of the "flame and thunder" produced within them, the image of clouds is stripped of any feminine identity. This process is repeated in the second cloud reference: "his great ordnance, rends / The clouds which, big with horror, ready stand / To pour their burdens forth at his command" (2.44–46). "Their burdens" that they are "big with" invoke the image of a pregnant woman, but the clouds have become God's "ordnance," a pregnant gun ready to fire on God's command. The imagery of motherhood, and the usual link to the feminine, are turned here instead into a weapon without any gendering pronouns.

Hutchinson's account of the production of Earth's creatures again draws upon imagery linked to pregnancy: "God commands the teeming earth to bring / Forth great and lesser beasts, each reptile thing / That on her bosom creeps" (2.327–29). The "teeming" womb is finally accorded a female pronoun, as it is "on her bosom" that "each reptile thing . . . creeps" (2.328–29). Yet this female pronoun, oddly positioned in the phrase in such a way that it almost appears to modify "each reptile thing," does not accord any agency to "teeming earth." Only a repository, "the Word" is "obeyed" and prompts the creative act: "Immediately were all the creatures made" (2.329–30). The "Word" of God, not an active Earth, takes over the procreative role. Hutchinson's choice to deemphasize conventionally female procreativity is further highlighted by comparison with the analogous line in Milton's poem.

Throughout Book 7 of *Paradise Lost*, Milton has gendered images as male, such as "the rising Birth / Of Nature," which the poem describes as "His genera-tion." Yet in Milton's account of the animals' creation on the sixth day, the Earth is very explicitly gendered female: "The Earth obey'd, and straight / Op'ning *her* fertile Womb teem'd at a Birth / Innumerous living Creatures, per-fet forms, / Limb'd and full grown" (7.453–56; my emphasis). While Milton has consistently described in gender-neutral terms the material and the process of creation, he ties the act of creation to a female, generating womb, stressing the "perfet forms" emerging from her.[17]

In the early part of Hutchinson's poem, the emphasis on the degendering of Creation, and thus the deemphasis of the productive creativity of the female body, is so significant because she transforms this imagery as the poem moves forward. Comparison with Milton highlights their parallel promotion of a male creative God, but it also allows us to observe where Hutchinson modifies her representation of female reproduction; her break with Milton occurs in her account of Eve and her role of genetrix. While initially according the male creator procreative power, such that even female-gendered imagery of birth and wombs are deemphasized, Hutchinson emphasizes reproduction in the marriage scene. Thus, following her initial suppression of metaphoric mater-nal power—poetically prominent in Lucretius and yet challenging to a view of a Christian God's Creation—Hutchinson offers a resurgence of maternal power by Canto 3. She stresses generative imagery in generational narratives, and consequently her "meditations" on Genesis begin to highlight the role of the wife and mother as she frames a response to political theory that deempha-sizes the maternal component of generational authority.

In the course of her Creation sequence, Hutchinson establishes a connec-tion between Eve's maternity and the politically resonant language of "domin-ion." As a result, she expands the power of the mother within the context of marriage, combining a significant rewriting of Genesis with a gesture toward revisions within contemporary marriage laws. The focal point of Hutchinson's revision of traditional commentaries on and renditions of Adam and Eve's creation thus occurs at the moment of their marriage. Since male authority in marriage serves as an originary point for arguments for and against monarchy during the seventeenth century, Hutchinson's choices in this textual moment il-lustrate her engagement with the cultural debate over political obligation and the role of contract. In revising biblical commentary while integrating contem-porary modifications to the marriage ceremony, Hutchinson locates a crucial matrix of maternity, marriage, and political authority in her account of Adam and Eve's creation and union.

As critics from Mary Nyquist to David Norbrook have remarked, the inter-polation of Genesis 1 and Genesis 2 by commentators and poets is the crux in any writer's account of how gendered authority is derived from the Bible.[18] As Nyquist explains, the Priestly (P) creation account in Genesis 1 offers a potential vision of equality between man and woman as "male and female created he them," while the Yahwist (J) account in Genesis 2 inscribes Adam's superiority over Eve: here, she is created second and was created from Adam. Milton fuses the P and J texts in Raphael's Book 7 speech, "this splicing economically mak[ing] from two heterogeneous accounts a single one that is both intellectually and aesthetically coherent" (Nyquist, 116); this fusion clarifies that "man" is Adam, not Adam and Eve. The consequence, according to Nyquist, is that the tension between the two Genesis narratives is resolved as Adam is given priority and, most significantly, single access to dominion. In Book 8, Adam's account of his creation clarifies who receives God's injunction to rule the world. Prior to Eve's creation, God says to Adam, "This Paradise I give *thee*, count it *thine* / To Till and keep, and of the Fruit to eat" (8.319–20; my emphasis). Nyquist argues that Adam's account of receiving Paradise from God before Eve's creation clarifies who has been awarded "rule" and "Dominion" in the poem: Adam alone.

Hutchinson dramatically restages this scene in *Order and Disorder*, fusing the P and J texts to highlight that dominion is given to a unified Adam and Eve. Furthermore, the award of dominion over all the world in Hutchinson's poem occurs within their marriage ceremony. By combining the first and the second book of Genesis in this section of *Order and Disorder*, Hutchinson has Adam and Eve receive God's commands while together; God "give[s] you right to all her fruits and plants, / Dominion over her inhabitants . . . Are all made subject under your command" (3.419, 421–22, 426). Adam and Eve are thus given dominion as part of their union in marriage. Furthermore, the language stresses their unity through this marriage ceremony: "We, late of one made two, again in one / Shall reunite" (3.406–7).

Adam and Eve's unification as "one" as they receive dominion occurs when Adam, not God, announces this "marriage" in which "male and female doth combine" (3.415). Adam thus speaks the Genesis 2:24 line here, a significant revision of traditional marriage commentaries. By attributing lines 412–15 to Adam, Hutchinson positions the ceremony in a more secular context: Adam, not God or a figure for the church, speaks the lines that conclude the marriage: "So men hereafter shall their fathers leave, / And all relations else which are most dear, / That they may only to their wives adhere; / When marriage male and female doth combine" (3.412–15).[19] While God confirms the "sacred knot" in the following line, the spoken contract between man and wife at the center of a 1653 revision to marriage laws appears reflected in Hutchinson's scene.[20] The 1653 marriage act required a spoken contract between the husband and wife, one observed by witnesses while a justice of the peace presided over the union; besides legislating a secular marriage, the act required mutually expressed consent.

While Hutchinson's narrative does not stage Eve's verbal assent to the marriage contract,[21] Adam's language of union followed by Hutchinson's use of imagery from the Canticles affirms their joint acquisition of "dominion." Sixty lines after the account of Adam and Eve's union in marriage, the allegory of marriage as prefigurative of Christ's love for the church enters the poem. "Henceforth no longer two but one we are," states Christ to his spouse, while the couple is presented as sharing a spiritual dominion: "From heaven I did descend to fetch up thee, / Rose from the grave that thou mightst reign with me. . . . Thou dost my merit, life, grace, glory share" (487, 485–86, 488). The unity characterizing both marriage and the relationship of husband and wife is consequently highlighted by Christ's language. While the more secularly located contract of marriage from the Interregnum marriage legislation is gestured at in Adam's earlier language, the allegorical treatment of marriage continues Hutchinson's stress on the unity of man and wife.[22]

This jointly appointed dominion is further affirmed in Hutchinson's alignment of the act of marriage with that of reproduction. In perhaps Hutchinson's most significant revision of traditional commentaries on marriage, the language of union, which is the marriage ceremony from Genesis 2, is combined with the command to "be fruitful and multiply" in Genesis 1:

> . . . as unto thee,
> Ravished with love and joy, my soul doth cleave,
> so men hereafter shall their fathers leave,
> And all relations else which are most dear,
> That they may only to their wives adhere;
> When marriage male and female doth combine,
> Children in one flesh shall two parents join. (3.410–16)

The primacy of marriage in this sequence is fused with the emphasis on generation, an interpretation of the language of "one flesh" that distinguishes Hutchinson's account from standard biblical commentary. The imagery of "one flesh" is conventionally interpreted only as the act of marriage. Hutchinson's reference to Matthew 19:4–6 in the margin underscores her revision of the biblical text in order to stress the act of reproduction. The passage (New King James Version) describes the act of marriage as follows:

[4] And He answered and said to them, "Have you not read that He who made them at the beginning 'made them male and female,' [5] and said, 'For this reason a man shall leave his father and mother and be joined to his wife, and the two shall become one flesh'? [6] So then, they are no longer two but one flesh. Therefore what God has joined together, let not man separate."

This passage gives us the language of the marriage ceremony, but it does not allude to the children who, in Hutchinson's account, become the "one flesh" that "combines" man and woman in reproduction. Furthermore, none of the biblical references she provides in the margin use the "one flesh" phrase to describe the production of children; the gesture to Genesis, Matthew, and Ephesians in the margin only confirms Hutchinson's different application of the phrase. While Hutchinson makes explicit the metaphor embedded in the "one flesh" phrase, the consequence is to make the production of children—and thus the act of reproduction—much more central at this moment in her poem.

Adam and Eve are thus described as in a union that allows both of them access to "dominion" through their act of reproduction. Since the passage that immediately follows offers "dominion" to the mother and father, Hutchinson's portrait of the first union of man and woman suggests how fully maternal power and dominion are linked. The mutuality gestured at in the marriage contract between Adam and Eve is consolidated by the language of generative authority, as the "one flesh" of the child joins the "two parents" in their authority over the world. I am suggesting, then, that the figure of the mother in Hutchinson's account is given greater consequence within marriage because of the intersection between the reproductive act, their dominion as provided by God, and the resonances to the marriage contract. Hutchinson's "response" to Milton comes to include, not just the reconfiguration of "dominion" now awarded to Adam and Eve as "one," but a correspondingly representation of female authority as linked to maternal production. This greater emphasis on Eve's involvement in reproduction and control are reinforced by an account of a marriage that invokes the mutual consent of a contracted union. As we will see, the possibility of greater participation in the contracted union becomes embedded into the role of mother and wife in *Order and Disorder*.

Given the cultural and political significance of the act of marriage, Hutchinson's focus on this event speaks directly to the issues of political and gender hierarchy dominating the period. As with most debates over marriage at the time, a discussion about the organization of the family was simultaneously about state organization; the family-state analogy that lay at the base of patriarchal theory meant that the status of marriage could not be extricated from political debates about the relationship between a monarch and his people.[23] Hutchinson's treatment of the marriage ceremony in *Order and Disorder* illustrates her engagement with the complicated question of contractual relationships, both in the personal contract of the marriage ceremony and in the emerging social contract between citizen and state.[24] Furthermore, Hutchinson's linking of a more mutual act of contracting marriage with an award of dominion and a complementary emphasis on generation offers a vision of the family unit at the moment of creation. The connection she establishes between the language of dominion, its relationship to gender, and the location of control within the structure of the family shows her explicit engagement with the issue of contract in seventeenth-century political theory.

As Anthony Fletcher has stated, "the great battle between patriarchalists and social contract theorists" was the "master theme of seventeenth-century political theory" (292). Theorists articulating patriarchal positions throughout the early seventeenth century included Jean Bodin, Sir Edward Coke, and

Henry Spelman, though Robert Filmer is considered to be the best known and most effective articulator of patriarchal theory. A significant political debate emerges between these theorists and contract theorists such as Thomas Hobbes, James Tyrrell, Algernon Sidney, and John Locke. And a "great battle" this was indeed, raging before, during, and after the Civil War as these thinkers debated the very underpinnings of political organization in England. As a staunch Parliamentarian, Lucy Hutchinson would unquestionably have been familiar with the terms of the debate between contract and patriarchal theorists; countering the claims in patriarchal theory was immensely important for Republicans. As I will suggest, this debate shaped Hutchinson's vision in *Order and Disorder* of the first marriage, the organization of family unity, and the status of political organization.

Patriarchalist theory was a body of political thought that emerged in the seventeenth century seeking to justify the origin and the authority of monarchy through a genetic argument: according to this pro-monarchical school of thought, the authority of monarchy had been inherited, and Adam had first received this grant of authority. While Robert Filmer is one of many patriarchal theorists in the seventeenth century, his ideas have often been considered a composite of its principles.[25] His most significant work is *Patriarcha*, the text to which Locke will respond in the *Two Treatises*. While *Patriarcha* was not published until 1679 and 1680, it was written much earlier, perhaps as early as the late 1620s to 1640s. Furthermore, Filmer's theories would have been known from a series of other publications in the 1640s, when many of the ideas outlined in *Patriarcha* were first expressed. *Patriarcha*, though, offers the most "concise statement of the traditional political beliefs" that defined patriarchalism as a system of thought (Schochet, 121).[26]

Grounded in the analogy between a father's rule over his family and the political application of the analogy to justify the monarch's right to rule over his subjects, the primary premise directing all of Filmer's thought was the equivalent, identical relationship of the family and state. As Gordon Schochet explains, Filmer saw "the relationship of regal and paternal authority . . . as *identical*, not merely *similar* or in some way analogous" (146). The metaphoric logic at the base of patriarchal theory fuses with the biblical story to provide the ideological ground for this system of thought: the basis for monarchical power was established not simply by the Bible but in the Garden itself. The authority of the monarch exists because of Adam's initial acquisition of dominion: monarchical power is initiated by God, and granted to Adam, in the first moments of creation. According to Filmer, since God had granted this right to Adam, all subsequent patriarchs had the right to rule as monarchs, their power derived from the initial patriarch: "This lordship which Adam by creation had over the whole world, and by right descending from him the patriarchs did enjoy, was as large and ample *as the absolutist dominion of any monarch* which hath been since the creation" (7). For Filmer, dominion was given to Adam and thus fatherly authority, and simultaneously kingly authority, is owed to him.

Hutchinson's linking of the language of dominion with that of parental identity suggests how engaged she was with the premises of patriarchal theory. I will be suggesting that in her treatment of the relationship between the family and dominion, Hutchinson goes to the very heart of the theories of thinkers such as Filmer. Furthermore, her gesture toward the contractual ground of marriage, as legislated by the Barebones Parliament, establishes a further connection between political contract theory and her representation of marriage. As a staunch supporter of Parliament—and thus as philosophically strongly anti-monarchical—Hutchinson is returning to the story of Genesis not simply for vindication. She is also returning to the very ground from which pro-monarchical theorists, who expounded the theory of patriarchalism, argued their positions.

First, we can see how much Hutchinson's treatment of the Garden story differs from the account that comes out of patriarchalist writings. Unlike Filmer or any other patriarchal theorist of the period, Hutchinson does not locate dominion only in Adam; her account of the award of dominion describes a plural "you" who receives this grant of control. Either the "you" is Adam and Eve, in which case Filmer's narrative of the single male monarch is undercut, or the "you" describes men and women (i.e., humankind) receiving the grant of dominion. In either case, her account of the marriage and dispensing of authority counters the singular award of authority upon which all of Filmer's theory rests. Hutchinson's anti-monarchical sentiment, then, shapes her representation of this award of dominion to Adam and Eve.

This moment in the Garden, then, is the basis of the "genetic" theory of monarchy. All subsequent monarchies, in patriarchal thought, derived their right from this origin of Adam's award of dominion. This derivation of political authority from the originary moment of Adam's receipt of "dominion" means that mankind has no power to reject the power of the monarchy. Filmer summarizes the consequence of this event in the Garden to our subsequent political obligation: "I see not then how the children of Adam, or of any man else, can be free from subjection to their parents. And this subjection of children is the only fountain of all regal authority, by the ordination of God himself" (7). If Hutchinson's account of the awarding of dominion challenges Adam's singular award of this power, it also undercuts a contingent theory of inherited monarchical power; if she counters Adam's identity as a monarch through this award, she challenges—through competing narratives of Genesis—Filmer's subsequent continuation of political obligation.

Hutchinson's framing of the awarding of dominion within an account of marriage and reproduction challenges another crux in patriarchal theory. Central to patriarchalism was the fifth commandment, "Honor thy father and thy mother." In Filmer, his dependence on this commandment—and the subsequent building of a patriarchal basis for power—depended on the elision of the mother in the commandment:

> To confirm this natural right of regal power, we find in the decalogue that the law which enjoys obedience to kings is delivered in the terms of 'honour *thy father*' as if all power *were originally in the father*. If obedience to parents be immediately due by a natural law, and subjection to princes by the mediation of an human ordinance, what reason is there that the law of nature should give place to the laws of men, as we see the *power of the father over his child* gives place and is subordinate to the power of the magistrate? (11–12; my emphasis)

In this passage, the commandment is truncated to allow for power to reside only in the male parent.[27] The slide from parental to paternal is the basis of Filmer's theory of both family and political obligation and power; this elision of mother and thus of women in Filmer's theory will be variously attacked by Hobbes and Locke. Central to the debates of the seventeenth century, the position of the mother becomes central in Hutchinson's account of Genesis, both the relationship described between Adam and Eve and the accounts of later mothers. Hutchinson uses her account of Genesis to make a counter-claim about origins by articulating the role of mothers in this narrative with significant consequences for seventeenth-century political thought.

While continuing to balance the granting of patriarchal creative power to God with the politically resonant presence of the mother, Hutchinson initiates praise of both marriage and reproduction, as she establishes a trajectory within the poem that argues the wife and mother's role within the award of dominion. A defense of marriage quickly follows her fusion of Genesis 1 and 2: marriage has not "yet . . . grown less sacred since / Man fell from his created excellence" (3.439–40). Marriage is recuperative, for it "repairs time's daily wastes with new supplies" (3.448), and it is compared to the regenerative aspect of reproduction: "When the declining mother's youthful grace / Lies dead and buried in her wrinkled face, / In her fair daughters it revives and grows / And her dead cinder in their new flames glows" (3.448, 449–52). Regeneration is gendered female as a line of mother to child—in fact, to daughters—is established. Thus, the rebirth imagery for mankind granted to a woman at the end of *Paradise Lost*'s Book 12 becomes a fixture in Hutchinson's account immediately after the appearance of Eve.

From Cantos 3–6, the position of the womb—which had been linked to God's acts of creation—becomes gradually located in Eve's body. Reproductive imagery and the defense of marriage positively represent the generative activity of women in the opening cantos. In Canto 3, Hutchinson links the reasons for a mate with the future generation of mankind, a sequence that culminates in the floating signifier of the womb. In an extensive discussion by the narrator on the reasons for a mate, Hutchinson counters a tradition playfully summarized in Marvell's "The Garden": mankind would have been better off had woman never been created, thus "Two paradises 'twere in one / To live in paradise alone" (63–64). In the service of countering this common attack on women—and especially on Eve—the womb reappears in Hutchinson:

Man's nature had not been the sacred shrine,
Partner and bride of that which is divine;
The Church, fruit of this union, had not come
To light, but perished, stifled in the womb. (3.329–32)

Here the "womb" initially appears ungendered, even unattached to a reference or body: there is no Eve yet, and thus no "womb" to produce the "fruit of this union." But the sequence is actually constituting the mate that Adam needs, and the reproductive potential she represents. Eve's creation sixty lines later will give this productive, floating signifier a signified upon which to attach itself. At that point, the positive outcome of reproduction will become emphasized.

Thus, Eve emerges as a central agent in the poem. The image of a dormant womb described above becomes linked to action, movement, and forward direction that implies future lines of genealogical descent. In the second rhyming of "womb" and "come" in Hutchinson's text, the devils, wishing to destroy mankind through his/her sin, "hoped death would prevent the dreaded womb / From whence their happier successors must come" (4.158–59). The generative identity, and power, of Eve causes their fear; as her "dreaded womb" emerges in the narrative, Eve's body becomes a site of power.

It is when the womb is placed into action, both that of Eve and of other women, that it becomes linked to generational identity and authority. A very detailed account of childbearing in Canto 5 is followed by this statement about woman's role as genetrix, one that reintroduces the relationship between procreative power and authority:

The next command is, mothers should maintain
Posterity, not frighted with the pain,
Which, though it make us mourn under the sense
Of the first mother's disobedience,
Yet hath a promise that thereby she shall
Recover all the hurt of her first fall
When, in mysterious manner, from her womb
Her father, brother, husband, son shall come.
Subjection to the husband's rule enjoined
In the next place. (5.221–30)

In striking contrast to Milton's generative imagery of what is "to come / Out of [Adam's] loins" (11.454–55), all males "come" from Eve's "womb." Now the future of the human race, its future history and thus existence, will "come" from her body. The forward movement of generation, highlighted again by the "womb"/"come" rhyme, is shown to be a function of womankind, thus implying a potential position of strength through the assertion of female generative power. The text appears to recognize how significant this gendered assignment of creative power is: immediately, patriarchal dominion is asserted as Eve and women are placed under biblically mandated male "Subjection."

While the poem moves toward the concrete female womb in Cantos 4 and 5, in Canto 6 the account of Cain's and Abel's own genesis illustrates Eve's body as at the genetrix of all male figures. Canto 6 becomes a ground zero for the biological and political implications of generation. Hutchinson's rejection of the grounds of patriarchal theory—particularly the elision of mothers within Filmer's discussion of authority—determines the account of Cain's and Abel's birth. As Hutchinson's text will detail, Adam's position as father requires the body of the mother to make him such. Again, the very ground on which all of patriarchal theory depends—Adam's singular identity as and power as parent—is renarrated by Hutchinson. Her Genesis account now insists on inserting the biological "mother" explicitly into the narrative, a narrative that—as we see with Milton—can be told without the mother. And yet, while Hutchinson's emphasis on maternal activity counters the royalist, monarchical impulses of patriarchal theory, she does not rewrite basic biblical tenets. Her attempts to counter patriarchal theory are balanced with God's power.

In Canto 6, Hutchinson revises the biblical text in order to highlight the role of the mother, yet that power does not escape God's direction.[28] Finally in this sequence, physical generation is to occur: Adam will become a father, making this a significant political moment in a theory of paternal and monarchical authority: once Adam is a father, for example, Filmer can apply his theory of awarded dominion. Since according to Filmer the "subjection of children is the only fountain of all regal authority" (12), monarchy is actually set into motion once Adam's children are born. Yet Hutchinson's engagement with the mechanisms of patriarchal theory continues. Eve's body—whose procreative future has been alluded to generally in the previous cantos—now becomes the productive site of the story. Accounts of her producing body, "Promising life to enter through her womb," and of "Her teeming womb with new fruit swelled again" are described in relation to God's power, not Adam's (22, 27). The female producing womb, here identified in pregnant detail with Eve, must concede agency to God, who "made the woman man's first fruit conceive" (6.17). God is the "maker," while her body operates as a vessel.

While Hutchinson will offer Cain as "man's first fruit," an epitaph that does not highlight Eve's generative power, the sequence introduces the language of parental, not paternal, possession and authority. Eve asserts possession over her and Adam's "fruit": "Then brought she forth; and Cain she called his son, 'For God,' said she, 'gives *us* possession'" (6.25–26; my emphasis). Eve remembers the marriage ceremony well. In reproduction, the process through which "Children in one flesh shall two parents join" (3.416), man and women are fused into one, and that unity offers them both "Dominion over her inhabitants" (3.422). Subjugation to their husbands, to which women are condemned after the Fall, does not equal the erasure of either the mother or allegiance owed to the mother; the mutuality implied by the marriage contract continues to mark the processes of and in the family. Thus, at the very moment that Adam is made a "father" and consequently becomes able to claim monarchical authority in patriarchal theory, Hutchinson's Eve insists that children owe obligation to father and mother: Both have "possession" of the child. Since reproduction makes Adam a father, Hutchinson explicitly works to counter a thinker such as Filmer at this moment of her narrative.

Eve's maternal claim to a form of dominion over the child is reinforced by her naming of both Cain and Abel: "and Cain she called his son"; "Abel she called the next" (6.25, 29). Naming is traditionally acknowledged as a form of power in the Genesis story: Adam's naming of the animals enacts his "dominion" over them. Thus, Eve's act of naming indicates a form of her authority over children, one articulated in the poem in conjunction with Adam's control over her. Eve's naming of Cain and Abel has been preceded by Adam's naming of her: she becomes pregnant, "In hope of which her husband called her Eve" (6.18). Hutchinson's balance between the mother's power over the children and the relationship between husband and wife is also highlighted by her placement of Eve's naming by Adam: in Genesis, Adam "called his wife's name Eve" in the Garden. Hutchinson moves this act of naming out of the Garden, and ten lines later adds the account of Eve's naming of their sons: no such account occurs in Genesis. Hutchinson's rearrangement, and creation, of these details offers a parallel parental form of authority granted to Adam and to Eve, one that reinforces Hutchinson's version of the marriage scene.

While Hutchinson does not erase the biblical punishment that "your husband . . . shall rule over you," the production of children throughout *Order and Disorder* provides an assertion of individualized power for the mother, one that joins the two parents in the more mutual union characterized as "one flesh." Her explicit, and sustained, refutation of the tenets of patriarchal theory through her biblical narrative resembles the discussion of motherhood, obligation, and authority that marks the thought of another mid-seventeenth-century political theorist: Thomas Hobbes. One of many contract theorists in the period, Hobbes explicitly considers the relationship between marriage, maternity, and contract. Engaged in the same debate that we see shape Hutchinson's engagement with patriarchal theory, Hobbes offers a suggestive parallel to Hutchinson's representation of marriage and maternity in *Order and Disorder*.[29] Both are engaged in this significant cultural debate, finding answers to questions raised by the conflict between patriarchal and contract theorists that drew the family, rather than just the father, into accounts of political dominion.

As Locke will do much later in the *Two Treatises*, Hobbes is engaging patriarchal theory, especially the premises of paternal power and uses of maternal power, in order to counter thinkers such as Filmer. In both *De Cive* (translated as *On the Citizen*) and *Leviathan*, Hobbes discusses the dominion accorded the mother. While the basis of his argument lies in a combination of his contract theory and the fourth law of nature he posits—that of obligation—the process of biological reproduction becomes the site of the mother's power. By "*right of nature* Dominion over an *infant* belongs first to the one who first has him in their power. But it is obvious that a new-born child is in the power of his *mother* before anyone else, so that she can raise him or expose him at her own discretion and by her own right" (108). Furthermore, Hobbes voices an explicit link between mothers—the productive source of a child—and power: "And in this way in the state of nature every woman who gives birth becomes both a *mother* and a *Mistress*" (*De Cive*, 108). The language of "dominion" thus resonates through Hobbes's passages in *De Cive* and *Leviathan*: "If there be no Contract, the Dominion is in the Mother" (254). As always, the question of when and where the state of nature applies is a complex question in Hobbes, though he does suggest in the Latin edition of *Leviathan* that the state of nature described the conditions of Cain and Abel.

While Hobbes does designate this greater power of the mother as occurring in the state of nature, the pre-political contractual space that Hobbes is describing accords with Hutchinson's narration of the first part of Genesis, particularly her reconfiguration of the P and J texts of Genesis. In such a not yet contractually determined space, dominion is accorded to the mother through her reproductive power. More significantly, Hobbes's conclusions about the formation of commonwealths, which supplant the state of nature, again illustrate how Hutchinson's narrative engages the mechanisms—including female reproduction—by which political organizations are formed in the biblical source. Her continuing conversation with the tenets of patriarchal and contract theory includes her sustained resistance to accepting divinely assigned monarchical authority within the early events narrated in Genesis. As such, Hobbes's developmental narrative of the evolution of commonwealths, which allows him to argue for a consent-based theory of governance that follows a state of nature, could have provided to Hutchinson an interesting, effective theoretical model with which to counter Filmerian assertions.

Hobbes also provides a narrative of political development that allows for the gradual formation of governmental structure in the narrative of Genesis. He does not explicitly use the events of the Bible, as do Filmer, Hutchinson, and even Locke, to describe the birth of government structures. But like Hutchinson he is drawing on his initial willingness to accord some element of "dominion" to mothers, as well as his narrative of the development of consent-based governmental structures. While Hobbes patterns a connection between women's generative activity and the formation of generational authority, Hutchinson interweaves these events. Hobbes highlights the language of dominion once the state of nature is left behind: gender equity or even greater female power does not remain, as he describes in *Leviathan*: in most commonwealths the "sentence is in favour of the Father, because for the most part Common-wealths have been erected by the Fathers" (139–40). But the mother has to be subject to the father for the dominion over the child to pass away from her: "If the Mother be the Fathers subject, the Child, is in the Fathers power: and if the Father be the Mothers subject, . . . the Child is subject to the Mother; because the Father also is her subject" (140). In the noncontractual space of the Garden, where both Adam and Eve are given "dominion," the subjection of Eve, and the erasure of the power of the Mother, has not occurred.

Hutchinson's realignment of the Genesis stories to frame the issue of dominion in marriage and reproduction allows her to intercede in the political debates around familial and monarchical power that mark the writings of Hobbes and other contractual theorists. Her responses to Filmerian concepts, shaped by the space for maternal "dominion" that a writer such as Hobbes theorizes, extend throughout her account of Genesis. She turns to contractual theory in order to highlight the presence of the mother elided by both Milton's poem and the patriarchal theory of Filmer. Consistently revising her biblical text, Hutchinson both grants the mother possession over the child—awarded consistently to the father in Genesis itself—and highlights the generative line of the mother. The language of maternal generation becomes significantly highlighted once figures of female production, such as Sarah, are at the center of Hutchinson's narrative (as well as that of the Bible). The consequences of her emphasis on a maternal claim to children—while it does not undercut the power of God's greater creating power—politicizes her representation of biblical families in light of debates within seventeenth-century political theory.

While Hutchinson's Genesis poem is framed by the events within the biblical narrative, she consistently changes biblical language that describes the production of children. Language in the Bible asserts that women produce children for men, as in the account of Sarah's production of a child: whether through the body of Hagar or her own body, the language stresses Abraham's possession of the child: "Sarah your wife shall *bear you a son*"; "For Sarah conceived and *bore Abraham a son*"; "And Abraham called the name of his son *who was borne to him*" (17:18, 21:2, 21:3; New King James Version; my emphasis). Sarah describes her production of a son for her husband in exactly the same terms: "For I have *borne him a son* in his old age" (Genesis 21:7; my emphasis).

This language of the child produced for the father is modified in a number of ways in Hutchinson's poem. The seeming transition of power from mother as the source to father as the authority figure to whom the child is delivered is revised extensively in her account of Sarah: "To comfort their disgrace, now Sarah's womb / Grew pregnant with that promised fruit in whom / A blessing was designed for the whole earth, / And the ninth moon disclosed the joyful birth" (14.253–56). Sarah does not bear a son for Abraham; they together share in the joyful birth, a modification that Hutchinson's use of a collective pronoun illustrates. Canto 14 provides this unified vision of Sarah and Abraham, one that recalls the marriage sequence of Adam and Eve and the language of producing children: "*they* call their son" Isaac since his "name implies / *Their* gladness" (14.257–58; my emphasis). Sarah bears them a son, not Abraham, and this change is reflected in language offering Sarah continued, even individualized, possession over her son: God states that "I will thy Sarah bless / And *her son* shall the promised land possess / And mighty nations out of her shall grow. Upon *her nephews* I will thrones bestow, / My covenant establish with *her seed*" (12.179–83; my emphasis). God then reiterates that "Sarah's [sons] shall my covenant retain" (188). Hutchinson does not negate the language of male seed; Abraham has just received the covenant following a promise that "Thy seed shall be abundantly increased / And spread their families in the spicy east" (155–56). But Hutchinson's modifications to biblical language suggest that mothers maintain a possession of and over their children, one which they share, but do not have to concede to, their husband or master.

This language of shared possession of children, even the restoration of a maternal line, characterizes the final third of the poem. Every direct comparison between the language of generation in Genesis and *Order and Disorder* illustrates Hutchinson's rewriting of accounts of women producing for men. In Canto 15, we hear that "with eight sons which his wife, fair Milcah, bore, / To whom his concubine has added four" (303–4). While Milcah retains a possessive title over her children in Hutchinson's line "Of Milcah's eight sons" (15.305), all such title to one's children seems denied to her, and the concubine, in the biblical source line: there, we hear that "Milcah also has borne children to your brother" (22:20), a statement reinforced with "These eight Milcah bore to Nahor" (22:23).

These revisions by Hutchinson prepare, in the final few cantos, for the production of a more maternally identified line. While patriarchy is hardly overturned in *Order and Disorder*, the language suggests how Hutchinson is simultaneously highlighting maternal possession and connection. The children of Rebecca, Jacob and Esau, are directed in Genesis to lands or women identified through the paternal line: "go to Padam Aram, to the house of Bethuel *your mother's father*, and take yourself a wife from there of the daughters of Laban *your mother's brother*" (28:2, my emphasis). In the biblical language, Rebecca's maternal heritage is defined through male relatives, a situation repeated in the directions given to Esau to get a wife. Further, the affiliation of the wife is entirely circumscribed by the male line: "So Esau went to Ishmael and took Mahalath the daughter of Ishmael, Abraham's son, the sister of Nebajoth" (28:9). In Genesis, Mahalath is defined in Genesis by three male relationships—father, grandfather, and brother.

Hutchinson will reintroduce the missing mother into her account, translating these into maternally affiliated lines of association. When Jacob is directed by Isaac "to thy mother's native country go" (18.230), Hutchinson stresses that the line is derived through Rebecca: Esau "brings from thence / Bashemath whom Nebajoth's mother bore, / Ishmael's fair daughter" (18.338–40). Paternal identity does not disappear—she is still identified as Ishmael's daughter—but Hutchinson has reintroduced the mother, who was entirely erased in accounts of male association. These sequences recall Hutchinson's Canto 5 remark on the productive role of the mother: "from her womb / Her father, brother, husband, son shall come" (5.228–29). While my claim is not that Hutchinson insists on some singularly female identification of family line, she consistently realigns accounts of familial production to reintroduce the mother. These maternal figures do not produce children for male patriarchs, but are instead a generative force that produces a matrilineal line, or produces in concert with the husband/father.

Hutchinson's consistent rephrasing of the language of maternal production corresponds to her choice to streamline many parts of Genesis that offer extensive male-derived lists of "begetting." Her choice to compress such moments in Genesis is particularly notable since she extensively relies on the biblical narrative. The consequence of her expansion and contraction of the story is a subtle but consistent highlighting of maternity and downplaying of patriarchally derived family units. The most overt "begetting" chapters in Genesis—10, 11, 25, and 26—are the most significantly compressed, and parts are entirely dropped. Hutchinson's narrative sensibility prompts her choice to replace them with expanded narrative accounts of Sarah, Rebecca, and Rachel. The effect is to put stress upon and elaborate on their roles as wives and mothers.

Hutchinson's compression of the language of "begetting" in the biblical text also further undermines the grounds of Filmerian, patriarchal power. As we have seen, Filmer's patriarchal theory rests on the transfer of power from father to son, an uninterrupted process of power inherited from Adam and then handed down to contemporary monarchs. This detailing of paternal begetting practices occurs in the very chapters of Genesis that Hutchinson compresses: as Filmer argues,

As this patriarchal power continued in Abraham, Isaac and Jacob, even until the Egyptian bondage, so we find it among the sons of Ishmael and Esau. It is said: "These are the sons of Ishmael, and these are their names by their castles and towns, twelve princes of their tribes or families" (Genesis 25, 16). "And these are the names of the dukes that came of Esau, according to their families and their places by their nations" (Genesis 26, 40)." (8–9)

Hutchinson downplays these narratives of sons and their inherited authority, making room instead for accounts of the family-based process of generating offspring. She unwrites many of the phrases upon which patriarchal theory more generally, and Filmer more particularly, relied to establish patrilineal monarchy. Thus, her narrativizing of the biblical story counters the main principles of patriarchal thought. In awarding dominion jointly to Adam and Eve, enhancing maternal lines within her poem, and consistently reintroducing the mother throughout her verse, Hutchinson offers critical, even devastating, commentary on patriarchal theory just as will political writers Algernon Sidney, James Tyrrell, and John Locke in the early 1680s.

As we have seen, Hutchinson explores what extending dominion to mothers does to the narrative of Genesis. Her presentation of the maternal has consistent political implications throughout *Order and Disorder*. Where she chooses to expand the stories, the emotions, and the conflicts of mothers are the portions of the biblical narrative where governmental organization—represented in positive terms—is originating and spreading. The productive female body becomes stressed throughout the latter third of *Order and Disorder*, as in the description of Rebecca: Hutchinson details extensively "Her pregnant womb," the quickening, and the painful experience of pregnancy. And these wives' birthing experiences are being highlighted at the moment in the text when expansion of their families and tribes is occurring. As Abraham becomes "great in wealth and power" (15.1), we observe the expansion of this familial-based form of the commonwealth and, with it, a greater emphasis on the maternal line and the identification of the mother as a powerful figure.

While we have seen the detailing of individual mothers' claims to their children, Hutchinson now returns us to the metaphoric figure of Mother Earth, an image she so resisted in the earlier part of the poem. Abraham's final moments are encompassed by power of the mother: "Eight score and fifteen years now from his birth / Expired, his flesh returned unto the earth, / That universal mother whose vast womb / Doth all her own productions reintomb" (16.307–10). This language is entirely Hutchinson's addition; she allows the language of the earth to regain its traditional gendered identity and the power that derives from this.

Hutchinson seems to be making a distinction between the expanding protocommonwealths of Abraham and his sons and earlier accounts of Noah, a distinction that is also marked by the presence or absence of women's bodies. In *Patriarcha*, Filmer details the handing down of this monarchical power to Noah and his heirs following the flood. This is a central genetic aspect of Filmer's theory to which numerous contract theorists—and I am suggesting Hutchinson as well—will react:

Not only until the Flood, but after it, this patriarchal power did continue—as the very name of patriarch doth in part prove. The three sons of Noah had the whole world divided amongst them by their father, for of them was the whole world overspread, according to the benediction given to him and his sons. (7)

One might read her opening to Canto 10 as rehearsing a parallel, patriarchal inheritance of monarchical power from father to son: "Now several sons were born to Noah's sons / And those sons fathers of great nations" (10.1–2). Yet this statement is undercut in a variety of ways within Hutchinson's narrative, which Norbrook has argued is strongly anti-monarchical and republican: the stories of Noah, Ham, and Nimrod are frequently used to argue against monarchy.[30] Also, as we will see, these lines introduce us to a section of the poem entirely devoid of female figures.

The founding of nations that Hutchinson will describe here occurs through a Filmerian-style transfer of power from father to son. But this transfer of power which forms the basis of all patriarchal claims of authority results in the first monarch and tyrant: "Nimrod the regal title first assumed. / In Babylon did he his throne erect / And all the neighbours by his powers subject" (10.10–12). Hutchinson's account of Nimrod's rise to power, and subsequent transfer of authority to his sons, may lack the outrage expressed by Adam in Milton's poem. There, Noah's family did "spend thir days in joy unblam'd, and dwell / Long time in peace by Families and Tribes / Under paternal rule; till one shall rise / Of proud ambitious heart, who not content / With fair equality, fraternal state, / Will arrogate Dominion undeserv'd / Over his brethren, and quite dispossess / Concord and law of Nature from the Earth" (12.22–29). Hutchinson offers instead a critique of the process: "Thus the first mighty monarchs of the earth / From Noah's graceless son derived their birth" (20). She makes this patrilineal line—one on which Filmer relies when he explains that "the division [of land] itself was by families from Noah and his children, over which the parents were heads and princes" (8)—fundamentally problematic. Noah's "graceless son" Ham becomes the father of the first monarch and tyrant, and yet his "prince" Noah had condemned him. Furthermore, as Norbrook has noted, the description of Noah does little to validate patriarchal theory (xl): "Noah, the new world's monarch, here lies drunk / His awful dread is with his temperance sunk" (9.187–88). And as she has done throughout the poem, Hutchinson uses techniques like the poetic compression of this line to effectively underscore the republican, anti-monarchical point. Patriarchal theory, the inheritance structure validated by the narrative of biblical events, is shown to lead to tyranny, but also to rely on faulty, even parodic, modes of power transfer.

Both Hutchinson's and Milton's poems can be seen as engaged in the theoretical battle between contract theorists and proponents of patriarchalism, and passages abound in *Order and Disorder* that explicitly counter the "genetic" theory of political origins. While Filmer, for example, sees this dominion as residing in Adam's and his descendants' monarchical power, Hutchinson counters such an assertion explicitly. She states in Canto 3 that "his fall'n sons...arrogate / [Adam's] forfeited dominion and high state" (630–31). Because of the Fall, Adam has "forfeited dominion." Fallen sons have no more right to this dominion, she seems to suggest, than a fallen Adam. While initially denying a basic tenet of patriarchal thought, she continues with an account of kings' relationships to subjects that accords with aspects of consent theory: "God . . . did ordain / That kings, hence taught, might in their realms maintain / Fair order, serving those whome they command / As guardians" (3.632–35). While she continues to suggest limitations on kings' ownership of land and constraints on their behavior, her language of guardianship and of kings "serving . . . whome they command" insists on the responsibilities of kings to their subjects. This assertion is entirely counter to the God-given right of kings argued for by patriarchal theorists and to the corresponding responsibilities of subjects because of this granted domination.

But the republican nature of Hutchinson's response is only half of the significance of her manner of engaging, and rejecting, the main tenets of patriarchal theory. Her engagements with patriarchal thought are fought out through the presence or absence of the maternal figure. At points in the poem when women's bodies have entirely disappeared from the narrative, she offers accounts of the dangers of an entirely male-determined line of authority. Thus, the presence of the maternal that characterizes her accounts of Abraham and his offspring confirms his appropriate acquisition of "wealth and power" (15.1) and the corresponding expansion of governmental authority. Abraham is not represented as the drunk patriarch, embodying monarchical power. And his interactions with other kingdoms are described in the resonant language of "consent" and "covenant." While the account of Nimrod is marked, and marred, by the anti-Parliamentarian assumption of "the regal title first," he further "subject[s]" his neighbors (10.10, 12). Abraham instead "contracts / a league with [Gerar], that not by hostile acts / Nor secret practices each should invade / The other's right, and that this covenant, made / By them, their next successors should include, / And to their generations be renewed" (15.7–12). In an event that establishes long term peace through the "contract," aspects of a commonwealth emerge along with political stability. In a narrative engaging the main elements of the debate between Hobbes and Filmer, Hutchinson also draws upon consent theory in such a way that her narrative appears predictive of Locke's social contract.

Yet Hutchinson is offering a more familially located narrative of empire creation and the expansion of government. Her reintegration of the female body into many of these accounts from Genesis has the effect of offsetting, and sometimes explicitly rejecting, the premise of patriarchal inheritance. Narratively, she offers an increasingly domestic vision of marital union in the stories of Sarah, Rebecca, and Rachel. The consequence is a vision of governmental structure as revolving around, and as produced by, the family unit that is the result of a mutually contracted union of marriage. Furthermore, these accounts of the family unit stand in contrast to the portions of the narrative which become separated from the language of maternity. Hutchinson, then, re-embodies moments in the Genesis narrative in order to counter the patriarchal, father-to-son derived theories of Filmer. While granting God's preeminent power over the female body, allowing the "invisibility" of which Froula speaks to characterize God's form of creativity, the poem links the female body to both the generation of bodies and of governments. Her politicizing of the family through an emphasis on the female body allows Hutchinson to counter the erasure of women in the political hierarchy while arguing against patriarchal theory's principle of male lineal descent.

We have thus seen the complex influences on Hutchinson's *Order and Disorder*, which negotiated the period's debate between contract and patriarchal theories. She uses Lucretius's promotion of female-gendered creativity and Milton's *Paradise Lost* to promote politically resonant creative power in the Genesis narrative of human begetting. The result is a narrative account of the Bible that can challenge the threatening aspects of Lucretius's text, rewrite the degendering of female power that marks much of Milton's poem, and gesture toward reintroducing the "mother" into an account of biblically derived human history. But I would like to suggest that the parameters of Hutchinson's conversation extend even further. In returning to the biblical narrative to engage issues of gendered culpability for the Fall, and the consequent mode of establishing governmental authority, Hutchinson's poem, likely composed in the late 1670s, is part of a contemporary foment of political theory. The publication of the first five cantos in 1679 locates *Order and Disorder* right around the 1679 publication of Filmer's *Patriarcha*, his culminating statement of patriarchal theory. The poem is productively placed in conversation with patriarchal theory. Hutchinson's reactions to biblical narrative employed to support patriarchal political theory parallel the most significant response to Filmer produced in the seventeenth century: Locke offered an extended rebuttal to *Patriarcha* in the *Two Treatises of Government*, a tract published in 1690 but considered by some to have been composed between 1679 and 1681.

Like Hutchinson, Locke is invested in providing a powerful counter to patriarchal thought as summarized in Filmer's *Patriarcha*, and Locke attacks many aspects of patriarchal thought within Filmer's writings. Locke's *First Treatise* aligns closely to *Order and Disorder* both ideologically and in its use of biblical authority. Hutchinson's fusion of Genesis 1 and 2 in the marriage scene of Adam and Eve, for example, is the same refutation that Locke will employ: "It is false," Locke maintains, "that God made that Grant to Adam, as soon as he was Created . . . it is plain it could not be spoken to Adam till after Eve was made and brought to him" (152). This reintroduction of Eve into discussions of dominion is echoed in Locke's restoring of the mother to a discussion of authority. According to Locke, if there is an "Absolute Power" that parents have been granted over their children,

This would give the *Father* but a joynt Dominion with the Mother over them. For no body can deny but that the Woman hath an equal share, if not the greater, as nourishing the Child a long time in her own Body out of her own Substance . . . the Mother cannot be denied an equal share in the begetting of the Child, and so the Absolute Authority will not arise from hence. (1.55)

In denying the absolute authority of the father, and thus the basis of Filmerian patriarchal theory, by arguing through the biblical story in the *First Treatise of Government*, Locke follows in the line established by Hobbes but refined by Hutchinson's Genesis poem.

The presence of maternal authority—and of Eve—is short-lived in Locke's text: by the *Second Treatise*, Locke can evade the consequences of returning women to discussions of familial authority—and therefore the possibility of a more public form of maternal power—by dividing the family from the state. Yet these parallels with Locke highlight the significance of Hutchinson's introduction of the mother into a discussion of familial and state authority. Hutchinson is theorizing—as does Locke—the effect of the figure of the mother on the foundation of the state. But her gendered engagement with political theory in the late seventeenth century suggests a possibly more prominent view of the role of the woman and the family in the formation of government than that which emerges in the *Two Treatises*. *Order and Disorder*'s mode of gendering political theory highlights that alternate conclusions existed in the seventeenth century about what would become the modern division of the family and state. Hutchinson is attempting to define a familial unit that is linked to the state. Locke, through returning women to a discussion of familial power, evades the consequences of political, maternal power by dividing the family from the state.

Rachel Weil has suggested that, far from being a consistent theoretical position, the family/state division is a consequence of Locke's attempt to argue against Filmer's genetic and analogous theory of monarchy.[31] For the purpose of evaluating Hutchinson's entrance into this sphere of political theory, what seems most significant is that she does not pull away from the implications of maternal control. She seems to try to present—in a narrative, unsystematic manner—a view of the family as a governmental unit without resorting to a theory of masculine absolute authority. Interestingly, as Weil has also noted, the political theory published by "Whig" writers such as Algernon Sidney, James Tyrrell, and Locke suggests numerous possibilities for developing republican, antimonarchical theory. Hutchinson can be seen as participating in an emergent discourse, one that will become codified in Locke. But her gendered engagement with the state of political theory in the late seventeenth century suggests an alternate view of the role of the woman and the family in the formation of government than will emerge in the *Two Treatises of Government*.

The conversation Hutchinson is having with writers, including Milton, certainly, and Hobbes and Filmer, probably, over the establishment of social and governmental authority also highlights the continuity of the biblical narrative in "modern" visions of the state. When Hutchinson reads and responds to Milton, she is engaging the very question of gendered authority on which women's social and political status depended. While it would be hard to establish a direct line from Hutchinson to Locke, striking parallels exist between their writings: they similarly negotiate the story of the Fall, and they construct authority based on the gendered implications of Eve's presence and practice. Hutchinson's negotiation of Genesis, with its central issues of women's culpability and their relationship to power, highlights key elements in Locke's construction of a "modern" state. The consequence of Hutchinson reading Milton, then, is—at least—twofold. *Order and Disorder* illustrates the highly productive space for poetic and political female authorship that Milton's *Paradise Lost* created. Furthermore, her interpolation of a discourse about female culpability and authority helps expose how the ground from the Garden becomes the plot upon which we have built our ideas of the modern state.

The last two chapters have offered a multiplicity of interpretive possibilities that such studies in influence can provide. Milton's engagement with female prophets in Chapter 3 can reconfigure a psychoanalytically inflected reading of Milton's repression or perversion of the maternal: the female prophet instead draws the poetic voice toward political engagement. While my focus here on Milton's portrait of the reproducing female body might seem to return to such critical, in both senses of the word, approaches to Milton, I would point instead toward the opportunity this imagery offered for Lucy Hutchinson: she returns to the same political female body that Milton had engaged through discourses of prophesy. These differently oriented readings of Milton's poem illustrate the rich interpretations made possible by reconfiguring "influence." The polyvocal nature of *Paradise Lost*, in which Milton can expose the creation of anti-feminist language while simultaneously recording the voices countering or revising this tradition, allows for divergent readings to coexist within the text. The very influences that *Paradise Lost* has on other writers further underscores the polyphonic nature of the text. Hutchinson does not reject nor does she repeat the repression of the maternal: she employs this to create a new, alternate reading of Genesis. While an older style of "influence" imagined a singular line of influence, I am charting instead how the use of the female body can resonate differently in distinct contexts; differently configured layers of texts, writers, cultural influences and pressures alter the meaning of that body within discrete moments of Milton's and Hutchinson's poems. Cultural, biographical, historical, textual, and ideological "influences" all participate in this process.

As I turn to the work that John Milton's and Margaret Cavendish's texts are doing in Chapter 5, we will see the cultural influence of emerging scientific discourse on two texts that centrally consider the acquisition of knowledge and the implications of this for gender. These two texts, produced essentially in the same year, could not, as it were, "know" each other. Thus, the prominent form of "influence" in this chapter will be the cultural discourses of the Royal Society. And yet, by placing these two texts into a cultural conversation with the language of experimental philosophy, the work that each of these texts performs highlights the cultural, literary, and theological motivations shared by and differentiating Milton and Cavendish. While one text would almost certainly have been unable to influence the other, positioning them side by side will have a profound impact on how we can perceive the influences onto and shared between Milton's *Paradise Lost* and Margaret Cavendish's *Blazing World*.

The Two Faces of Eve: Gendering Knowledge and the "New" Science in *Paradise Lost* and Margaret Cavendish's *Blazing World*

As the previous two chapters have explored, the female body is invoked amid prophetic language at the mid-century and then deployed within *Order and Disorder*'s "Meditations" on the marital and maternal role in governmental organization. In this chapter, I will be reinserting women, in particular the figure of Eve, into another central discourse of the period: the rise of science and the concomitant discourse about the process of acquiring knowledge. Within *Paradise Lost* and Margaret Cavendish's *Blazing World*, we observe as Eve, or an Eve-like figure, engages the problem of knowledge within a Paradisical space. Inflected by discourses of the Royal Society, whose formation significantly propelled the rise of science in the period, Milton's and Cavendish's stories of the Garden event negotiate Restoration practices of controlling knowledge in the period. This mode of intertextual and intercultural reading resembles the now very familiar practices of new historicist methodology. Yet in keeping with my emphasis on influence in this study, I would like to stress the productive nature of examining the intersection between these three "texts" in the context of Restoration culture. Milton's *Paradise Lost*, Cavendish's *Observations upon Experimental Philosophy* with *The Blazing World*, and texts affiliated with the Royal Society intersect with one another at the nexus of three ideological discourses: emerging seventeenth-century scientific practices; the theological implications of knowledge and gender; and debates about political organization. These overlapping interpretive frameworks provide a context for engaging the "influence" of Royal Society discourses onto essentially simultaneously produced texts: *Paradise Lost* and *The Blazing World*. The conjunction of Milton's and Cavendish's published texts consequently illuminates the practices of gendering and politicizing knowledge during England in the 1660s.

Critical discussions, and debates, surrounding both Cavendish and Milton have variously located them among discussions of science in the period. For Cavendish, entering this discursive space was an overt goal of many of her publications. As the history of science has documented for us, during the 1660s through 1680s the growing ascendancy of experimental philosophy would effect the gradual demise of natural philosophy[1]: texts such as Cavendish's *Observations upon Experimental Philosophy* with the appended *Blazing World* would be on the losing side of this debate. They are nonetheless part of its history as is Cavendish, who asserted herself into this debate: to employ Cavendish's terms, the "speculation" that she elaborates within the *Observations* "must need go before [the] practice" of the "experimental philosopher" (*Observations*) because the organization of the world is better derived from "reason"—or natural philosophy—than from the "sense" that propels experimental philosophy. Cavendish's *Observations upon Experimental Philosophy*, then, offered one of many sustained criticisms, including an attack by Hobbes, of experimental scientists such as Robert Boyle and Robert Hooke.[2]

In contrast to Cavendish's explicit investment in the debate over experimental science, Milton critics have debated his involvement in, investment in, even knowledge of the "new science." While an older tradition of criticism had distanced Milton from any engagement with late century developments in science, more recent scholarship has contextualized Milton's writings amid the cultural impulses that helped to form the Royal Society.[3] The main debate among critics: what side would Milton privilege? That argued by Margaret Cavendish and Thomas Hobbes? Or that represented by Richard Boyle and Robert Hooke? Considering Milton and Cavendish together helps to construct a more nuanced answer to this question. The philosophical parallels between Milton and Cavendish, well established by critics, would tend toward aligning them with a negative view of the "new science." Both Milton and Cavendish are decidedly materialist and monist in their thinking by the 1660s; committed, as John Rogers has illustrated, to vitalism as a philosophical counter to a Hobbesian mechanistic world view, their philosophies evolved, if not in step, in a parallel direction. Cavendish's early embracing of Epicurean atomism soon turned to what Eileen O'Neill calls the "organicist materialism" that marks her works produced in the 1660s (xx).[4] In the philosophical balancing act between the mechanist universe postulated by Hobbes and Descartes and the Platonism of writers such as Henry More and Ralph Cudworth, Cavendish comes to occupy a space, as well as an intellectual trajectory, close to that of Milton. John Milton's own movement away from his earlier neo-Platonic views—observable in *Comus*, for example—occurs in concert with his rejection of the mechanistic world of Hobbes and the challenges posed by Descartes's mind/body division.[5] The two thinkers are developing in similar philosophical directions in the shifting intellectual sands of the seventeenth century, their parallel evolution possibly suggesting Milton's interest in Cavendish's growing resistance to the new science. Their mutual monist rejection of Cartesian dualism and their embracing of vitalism to counter the agency-less mechanistic world offer a new perspective onto Milton's (largely resistant) response to the "new science."[6]

Further, the simultaneous publication of narratives of Paradisical spaces provides an opportunity to evaluate Milton's views about the new science through the lens of Cavendish's reactions. Milton's *Paradise Lost*, published in 1667, was encircled by the publication of Cavendish's *The Description of A New World, Called The Blazing World*; it first appeared in 1666 and was then reissued in 1668, appended both times to her *Observations*. Both of these texts thus emerge during a significant debate around the practices of science and philosophy during the Restoration. At almost the exact same moment in the 1660s, Milton's portrait of Eve and the Eve-like figure of the Empress in Cavendish's *Blazing World* engage the relationship between the acquisition of knowledge, the Fall, and the implications for a portrait of a gendered hierarchy. And they do so through language that engages emerging discourses of science, specifically texts affiliated with the Royal Society.

Founded in 1660 and granted a royal charter in 1662, the Royal Society followed the precepts of Francis Bacon in developing, among other interests, a program of experimental philosophy usually considered the foundation for modern science. Yet this narrative, often linked to an emerging modernity, is told in part through the story of Genesis. Members and eulogizers of the Royal Society describe their endeavors as enabling their return to the Garden. The invocation of the Genesis narrative within texts promoting the Royal Society consequently asserts a powerful link between emerging scientific practices and our eviction from the Garden: in poems, scientific tracts, even designs for the Society, the Royal Society's activities are described as remedies for our postlapsarian identity. Certain modes of acquiring knowledge are thus imagined as a way to return to Paradise. And yet, the redemptive return to Eden sustains its traditional grounding in the connection between gender and knowledge. If Eve's actions precipitated the Fall, now the actions of male experimental philosophers, who consistently praise the "masculine" nature of their activities, will allow a reclamation of the lost prelapsarian space.

Thus the writings of members of the Royal Society, as well as Cavendish's and Milton's narratives, all (re)consider the relationship between accounts of the Garden and practices of the "new" science. Hooke's implied narrative of regaining Paradise becomes enacted within aspects of Milton's and Cavendish's accounts of our previously lost Paradise, in which gender theologically and historically shapes our understanding of the acquisition of knowledge. In previous chapters, I indicated that early seventeenth-century female defenders of women, such as Rachel Speght and Aemilia Lanyer, reconfigured this inherently gendered narrative of access to knowledge. Now, the discourses of the Royal Society will rewrite that traditional gendering of knowledge within an emergent discourse of science, prompting Milton and Cavendish to represent the gendered acquisition of knowledge in distinct ways. Both writers will then employ the story of the Fall to interrogate the various boundaries that the Royal Society placed around experimental science and the larger category of knowledge itself.

In overt practice, policy, and reflections on methodology, experimental philosophy or the "new science" was gendered male. The Royal Society limited membership to gentry and noble men; some critics have even suggested that the physical barriers to women's involvement in experimental science may well have shaped Margaret Cavendish's philosophical positions.[7] Milton's and Cavendish's similar—while still significantly divergent—portraits of Eve and their representation of knowledge acquisition in the Garden can, in part, be read as reactions to the gendered implications of "experimental" redemption. If the way back to the Garden is male-produced science, then this "postlapsarian" cure will bring with it social order. Yet as Eve Keller has argued about these Royal Society views, "science . . . creates paradise, but not for all" (465).[8] In restaging that narrative with her Eve figure, Cavendish explicitly attacks these assumptions through the category of gender: she genders experimental philosophy as male, but narrates a language of restoration to political power and to the Garden itself in order to grant authority to her female natural philosopher, the Empress of the Blazing World. Milton associates Eve, more so than Adam, with experimental philosophy, defying the gender boundaries established by the Royal Society. Their portraits of Eve thus specifically engage, even refute, the rewritten Garden narrative employed by the Royal Society, one which constructed a philosophical and political Golden Age of gender or political exclusivity.

Just as the theological implications of a "restor'd" state would not have been lost on either Milton or Cavendish, neither would the political ones: in the context of the language of "restoration" to the Garden of Eden, the uses of the narrative of the Fall were as inherently political as they were theological. Even as the practitioners of the Royal Society proclaimed their distance from the potentially divisive politics of the Restoration, their language gestured at a "restor'd" monarchy while narrating "restor'd" Edenic access. As Steven Shapin and Simon Schaffer have illustrated in *Leviathan and the Air-Pump*, the practices of the Royal Society were thus powerfully linked to the maintenance of political order. Simultaneously, the entirely male membership of the Royal Society limited its form of "knowledge" to that which only men could access. What will become a politically regulated performance of social order rests on the exclusion of women. At the very intersection of the political and the "scientific," we see Cavendish and Milton reassert the figure of Eve as a mode of engaging the terms of Royal Society rhetoric.

Furthermore, in both Milton's and Cavendish's texts, access to natural or experimental "truths" becomes explicitly linked to access to political power: if for Cavendish's Empress female political power makes control over knowledge production and distribution possible, in Milton, confusions about the limits of knowledge become the confusions of a gendered, social hierarchy. Thus, both Milton and Cavendish offer, through the narrative of acquiring scientific knowledge, an account of social disruption. And as such, they powerfully counter the goals of the Royal Society. As Eve Keller notes, when Cavendish's Empress encourages her experimental scientists, disagreement ensues, potentially threatening social disorder.[9] Her role as a redeemed Eve allowed back into the "Paradise" that is the Blazing World exposes the very connection between (scientific) knowledge, gender, and political organization hidden from view by the Royal Society's gender exclusivity.

While exposing gender inequalities is a major goal in Cavendish's description of the Royal Society, gender also serves Milton as a weapon to counter the Society's claims about the boundaries that can be placed around knowledge. In fact, both writers will reverse the claims made by Royal Society members: in the case of Milton, engaging in the practices of experimental science leads to the Fall itself. Alternately, in Cavendish's *Blazing World*, such experimental science will threaten a potential fall from a vision of prelapsarian social harmony. Of course, the political differences between Cavendish and Milton might initially give us pause; I am suggesting a parallel resistance from a fallen Republican and restored Cavalier to an institution upon which Charles II had bestowed a royal charter. Yet both writers draw upon the narrative of the Fall, and its associations with the "new science," to critique the resulting political structure of exclusion. Thus, the Edenic narrative is once again employed as a crux for exploring the relationship between social order and gendered relations in England's "restor'd" state.

In interrogating the practice of science during the Restoration, we continue to pursue the main theme of this book: gendered hierarchies and their importance as the basis for political organization. An interesting analog exists between the gender exclusivity of the new science and the narrative of "liberalism" and the formation of the social contract as outlined by Carole Pateman. The construction of "modern science" follows a similar line, making women as invisible to the transactional processes of modern science as they become to the formation of the modern state. The larger point of this chapter is not to rehearse Pateman's well-known thesis. Instead, as we have seen throughout the other chapters of this book, at the intersection of Milton's and Cavendish's texts, alternate visions of that gendered exclusivity are imaginable in the world preceding the Lockean social contract. While the options formulated by Milton and Cavendish have their own limitations in terms of both gender and class, both *Paradise Lost* and *Blazing World* were imagining alternatives to political organization in the mid-1660s. These options are revealed to us as a result of viewing these contemporary texts in concert: parallels and distinctions highlight each writer's interventions in the cultural debate about the emerging discourse of experimental science.

Despite a modern vision of science as existing outside a set of religious beliefs, the belief system of the Royal Society was still very much embedded within religious beliefs and practices of the period. In various pieces of propaganda for, and writings by, Royal Society members, experimental philosophy was imagined as offering a return to the prelapsarian state. Knowledge, instead of causing our Fall, could be transformed by members of the Royal Society into access to Eden. Recasting the Fall in the "Preface" to *Micrographia*, Hooke explicitly positions experimental philosophy as our redemptive return to the Garden:

And as at first, mankind fell by tasting of the forbidden Tree of Knowledge so we, their Posterity, may be in part restor'd by the same way, not only by beholding and contemplating, but by tasting too those fruits of Natural Knowledge, that were never yet forbidden.[10] (Ab2r–Ab2v)

The "restoration" to the Garden can now be accomplished by a redefined act of acquiring knowledge, a validating "tasting."

These sentiments about the theologically restorative nature of experimental philosophy were expressed equally by eulogists for the Royal Society. In "To the Royal Society," Abraham Cowley describes the reentry to the previously lost garden space, opened up, as it were, to (experimental) philosophy through Francis Bacon:

The orchard's open now, and free;
Bacon has broke that scarecrow deity;
Come enter, all that will,
Behold the ripen'd fruit, come gather now your fill.
Yet still, methinks we fain would be
Catching at the forbidden tree,
We would be like the Deity,
When truth and falsehood, good and evil, we
Without the senses aid within our selves would see;
For 'tis God only who can find
All Nature in his mind. (58–68)

Cowley describes the breaking of a "scarecrow deity," a seeming deflation of the angel who guards the entrance to the Garden, flaming swords in hand, to a garden gnome. As a result, the "orchard's open now, and free" from the restraints the first Garden space posed on knowledge acquisition. Thus, Bacon's inheritors are now able to "behold the ripen'd fruit" as practitioners of science are "invited" to "gather now your fill."

In previous chapters, we have seen the uses that women writers such as Speght and Lanyer made of a reconfigured Garden into which a redeemed Eve could enter. This imagery employed by members and eulogizers of the Royal Society offers, instead, an expressly male reclamation of the Garden space that was consistent with the overt gendering of the Royal Society and their practices as male. Only male members were accepted and, except for Margaret Cavendish's much discussed visit, women were not even allowed as visitors. Even when this woman, singular in so many ways, was allowed entrance into the Royal Society, her visit "only underlined her exclusion from the experimental site"; as Elizabeth Spiller notes, Cavendish did not actively participate as a witness to the experiments, an obligation for any other, male, visitor to the Society (212). By gendering science, the Royal Society actually accomplishes the gendering of redemption; entry back into the Garden becomes dependent upon one's position within the Society and is accomplished through an alignment with our unfallen forefather.

While Cowley discusses entrance back into the Garden, Henry Power focuses on Adam's actions in the prelapsarian Garden. Employing a link between our first father's prefallen abilities and those of experimental philosophers, Power describes the prosthetic uses that Adam could have made of "the Telescope or Microscope" (A4r):

> for howsoever though the faculties of the soul of our Primitive father Adam might be more quick and perspicacious in apprehension, than those of our lapsed selves; Yet certainly the Constitution of Adam's Organs was not divers from ours, nor different from those of his Fallen Self, so that he could never discern those distant, or minute objects by Natural Vision, as we do by the Artificial advantages of the Telescope or Microscope. (A4r)

The leveling of the distinctions between Adam and members of the Royal Society sets the stage for experimental science in the Garden. The limitations of Adam's senses are equated with those of "our lapsed selves"; just as for modern men, without "Artificial advantages," Adam's sight in the Garden is constrained. Man is a diminished version of the original father, the passage concedes: this is a result of the Fall but also a function of the distance from the oft-asserted grandeur of our original parents. Yet this debasement can be offset by the "Artificial advantages of the Telescope or Microscope" (A4r). These devices become prosthetic tools to allow Royal Society members to reclaim Adam's inheritance of the Garden through portraying him as a potential member of the Society. In fact, because Adam was disadvantaged by his lack of scientific instruments, the narrative allows these members to supersede our original father who "could never discern those distant, or minute objects by Natural Vision" which now some men can. Science thus can restore certain men to a prelapsarian condition, the "unique promise of Paradise regained," as Eve Keller describes the Baconian promise (455).[11]

The garden motif comes to characterize many aspects of Royal Society practices, propaganda, and plans, and is sustained within Abraham Cowley's 1661 architectural plan for a College of Experimental Philosophy. Though this plan for building an actual college never came to pass, Cowley's detailed account of an imagined proper establishment engages the imagery employed by Cowley and Hooke.[12] In his description of the college's buildings (following detailed segments on personnel and resources for the College), gardens emerge as a structuring architectural motif within both the scholars' residences and their work areas. Organizing the buildings around cloisters, Cowley imagines "little Gardens" for each of the "Professors Lodgings" "after the manner of the Chartreux beyond the Sea" (22). Modeling the buildings upon a Carthusian monastery, these cloistered gardens literally become an emblem for the prefallen garden space invoked by this convention of religious architecture. Just as Adam is imagined as a member of the Royal Society itself, Cowley offers a working garden, one where the very pursuits of experimental philosophy will bring its members closer to discoveries, and thus to redemptive knowledge: "that the second enclosed ground be a Garden, destined only to the tryal of all manner of Experiments concerning Plants, as their Melioration, Acceleration, Retardation, Conservation, Composition, Transmutation, Coloration, and whatsoever else can be produced by Art either for use or curiosity" (26). Milton's Adam labored within the Garden as will the members of Cowley's science college, who will now test scientific ideas rather than prune the plants of this reclaimed Edenic space.

While a previously barred entrance into the Garden space was unlocked by experimental science, the limitations placed upon this form of "restoration" were highly politicized as well as gendered. In what resembles—and possibly helped form—our culture's current insistence on the political "objectivity" of science, Abraham Cowley's *Proposition for the Advancement of Experimental Philosophy* delineated the apolitical nature of the future Royal Society: "Neither does it at all check or enterfere with any Parties in State or Religion, but is indifferently to be embraced by all Differences in opinion, and can hardly be conceived capable (as many good Institutions have done) even of Degeneration into any thing harmful" (D6r). Yet despite the attempts to distance the Royal Society from the political and social divides that marked the period of the Restoration, Shapin and Schaffer have illustrated the resonantly political nature of the Society.[13] In receiving a charter from Charles II, freedom to publish, and financing for their experiments, the Royal Society promoted the "Restored" monarch. Just as politically the Restoration was seen as the return to a redemptive Golden Age, the king's scientists continued to work toward returning themselves to the Garden.

Thus, Cowley was denying in *A Proposition for the Advancement of Experimental Philosophy* what was overt in practice: scientific activities were linked at multiple levels to political patronage, political activity, and, possibly, to political disruption. Other critics of experimental philosophy overtly articulated the profound links between philosophical positions—whether natural or experimental—and the period's politics. When Hobbes attacks experimental philosophy because of its inability to accommodate his theories of motion, he delineates the overlapping sites of politics and the emerging science. In *Dialogus Physicus, sive De Natura Aeris*, Hobbes's engagement of Boyle's *New Experiments Physico-Mechanicall*, theories about politics and of the natural processes of the world can not be detached.[14] In this dialogue, the interlocutor who is challenging Boyle's air-pump experiments asserts this very connection: "Meanwhile, content with Hobbesian physics, I will observe the nature and variety of motion. I will also use the same Hobbesian rules of politics and ethics for living" (Hobbes, *Dialogus*, 391). Refusing to detach the "physics" or motions of nature and of society, the figure most like Hobbes within the dialogue asserts the parallel, analogous functioning of nature and society's political organization. As the debate comes to a close, the seeming defender of the Society and of Boyle's experiments will concede defeat to Hobbes's objections about the explanation of the air pump experiment.

But more significantly, he will associate, even align, political and "scientific" practice: "Indeed, you are quite right about politics. For like our physics, that is experimental: for it is well confirmed by almost twenty years of superior experience" (391). The greater victory—in this stated dialogue—is the acquiescing to the parallel "motions" of the world of nature and the world of men. Even when Cowley establishes boundaries around experimental philosophy, insisting that it can be insulated from political factions, his language concedes the possible connection of interfering "with any Parties in State or Religion" (D6r). Such a defense was necessary against Hobbes as well as against a (valid) cultural anxiety that competing forms of knowledge would by necessity have political, and socially disruptive, implications. The very attempts to construct experimental practice as apolitical thus highlight the overtly political stakes of knowledge and acquiring it during the Restoration. While apolitical investigation is the imagined ideal within the Royal Society, political and social upheavals mark both Milton's and Cavendish's exploration of knowledge's limits in their narratives of prelapsarian spaces.

The terms of Margaret Cavendish's response to the practices of and ideology of the Royal Society include: explicitly responding to publications by their main members; framing her narrative to engage the practice of experimental philosophy; and reflecting—though perhaps not overtly critiquing—the implications of the ideological framework of the Society. I have noted above Cavendish's explicit valuing of sense over reason in philosophy, one which draws her to respond to a range of experimental scientific texts. Eve Keller has discussed how Henry Power's 1664 work on experimental philosophy drew Cavendish's attention.[15] Aspects of the narrative within *The Blazing World* and specific details from the *Observations* also suggest that Cavendish's 1666 texts are timely responses to Robert Hooke's *Micrographia*, published only a year before in 1665. Specific references and phrases within Hooke's "Preface" are explicitly countered by Cavendish, in particular his discussion of "Celestial Observations." Hooke states,

In Celestial Observations we have far exceeded all the Antients, even the Chaldeans and Egyptians themselves, whose vast Plains, high Towers, and clear Air, did not give them so great advantages over us, as we have over them by our Glasses. (Ad1v)

To counter Hooke's elevation of such prosthetic scientific devices—a favorite theme of experimental scientists—Cavendish revises Hooke's judgment of the "Antients" by undermining the utility of such celestial instruments:

I doubt not but they had as profitable and useful arts and knowledges . . . it may be they had no microscopes nor telescopes, but I think they were the happier for want of them, employing their time in more profitable studies. What learned and witty people the Egyptians were, is sufficiently known out of ancient histories. (196)

Here the specificity of the attack on the microscope shows that *Micrographia* is Cavendish's target. Her rejection of the prosthetic uses of such equipment is unapologetic, unlike Milton's less stable use of the telescope throughout *Paradise Lost*. Yet these specific moments become woven into a narrative reconsideration of any experimental philosophical path leading back to Paradise. In her *Blazing World*, specific textual engagements with Hooke and his metaphors become expanded into a satirical representation of the Royal Society, at the core of which is a rewriting of their narrative of a Paradise regained, or "restor'd," through male experimental scientists. This narrative thus allows her to engage the practices of, and the arguments of, the Royal Society, which undermine their account of the benefits from "new science."

Recalling the use that members of the Royal Society made of the motif of Eden, as well as reentry into it, Cavendish's narrative of the *Blazing World* makes as its central site the original "Paradise" (9). Introduced as such in the opening pages of the narrative, the seat of the Emperor is later confirmed to be the Paradise of Genesis: "That Paradise was not in the world she came from, but in that world she lived in at present; and that it was the very same place where she kept her Court, and where her Palace stood, in the midst of the Imperial City" (71–72). Into this space, our main heroine, later the Empress, enters: she thus assumes an identity much like that of Speght, Sowernam, or Lanyer as she occupies the role of a redeemed Eve (re)entering Paradise. What is implied throughout the first part of the *Blazing World* is finally confirmed just before the "Second Part" of the narrative: this is a prelapsarian world into which our heroine wandered, geographically removed from the postlapsarian world from which she came. In the course of the narrative, certain innovations have introduced potential danger into the Blazing World, and if changes are not made, "it may in time prove as unhappy, nay, as miserable a World as that is from which I came . . . all which . . . is a great misery, nay, a curse, which your blessed Blazing-World never knew" (121). What is the cause of the threat, this potential fall into a "miserable" postlapsarian world? The innovations introduced by experimental philosophy.

In order to retain this prelapsarian "Paradise," the Eve-like Empress who rules over it will need to regulate the practices of experimental philosophy. As her activities illustrate, experimentation is not a redress for the postlapsarian state, but instead the path to it. In *The Blazing World*, the Empress poses the question about the movement of the sun, stars, and planets to her Bear-men "Experimental Philosophers." Addressing the same question that both Adam and Eve will pose in *Paradise Lost*, the Bear-men begin a dispute as to whether the Sun moves around the Earth, or the Earth the Sun; in addition, they query the movement of stars, asking whether they "fly from place to place, especially at such a vast distance" (27). Unable to agree in their observations, the Bear-men attempt to settle these questions by turning to the use of telescopes. Yet the truth is only obscured by these attempts. The Empress's response is the strongest rebuke Cavendish provides in her satirical portrait of the Royal Society: "I do plainly perceive, that your Glasses are false Informers, and instead of discovering Truth, delude your Senses: Wherefore I Command you to break them, and let the Bird-men trust only to their natural eyes, and examine Coelestial Objects by the motions of their own Sense and Reason" (27). Cavendish's rejection of assertions within Hooke's *Micrographia* becomes here a portrait of an alternate, unfallen world that illustrates the failure, even danger, of such prosthetic devises. As many critics have remarked, Cavendish's principles in the *Observations*—that the "deluding experiments" of the experimental philosophers are shown to be less satisfying than the "speculation" that marks her, and the Empress's, approach to truth (196)—are expressed in narrative form.

When the Empress mistakenly allows her Bear-men philosophers to continue their experiments within their societies, it allows Cavendish to employ the Royal Society's tropes in order to attack their practices. As in Hooke's and Cowley's embedded narratives, Cavendish has narrated a return to "Paradise" in her "romance." Yet the account of the Empress's actions allows Cavendish to explicitly refute the redemptive narrative of the Royal Society. A female, conversant in natural philosophy, enters and reigns over Paradise, containing the unruly, and politically and socially disruptive, academies of experimental philosophers. Many of the scientist animal figures are shown to be foolish. Yet in an explicit counter to Hooke's portrait of experimental philosophers as offering redemption, these "philosophers" are shown to cause the most disruption. At the very end of the first part of *The Blazing World*, the Royal Society's language of restoration to a prelapsarian state becomes instead a threatened reenactment of the Fall:

there are such continual Contentions and Divisions between the Worm- Bear- and Fly-men, the Ape-men, the Satyrs, the Spider-men, and all others of such sorts, that I fear they'l break out into an open Rebellion, and cause a great disorder; and the ruin of the Government. (120)

Further, in what is an overt challenge to the frequently asserted apolitical nature of the Royal Society's practices, we see here that they create the very social and political "divisions" denied by the Society. The Empress does take some blame for the situation; she admits that it is "the nature of Women being much delighted with Change and Variety [that] after I had received an absolute Power from the Emperor, did somewhat alter the Form of Government from what I found it" (120). Yet her double, the Duchess, suggests how to restore unity and prevent the fall into a postlapsarian and politically rebellious state: end the experiments.

Thus, employing but inverting the very same narrative, Cavendish explicitly links the practices of science to political conflict. As such, she is countering one of the most significant arguments for, and concerns about, the Royal Society: that division in opinion not be allowed to effect the political landscape. For, as Abraham Cowley's *Proposition for the Advancement of Experimental Philosophy* asserted, "Neither does it [experimental philosophy] at all check or enterfere with any Parties in State or Religion, but is indifferently to be embraced by all Differences in opinion, and can hardly be conceived capable (as many good Institutions have done) even of Degeneration into any thing harmful" (D6r). Cavendish explicitly counters this assertion: "wheresoever learning is, there is most commonly also Controversie and quarelling . . . which must breed factions in their Schools, which at last break out into open Wars, and draw sometimes an utter ruin upon a State or Government" (122). Yet her locating the threat of the Fall amid the male-gendered practices of the Royal Society provides a much more profound critique of the institution and its practices. The "masculine" activities that have generated these intellectual "Contentions and Divisions" redirect the story of the Fall away from our Eve figure in Paradise. She thus effectively places the fault for the Fall squarely on the shoulders of male scientists. While the members of, and eulogists for, the Society had attempted to appropriate the figure of a redeemed Eve in their accounts of scientific inquiry, Cavendish now turns that portrait on them, redirecting blame onto those men who push the boundaries of knowledge.

Cavendish's method keeps her closely tied to, though highly critical of, the gendered practices and ideology of the Royal Society in her send-up of their "philosophy." From the opening of her *Observations*, Cavendish had recorded the boundaries of both practice and intellectual acceptance that marked the organization. In the "Preface" she states that experimental philosophers "will perhaps think me an inconsiderable opposite, because I am not of their sex, and therefore strive to hit my opinions with a side-stroke" (10). As a woman, she was below the notice of male experimental scientists because she was their "opposite" (10). They actively resisted women's involvement in experimentation, or their contributions to natural philosophy, by denying women entrance to the Society. But the fact of her gender, Cavendish suggests, would also prompt a more aggressive response to the "opinions" of a woman. While Cavendish records her criticism in her *Observations*, she animates them in *The Blazing World* as appropriate limits of knowledge are discovered by a redeemed figure of Eve, one who practices an intellectual process that Cavendish's narrative has both feminized and valorized.

The gendering of philosophical practice initiated by members of the Society is employed further by Cavendish as she turns yet another series of linguistic conventions employed by the Royal Society against itself. As a number of scholars of the Royal Society have noted, the Society's gendering of experimental practice complemented their gendering of language to describe forms of knowledge. For example, the elevating of a "masculine" style of science within Thomas Sprat's *History of the Royal Society* privileges "Masculine Arts of Knowledge" over the "Feminine Arts of Pleasure" (Nate, 408). In undertaking to gender forms of philosophical practice, Cavendish distinguishes between male and female forms of knowledge in a manner that parodically replays the strategies of the Royal Society.[16] In her hands, such categories argue for her view of the proper modes of querying the natural world. Again using the very propaganda of the Royal Society against itself, Cavendish can declare a victory over the competing claimants to knowledge in the period's philosophical circles.

Gendered modes of acquiring knowledge, defined by the Royal Society and reconfigured by her narrative, thus profoundly shape Cavendish's satire of the Royal Society. Cavendish's reassignment of the value of masculine or feminine modes of knowledge is enacted through gestures toward the narrative of the Fall within *The Blazing World*. First, Cavendish highlights the threat posed by experimental philosophers to the Blazing World by comparing the consequences of natural philosophical inquiry to that of her experimental scientists. Then, within a sequence at the center of *The Blazing World*, Cavendish takes up the story of Paradise which she fundamentally rewrites through the actions of her Eve-like Empress. A range of fallen, or misdirected, masculine practices of inquiry are contrasted to those of the Empress within a dialogue that occurs between her and the "Immaterial Spirits." In this exchange, the normal conclusion to the Genesis story—that the Fall is caused by woman's acquisition of knowledge—is rewritten. In a dialogue that explores the world through modes of inquiry much closer to the practices of natural philosophy, we watch as this Eve figure pursues the boundaries of appropriate knowledge.

Within the first part of *The Blazing World*, the prelapsarian nature of Paradise and the potential threat posed to that unfallen state are positioned as bookends to a narrative all about the boundaries of knowledge. Between these two instances of discovering the disruptive political challenges produced by experimental philosophy, the Duchess speaks with the Immaterial Spirits for ten pages. For, at the very center of the text and almost the exact mid-point between the Empress's two discussions about the postlapsarian consequences of experimental philosophy, the narrative of the Fall is explicitly invoked. The Empress now asks the Spirits "Whether they [the Immaterial Spirits] were none of those Spirits that frighted Adam out of Paradise," inquires about the composition of the Serpent by whom "Eve was tempted," and "desired the Spirits to inform her where the Paradise was" (71–72), thus interweaving questions about the limits of knowledge with the original narrative of the Fall.

In Cavendish's meditations on and challenges to experimental philosophy, as well as to a range of philosophical ideas circulating in the late seventeenth century, issues of gender continue to shape this *Blazing World* sequence and Cavendish's parsing of these schools of thought. The narrative of this Fall sequence has been framed by the much more culpable, male-gendered forms of acquiring answers to the workings of nature: experimentation. And while the exclusive male practice of experimental philosophy threatens to repeat the Fall, the actions of a female natural philosopher suppress Eve's culpability within the *Blazing World*'s re-narrative of the Fall. Within *The Blazing World*, forms of science are not simply gendered. Cavendish uses the story of the Fall to move beyond an inversion of the gendered practices of the Royal Society with implications for the postlapsarian marital, social, and political hierarchies, fundamentally replotted by the center of, and at the center of, Cavendish's narrative.

Ultimately, Cavendish's sustained interspersing of discussions of our Fall from Paradise with accounts of knowledge acquisition shows the redemptive power of knowledge to lie not with experimental science, but instead with her form of natural philosophy. These specific uses of natural versus experimental philosophical modes of inquiry will be much less discernable within *Paradise Lost*. Yet here, as in Milton's narrative, we see how integrated the acquisition of knowledge is within accounts of Paradise, the (potential) loss of Paradise, and the gendering of responsibility for Paradise's loss. What Cavendish does, after framing this sequence with a male-gendered portrait of dangerous knowledge, is to offer a redeemed image of an Eve who discovers, and respects, the boundaries of knowledge. At the exact midpoint of Cavendish's narrative, the Spirits answer that "Natural desire of knowledg . . . is not blameable, so you do not go beyond what your Natural Reason can comprehend" (85). This moment will simultaneously invoke and repress the narrative of the Fall. The statement by the Immaterial Spirits, which praises the Empress's, and Cavendish's, form of natural philosophy while implicitly critiquing experimental philosophy, is prompted by the Empress's question about the Fall. As her sequence of questions turns to the original Genesis tale, she queries its cause: "Then she would fain know, how it came, that both Spirits and Men did fall from a blessed into so miserable a state and condition as they are now in" (85), her question mirroring Milton's epic question, "say first what case / Mov'd our Grand Parents in that happy State . . . to fall off / From their Creator, and transgress his Will" (1.28–31). Yet here, the question is posed by a female character who is explicitly a stand-in for the female author. Nor is this the only place that the Genesis narrative has been invoked in the exchange with the "Immaterial Spirits": the Empress has recalled the entire narrative of the temptation for the reader when she asks about our eviction from Eden: she had asked whether it was "an evil Spirit that tempted Eve . . . or . . . the Serpent?" (81).

By explicitly recalling the event in the Garden, the Empress returns us to the question of Eve's culpability at the center of this Fall narrative. Yet while the scenario of the Fall is recalled for us, it is not replayed. This entire sequence or conversation consequently presents a double vision of the story of the Fall. The event that occurred—Eve tasting the fruit—stands alongside a rewritten version of it, but now one where Eve does not take the fruit. In the exchange with the Immaterial Spirits, the possible answers to the question of how mankind fell from a blessed state are evaded. When the Empress asks "how it came that both Spirits and Men did fall from a blessed into so miserable a state and condition," she is told "By disobedience." But when she inquires "Whence this disobedient sin did proceed," the Spirits assert instead the boundaries of knowledge: "But the Spirits desired the Empress not to ask them any such questions, because they went beyond their knowledg" (85). Instead of providing an answer, the Spirits model an alternative ending to the story of our temptation. In stating that they cannot go "beyond their knowledge," they initiate another version of the story of the Garden. What goes "beyond their knowledge" becomes the very "knowledge" that lead to the Fall. Part warning, part lesson, this expression of knowledge's necessary bounds allows the Eve-like Empress to replay the Fall. Since the story is not retold to us, Eve's initial culpability is deemphasized. We also see the boundaries of knowledge observed, not transgressed. This new story can occur, of course, because of the Eve-like figure who transforms the end of the story. As Cavendish ironically restages the Fall, she offers us a questioning Eve/Empress at the original site of Paradise who does not "go beyond" the boundaries of knowledge: "Then I'le ask no more, said the Empress, for fear I should commit some error" (85). First redeemed through her entrance back into Paradise, and then later by her acquiescing to appropriate boundaries placed around experimental philosophy, the Empress becomes a redeemed version of Eve.

While critiquing experimental philosophy through her replaying of the story of the Fall, Cavendish will simultaneously reject another seventeenth-century interrogation of the Genesis text: Cabbalistic interpretations of the Fall, which were a central goal of philosophers like Franciscus Mercurius van Helmont, who engaged the opening Genesis books of the Bible. Interwoven into the Empress's discussion of the Immortal Spirits are repeated references to Cabbalistic practices through which Cavendish rejects this alternate route to accessing, and understanding, Genesis. In the voices of the Immortal Spirits, the men searching for the "Jews Cabbala" are ruled "mere Cheats" by the spirits (66), who also insist that "not all Cabbala's are true" (72) and reject any "mystery in Numbers" (74) common to Cabbalistic study. They conclude, "We think . . . that *Cabbalists* have nothing else to do but to trouble their heads with such useless Fancies" (74). In what appears an analogous rejection of their intervention into, and attempts to understand, the Garden narrative, Cavendish elevates her engagement of the Garden and the story of the Fall over that of experimental philosophers and Cabbalists alike. Perhaps she saw the highly gendered linguistic barriers to Cabbalist study—women rarely learned Hebrew—as paralleling the barriers imposed by the Royal Society's scientific experiments. This rejection of these lines of philosophical thought promising "answers" about the original Garden highlights her own discovery—through the dialogue with the Immortal Spirits—of a proper realignment between knowledge and women. Offering her own interrogation of the "secret" of the Fall, one might say that Cavendish constructs her own Cabbala, even concluding that she will write her own "literary" Cabbala. Yet her "discovery" about the Garden, revealed through the Empress's dialogue with these Spirits, rewrites the original narrative of the Fall by placing limits around access to knowledge. This female Eve figure thus uses her own version of natural philosophy to reason past the limits of the new science and the esoteric inquiries embedded in the "secrets" of Cabbala.

A portrait of the original Eve at the scene of temptation, then, is offered to the reader only to be evacuated of her postlapsarian significance. As we have seen throughout *Engendering the Fall*, of course, women's status after the Fall plots the mechanism of hierarchy upon which political authority rests. This restaging and regendering of the story of the Fall thus has profound implications for hierarchy within marriage as well as within the political structure of Cavendish's Paradise. In this prelapsarian space, a wife can receive "absolute power to rule and govern all that World as she pleased" (13) as the Empress does from the Emperor. The Fall is not presented as the cause of awarding of authority to one or the other member of the marital unit. For Milton, of course, the awarding of inappropriate, politically inflected authority to a woman leads to Adam's inevitable fall: Adam's description of Eve as "so absolute" directly precedes the Fall (8.547). Yet in the prelapsarian Blazing World, the Emperor can accord his wife "absolute power" without destroying this "peaceful Society" characterized by "united Tranquility, and Religious Conformity" (102). Thus, Cavendish provides an alternative marital and political structure that can exist because of the restaged Garden moment. By acceding to the boundaries of knowledge, and eschewing the "disobedience" that caused the first Fall, the Empress can replay Eve's role by redeeming women from the subsequent hierarchy plotted onto marital and political structures.

The utter disappearance of the Emperor, in whom power would normally reside, throughout most of the first book of the *Blazing World* underscores the suspension of postlapsarian strictures on a gendered hierarchy in marriage. When the Emperor does reappear in the second book, his interactions with his wife resemble those between consulting heads of state as they discuss an invasion plan into the Empress's native ESFI. We see how intimately the plotting of an alternative view of female political power depends on the structure of the very first marriage. The form of autonomy that the Empress receives from her husband is simultaneously marital and political: the Empress operates independently throughout the narrative, traveling to other worlds with her friend and scribe, the Duchess, and invading hostile countries. No femme covert she, these actions seem possible precisely because of the Blazing World's identity as

Paradise. Thus, as the Empress assumes political power to free her homeland, the limitations of a gendered hierarchy of power are transgressable precisely because the Empress did not violate (appropriate) boundaries of knowledge. Rewriting the narrative of the Fall thus simultaneously makes possible the rewriting of women's relation to political authority.

This disruption of the alignment between marital and political authority explains the appeal for Cavendish of embedding echoes to Queen Elizabeth within her account of the Empress.[17] Certainly, invoking the political acumen of the Virgin Queen assigns to the Empress even more associations of and to power. Yet this reference back to Elizabeth also highlights the revisions that Cavendish has accomplished in her text. Traditionally, a married women would have been unable to rule because a subservient wife cannot be a power-wielding queen. Now, a wife can have imperial power because Cavendish's prelapsarian utopia has rewritten the originary narrative of marital authority.[18] The second book's invasion of ESFI thus allows for a doubled "restoration" within the narrative; the Eve-like Empress can return to her own world and be "restor'd" to a form of political power that women had been denied because of the Fall. Redeemed by her entrance into Paradise at the opening of *The Blazing World*, the Empress gains in this world what all women have lost. Restaging the Fall, combined with portraying male philosophers as posing the greater challenge to remaining in Eden, makes it possible for this self-determining Empress, wife, and woman to achieve a politically and theologically inflected "restoration."

Philosophy thus redeems the Eve-like Empress as Cavendish reimagines the restorative power of (types of) knowledge. Just as Milton will insist upon, the "new science" cannot, despite the assertions of the Royal Society, be separated from social and political organization. Cavendish's narrative of the new science creates space for an alternate marital structure and consequent female political autonomy. In doing so, Cavendish could be said to actively reject the basis of Filmerian monarchical justification. Simultaneously she offers a radically different portrait of women within the political sphere than Locke will offer in the *Two Treatises*. That Cavendish comes to engage political issues in her treatment of natural and experimental philosophy suggests once again that considerations of the "new science" could not occur outside of larger debates surrounding political organization and disruption. This is where Cavendish's and Milton's engagement with scientific discourses are so similar. Knowledge acquisition is a cultural, social, and political practice. It can not be walled off in Restoration England. Much, of course, differs in the answers that each provide. Cavendish's redemptive portrait of Eve is accomplished through an attack on the masculine prerogative of scientific knowledge and affects the necessary reign of husband over wife. But Cavendish's Eve figure is not simply less culpable: direction from the Countess actually results in the prevention of a fall into social discord. When the Empress realizes the potential for political upheaval as a result of experimental philosophy, she takes action—the dissolution of her societies—to prevent such a fall from this prelapsarian Paradise. Cavendish thus entirely rescripts the Garden tale, and its many social and political implications, through a rejection of experimental science.

This very detailed response by Cavendish is generalized in Milton's narrative. His consideration of the appropriate boundaries to knowledge, the consequences of gendering knowledge acquisition for the purposes of social order, and the language that characterized the investigations of the "new science" embedded into his poem will not repeal the Fall. Nor will he generate as radical a revision of marital authority. Yet both Milton and Cavendish are posing a similar question about the practices of the Royal Society and offering answers through their portrait of Eve. The distinction in their responses only furthers the productive nature of considering these two texts in concert. How they treat the discourses of and around the Royal Society is set into a relief that draws out the details in their responses: the very shadows cast by the other text bring its texture into focus for the reader.

In *Paradise Lost*, Milton considers the implications of acquiring "knowledge" in the context of the Restoration project of promoting aspects of experimental science, a search for knowledge the Royal Society claimed could occur without threat to social or political order. *Paradise Lost* consequently engages aspects of the new science in initially broader terms than does Cavendish: Milton represents the dangers that knowledge poses, his poem refuting the possibility that "knowledge" could be seen as a nondisruptive force, an avenue into, rather than than the cause of eviction from, Eden. Again gendering access to knowledge, Milton's poem seems to imply that the more disruptive force is female: Milton's Eve does transgress the boundaries of knowledge, while Adam transgresses the boundaries of gender authority. The consequences are distinct forms of culpability borne by Adam and Eve, and thus subsequently all men and women. But these distinctions continue to assert the connection between social disruptions posed by knowledge and by destabilized gendered hierarchy. Thus, the "scientific" inquiries made by both Adam and Eve point to the very social disruption to which knowledge acquisition will necessarily lead, countering the models of knowledge production promoted by the Royal Society.

Shapin and Schaffer have illustrated how the Royal Society modeled a form of knowledge production that could be detached from larger political and social divisions, accomplished largely by establishing boundaries around the experimental philosophers and the space in which they performed their experiments. The members of the Society were limited to those who were seen as invested in a portrait of intellectual cooperation, not of dissent. Competing notions of knowledge, in religion as well as philosophy, had been a major force in producing insurgent religious sectarians and political rebels during the 1640s and 1650s. The Royal Society would thus offer an alternative model, based on limited membership, rules for producing truth, and a strategy based on producing consent. For this very reason, many suspect Hobbes was excluded from membership. Both his model of society described in the *Leviathan* and his personal antagonism for experimental science testified to his unwillingness to model philosophical, or political, agreement and consent. Further, the conducting of these experiments in private, to which Hobbes explicitly objected, had the effect of further sequestering the dangers of knowledge from the rest of the culture. Generating themselves as a kind of intellectual elite, even as "priests of nature" (Shapin and Schaffer, 319), members of the Royal Society could conduct investigations outside of public spaces that theoretically would prevent disruption of the political or social order.

The goal was the production of knowledge in a form that would no longer disrupt the culture. Henry Oldenburg, in correspondence with Milton in the last half of the 1650s, described "knowledge" as that which "does not disquiet the mind but settles it" (quoted in Shapin and Schaffer, 299), a statement beautifully summarizing the project behind the Royal Society. The political implications were enormously significant: "The experimental philosophers aimed to show those who looked at their community an idealizing reflection of the Restoration settlement" (Shapin and Schaffer, 341). A propagandistic force for intellectual inquiry, the Royal Society supported the (fragile) restored monarchy of Charles II, and thus definitely not Milton's views. The ties between the Royal Society and Charles II meant, of course, that the language of a "restoration" spoke to the political conditions of the 1660s as well as to the theological narrative of Genesis, forms of "restoration" we saw interwoven into Cavendish's narrative. The King's connection to the Society was also overt at numerous moments: his awarding of a charter in 1662; the Society's right to publish under their own imprimatur; and Charles II's personal involvement with the Society. In his response to Hobbes's *Dialogus Physicus*, Boyle does not just count the King as a supporter of the Society; he describes Charles as a practitioner. In defending his experiments, Boyle recounts "that Monarch of the *Virtuosi*, the King" who joined them as a participant in an experiment: "so great a Monarch, and so great a *Virtuoso*," they bring to "his Majesty" proof of a particular process (*New Experiments . . . An Examen of Mr. Hobs's Doctrine*, 147 [L2r], 297 [U5r]). As a "virtuoso," Charles is counted as a participant in the gathering of information, as well as a financial supporter of the activities of the scientists.[19] Despite declarations of their experiments as standing outside of social or political conflicts, praise of the nation's monarch as a reigning "Virtuosi" politicizes the activities within the Society. As the boundaries established to prevent political disagreements were dropped to allow the restored monarch into their Society, the fictional nature of such boundaries became exposed.

As Shapin and Schaffer have illustrated, "Solutions to the problem of knowledge are solutions to the problem of social order" (332); their formula thus suggests that problematizing the status of knowledge threatens to disrupt social order. Their analysis of the debates between Boyle and Hobbes thus highlights the politically fraught category of "knowledge" during the Restoration while providing a broader context for considering both Cavendish's and Milton's engagement with the status of knowledge in the Garden. While Cavendish explicitly engages the practices and methodologies of the Royal Society to regender disruptive knowledge, including the Society's masculine exclusivity, Milton considers the socially disruptive nature of knowledge through his portrait of Adam and of Eve. He expresses knowledge's disruptive nature through one of the most contested scientific concepts in Renaissance culture and interpretative cruxes in Milton criticism: the possible Copernican structure of the universe argued within Galileo's writings. In choosing the immensely contested issue of a heliocentric versus geocentric universe, Milton selects perhaps the most ideologically disruptive scientific debate of the period through which to explore the problem of knowledge.

Much excellent work has been produced by literary scholars attempting to unravel the question of Milton's relation to Galileo, and specifically Raphael's condemnation of the pursuit of knowledge of the cosmos in Book 8. Does the prelapsarian condition in the Garden suspend this seeming condemnation of Galileo? Or does Milton employ Raphael's language of the uncertainty of knowledge to evade a decisive answer about the construction of the universe? Milton's biography resists stable answers. Amy Boesky's "Milton, Galileo, and Sunspots: Optics and Certainty in *Paradise Lost*" argues convincingly for Milton's detailed knowledge of and engagement with Galileo's ideas in the *Sunspot Letters*, though she sees Milton's invocation of the sun "spots" as "at once sites of certainty, courage, . . . genius, and contradictorily blind spots, markers for the limits and dangers of scopic power" (40). Milton's sympathy for Galileo's besieged position seems much more certain: he expressly condemns Galileo's treatment in his 1644 *Areopagitica*, "a prisoner to the Inquisition for thinking in astronomy otherwise than the Franciscan and Dominican licensers thought" (738).

While the Galileo question in Book 8 will continue to be debated, the larger context of Restoration science and its relation to social (dis)order becomes invoked by Milton's engagement of the universe's workings. Raphael's asserting of "boundaries" to knowledge could well be aligned to the limitations placed around knowledge production and dissemination by the Royal Society. While I have no interest in reading Raphael as a figure for the Society, the pursuit of explicit scientific truths in *Paradise Lost* does lead to a major disruption in the community of the Garden. The Book 8 engagement with astronomy, and specifically Galileo's challenge to the religious establishment of Italy, thus needs to be viewed through the attempted containment of "knowledge" during England's Restoration period. The Royal Society postulates the existence of "scientific" debate outside of political upheaval. Yet Milton's discussion of the boundaries of knowledge in Book 8 exposes as unworkable the Royal Society's attempts to sequester knowledge from social conflict. Further, by engaging, in gendered terms, the question of boundaries around the members practicing scientific inquiry, Milton suggests how the pursuit of knowledge will escape both rigorously established lines of pure, apolitical inquiry as well as the boundaries of gender: Eve will participate in knowledge production and, ultimately, its fatal acquisition. While Cavendish will use gender to argue against experimental philosophy and embodying controlled knowledge within her Eve-like Empress, Milton will illustrate the unboundable threats of knowledge that Adam and Eve alike expose. Employing gender for different purposes, Cavendish and Milton nonetheless jointly challenge, even penetrate, the boundaries around debate that the Royal Society attempted to establish.

In both *Paradise Lost* and *The Blazing World*, the very same question about the organization of the cosmos becomes the opportunity to establish the limits of observational science. The very repetition of the Galileo question in these two texts suggests how central the issue of socially disruptive knowledge was in the mid-1660s. One of the Empress's strongest criticisms of her Experimental Philosophers emerges as they struggle with Galileo's assertions: "for some said, they perceived that the Sun stood still, and the Earth did move around it; others were of the opinion that they both did move; and others said again, that the Earth stood still, and the Sun did move" (26).[20] For Cavendish, the resulting "disputes" (26) argue for the significant, political conflicts produced by aspects of this "new science." In this way, the concerns illustrated in her romance accord with those in Milton's prelapsarian tale.

Adam's well-known question about the structure of the universe introduces the dispute that challenged the Empress's society and was the prompt for Galileo's trial by the Inquisition: does the Earth move around the sun? Do the stars "roll/ Spaces incomprehensible" to accommodate a "sedentary Earth" (18.19–20, 32)? Raphael's response initially articulates the intricate layers of knowledge embedded in the question:

. . . What if the Sun
Be Centre to the World, and other Starts
By his attractive virtue and their own
Incited, dance about him various rounds?
Thir wandring course now high, now low, then hid,
Progressive, retrograde, or standing still,
In six thou seest, and what if sev'nth to these
The Planet Earth, so steadfast though she seem,
Insensibly three different Motions move? (8.122–30)

Occupying the same role that the Empress plays in the *New Blazing World*, Raphael appears to establish intellectual boundaries for the poem—and thus to express an opinion much like that of Margaret Cavendish:

. . . Heav'n is for thee too high
To know what passes there; be lowly wise:
Think only what concerns thee and thy being;

Dream not of other Worlds, what Creatures there
Live, in what state, condition or degree,
Contented that thus far hath been reveal'd
Not of Earth only but of highest Heav'n. (8.172–78)

Raphael's placing of limits onto knowledge also guides his critique of tele-scopes. In detailing that the design of the cosmological map of the universe is partly meant to dissuade certain human investigations, Raphael states that "God to remove his ways from human sense, / Plac'd Heav'n from Earth so far, that earthly sight, / If it presume, might err in things too high, / and no advan-tage gain" (8.119–22). Milton's placement of the reference to Galileo, the "Tus-can artist" using his "optic glass," in the Hell of Book 1 could be read as reenforcing Raphael's seeming critique of the instrument, the very tool banned by the Empress because telescopes are deluding "false Informers" (27).[21]

These invocations of Galileo in both Cavendish's and Milton's narratives underscore the threats associated with Galileo's thought during the period. The most significant scientific disagreement in the seventeenth century, Galileo's "thinking in astronomy" posed the most ideologically revolutionary alternative to the structure of the universe. Tried and found guilty by the In-quisition for supporting a Copernican universe in his *Dialogues*, Galileo's text was placed on the Catholic Church's index of banned books in 1633. A trial that intellectuals in Europe followed closely, it illustrated the power of the Catholic Church to control freedom of inquiry while simultaneously showing the severe consequences of holding, and publishing, heretical ideas. Its effect on free inquiry was chilling: Descartes even modified his publishing plans for "Le Monde," a text in which he followed Copernicus.[22]

Galileo's experience, which Milton not only knew but could well have heard from the astronomer himself, defined the individually and culturally disruptive possibilities of scientific ideas. Yet it also illustrated how intertwined religious dissent and dispute were within scientific innovation. Galileo's example thus explicitly countered the assertions of the Royal Society that scientific discov-eries could be insulated from cultural dissent and social unrest. While Cavendish illustrates specific political dangers posed to the Blazing World as a result of determining truth through the telescope, Milton considers broad po-litical and social disruptions necessarily prompted by modes of inquiry such as those of Galileo. By redirecting a reading of the "Galileo question" toward the issue of science's disruption of the social and political realms, the interpre-tive milieu for evaluating Milton's gesture to Galileo and other experimental practices becomes the necessarily politicized identity of the Royal Society. One advantage of this approach is the opportunity to avoid a reading overly influenced by Milton's biography: the Book 8 inquiry about the cosmos is bet-ter evaluated through the broader "question" of the production of scientific knowledge during the Restoration.

While references to Galileo occur three times within the epic, allusions to

Galileo's theory are embedded within recurring descriptions of the workings of the cosmos. Book 8 offers the most highly contested exchange between Raphael and Milton, beginning as a question about how the universe works and ending in Raphael's statement about appropriate limits to knowledge. Yet earlier, uncontested gestures toward the structure of the cosmos dot the text. In Book 4, as Uriel looks over the universe, the Copernican and Ptolemaic systems are both offered to us through an "or," suggesting an absence of contention over the irresolvability of the question:

. . . whither the prime Orb,
Incredible how swift, had thither roll'd
Diurnal, or this less voluble Earth
By shorter flight to th' East. (4.592–95)

Here, the narrator casually offers both options to the reader. As many critics have suggested, Milton appears to appropriate the multiplicity possible within Galileo's practices to evade the certainty of one system over another. Even in his only explicit invocation of Galileo, Milton's representation of the astronomer's practice is marked by absence of certainty: "by night the Glass / of Galileo, *less assured*, observes / Imagin'd Lands and Regions in the Moon" (5.261–63; my emphasis). Here, the mechanics of the cosmos are expressed independently of questions about social or political organization; before the creation of Adam and Eve, the status of cosmological organization operates outside of the (human) social consequences of knowledge. I will be suggesting that disputes over the cosmos must emerge when such scientific issues are interwoven with social or political issues.

Within Book 8, prompted by Eve's Book 4 question and articulated by Adam, the social significance of Galileo's discoveries transforms an account of cosmological possibilities into explicit commentary on the social and gendered nature of the human world.[23] Posing problems to a gendered hierarchy will make knowledge dangerous, and Book 8's discussion of the cosmic order quickly becomes a metaphor for the organization of the body politic—an order necessarily plotted onto a gendered hierarchy. Thus, as in Cavendish's return to Paradise, humans' access to knowledge, in its various forms, is inflected by issues of gender. As many critics of this sequence have noted, the perfectly balanced Book 8 introduces us to questions about an inversion of hierarchy—here in the cosmos—and concludes with an inversion of gendered hierarchy.[24] Unlike pre-Edenic references to the organization of the cosmos, Adam's questions to Raphael insist, through his language choices, on the connection between the Copernican debate and social order. In describing the seeming "disproportions" of "Nature" that did "So many nobler Bodies . . . create" to encircle "the sedentary Earth, / That better might with far less compass move" (27–28, 32–33), Adam suggests that an appropriate social hierarchy has been disrupted, even inverted: by his calculations, the Earth is

"Serv'd by more noble than herself" (34). Raphael's response clarifies the terms of Adam's inversion of hierarchy: in supposing "That bodies bright and greater should not serve / The less not bright," Adam is privileging appearance (87–88). In response, Raphael insists "Great / Or Bright infers not Excellence" (90–91).

This focus on appearance and the subsequent misreading of what is more "noble" produce Adam's greater misapprehension. Social order—the "greater" serving the "less"—is potentially disrupted by scientific inquiry. But more fundamentally, gendered order is disrupted. The gendering of the Earth as female bridges Adam's opening discussion with Raphael and the stark upbraiding Adam receives at the end of Book 8. Just as the female Earth is "Serv'd by more noble than herself," so too will Eve be served by her "more noble" husband. In Adam's initial theory, the stars and sun will circle around the "fruitful Earth" just as Adam imagines himself as circling around Eve in his description at the book's end. Nor are Adam and Eve, and man and woman, the only gendered objects here: the sustained gendering of the cosmos reinforces this inverted hierarchy. As John Guillory details for us, the sun which may circle around the (female) Earth is male: "Whether the Sun predominant in Heav'n / Rise on the Earth, or the Earth rise on the Sun, / He from the East his flaming road begin" (160–62).

The gendering of Earth and Sun, and thus the powerful domestic implications of cosmological order, prepares us for Adam's second, perhaps even greater, error within his conversation with Raphael. Just as Adam initially interpreted the sun as more noble than the earth, he has now "attribute[ed] overmuch to things / Less excellent" by focusing on the "fair" "outside" of Eve (565-66, 568). Though Adam realizes that Eve is "in outward show / Elaborate, of inward less exact," he nonetheless seems to "serve" her despite his greater nobility as a man:

For well I understand in the prime end
Of Nature her th'inferior, in the mind
And inward Faculties, which most excel,
In outward also her resembling less
His Image who made both, and less expressing
The character of that Dominion giv'n
O'er other Creatures; yet when I approach
Her loveliness, so absolute she seems
And in herself complete, so well to know
Her own, that what she wills to do or say,
Seems wisest, virtuousest, discreetest, best. (540–50)

The language of "Serv'd by more noble than herself" is repeated in his account of how "Authority and Reason on her wait," as the "nobleness" that should belong to the greater, male, figure is now accorded to Eve.

While Adam was clearly expected to model his thoughts based on the ear-

lier rebuke he received on the boundaries of scientific investigation, the astronomy and gender hierarchy lesson has been equally lost on him: while he may
be "attribúting overmuch to things / Less excellent," he seems not to "per-
ceiv'st" this (8.565–66). His perception faulty, he misreads through "sense"
rather than being directed by "reason." Through the subject of Eve, then, we
are returned to the problems of scientific inquiry. We have seen this same move
in Cavendish, who reminds us of the distinction between "sense" and "reason"
at the core of the disagreement between experimental philosophers and natural philosophers: "Reason must direct first how sense ought to work; and so
much as the rational knowledge is more noble than the sensitive, so much of
the speculative part of philosophy more noble than the mechanical" (196).
Adam apprehends the world through sense, which prompts scientific questions
for which he will be rebuked. Furthermore, this same focus on sense, on the
"outward" appearance of Eve, results in his violation of the social and gendered order. As in Cavendish's narrative, where the faulty pursuit of "sense"
over "reason" will result in the Fall, Adam's questions on the stars simultaneously disrupt an hierarchical account of gender relations that will ultimately
lead to (his) fall. Adam's Book 8 exchange with Raphael illustrates that the Fall
is prompted by a two-pronged violation of appropriate boundaries: searching
for knowledge, which will disrupt a gendered, and thus political, hierarchy.[25]

Eve's fall in Book 9 is equally framed by many of the issues within Adam's
exchange with Raphael. And yet here, the more general issues of scientific inquiry become specified through certain motifs that characterized the practices
of the Royal Society and become embedded into Milton's account of the Fall.
While I will be reading the central moment of the Fall against these details of
experimental philosophy, my broader claim is that Milton's opposition to the
Royal Society was, if you will, more political than philosophical[26]: the claims
of apolitical knowledge, of acquiring information outside of—and without dis-
turbing—the bounds of social or political practices was, for Milton, untenable.
As we saw in discussions of the cosmos, the structure of the universe can be
presented without conflict before the introduction of Adam and Eve. Once a
social context for knowledge exists, though, that social framework will interact
with, even interfere with, "scientific" knowledge. This broader statement thus
allows me to both agree and disagree with aspects of Karen Edwards's *Milton
and the Natural World*. The book's larger claim, that access to the natural world
provided by experimental philosophers such as Hooke had an appeal for Milton, is thorough and convincing; she effectively records the many ways in
which the Book of Nature is consulted and reconfigured in Milton's Edenic
narrative. In terms of the specific uses that Milton will make of terms and
method within Royal Society practices, though, I disagree with elements of her
argument. The representation of the figure of Eve in Book 9 sustains the very
problem of bounding knowledge illustrated in Book 8; simultaneously distinctions between natural and experimental philosophy appear integrated into

Eve's actions. As in the Book 8 sequence, Milton appears to introduce the category of gender in order to dispute the broader apolitical claims of the Royal Society; their "scientific" inquiries and specific modes of apprehending the world generate the very social disruptions recorded in the poem.

In *Milton and the Natural World,* Karen Edwards offers an intriguing reading of Eve as a "new philosopher"; Edwards even accords to Eve "the instincts of a Boylean witness. [Eve's] attitude perfectly combines experimental skepticism and open-mindedness" (21, 36). I find immensely convincing, but for different reasons, Edwards's portrait of Eve as an experimental philosopher. Later, I will suggest that Eve's reaction to the temptation actually appears to internalize one of the central tenets of experimental philosophy: the valuing of sense experience over reason that we saw embedded into Adam's exchange with Raphael. But first, any discussion of Eve's affiliation, positive or negative, with "experimental science" in the period needs to consider the heavily overdetermined word "experiment"; both the historical context of the word and its narrative role in the poem require our attention when valuing Eve's identity as an "experimental" philosopher.

As we know, Eve tempts Adam in Book 9 with language that invokes the theological sense of "experience": "On my experience, Adam, freely taste," she encourages her husband. In a critical tradition that goes back to Stanley Fish's *Surprised by Sin,* this word "experience" has been linked to "empirical science," an anachronistic meaning when applied to this poem (Edwards, 18). Yet a more historically appropriate word is the one that Eve employs once she recognizes the full weight of her crime: in Book 10, Eve turns instead to the term "experiment" [27]:

Adam, by sad experiment I know
How little weight my words with thee can find,
Found so erroneous, thence by just event
Found so unfortunate. (10.967–70)

Eve's use of the phrase "sad experiment" in this passage might appear to mean that Eve has tested and found her "words" to have little weight at this moment in the story. Yet, at this very moment in the narrative of Book 10, Eve's words have had extraordinary weight: her pathos-filled language of fault that proceeded this statement prompts Adam's "reconcilement" with Eve 25 lines earlier (10.943). The words she has just uttered, those that follow the "sad experiment" of her fall, prove to be neither "erroneous" or "unfortunate." Thus, the "sad experiment" is, instead, her testing of the injunction: her act of falling is the "sad experiment" that has proved "so erroneous . . . so unfortunate" (10.969–70).[28]

To describe her fall as a "sad experiment" casts significant doubt on a positive, or even ambivalent, treatment of experimental philosophy in the poem. The word "experiment," particularly to describe the activities of Boyle, graced numerous titles of works coming out of the Royal Society in the earlier 1660s: *New experiments Physico-Mechanicall, Touching the Air* in 1660, "A Physico-Chymical Essay, containing an Experiment . . ." and "A Proëmial Essay . . . with some considerations touching Experimental Essays in General" in 1661, *Some Considerations touching the Usefulnesse of Experimental Natural Philosophy* in 1663, and *Experiments and Considerations Touching Colours* in 1664 show the prominence, and specificity, of this term in the years preceding Milton's publication of *Paradise Lost*. Among all authors, Boyle uses the word most frequently to signify his form of philosophy, though participants in the emerging area of experimental science also publish tracts employing the word "experiment." Abraham Cowley's 1661 *A Proposition for the Advancement of Experimental Philosophy* is a blueprint for the organizational, even architectural, structure of a college like that of the Royal Society. And Henry Power's 1664 *Experimental Philosophy, in Three books: containing New Experiments Microscopical, Mercurial, Magnetical . . .* details its participation in Boyle's definition of experimentation within its title. Even Margaret Cavendish, a strong and satirical voice against experimental philosophy and the practices it incorporated, titles her 1666 text *Observations upon Experimental Philosophy*, a clear indication, according to Judith Moore, that Cavendish perceived the growing market share of experimental philosophy when invoking this specific meaning of "experiment" (9). While instances of the use of "experiment" that accord to our modern definition of "experience" occur in some titles, the publications of Boyle and his associates largely redefine the meaning of the word: "experiment"-ing becomes the practice of acquiring (scientific) knowledge.[29]

This failed "experiment" of Eve's—of tasting and then falling—prompts us to consider other uses from the vocabulary of Royal Society scientists that echo through this narrative of the Garden story. Eve's reaction to the temptation actually appears to internalize one of the central tenets of experimental philosophy: the valuing of sense experience over reason. Figures like Cavendish and Hobbes make parallel distinctions between the modes of, and hierarchy of, knowledge in natural versus experimental philosophy. In her *Observations*, Cavendish asserts:

Reason must direct first how sense ought to work. . . . But our age being more for deluding experiments than rational arguments . . . doth prefer sense before reason, and trusts more to the deceiving sight of their eyes, and deluding glasses, than to the perception of clear and regular reason. (197)

In fact, this age will "pronounce the truth without any appeal to reason" (197), since the "bare authority of an experimental philosopher" derives from sense alone. Like Cavendish, Hobbes also denies such authority to sense: "Philosophy is such knowledge of Effects or Appearances, as we acquire by true Ratiocination from the knowledge we have first of their Causes or Generation: And again, of such Causes or Generations as may be from knowledge first their Effects" (*Elements of Philosophy*, 2).[30] Hobbes, too, elevates "Ratiocination," since this was how one acquires "knowledge" of "Appearances." In contrast to these natural philosophers' privileging of reason or sense, experimental philosophers—in whose midst I will place Eve—were concerned with extending the dominion of the senses. Robert Hooke's aim was the "inlargement of the dominion, of the Senses," which could be achieved through instruments, resulting in the improvement of "our other Senses, of hearing, smelling, tasting, touching" (Aa2r, Ab2v).

In line with Hobbes's and Cavendish's resistance to elevating "sense," "appearances, or apparent effects" over "reason" or "ratiocination," Milton values reason over sense in his representation of Eve's fall. In fact, it is Eve's very privileging of sense that becomes her fall.[31] Responding to what she sees, Eve is prompted by the talking snake to start down an intellectual path that moves her farther and farther away from "reason."[32] Ultimately, she becomes entirely controlled by her senses:

Fixt on the Fruit she gaz'd, which to behold
Might tempt alone, and in her ears the sound
Yet rung of his persuasive words, impregn'd
With Reason, to her seeming, and with Truth;
Meanwhile the hour of Noon drew on, and wak'd
An eager appetitie, raised by the smell
So savory of that Fruit, which with desire,
Inclinable now grown to touch or taste,
Solicited her longing eye . . . (9.735–43)

This passage is characterized by the sensuousness of sight, sound, touch, and taste that finally overpowers Eve. As her senses direct her, rather than her rationality, Eve appears to give into the very "empire of the senses" praised by Thomas Birch in his description of Robert Hooke's, and the Royal Society's, experimental goals.[33] That "empire" was not only of the senses but of a controlling mode of sensuality. Of particular importance in Hooke's language in the 1665 *Micrographia* was the trope of rapture:

And I do not only propose this kind of Experimental Philosophy as a matter of *high rapture* and *delight* of the mind, but even as a material and sensible *Pleasure*. So vast is the variety of Objects . . . that I dare compare the contentment which they will injoy, not only to that of contemplation, but even to that which most men prefer of the very Senses themselves. (Ad2r, my emphasis)

As in the account of Eve, Hooke describes the experience of experimental philosophy through its tactile satisfactions, stressing "delight" and "material and sensible Pleasure." The language of "high rapture" in the face of such "delight" seems equally relevant to Eve's willing concession to her senses. The "delight" she experiences could be described as nothing less than a rapture: "Intent now wholly on her taste, naught else / Regarded" (9.786–87).

Such "delight" granted by her elevated senses finds common ground with the constellation of images, and pleasures, in Hooke's "Preface." If Satan serves to heighten the senses through his promotion of the fruit, Hooke imagines just such possibilities for "an inlargement of the dominion . . . of the Senses" (*Micrographia*, Aa2r). His enthusiasm for the newly discovered practices of experimentation fuels language about the luxuriousness of the senses that should be preferred to reason:

> For the Members of the Assembly having before their eys so many fatal Instances of the errors and falshoods, in which the greatest part of mankind has so long wandered, because they rely'd upon the strength of humane Reason alone, have begun anew to correct all Hypotheses by sense . . . and to this purpose it has been their principle indeavour to enlarge and strengthen the Senses. (Ag1r)

Summarizing the Royal Society's methodology, we are told that "humane Reason" has, instead, been the cause of man's errancy. As the "Preface" continues, these senses to be "strengthened" and "enlarged" are described at great length. Beginning with sight, Hooke describes the amplification of the power of perception through all of the senses: "And as *Glasses* have highly promoted our seeing, so 'tis not improbable, but that there may be found many *Mechanical Inventions* to improve our other Senses, of *hearing, smelling, tasting, touching*" (Ab2v). And as Hooke details how such strengthening and enlarging of the senses should proceed, tasting is highlighted: "'Tis not improbable also, but that our *taste* may be very much improv'd" (Ac2r).

Eve's own experience of the enlargement of her senses and her progression through them seem suggestively patterned in Hooke's account. Just as Hooke chronicles the senses that will be heightened, ending notably with taste, so too is Eve's fall propelled by the progressive rapture she experiences as a result of her, increasingly powerful, senses. Her "gaz"ing leads to the "sound" of Satan's temptation, which "rais'd by the smell" of the fruit makes Eve "Inclinable now grown to touch or taste" (9.735, 736, 740, 742). At the "evil hour" at which she rashly reaches out, "In Fruit she never tasted" "such delight" (9.787).

This emphasis on the rapture of the senses and the ultimate act of tasting is explicitly integrated into Milton's Garden narrative as it was into Hooke's restorative methodology of experimental philosophy. Hooke takes us back into Paradise, imagining the restorative power of experimental philosophy:

> And as at first, mankind fell by tasting of the forbidden Tree of Knowledge, so we, their Posterity, may be in part restor'd by the same way, not only by beholding and contemplating, but by tasting too those fruits of Natural Knowledge, that were never yet forbidden. (Ab2r–v)

I would not want to suggest that the multivalence of Milton's account of sensual temptation be reduced only to a critique of the "empire of the senses" valued by members of the Royal Society. Nor is Milton's (re)turn to the Garden solely a response to Hooke's 1665 *Micrographia*. Eve's affiliation with the body rather than the mind in this sequence of *Paradise Lost* derives from a longstanding association of women's nature with a sensually and sexually inflected account of the Fall. But the "scientific lady" that she comes to be in this scene sustains the connection between sexuality and the acquisition of knowledge rather than dampening it[34]; the classical, philosophical, and theological conventions about "woman" and the temptation fuse with Eve's "experiment," illustrating the failure of "reason" to direct "sense" how to "work." Following the pattern established by the "empire of the senses" so lauded in accounts of the Society, Eve takes on the role of an experimental philosopher, ultimately relying on the "senses" and thus overriding reason. Milton may be suggesting that experimental philosophy, with its emphasis on sense over reason, is partly the cause of the Fall.[35]

Milton's portrait of Eve's mode of, and the consequences of, questioning the world around her thus differently genders access to, and the creation of, knowledge. The specifics of Eve's queries, first to Adam and then to the nature of the fruit of knowledge itself, continue to align her with the "realm of the senses" so valued by experimental philosophers. When Raphael admonishes Adam about the limitations of knowledge, and the ordering of gender hierarchy, he is responding to her earlier Book 4 question: "wherefore all night long shine these, for whom / This glorious sight, when sleep hath shut all eyes" (4.657–58). She has thus introduced the question of proportion implicit in Adam's question to Raphael.[36] While the narrator may assert that "woman's happiest knowledge and her praise" is to "know no more that what thou bidd'st," her actions speak to a different truth about gendered modes of knowledge acquisition (4.638, 637, 635).

Eve's queries exemplify the poem's significant questions about, and limits set onto, knowledge. While showing that knowledge will violate the boundaries of social stability, Milton also illustrates the permeable walls of science's gendered nature. While a large part of the control over knowledge production within the Royal Society was to be accomplished through limited, and of course an all-male, membership, both Adam and Eve query the nature of the world in the course of *Paradise Lost*. While Royal Society members imagine such limited membership as the mechanism that will allow us to regain the Garden, Milton represents female inquiry as inevitable. Most importantly, the walls the Royal Society erected around knowledge production cannot prevent our fall. The unquenchable desire for knowledge cannot be controlled, in men or women. I have thus presented an argument for Eve as an experimental philosopher, whose inquiries do not "restore" us to but rather evict us from the Garden since the acquisition of knowledge, the search for truth, will necessarily threaten the stability of a culture. Thus, by linking these men's discourses and theories to the falling Eve, Milton challenges the restoration to the Garden, while countering one of the propaganda machines promoting the Stuart "Golden Age."

Promoted by divergent elements within Royal Society practices and ideol-

ogy, Milton and Cavendish frame responses to the nexus of knowledge and social and political organization through the mechanism of gender. Any interpretive strategy, as this intertextual reading, should provide us a new
perspective onto literary and cultural texts. By viewing *The Blazing World* in
concert with *Paradise Lost*, a sustained political narrative emerges within
Cavendish's account of a Paradisical shadow-world. Such a reading updates
the solipsistic, even apolitical, Margaret Cavendish that Catherine Gallagher
introduced in 1988. As Gallagher suggested, the political implications of the
"Golden Age" trope that characterized representations of Charles II's restored
England would not have jarred with Cavendish's unremitting Royalism. In
fact, Cavendish's "restored" Paradise can participate in the celebration of
Charles's political success. She will, though, need to recast, and in fact regender, that Golden Age. For Cavendish, a reassignment of gender authority can
offset our fall into, among other things, a solidified gender hierarchy: the
"restor'd" world of the Stuart Restoration can be accepted, but only if a place
for female, or at least a place for this female's, authority is acknowledged. She
accomplishes that through the female-gendered natural philosophy that resists
the Fall otherwise precipitated by experimental philosophy: in her narrative,
"Eve" and women will not fall.

Milton and Cavendish, then, employ many of the same pieces of the "new
science" puzzle, but arrange them differently. As in Book 8, Milton's account of
the Fall integrates Eve's experimental practice with representations of imagined, or more accurately transgressive, innovations in social and political organization; through the new "science," Adam and Eve imagine, or at least make
imaginable, the very disruptions to gendered hierarchy that generate social disorder. This underscores the "political" response that Milton provides to Royal
Society practices. The Society's language of a "restor'd" Eden buttressed a
broader-based claim for the restoration of a Golden Age through Charles's return. The language in coronation broadsides and commendatory poems asserts
that Charles's "presence shall makes ours a golden age," "For now's return'd the
golden age again" (Pordage, C1r, C2v). "Wee'l live as if the golden age were
now / Return'd," and, as a result, "Wee'l blessed live in innocence" ("Festa
Georgiana," B1v, p. 6). Thus, Charles returns England to this prelapsarian state
of innocence as its redemptive savior: he will "Redeem thy people" as he "assume[s] thy own" country again (*The manner of the Solemnity of the Coronation*). But
the Royalists' Golden Age was Milton's fall from republicanism itself. Milton
would resist such "redemptive" language of the Restoration. And he can reject
this discourse by interweaving, and undermining, the analogous discourse from
the Royal Society's "restorative" Garden narrative into his poem.

As Mary Ann Radzinowicz points out in "The Politics of *Paradise Lost*," the
generic choice of the Genesis story, "radicalized by the Puritans in general and
by Milton" (217), is the inverse of the Utopian, conservative narrative of the
fully Restoration *Blazing World*. Just as her politics, Cavendish's utopian narra-

tive supports the conservative politics of the restored Stuart monarchy. Yet despite their political and generic differences, both of these stories of the Garden narrative interrogate the relationship between scientific knowledge, political stability, and the foundational nature of gender in that relationship. In Chapter 3 we were reminded of the use that Milton makes of the female prophetic voice and body: as with the deployment of Eve's "scientific" inclinations, Milton actually turns the female body against the practices of standardizing and stabilizing meaning in the post-1660 period. Milton's portrait of Eve introduces, through the language of the "new science," the immense power of gender in establishing and maintaining political legitimacy. Because the relationship of the first couple remains that upon which governmental organization rests in this period, the narration of that relationship can also illustrate the government's absence of legitimacy. Though Eve will need to sin in Milton's non-utopian narrative, her significance to the structure of political legitimation is of tantamount importance in the late 1660s. The state necessarily relies on the first relationship to describe, and validate, political authority and order. Instead of locating Eve outside of the acts of constructing political authority, both *Paradise Lost* and *The Blazing World* place her at the center of that story.

Milton's conversation, though not explicitly with Cavendish, occurs over the same issues of science, knowledge, and gender that Cavendish had engaged only a year before. Both of their narratives of Paradise sustain this project's emphasis on the productive nature of the female figure and the female writer within discussions about political organization and order. As we have seen with Hutchinson, Milton could enable writers through his portrait of Eve. Later writers will transform this portrait, rewriting the boundaries he attempts to construct around Eve into enormous possibilities in the last two decades of the seventeenth century. In the final section of the book, I will consider Mary Chudleigh's, Aphra Behn's, and Mary Astell's return back to *Paradise Lost*; the poem aided them in their own boundary-crossing reflections on the gender order and the implications for hierarchy, social and political. In the first of these, we will see Mary Chudleigh return to, and profoundly rewrite, the terms of the "boundaries" that both Cavendish and Milton had attempted to set about knowledge. What lies beyond these boundaries for Chudleigh is both a quite radical rethinking of Milton, marriage, and the gendering of souls themselves. The Genesis narrative thus remains a core motif that late Restoration women writers engage in order to interrogate the social construction of familial and political hierarchies into the late seventeenth century.

Part III
Influences

The final section of this book moves us to the late seventeenth century, taking us to writers—Mary Chudleigh, Aphra Behn, and Mary Astell—who would have looked back historically onto Milton and his narrative of the Fall. More importantly, the Milton they were to engage would have been associated with, and in the eyes of many disgraced by, his regicidal republican politics: the terms of his status as a major canonical figure were thus still being debated by late seventeenth-century critics. The final section of this book also shifts to the historically destabilizing energies located around James II's reign and then the 1688-1689 accession to the throne by William and Mary, a period which saw gender's role in supporting theories of government significantly revised.

As we have seen, the family/state analogy remained prominent throughout the Civil War period: a prophet such as Elizabeth Poole takes it up explicitly in her addresses to the Parliamentary Council, while Lucy Hutchinson is engaging tenets of Filmerian thought throughout *Order and Disorder*. The debate over the family/state analogy will of course receive Locke's sustained attention in the *First Treatise*, where he challenges Filmer's arguments in *Patriarcha*, published posthumously in 1680. While it might be argued that the language of patriarchalist theory had less currency after the 1688 Glorious Revolution, the attacks on Locke's *Two Treatises* into the early eighteenth century show that this theoretical formulation still had followers until the end of the century.[1] In fact, during the late 1680s and 1690s, the relation between marriage and government receives renewed attention as it is first placed under pressure during the Exclusion Crisis and then used to support the terms of the "Glorious Revolution." As Rachel Weil and Lois Schwoerer have detailed, the role of gendered authority in marriage is particularly prominent within the theoretical justifications provided for William and Mary's joint assumption of the throne. While the family and the marital relationship had been debated as models for commonwealth formation or governmental organization during the mid-seventeenth century, the specific details of the marital union now became of central concern. Thus the relationship between the marital and political state clearly remained part of the cultural psyche through the 1690s.

While Locke's treatment of the actual terms of the relationship between a husband and wife was more cursory, the writings of Mary Chudleigh, Mary Astell, and, for different reasons, Aphra Behn begin to explore that relationship in detail. All three writers offer extensive critiques of the union as constituted, consequently challenging—with different goals and different results—aspects of the patriarchialist analogue deployed, and debated, through the Civil War and early Restoration period. Nor does such a focus on the practices and realities of married life (or faux married life, in the hands of Behn), as some critics have suggested, draw these women's writing into the domestic sphere.[2] Chudleigh's, Astell's, and Behn's writings—whether in the novelistic form of the *Love-Letters Between a Nobleman and his Sister*, the utopian essay form of the *Serious Proposal*, or the poetic narrative of the *Song of the Three Children Paraphras'd*—are also works of and on political theory. As I will explore more fully in the conclusion on Locke and the possible inflection of these women's writing into his *Two Treatises*, these writers explore the marital relationship so central to his major governmental treatise.

This historical shift to the last years of the seventeenth century also reconfigures the directions in which influence flows within two chapters and a conclusion. Contemporaries, John Locke, Aphra Behn, Mary Astell, and Mary Chudleigh are exploring the implications of a more nuanced treatment of the institution of marriage in the later seventeenth century. These writers still engage Milton: his version of the Fall remains central to their own interpretations of women's status in the period. These women writers are also negotiating more developed contractarian theory that delivered significant blows to a patriarchalist view of monarchy in both the Exclusion debates and in tracts justifying the ascension of William and Mary. All three writers take up the patriarchalist analogy of the family and the state. Yet they will turn it inside out as they examine how marriage as an institution functions and fails. In the process, these late seventeenth-century writers deploy Milton's own narrative of the first marriage in their own interrogations of an institution that, by century's end, came to be associated with the very "tyranny" Milton decried within the state itself. Milton's political theory as his poetry thus continue to provide these writers access to debates over the family, state, and the institution of marriage into the eighteenth century.

Rewriting Creation: Mary Chudleigh's *The Song of the Three Children Paraphras'd* and *Paradise Lost*

Mary Chudleigh's most anthologized of poems, "To the Ladies," announces her investment in interrogating the institution of marriage and its relationship to governmental organization in the late seventeenth century.

Wife and Servant are the same,
But only differ in the Name:
For when that fatal Knot is ty'd,
Which nothing, nothing can divide:
When she the word *obey* has said,
And Man by Law supreme has made,
then all that's kind is laid aside,
And *nothing left but State* and Pride:
Fierce as an Eastern Prince he grows,
And all his innate Rigor shows:
Then but to look, to laugh, or speak,
Will the Nuptial Contract break.
Like Mutes she Signs alone must make,
And never any Freedom take:
But still be govern'd by a Nod,
And fear her Husband as her God:
Him still must serve, him still obey,
And nothing act, and nothing say,
But what her haughty Lord thinks fit,
Who with the Pow'r, has all the Wit.
Then shun, oh! shun that wretched State,
And all the fawning Flatt'rers hate:
Value your selves, and Men despise,
You must be proud, if you'll be wise. ("To the Ladies"; my emphasis)

In this poem published in 1703, Chudleigh's mode of invoking marriage, and its relation to the state, differs from the use of family/state analogy used twenty years earlier.[1] In 1679–1680, a two-year span that saw the publication of Lucy Hutchinson's first five cantos of *Order and Disorder*, the publication of Filmer's summary of patriarchalist theory, and the possible drafting of Locke's *Two Treatises*,[2] the language of the family was explicitly used in accounts of governmental structure or justifications. Here, Chudleigh inverts such earlier uses of the metaphor. Once a woman enters into a "Nuptual Contract," according to Chudleigh, she loses all "Freedom" as she becomes "govern'd by a Nod." The extremity of a husband is recorded in one of the most egregious images of tyranny, the "Fierce . . . Eastern Prince" who can, and the poem implies does, show "all his innate Rigor" once the act of marriage makes "her Husband as her God." Chudleigh thus critiques the marriage contract through the application of inappropriately applied political hierarchy: instead of employing the family unit as a metaphor to think through the state, Chudleigh employs examples of inappropriate governmental structures to critique the marriage contract.[3]

Chudleigh also goes one step further in her poem: she suggests that, given the inequitable application of hierarchy within this contract, women should avoid marriage itself. She appeals to women to "Then shun, oh! shun that wretched State. . . . Value your selves, and Men despise." Using structures within an earlier patriarchal theory against itself, Chudleigh calls upon women to reject the private, despotic tyranny that is marriage. Women thus can be freed from marital oppression, can exist, in Mary Astell's words, outside of "Subjection" if they remain unmarried (*Reflections*, 10).[4] Yet this conclusion, that the contract itself is too onerous and thus women should not enter into it, is significant in another way. When Chudleigh calls upon women to step outside of this system, she fundamentally undermines the hierarchy of the family unit that certain theorists deployed to justify forms of governmental organization. Chudleigh redefines hierarchy within the family by exposing it as a function of a "Nuptial Contract," but not as a function of the category of gender. The larger consequence is Chudleigh's resulting fundamental challenge to gender as a category upon which governmental hierarchy can be built. Since it is the choice of a woman to enter into a nuptial contract, women can choose to be outside of this. Specific acts by individual women (marriage) will necessitate that they follow the biblical injunctions upon which patriarchal authority rested. But hierarchy—especially political hierarchy—no longer can rely on the biblical injunctions that rest solely on the category of gender.

I am suggesting that Mary Chudleigh exposes, and warns against, the basis of marital oppression while proposing an alternative that threatens certain theoretical justifications for the monarchy. This is a rather radical claim about a poet often linked in politics and style to Tory encomiasts such as John Dryden and Mary Astell. Nor will this be the last such radical claim I make about Chudleigh in this chapter, which will highlight Chudleigh's innovations with marital theory and the category of gender itself. The author of an extensive collection of poems (1703), at least one, possibly two, defenses of women that engage the institution of marriage,[5] and a 1710 essay collection, Chudleigh engaged a series of English cultural debates in concert with philosophical and poetic traditions from her country home near Exeter. She was recognized during her life by Dryden, corresponded with Mary Astell, and lived on in four editions and anthologies throughout the eighteenth and nineteenth centuries. Perhaps it is her Dryden-like style that accounts for her current exclusion from the Norton Anthology of English Literature; alternately, she may have become overshadowed by Astell's rising popularity over the last few decades of canon (re)formation. Yet the range of Chudleigh's writings, the lyrical and political complexity of her verse, her investment in Cambridge Platonist philosophy, and the ideological intervention she makes into debates over marriage in the period, make her a late Restoration figure of significant interest to feminist scholars, intellectual historians, and cultural historians of the period.[6] And as we will see, she is neither an insignificant echo of Astell nor a dismissible writer of "Drydeniana," as her poetry collection is described in the front leaf of a 1703 edition in the Folger Shakespeare Library's collections.

While Chudleigh's emphasis on marriage in "To the Ladies" and in the dialogue poem *The Ladies Defence* links her views to the much better known Astell, Chudleigh's Tory qualifications are less solid. Members of both her husband's and her own Devon-based family had been Parliamentary supporters during the mid-century, though they were "firmly in the Royalist camp" by the Restoration (Ezell, xix). Recent research on Chudleigh suggests, and this chapter will concur, that her affiliation with nonconformists during the late seventeenth century challenges any such unassailable Tory political affiliation. Further, Chudleigh's sustained negotiation of Milton's works, particularly *Paradise Lost*, within her own writings forces us to rethink Chudleigh's poetic strategies as well as political identity. I will be tracing in this chapter the disquietingly—both for the currently accepted view of Chudleigh's political affiliation and possibly for Chudleigh herself—internalized voice of Milton in her works: he appears to provide a narrative framework for some of Chudleigh's works as well as serve as a poetic model.[7] Through what I will be calling a suppressed form of influence, one in which Milton's voice is prominent while ostensibly hidden, we revisit the radical implications of Chudleigh's statements about marriage through parallel rebellious strategies. These are, I will argue, mediated through the figure of Milton, in particular the political valences of his choice of rhyme.

This chapter will thus initially provide a historical framework for considering discourses about marriage, ones revitalized, if you will, by the political implications of William and Mary's theoretically joint rule. Chudleigh's response to these discourses and the constraints of marriage that they delineate in the period lead her to an engagement with Milton's poetry and the late seventeenth-century debate over the aesthetics and politics of rhyme. Her "rebellious" negotiation of Milton becomes embedded into her commentary on the politicized discourse of late seventeenth-century rhyme. An explicit, if suppressed, negotiation of Milton becomes most prominent in Chudleigh's longest poem, *The Song of the Three Children Paraphras'd*; the strands of marital confinement, the political stakes of marriage, a philosophical portrait of the universe and souls within it, and the implications of drawing on Milton's narrative of the Fall will frame the close reading of the *Song* that closes this chapter, one in which the strategy and stakes of Chudleigh's subtle but substantial negotiation of Milton become explicit.

In the *Song*, Chudleigh will challenge the socially organizing practice of the marriage contract by positing and developing a nongendered narrative of souls. A mini-epic, this poem replays the Creation and the Fall through a Platonic spiritualized world, one that allows Chudleigh to escape the limitations placed onto women within the marriage contract. A rewriting of *Paradise Lost*, the *Song* restages Milton's portrait of the Fall and the narrative of postlapsarian culpability. Chudleigh's engagement with the (politicized) debate over rhyme and its associations with revolutionary inclinations thus become overt in the *Song*. This affiliation, interwoven as it is with Milton's political identity as "impious" and even "diabolical" (Joseph Jane, tp) in the late seventeenth century, enables Chudleigh to adopt and adapt the Satanic "gaze" of *Paradise Lost* into her *Song of the Three Children*. By deploying Milton's political identity at the end of the seventeenth century through echoes of the poet, Chudleigh is able to return to, but also to fundamentally reframe, her "radical" claims about gender and marital unions through a portrait of a universe shaped by Platonic thought. Invoking Milton's Creation narrative and appropriating Satan's perspective in the poem, Chudleigh can offer—refracted through the two rebellious figures of Milton and Satan—a revised Creation narrative in which gender is erased. With that erasure comes the suspension of gendered culpability upon which the hierarchy of marriage rests in the period.

By interrogating both the poetic and political implications of Miltonic echoes in Chudleigh's work, this chapter will consider the subversive uses to which the frequently dormant strategy of influence could be put. The suppression of what is generally considered the "authority" conferred by the influence of major poems becomes the central methodological story in Chudleigh's *Song*. Yet this continues the narrative, which we have observed within previous chapters, of the enabling possibilities Milton offered to writers such as Lucy Hutchinson. While the gender politics of Milton's poem are likely perceived by a twenty-first-century audience as stymieing female voices, Chudleigh's innovative enactment of the poem's political and gendered possibilities allows her to inhabit a radical literary and ideological position at the end of the seventeenth century.

Framing Mary Chudleigh's *Ladies Defence*: The Political Dimension of Marriage in the Late Seventeenth Century

While the terms of the family/state analogy are remodeled by the end of the century, the issue of authority in marriage and its relationship to the political world nonetheless would have been inescapable in the last fifteen years of the seventeenth century. As Rachel Weil has illustrated, though contract theorists such as Locke claimed to be rejecting the family/state analogy, the relationship between family authority and monarchical/governmental power continued to be at the core of many political negotiations, especially that of the joint monarchy of William and Mary. In 1688, it became necessary—in order to gain support from the English people—to accord to Mary the role of joint monarch.[8] And yet a crucial provision, that the administration of the kingdom resides in William alone, enacted the analogy of family and state that otherwise would seem to have been displaced by the very contractarian theory that had justified the "Glorious Revolution."[9] By placing a royal couple—as opposed to just a king—on the throne, the problem of gendered authority in marriage became reenacted at the level of the state.

Thus, while contractarian language helped to support the removal of James II as king, the analogy between the family and state was literally enacted during Mary's few years as joint monarch. Weil highlights how debates around the awarding of the monarchy and representations of Mary II maintained the necessary portrait of female submission within government as in marriage. Henry Pollexfen, in arguing for William, explicitly employed the necessity of male authority in the family to maintain a stable state.

And does any think the Prince of Orange will come in to be a subject of his own wife in England? This is not possible, nor ought to be in nature. If you stay till the princess please to give the government to the prince, you gratify the prince, by taking away his wife from him, and giving her the kingdom. If we are for unity and the protestant interest, I hope this marriage was made in heaven, and I hope good effects of it. (Grey, 9.64).

The imagery surrounding Mary II functioned in a similar fashion, reinscribing the analogy of the state and family through accounts of Mary's unity with William. With the analogy still actively structuring this supposedly "contractual" version of government, peace within marriage and peace between these joint monarchs had to be maintained, as well as asserted. Thus, the inconceivability of Mary disagreeing with her husband/joint ruler was constantly expressed. James Abbadie describes that Mary's "love and admiration for him made her submission a delight to her" (quoted in Weil, 115). Paeans to the Queen describe this "Strange paradox of power" which reinscribed a familiar ideological position: the basis for all governmental organization was female submission in marriage. While Mary might "govern," "still [as] the wife [she] obeyed!" (quoted in Weil, 116).[10]

Chudleigh's discussion of marital authority thus occurs within a much broader social and political context, one that may well explain many of her modes of representing women's limitations in marriage. In Chudleigh's first published work, the 1701 *Ladies Defence, or The Bride-Woman's Counsellor Answer'd,*

she embeds extensive political language into accounts of the relationship between men and women, invoking the same imagery of the Eastern tyrant that
characterizes "To the Ladies." The female interlocutor, Melissa, will initially
critique marriage as "Bondage" for women, recommending that they reject
husbands as "Abridgers of their Liberty," who "inslave" wives (165, 166, 170).
The Parson, while ostensibly responding to Melissa, nonetheless confirms
these traits of the "Marriage State": "If to your Lords you strict Allegiance
pay'd, / And their Commands submissively obey'd: / If like wise Eastern Slaves
with trembling Awe / You watch'd their Looks, and made their Will your Law,"
then wives would be treated with "Kindness and Protection" (178–83). Melissa
stresses the abridgement of women's liberty and the loss of their rights, a situation that the Parson validates, echoing Chudleigh's critique of marriage in
her poem "To the Ladies" as she aligns marriage with the practice of Eastern
tyrants. The "Skill to Govern" (189) attributed to husbands by the Parson attempts to naturalize their politically inflected rights, but the overtly political
nature of their rule is exposed—rather than naturalized—by such references
to Eastern tyrants.

While this language suggests the continuance of the family/state metaphor,
the problems of governmental organization haunt this account of marriage.
Now, the battle over the relationship between the subject and governmental
authority—the king—is debated within the family. Further, through Melissa's
language, women are imagined as subjects with "liberty" that marriage forces
them to give up. The language of an individual's political rights becomes located within the center of the very organizational unit that comes to ground
political authority: marriage. While repeating this inversion of the analogy that
marked "To the Ladies," Melissa's language of women's lost "liberty" contains
a nostalgic nod to republican language from earlier in the century. In what
might well be seen as the first echo of Milton's writings, as well as a trace of
his politics, Chudleigh's political image of the Eastern tyrant, emblem of
monarchical oppression, dominated the account of Satan's transformation
into a monarch at the opening of *Paradise Lost*'s second book: "High on a
Throne of Royal State which far / Outshone the wealth of *Ormus* and of
Ind, / Or where the gorgeous East with richest hand / Show'rs on her Kings
Barbaric Pearl and Gold, / Satan exalted sat" (2.1–5). Husbands and monarchs
share the same ultimate image of tyrannical excess.

While I will suggest later that the political implications in Chudleigh's poetry are quite radical (if not revolutionary), here she turns away from the implications of the forcible loss of "liberty": her answer to this usurpation of
women's "liberty" in marriage is hardly rebellion. She will concede that
women will not "to Dominion once aspire"; further, men "shall be Chief, and
still your selves admire. / The Tyrant Man may still possess the Throne"
(657–59). Yet Chudleigh's "passive obedience" does offer a form of response.

"'Tis in our minds that we wou'd Rule alone" (660), a type of "rule" that she further details at the close of the *Defence*. Positioned as analogous to the internal "rule" that women will be able to exert in their lives, Chudleigh offers an account of leaving behind the material world, an ascent to a space outside of marital hierarchies and resulting oppressions.

Thus will we live, regardless of your hate,
Till re-admitted to our former State;
Where, free from the Confinement of our Clay
In glorious Bodies we shall bask in Day,
And with inlightened Minds new Scenes survey.
Scenes, much more bright than any here below,
And we shall then the whole of Nature know;
See all her Springs, her secret Turnings view,
And be as knowing, and as wise as you.
With generous Spirits of a Make Divine,
In whose blest Minds Celestial Virtues shine . . . (825–35)

In this nonphysical state, in which women will be linked with "Celestial Virtues" rather than (political) subservience, freedom and liberty will be rediscovered—but outside of the context of marriage contracts. For those women who reject Chudleigh's advice in "To the Ladies" and acquiesce to marriage, the future elevated plane will offer the freedom lost in marriage. Now they are offered a future in which they will lose their physical bodies, or "the Confinement of our Clay." With this loss of physicality comes an erasure of the consequences of, because of the erasure of the category of, gender: all beings will become souls sans gender. As we will see, Chudleigh adopts a philosophical distinction between the soul and the body in order to explore the possibility of a genderless soul.

In this move from embodied gender, and thus the cultural constraints that this entails, Chudleigh will prepare for her most significant poem, *The Song of the Three Children Paraphras'd*. This Creation poem constructs a disembodied, and degendered, spirit world that will complement, and in fact fulfill, this closing vision in *The Ladies Defence*. As I suggested above, in theme but also perhaps in metaphysics did Chudleigh find a sympathetic source text in *Paradise Lost*—though a source text that, until now, no one has commented upon. The ascent to a spiritual plane that Chudleigh offers to wives in particular, and women in general, is one of many simpatico moments that may bridge Milton's *Paradise Lost* and Chudleigh's *Song of the Three Children Paraphras'd*. The Book 5 account, to which I will return later, describes the "gradual scale sublim'd" to which "vital Spirits aspire" (5.483–84), one that allows men and women to escape "the Confinement of our Clay." Yet my claim about the sustained influence of Milton onto Chudleigh will require a broader context: before I consider closer stylistic or textual echoes of Milton, let me offer some thematic parallels linking Chudleigh and Milton, parallels that will also illustrate the political and poetic problematic of Milton in the late seventeenth century.

Dis(Quiet)ing Echoes of Milton in Chudleigh's Poetry, Or, The Problematizing Politics of Influence

An outline of Mary, Lady Chudleigh's published writings, as well as elements of her biography, makes a strong argument for her engagement with Milton's *Paradise Lost*. Issues of female culpability, the Fall, and the consequent implications for governmental organization embedded in the 1667 epic are layered into much of Chudleigh's corpus. Chudleigh's 1710 *Essays upon Several Subjects in Prose and Verse*, which structurally patterns itself on the narrative of the Fall, explicitly recalls Milton's literary treatment of the fallen angels. Within the preface of her collection of essays, Chudleigh discusses her strategy of representing one particular figure in the dialogue within the decade-earlier *Ladies Defence*. In defending herself against the "Clergy [who] will accuse me of Irreligion for making Sir *John Brute* talk so irreverently of them" (250), she insists that she represented him as such a man would speak: his thoughts, she clarifies, were not her own. She justifies this approach through Milton's strategy within *Paradise Lost*:

> The Poets are full of Examples of this kind, particularly *Milton*; he makes some of his Apostate Angels say blasphemous things of God, and yet the judicious part of Mankind have never blam'd him for it, because what they spoke was agreeable to their Nature, and expressive of their implacable Malice: 'Twould have been absurd in him to have made his Devils personate Saints. (250)

Sir John Brute, Chudleigh's representation of a tyrannical husband, is thus compared to Milton's fallen angels in Books 1 and 2 of the epic. This Milton reference consequently contributes to the method as well as the structure of this text: her reference to a fall caused by Satan's pride looks forward to the second essay in the collection, "Of Pride," while the larger theme of the Fall and its relation to knowledge are gestured at by the opening essay "Of Knowledge."

Most importantly, we observe how Chudleigh's *Essays*, as her first published work *The Ladies Defence*, interweave gendered authority into a narrative of the Fall and of woman's acquisition of knowledge. Central to *Paradise Lost*, such issues were often invoked through references to Milton's poem during the late seventeenth century. Even without having to accept Joseph Wittreich's assignment of Chudleigh's authorship of *The Female Preacher*, this 1699 defense of women illustrates how central Milton was within late seventeenth-century debates over gender.[11] In this pamphlet, at the point that the author is arguing for woman's creation as "a social help, not a servile one," he or she turns to Milton:

Woman's being created last will not be a very great argument to debase this dignity of the Female Sex. . . . The Great *Milton*, a very grave Author, brings in *Adam* thus speaking to *Eve*, in his *Paradise Lost*, lib. 9.

> *Of fairest of Creation! last and best*
> *Of all God's Works.* (21)

Texts taking up the very issue of the status of women thus considered Milton as an authority to whom one could turn, an authority who would defend women against harsh attacks. Alternately, Milton's tracts on divorce painted a dark portrait of the institution, a portrait that Chudleigh's *Ladies Defence* retouches to depict women's experience in marriage. In the next chapter, I will suggest that Astell was drawn in part to Milton because of his detailing of marriage's limitations, even dangers, within his Divorce tracts.

Chudleigh, meanwhile, engages Milton through specific references, through structure, and by drawing upon his cultural association with women's status; broad strokes of influence thus link the two poets. Yet within *The Song of the Three Children Paraphras'd*, we will begin to see explicit and detailed adaptations of Miltonic lines, ones that will work in concert with Chudleigh's greater metaphysical goal of freeing women from "the Confinement of our Clay." Within a number of these references, Chudleigh continues to privilege the opening two books of *Paradise Lost* as in her Preface to the *Essays*. In the first of such embedded references to *Paradise Lost* within the *Song*, Chudleigh explicitly cites a Miltonic line in her borrowed phrase: "*Thick as Autumnal Leaves* they lay" (1463; my emphasis). She derives this image from Milton's account of his fallen angels, "Angel forms, who lay intransit *Thick as Autumnal Leaves* that strow the Brooks / In *Vallombrosa* (1.301–2; my emphasis). As we will see, Chudleigh borrows half lines from *Paradise Lost* with some frequency. Yet she is invoking more than just the phrase "Thick as Autumnal Leaves" in her account of the Jews' flight from Egypt. The textual echo to Milton's epic simile begins by comparing the angels to fallen leaves, then moves to compare them to the Egyptians: "vext [by] the Red-Sea Coast, whose waves o'erthrew / *Busiris* and his *Memphian* Chivalry, / While with perfidious hatred they pursu'd / The Sojourners of Goshen" (1.306–9). Chudleigh thus draws upon Milton's phrasing while employing his metaphor in her account of the creation of the world. Chudleigh's 90-stanza poem depicts three 30-stanza cycles of creation: the poem follows the neo-Platonic theory of pre-existence, narrating spirits' union with the body, which enacts a fall. At this point in her narrative, Chudleigh has finished her narrative of the biblical human history, the final cycle of creation(s) and fall(s) in her poem that structures the *Song*. Consequently, she transforms a simile recounting the fall of the Angels in *Paradise Lost*, emblematized by their prone position on Hell's floor, into her narrative of human creation.

With Milton's poem as the best-known narrative of the Fall and of Creation at the end of the seventeenth century, Chudleigh would appropriately turn to *Paradise Lost* as a model. Yet, as we see here through an intricate textual echo, she will engage Milton's narrative, especially the first two books on Satan, to produce a cyclical account of the soul's and man's creation. The textual echo, then, gestures towards the larger thematic use to which she will put Milton's poem. Chudleigh transforms Milton's narrative of sin and Fall into one of redemption within her *Song*, intersecting this canonical poem with philosophical ideas that highlighted God's infinite goodness: overlaid on top of these three internal cycles is a division of the poem into two parts, the first forty-five stanzas describing the "Justice" that defines the Old Testament (45: 1016), the second forty-five stanzas depicting the "Love" that marks the covenant offered by the New Testament (46: 1036). Further, in keeping with her thematic concerns in "To the Ladies" and *The Ladies Defence*, Chudleigh reconsiders the role of gender in her exploration of redemption.

While here Chudleigh's "quoting" of Milton is quite overt, within her poetry more generally Chudleigh routinely echoes Milton's work, but compresses and even suppresses reference to him. Milton's presence in many of Chudleigh's writings is marked by misdirection rather than the acknowledgement of influence: for this reason, I suspect, there has been no sustained critical treatment of Milton's influence on Chudleigh.[12] I will trace this mode of compression and especially suppression through a poem ostensibly paying tribute to Dryden. In a process that will recall the constellation of images of political "liberty" in *Ladies Defence*, Chudleigh cannot risk showing the extent of her revision of certain cultural concepts about (gendered notions of) "liberty." As such, parallels with Milton appear coded. As I will suggest, the very role of rhyme and its association with political issues in the period necessitate Chudleigh's complex negotiation of Milton and of *Paradise Lost*. Resistance to Milton's politics and to his poetry went hand in hand in the late seventeenth century. While engaging Milton for her own purposes, Chudleigh gestures to this configuration of Milton's politically infused verse while attempting to distance herself from the "rebellious" title that could equally be applied to her reexamination of the marital structure as to her "source" poet. Milton enables but threatens Chudleigh; she needs central elements of his narrative and poem to achieve her goals, but she must control the consequent potential damage threatened by Milton's reception in the period.

We can see this doubled reliance on and distancing from Milton within Chudleigh's commendatory poem "To Mr. *Dryden*, on his excellent Translation of *Virgil*." In this poem, Chudleigh ostensibly praises Dryden as he is set within the tradition of English poets and presented as the poet fulfilling a national poetic tradition. Existing as it does within a poetic panegyric genre, the poem is hardly unusual, while its irregular Pindaric Ode form is an appropriate one in which to praise Dryden, who also employed the form.[13] And yet, the poem's language—ostensibly praising Dryden—is simultaneously, and significantly, evocative of Milton's *Paradise Lost*. Chudleigh begins her poem invoking a muse in order to praise Dryden, "Thou matchless Poet" (1), the asserted subject of her poem: "Permit my Muse in plain unpolish'd Verse, / In humble Strains her Wonder to rehearse" (5–6). As Chudleigh's muse acquires access to a greater view onto the topic of poetic achievement, the language of revealed sight and perspectival viewing characterizes (her) visual access: "From her low Shade she lifts her dazl'd Sight, / And views the Splendor and amazing Height" (7–8). The sight given to the muse, her movement from a "dazl'd," limited vision to access to a view of "Splendor," similarly marked the progression of Milton's muse in the opening invocation of *Paradise Lost*: "What in me is dark / Illumine, what is low raise and support" (22–23). Both Chudleigh's and Milton's lines delineate this gradual process of illumination; as "dazl'd" sight is transformed to perceivable sight, so is "dark"ness transformed into illumination. Further, in both lines this access to effective sight is accomplished through elevation to a perspectival position: Chudleigh's muse departs "From her low Shade" to be raised to an "amazing Height," a fusion of visual and physical elevation more economically fused within Milton's line. As Milton proceeds to tell the story of the creation of the world, Chudleigh now undertakes the story of the creation of a national line of poets.

Chudleigh's very detailed engagement with the language of Book 1, as well as her account of Milton's treatment of the angels in her borrowed line "Thick as Autumnal Leaves," supports her intimate knowledge of the opening books of *Paradise Lost*. And we see this thematic connection follow into the second stanza of the Dryden poem. Here, the language of Book 1 of *Paradise Lost* combines with the imagery of Book 2, most particularly Chudleigh's treatment of a past "Chaos" of poetic production. The language of creation shapes this "birth" of a national literary tradition in the second stanza where this "happy Birth of Light" invokes Milton's treatment of "Chaos" in Book 2 of *Paradise Lost*:

> Before the happy Birth of Light,
> E'er Nature did her forming Pow'r display,
>   While blended in their native Night,
>   The Principles of all things lay;
> Triumphant Darkness did her self dilate,
> And thro' the Chaos with resistless Sway
>   Her dusky Horrors spread;
> Such in this Isle was once our wretched State:
> Dark melancholy Night her sable Wings display'd . . . ("Dryden," 12–20)

This creative birth, in which Chudleigh invokes the beginning of the world as a metaphor for England's poetic darkness before Chaucer, recalls the opposition of light to the darkness of Chaos that marked Milton's extensive treatment of this unmolded space in Book 2. There, we hear Satan appeal to Chaos, promising to "reduce / To her original darkness" usurped portions of Chaos, thus "once more / Erect[ing] the Standard there of *ancient Night*" (2.983–84, 985–86). The connection between Chaos and "Dark melancholy Night" recalls

Milton's account of Chaos "Enthron'd" with "Sable-vested *Night*" (961–62). Within Chudleigh's language, the productive, even reproductive, identity of "Triumphant Darkness" continues to expand, to "her self dilate."[14] As such, it aligns Chudleigh's account of Night and Chaos with Milton's focus on Chaos as "The Womb of nature" whose power "in thir pregnant causes mixt / Confus'dly" (911, 913–14); this matrix of images is furthered by Belial's description of "the wide womb of uncreated night" (2.150).

Parallels to successive books of *Paradise Lost* thus appear within Chudleigh's poem to Dryden. Evocative imagery, such as the biblical association of the word and light, runs through the second stanza, though it is not until Book 3 of *Paradise Lost* that we are introduced to "Hail holy Light, offspring of Heav'n first-born" (1). For Chudleigh, the "happy Birth of Light" introduces a complex metaphor of poetic texts bringing light to England within the second stanza. Yet it is the genuine birth of light, rather than the "Lunar Beans" of Spenser or the "delusive Light" of Chaucer, that finally emerges at the opening of stanza 3: "With *Waller* our first Dawn of Light arose" (31). The third stanza, then, introduces us to the genuine light of Dryden's poems as "Dark Shadows" are "chas'd away": "Now all is clear, and all is bright" as access to Dryden—much as access to God in the third book of *Paradise Lost*—is finally achieved.

The use of the chaos motif and the birth of light characterizing Book 3 of *Paradise Lost* will join another invocation of Milton's poem: the ascent to the "sacred Hill" in the fourth stanza. By following Dryden, "we climb the sacred Hill," a site from which "our pleas'd Eyes with distant Prospects fill: / View all th' Acquests thy conqu'ring Pen has made" (45–47). Yet that "sacred Hill," and the poet's ascent to it, resonates with Milton's association of himself with Moses, who "on the secret top / Of *Oreb*, or of *Sinai*" was inspired to write his poem (6–7). Further, this praise of Dryden as leading English readers up "the sacred Hill" seems a rather odd image given the subject of Chudleigh's panegyric; Chudleigh's "To *Dryden*, on his excellent Translation of *Virgil*" is praising a secular, pagan, and obviously not Christian, *Aeneid*. While Chudleigh is clearly making "sacred" the production of English national poetry, the "sacred Hill" is one of many phrases that overtly describes Dryden while choosing language that gestures to Milton.

Given such resonance with the themes and language of *Paradise Lost*, the limited attention given to Milton within Chudleigh's poem becomes most notable. Chudleigh provides a conventionally canonical list of poets, beginning with Chaucer and then sequentially presenting Spenser, Waller, Milton, Cowley, and finally Dryden to the reader.

From Gloom, to Gloom, with weary'd Steps we stray'd,
Till *Chaucer* came with his delusive Light,
And gave some transient Glimm'rings to the Night:
Next kinder *Spencer* with his Lunar Beams
Inrich'd our Skies, and wak'd us from our Dreams:

Then pleasing visions did our Minds delight,
And airy Spectres danc'd before our Sight . . .
With *Waller* our first Dawn of Light arose,
He did the Beauties of the Morn disclose:
Then *Milton* came, and Cowley blest our Eyes;
With Joy we saw the distant Glory rise. (23–28, 31–34)

Despite the significance of Milton's poetic contribution to aspects of Chudleigh's writings and to the period, he receives a half line of praise, a line he must share with Cowley. Even Waller is provided two full lines, as are Chaucer and Spenser. In what could be seen as an ironic rehearsal of Chudleigh's own frequent use of Miltonic half lines, she gives him his due in the same half line form through which she will record snatches of his poetry.

Even taking into account a different aesthetic and a more belated understanding of Milton as one of the greatest of English poets, the veritable silence on Milton's contribution to the awaking of English poetry seems odd. Chudleigh's seemingly glancing reference to Milton is also out of step with Restoration literary tastes, in which Milton was accorded a canonical, if nonetheless contested, status.[15] This seeming avoidance of Milton is more striking in light of the significant figure he is for Chudleigh in other works, both in her description of method in *The Ladies Defence* and her "Autumnal Leaves" reference within *The Song*. I want to suggest that this seeming oversight of Milton in "To Mr. *Dryden*, on his excellent Translation of *Virgil*" is Chudleigh's purposeful misdirection about Milton's poetic significance for her. Such misdirection becomes clarified by the implications—aesthetic, political, and national—of rhyme about which Chudleigh writes in the poem. Seeming references to *Paradise Lost*, both thematically and linguistically resonant, are consolidated into an account of rhyme. Further, the close modeling of Miltonic themes throughout the first four stanzas adds greater significance to Chudleigh's subsequent discussion of rhyme.

In the final stanza of Chudleigh's poem, another odd invocation of Milton that is conveyed through his exclusion demands that we slightly broaden the context for considering Chudleigh's strategy: Dryden's use of Milton's primary poetic achievement. This shift to the wider context of Dryden's operatic reworking of *Paradise Lost* should allow us to answer this question: Why would Chudleigh mute Milton's importance in her poem? I want to consider the method through which Miltonic themes, even structure, are refracted within this panegyric, a method that becomes summarized for us by Dryden's own act of appropriating *Paradise Lost* within his adapted, and "tagged," 1677 opera. In *The State of Innocence, and Fall of Man*, based explicitly on *Paradise Lost*, Dryden opted to rhyme Milton's account of Paradise and the Fall.

Praise for Dryden's opera included testimonies to the period's preference for rhyme, ones expressed in concert with a general dismissal of Milton's choice of blank verse. In Nathaniel Lee's "To Mr. Dryden, on his Poem of Paradise," Lee gestures at Milton's fame while stressing the improvements made by Dryden:

To the dead Bard, your fame a little owes,
For *Milton* did the Wealthy Mine disclose,
And rudely cast what you cou'd well dispose:
He roughly drew, on an old fashion'd ground,
A Chaos; for no perfect World was found,
Till through the heap, your mighty Genius shin'd;
His was the Golden Ore which you refin'd.
He first beheld the beauteous rustick Maid,
And to a place of strength the prize convey'd . . . (A4r, 1677)

At first glance, Chudleigh's praise of Dryden at the end of her panegyric seems to accord with the very terms of Lee's encomium to *State of Innocence.* Chudleigh also praises Dryden for a similar focus on finding, and refining, that which Milton had left imperfect:

Our Language like th'*Augean* Stable lay,
Rude and uncleans'd, till thou by Glory mov'd,
    Th' *Herculean* Task didst undertake,
And hast with Floods of Wit th'offensive Heaps remov'd:
That ancient Rubbish of the *Gothick* Times,
When manly Sense was lost in trifling Rhimes:
Now th'unform'd Mass is to Perfection wrought . . . ("To Mr. Dryden," 68–74)

In fact, one might think that Chudleigh's praise of Dryden had been refracted through, or even redacted by, Lee's description in the commendatory poem to *State of Innocence.* The "heap," which is *Paradise Lost*, seems echoed quite directly in Chudleigh use of the terms "th'offensive Heaps," unformed poetry which Dryden reconfigures through his rhyming process. The "Chaos" of Milton's poem described in Lee's poem seems only slightly transformed into the "th'unformed Mass" of the more general tradition of English poetry that Chudleigh describes Dryden as reforming.

Though these echoes would suggest a parallel treatment of Milton by Chudleigh and Lee, this hardly accords with her engagement with *Paradise Lost.* More importantly, in such accounts of Dryden's artistic success, praise of Dryden appears to be literally built upon the edifice that is Milton: Dryden's play, in Lee's account, takes what Milton "rudely cast" out of the "Wealthy Mine" of *Paradise Lost*, reshaping the rich, raw materials of Milton's poem. Milton thus stands behind, through motifs and language, an account of Dryden's poetic success.

When Chudleigh engages the issue of rhyme, the rhyming couplets in *The State of Innocence* becoming the very "Ore" that "refin'd" a tagged *Paradise Lost*, she is not just entering the aesthetic battle over versification. She is profoundly engaging the political implications of versification, especially as this aesthetic choice related to Milton himself. The late seventeenth-century discussion of rhyme was, of course, a return to a much earlier debate, one staged in the Spenser-Harvey correspondence and in which Philip Sidney was a participant and experimenter; the problem of English and the appropriate form of versification consequently shapes much early Renaissance literary criticism and is taken up with even greater energy in the early eighteenth century. As in the sixteenth century, the use or rejection of rhyme was intimately linked with the status of English poetry.[16] As such, Chudleigh's emphasis on rhyme is a fitting close to a poem that makes its narrative the emergence of the line of English poets.

Yet rhyme also carried a great deal of cultural baggage. As we can see in both the Lee and Chudleigh poems, certain types of verse were considered "refin'd," a classification that had embedded into it notions of national pride and success for English poetry. Yet what constituted "refin'd" versus "Gothick" poetry became a significant disagreement among (emerging) literary critics. John Dennis, who first identified the "Gothick and Barbarous manner" of English poetry in 1701 (*Advancement and Reformation*, Aa2v), would link the "Gothick" to rhyme itself in his 1722 essay "On Prosody": Greeks and Romans "utterly contemned and rejected Rhyme," but "the Gothick or modern Poets vainly imagine that they can supply the Defect of Numbers in their unmusical Idioms by the Use of Rhyme" (282–83). As Chudleigh positions herself in this debate of rhyme through the use of the term "Gothick" in "To Mr. *Dryden*," she is simultaneously and necessarily positioning herself in the adjacent discussion of the political implications of rhyme. For the two conversations became fused in the late seventeenth century: Milton's epic had achieved, even among his sharpest critics, sublimity by eschewing verse. But his political reputation had become part and parcel of discussions of Milton's prosody: Isaac Watts in "The Adventurous Muse" (1706) thus describes Milton as "The noble Hater of degenerate Rhime [who] / Shook off the Chains, and built his Verse sublime" (152).

The very constellation of political views and prosody came to a head in discussions of Milton. When Chudleigh engages this debate in her praise of Dryden, with its suppressed praise of Milton, she models an issue for her readers and a solution for herself: the complexity of politicized prosody in the late seventeenth century and her resulting encoded engagement with Milton's poetry. Watts and then the Earl of Shaftesbury highlight how interwoven aesthetic critiques of Milton were with politicized language. Praising "Epick" Milton among others including Shakespeare, Shaftesbury describes how "those reverend Bards, rude as they were, according to their Time and Age, have provided us however with the richest Oar. To their eternal Honour they have withal been the first of EUROPEANS, who since the GOTHICK Model of Poetry, attempted to throw off the horrid Discord of jingling Rhyme" (217–18). His opposition to rhyme then joins his association of blank verse with "antient Poetick Liberty" that these poets have "asserted" (218). Watts's and Shaftsbury's associations of liberty through one's choice of prosody are overt references to Milton's own statement about prosody in *Paradise Lost*; it is "the first in English, of ancient liberty recover'd to Heroic Poem from the troublesome and modern bondage of Riming" (210). While Watts invokes Milton's use of "bondage" through his image of the "Chains" of rhyme, Shaftesbury highlights the politics of blank verse in his subtly rephrased "antient Poetick Liberty."

Other critics had, of course, interwoven their political judgments of Milton with assessments of his writings. Thomas Yalden charges that "thy seditious prose provokes our rage / And soils the beauties of thy brightest page" since "thy impious mercenary pen / Insults the best of princes, best of men" (quoted in Shawcross, *Critical Heritage*, 122). Reminding us that Milton frequently appears in poems on Dryden, Alexander Oldys's 1700 "An Ode by way of Elegy on. . .Mr. Dryden" creates a persona of Milton who admits " 'twas Verse alone / Did for my Hideous Crime attone, / Defending once the worst Rebellion" (B2v). William Winstanley, the most extreme critic of Milton, sums up the effects of Milton's actions on his legacy: "his Memory will always stink, which might have ever lived in honourable Repute, had not he been a notorious Traytor, and most impiously and villanously bely'd that blessed Martyr King Charles" (195).

But Lee's "To Mr Dryden, on his Poem of Paradise," the very poem prefacing Dryden's 1677 versification or tagging of *Paradise Lost*, links Milton's political identity to his blank verse most explicitly. Early in the poem, Lee praises Dryden for his transformation of Milton's "rudely cast" "heap" of a poem through rhyming it: because of the use of rhyme, it has been transformed into a beautiful "Virgin . . . Drest . . . with gemms" and "sweetest manners taught" (A4r). Lee then turns to language that interweaves poetic authority and political affiliation. Because Dryden has transformed this poem, he is "O mightiest of the inspir'd men," a "Monarch of Verse" (A4v). Most importantly, this language associates poetic practice with a particular political system. This process continues as Lee grants the crown to Dryden over Milton, embedding into this poetic transfer the very memory, and crime, of the regicide:

> . . . new Theams employ thy Pen.
> The troubles of Majestick *CHARLES* set down,
> Not *David* vanquish'd more to reach a Crown,
> Praise him, as *Cowly* did that *Hebrew* King,
> Thy Theam's as great, do thou as greatly sing.
> Then thou mayst boldly to his favor rise
> Look down and the base serpent's hiss despise,
> From thund'ring envy safe in Lawrel fit,
> While clam'rous Critiques their vile heads submit
> Condemn'd for Treason at the bar of Wit. (A4v)

The act of regicide is alluded to through "The troubles of Majestick CHARLES" while the appropriate punishment for those "Condemn'd for Treason" is staged for us. The two greatest flaws of Milton—his refusal to rhyme and his regicidal identity—are thus fused in this opening poem by Lee. The reference to regicidal "Critiques" perhaps most fully fuses the aesthetic choice of rhyme with the political choice of republicanism; those who would prefer the rhymeless *Paradise Lost* are regicides themselves.

References to rhyme as to Milton were thus heavily weighted topics at the end of the seventeenth century. Chudleigh, who had engaged these issues in "To Mr. *Dryden*," also turns to the political resonance of rhyme within the Preface to the *Song of the Three Children Paraphras'd*. In language that looks backward to Milton and forward to Shaftsbury, Chudleigh explains her choice of the Pindaric Ode for *The Song of the Three Children Paraphras'd*:

The Reason why I chuse this sort of Verse, is, because it allows me the Liberty of running into large Digressions, gives a great Scope to the Fancy, and frees me from the trouble of tying my self up to the stricter Rules of other Poetry. (169)

Chudleigh's aesthetic, of course, does not draw her away from rhyme; in fact, the form of the Pindaric ode, in which she composes the *Song*, aligns her to Restoration poets like Cowley and Dryden. Yet her justification of "this sort of Verse" by praising its narrative possibilities again invokes the political language of "Liberty." Even Milton's specific statement about the consequent "bondage" of Rhyme resonates in Chudleigh's desire to not "ty . . . my self up" to more constraining poetic forms. While stripped of some of its political energy, the political elements of verse—of which many of Chudleigh's contemporaries were conscious—thus remain as remnants in the preface to Chudleigh's longest poem.

This broader cultural context for understanding the politics of rhyme allows us to unpack Chudleigh's own discussion of rhyme in the closing stanza of her ode to Dryden. She now describes the "Herculean Task" Dryden faces of cleaning out the "Augean Stable" of "Our Language" which was "Rude and unclean's'd" until Dryden enters the British canon of poets (68-70): "That ancient Rubbish of the *Gothick* Times, / When manly Sense was lost in trifling Rhimes: / Now th'unform'd Mass is to Perfection wrought" (72–74). In praising Dryden's mode of rhyming, in particular distinguishing it from "trifling Rhimes," Chudleigh appears to align herself to an artistic and political majority in the period.

Yet the earlier suppression of Milton's significance within the canonical line of poets developed in "To Mr. *Dryden*" resurfaces in Chudleigh's discussion of verse. Chudleigh's account that Dryden is not guilty of "trifling Rhimes," and thus can preserve "manly Sense" in his verse, does not seem an accurate description of his *Works of Virgil*; it is translated entirely in couplets. While both Chudleigh's own aesthetic choices and her appreciation of Dryden should hardly have us conclude that she considered him the author of "trifling Rhimes," such an epitaph could never, of course, be applied to Milton. Chudleigh's choice of "Gothick" as the term by which to distinguish Dryden from earlier poets also invokes the debate over rhyme and the very history of English poetry. In Shaftesbury's account, "Gothick" is used to describe the very "jingling" rhyme that Milton had so completely rejected. Both he and Dennis would position Milton as the very example of non-"Gothick" poetry. The language of poetic "Perfection" used to praise Dryden consequently serves as another strange echo to the poet who, as in Dryden's *State of Innocence and Fall of Man*, stands behind Dryden's artistic production.

This odd, doubled, even misdirecting treatment of Milton needs to be read, I would argue, through *The Ladies Defence*. There, Chudleigh's upending of the categories of marital and political organization made her a radical, rebellious figure. As we will see, much in Milton's *Paradise Lost* would have made it an attractive text for Chudleigh. Like *Paradise Lost*, Chudleigh's longest work, *The Song*, is an expansive meditation on a very slight scriptural account: the apocryphal "Song" located within the Book of Daniel would have been very familiar as it appeared among the Morning Prayers of the Book of Common Prayer.[17] And while critics debate the influences of neo-Platonic thought upon Milton by the 1660s, the account of spiritual ascension in Book 5 could certainly be read as consistent with Chudleigh's extensive Platonic framework within the *Song*. This sequence in particular offered to Chudleigh an attractive model of freeing the soul from the gendered implications of the body. Yet, the standing of Milton—marked by, among other things, his rejection of rhyme—made alignment with him politically complicated.

While the weight of Milton's republican politics could have played a part in Chudleigh's careful negotiation of his poetic achievements, so too could her own family background. Though frequently linked to the Tory Mary Astell, Mary Chudleigh's own family as well as her husband's family were "distinguished for its activities on the Parliamentary side during the Civil War" (Ezell, xix). Barbara Olive, in her work on Chudleigh, has also stressed Chudleigh's alignment with nonconformists, both as a result of her family background and her uncle, Thomas Sydenham.[18] Chudleigh's own family history might suggest a desire to not align herself too explicitly with Milton; potential republican leanings might motivate Mary Chudleigh's poetic choices, but also help to explain her multilayered negotiations of a family past and her possible intellectual alignments. Chudleigh's structural as well as linguistic use of Milton's *Paradise Lost* thus agitates against his transformation into a half line afterthought: "Then Milton came."

As we will see in the next segment, a textual and poetic matrix of images testifies to Milton's importance in Chudleigh's poem. As in her interweaving of Miltonic echoes into "To Mr. *Dryden*," the stakes of invoking Milton were wrought with political implications. In her extensive reenvisioning of *Paradise Lost* through her major poem, *The Song of the Three Children Paraphras'd*, poetic engagements with Milton remain infused with political implications. Milton's poem allows Chudleigh to narrate an escape from the physical and gendered world that she initially proposed in *The Ladies Defence*. In the detailed reading of Chudleigh's major poem that follows, I will be considering what uses—poetic and political—Chudleigh could make of both Milton's verse and his identity in the late seventeenth century.

Boundless Creation and the Restaging of Perspective in the *Song*

Chudleigh's *Song*, which she labels a paraphrase of the apocryphal "Song of the Three Children," intricately redeploys a series of tributes to God, the angels, the earth, and creation within a neo-Platonic re-imagination of multiple creations and falls.[19] Clearly influenced by thinkers within the Cambridge Platonist school, the poem models certain central tenets in this body of philosophy, especially the soul's ability to achieve a higher plan. The *Song*, loosely following the structure offered by the sequential blessings of God within the apocryphal Song of the Three Children, introduces two creations and two falls into this narrative; the poem thus enacts both our fall into lower material forms and our souls' (possible) reascension. Within her Preface to the poem, Chudleigh explains the neo- or Cambridge Platonist thought that supports her successive creation accounts of a spiritual and then a physical world:

the Doctrine of Pre-existence, which supposes, that all Souls were created in the beginning of Time, before any material Beings had their Existence, and that they being united to Ætherial Bodies, were made Possessors of as much Happiness as they were capable of enjoying. From their sublime Station, and Bliss unexpressibly great, being by the Solicitation of their lower Faculties, unhappily drawn to a Love of Pleasure, and by adhering too much to the Delights of the Body, enervating and lessening the Activity and Strength of their noblest and most perfect Powers, which proportionably abated, as the other increas'd, they sunk by degrees into an Aerial State, from whence, such as by repeated Acts of Disobedience, and the too eager Gratification of their sensitive Appetites, are render'd unfit for the Exercise of their more exalted Faculties . . . fall lower yet, and lie in a State of Silence and Inactivity, till they are awaken'd into Life in such Bodies as by their previous Dispositions they are fitted for. (169–70)

Chudleigh thus interweaves into verses paying tribute to God an expansive narrative that reconsiders the bounds of creation, offering linguistic and thematic accounts of boundlessness that characterize her poem. Exploring the concepts of infinite space at the heart of Henry More's philosophy, the poem will illustrate the unbounded possibilities for the human soul; it can spiritually ascend to link one to the goodness of God.[20]

Of all of the tenets of Cambridge Platonism, Chudleigh appears to fully embrace the notion of the infinite nature of the universe. Her poem will unify a portrait of the boundless universe with a detailed engagement with, and rewriting of, Milton's language and narrative from *Paradise Lost*. Chudleigh utilizes Miltonic echoes to make temporal acts of creation boundless through their repetition within a Platonic schema. Furthermore, these reenactments of

Creation dissolve the boundaries of gender as they do of the material world itself. Chudleigh's Platonist thought and her consequent dematerializing of
human bodies and action can transform an event all too located onto a material, sinning, female body into an exploration of spiritual redemption and ascent. The narrative of culpability, one linked explicitly to gender and thus to
political governance and authority in the period, is consequently redrawn by
her poem through her sustained engagement with Milton's *Paradise Lost*.

Stylistic, narrative, and linguistic connections with *Paradise Lost* thus abound
within the *Song*. Because the *Song* is a story of creation(s), Milton's influence
could well be anticipated: *Paradise Lost* was the most significant and influential
poem produced on this topic in the late seventeenth century.[21] Yet Chudleigh's
mechanism for recording her debt to Milton occurs in the stylistic equivalent
of half lines: a series of echoes to Milton, when read cumulatively, reveal a
narrative of perspectival viewing and language about bounding and unbound-
ing which gestures at a project of much greater importance. The *Song* is thus
so much more than a poem influenced by Milton's *Paradise Lost*. Chudleigh will
actively engage the possibilities of Milton's reputation in the period, including
his "impious" and even "diabolic" identity, that could be linked to Satan himself. At the level of language and through the imagery of *Paradise Lost*, we can
observe a pattern of revision and of redemption, including the redeployment
of certain "Satanic" motifs into prelapsarian ones within Chudleigh's poem.
Many philosophers within the Cambridge Platonist school highlighted God's
existence by countering the atheistic implications of the mechanistic determinism of Hobbes or the theological determinism in Calvinist thought. Chudleigh
is equally engaged with this view of God, which shapes her emphasis on redemption rather than damnation.

These ideas frame Chudleigh's appropriation of Satan's language in *Paradise
Lost*, in particular her revision of the motif of "bounds" from which she frees
the soul. Ultimately, her poetic project allows her to fulfill the promise to re-
lease us from "the Confinement of our Clay." Boundaries placed upon Satan
become the language of a boundless creation in Chudleigh's *Song*, one inspired
by a Platonic philosophy that elevates souls and leaves behind both physical
form and gender. I will be exploring two language matrices—first that of
bounds and then of perspectival vision—through which Chudleigh makes extensive use of Milton. This rewriting, this appropriation of boundary viola-
tions and the visual gaze that characterizes Milton's Satan, becomes an
attractive, if transgressive, body of motifs through which Chudleigh can enact
her (rebellious) rejection of gendered hierarchy.

We have previously observed Chudleigh's use of "half lines" from Milton's
text. In her creation of a matrix of visual perspective, we will see Chudleigh
again turn to Milton as a source, drawing from the portrait of his fallen Satan
in order to redeem such motifs within a poem about falls, creations, and redemption. In stanza seven, which begins as praise of the stars, we are offered—

through the genre of this prophetic *Song*—a view onto the universe and our own globe:

> And there with boundless Freedom stray,
> And at one View Ten thousand sparkling Orbs survey,
> Innumerable Worlds and dazling Springs of Light.
> O the vast Prospect! O the charming Sight!
>   How full of Wonder, and Delight!
> How mean, how little, does our Globe appear! (164–69)

This perspectival position resonates strikingly with the Book 3 account of Satan looking down onto Earth. Satan stands amidst "innumerable Stars" (565) which Milton will then describe—and which Chudleigh will later echo— as "Innumerable Worlds" (166). These stars "seem'd other Worlds, / Or other Worlds they seem'd" to Satan in *Paradise Lost* (3.566–67). This mode of "half line" echoes will become expanded into a complex matrix of language about visual perspective upon which Chudleigh draws. Satan had looked from here down onto the Earth itself:

> So wide the op'ning seem'd, where bounds were set
> To darkness, such as bound the Ocean wave.
> *Satan* from hence now on the lower stair
> That scal'd by steps of Gold to Heaven Gate
> Looks down with wonder at the sudden view
> Of all this World at once. As when a Scout . . .
> Which to his eye discovers unaware
> The goodly prospect of some foreign land . . .
> Such wonder seiz'd, though after Heaven seen,
> The Spirit malign, but much more envy seiz'd
> At sight of all this World beheld so fair.
> Round he surveys . . . (538–43, 547–48, 552–55)

View; survey; prospect; and the production of wonder: these perspectival scenes, here observed from "innumerable Stars" and "worlds," create a pattern that will repeat itself again and again within Chudleigh's poem. While the perspective Chudleigh grants to the souls looking onto the Earth resonates with Satan's perspective in *Paradise Lost*, we see this language of Satan, specifically his acts of viewing in Book 4, explicitly echoed in Chudleigh's account of Adam and Eve. In the *Song*, just after God "did our happy Parents frame" (979), Adam and Eve "Then cast their ravish'd Eyes around, / Where e'er they gaz'd, they some new Wonder found" (987–88). Milton's Book 3 language, where he described Satan's view onto Earth, employed such a phrase. At his first view of Eden—the analogous moment in which we are shown Adam and Eve looking onto Eden in Chudleigh's *Song*—Satan's response is recorded: "Beneath him with new wonder now he views / To all delight of human sense exposʼd" (4.205–6). Both experience "new wonder" upon their gazing onto

Eden, as acts of viewing and perspective continue to link the Chudleigh and Milton's poems.

As with the transferral of Satan's nocent gaze into mankind's first view of God's creation, Chudleigh engages and rewrites the motifs of vision, perspective, and boundaries within *Paradise Lost* to rewrite the implications of the Fall itself: just as this body of Platonic thought stressed God's presence in the world around us, we see in Chudleigh the "nocent" actions of Satan transformed through her portrait of an infinite and inherently good universe.[22] Chudleigh's echoes of Milton thus draw us away from the Fall itself towards the redemptive act of Creation, one that occurs twice within Chudleigh's *Song*. As did other Platonist thinkers, she views human nature as inherently good; the consequences in her poem are a Fall narrative that deemphasizes profound evil. This rewriting of Milton's narrative of the Fall allows Chudleigh to establish an intertextual tapestry of visually oriented echoes between these two creation poems, reassigning and realigning words—such as the language of "bound"ing and words linked to visual perspective such as "view," "gaze," "ken, "survey," and "prospect"—that resonate throughout *Paradise Lost*. As she expands the visual boundaries of this Platonic concept of space, she will alter the manner, and meaning, of souls gazing onto this space.

I will be illustrating these connections between the language of bounds and of visual perspective first to establish the debt Chudleigh has to Milton. But it is a working debt, one producing profitable interest. Thematically as well as linguistically, Chudleigh revises Milton's invocation of boundaries in her poem. We are told that the view in Chudleigh's stanza 7 is "boundless," while in the Book 3 *Paradise Lost* episode, there are "bounds." Yet Chudleigh's engagement of the significant uses of "bounds" in Milton casts light on both her use of the word and Milton's deployment of it in his poem. In Book 3, for example, how are these "bounds" described to us? "So wide the op'ning seem'd, where bounds were set / To darkness, such as bound the Ocean wave" (3.538–39). The language of "bounds were set" is positioned in contrast to this "wide . . . opening"; the consequence is a beautifully ambiguous line. In *Paradise Lost*, "wide" expands the field of vision so broadly that it becomes difficult to locate its physical end at the indeterminate boundary of light. As the line continues, "such as bound the Ocean wave," the metaphor of the ocean as a boundary remains equally unclear. Here, the "bound" to the "Ocean wave" seems both a marker of limitation *and* an ironic account of that which cannot be bounded. Attempting to "fix" such boundaries proves elusive. When Chudleigh turns the "bounds" in *Paradise Lost* into the "boundlessness" that marks her rewriting of the phrase, we see Chudleigh expand upon the possibilities embedded into Milton's poem, transforming them into an important theme in her creation poem.

Linguistically and philosophically, Chudleigh found an effective source in Milton. "Bounds" without bounds are modeled for us in Milton's elusive language and in Satan's actions. Throughout *Paradise Lost*, Milton's Satan is characterized by his attempts to exceed the boundaries of the poem, in particular the "bounds" established by God: his entrance into Eden is marked by his "contempt"uous acts of violating God's physical boundaries: "At one slight bound high overleap'd all bound / Of Hill or highest wall" (4.181–82), an account repeated as Gabriel describes Satan as having "o'erleapt these earthy bounds / On purpose" (4.583–84). If Chudleigh thus overleaps the"bounds prescribed" (4.878) within *Paradise Lost*, we can trace from whence she derives some poetic inspiration.

In particular, Chudleigh's work with this image of the "bounded" ocean will recur multiple times within her text: it, as the Book 3 account of Satan's view onto earth, appears to be a Miltonic crux for Chudleigh. She engages this motif in order to transform "bounds" into re-creative possibilities, ones made possible by Platonic thought. Later in the *Song* when Chudleigh turns to this same image, we observe from an elevated perspectival position one of the many moments of creations in the poem:

Yonder, large Plains their verdant Beauties show,
And there, with noisie haste resistless Torrents flow:
Here, various Animals, and Herbs invite,
There, Towns we see, here Forests yield Delight,
And there, the mighty Ocean bounds our Sight. (827–31)

In *Paradise Lost*, the limitation to Satan's view or "ken" could be read as deriving from the oceanlike darkness which becomes a visual border to the created world. While our vision is "bound" by the "mighty Ocean" in Chudleigh, the context becomes the creation of the world, not Satan's (ultimately destructive) descent to Eden. While establishing a verbal matrix between her poem and *Paradise Lost*, Chudleigh's use of the language of boundaries thus allows her to refocus onto acts of creation. As we saw previously, Satan's "new wonder" precedes his preparation for our fall, while Adam and Eve's "new wonder" repositions this view into the prelapsarian moment of Creation.

In her first account of Creation, a closer verbal and philosophical echo between Milton and Chudleigh highlights her adaptation of Platonic thought to her rewriting of the Creation story, and thus her rewriting of *Paradise Lost*. During Creation, Chudleigh describes "th'obsequious Floods" that "gave way, / And each *within appointed Bounds* did stay" (493–94; my emphasis). Her line directly echoes Milton who, in his Book 7 account of Creation, "bid the Deep / *Within appointed bounds* be Heav'n and Earth" (7.166–67; my emphasis). This account of Creation at stanza 22 in Chudleigh, in addition to echoing a specific line, parallels Milton's own invocation of a Platonic view of creation. As Merritt Hughes says of Milton's Book 7 narrative of Creation, his is an "ultimately Platonic conception" of the "original differentiation of the four elements." At lines 237–42, we hear of the "fluid Mass . . . downward purg'd . . . then founded, then conglob'd / Like things to like." The result is an "Earth self-balanc't on her centre hung." Chudleigh appears to be drawn to Milton's specific language here because of elements of Platonic thought present in his vision of Creation. In her poem, the Earth "to a new made Centre fell / . . . On which a Mass of Liquids lay: / The lucid Particles together came" (476, 479–80). The rise of the lighter elements and the descent of the heavier ones align the two poems' accounts to the seventeenth-century Platonic theory Chudleigh employs in her poem.

Yet the use of the Miltonic "half line," the reference to "Within appointed bounds," further elaborates the philosophical appeal that *Paradise Lost* would have had for Chudleigh. In Book 5, Raphael offers to Milton the most explicit Platonic account of the (eventual) elevation of souls, an account in which this motif of the "bounds" reappears:

All things proceed, and up to him return,
If not deprav'd from good, created all
Such to perfection, one first matter all,
Indu'd with various forms, various degrees
Of substance, and in things that live, of life;
But more refin'd, more spiritous, and pure,
As nearer to him plac't or nearer tending
Each in thir several active Spheres assign'd,
Till body up to spirit work, in bounds
Proportion'd to each kind. . . .
And from these corporal nutriments perhaps
Your bodies may at last turn all to spirit,
Improv'd by tract of time, and wing'd ascend
Ethereal, as wee, or may at choice
Here or in Heav'nly Paradises dwell. (5.470–79, 496–500)

This articulation of the Platonic ascent of souls illustrates the philosophical significance of *Paradise Lost* for Chudleigh.[23] We also observe the same matrix of the language of "bounds" and of creation that marked Chudleigh's use of Milton's Book 7 "half line." And yet as we see in her transformation of such "bounds" to "boundlessness" in previous moments in her text, she will effect the same transformation in the category of gender. As her poem illustrates, the soul, as it "Ascend[s] . . . in a speedy Flight" in the opening line of the poem, will escape the "Proportion'd" "bounds" of gender.

Because of her Platonic theology, Chudleigh imagines spirits who descended to take on human form, a process she represents as a form of fall:

What, ye blest Spirits, what cou'd you excite
To leave your radiant Seats above?
Could mortal Bodies such Attractives prove?
Was Happiness grown your Disease?
Or were you surfeited with Ease?
O dreadful Lapse! O fatal Change!
Must you, who thro' the higher Orbs could range,

Survey the beauteous Worlds above,
And there adore the Source of Love,
Be here confin'd to Lumps of Clay,
To darksom Cells, remote from your Ætherial Day? (633–43)

Most important, this spirit world, created before Earth and Adam and Eve's sin, is a place of genderless souls. The pre-existence of souls consequently has a radical effect on both the narrative of creation(s) that Chudleigh relates as well as the story of our loss of Eden. Adam and Eve will both ascend to a spiritual place as well as existing in that state before the creation of Earth and mankind. The soul, not gendered, is released from Earth as it is released from a state of (gendered) difference.

I began this intertextual reading of Chudleigh and Milton by offering a "crux" linking the two texts thematically and linguistically. I want now to return to the matrix of visual motifs highlighted within that crux, ones Chudleigh revises in the course of the *Song*. As we initially saw in the account of "bound"ed-ness or "boundless"ness in both poems, the language of the prospect, of survey, even of wonder produced by them, is often placed into the mouth of Satan within *Paradise Lost*. As with the language of "bounding," Chudleigh engages the Satanic use of these terms, turning to the ultimate rebellious figure to engage a layered reworking of the language of perspective. It is at the juncture of the language of boundaries and of visual perspective, then, that we can unpack the significance of Chudleigh's Platonic thought. As we will see, Chudleigh's Platonic views allow her to reimagine the language of and acts of viewing in her poem; the consequence is her deemphasizing of the Fall while directing us toward a redemptive portrait that stresses acts of (re)creation.

Chudleigh will continue to un-"bound" elements of *Paradise Lost* through her reorientation of the use of the language of perspective in the poem. Thus, words such as "view," "ken," "gaze," "survey," and "prospect," which recur throughout *Paradise Lost*, will be employed alternately in *The Song of the Three Children Paraphras'd* as she traces an infinite and divine space of the universe. While Milton's poem stages a power struggle over the act of viewing, that power struggle will be transformed into Chudleigh's narrative of Platonic, and genderless, souls. For the *Song*, viewing becomes the purview of all ungendered souls. With Satan's appropriated control over perspective transformed into the gazing soul in the *Song*, the narrative of the Fall—if not "unwritten" in the *Song*—is profoundly deemphasized. Emphasizing the Platonic pre-existence of souls, these acts of creation also draw explicitly on the "boundless" nature of Chudleigh's poem. The pre-existing soul, able to acquire a visual perspective onto the infinite universe, is about to break another bound—that of gender. Our spiritual identities—like the genderless ethereal bodies of angels in *Paradise Lost*—are not bound by gender identification. By rejecting gendered souls, Chudleigh can reject this politically and socially restrictive category, a project she began in *The Ladies Defence*. Her return to *Paradise Lost*, then, produces a Platonic perspective of, and onto, souls released from the boundaries of gender.

In order to see how she engages *Paradise Lost*, and of course the portrait of Satan, let me outline what I see as the staged battle for visual perspective and power that characterizes *Paradise Lost* and will be recuperated in the *Song*. This battle is registered in *Paradise Lost* through the changing ownership of and associations with the language of viewing throughout the poem. While certainly the gradual diminishment of Satan in *Paradise Lost* accounts for fewer words of perspective applied to or used by him as the poem moves to its close, the middle of Milton's poem is characterized by Satan's usurpation of God's acts of, and language about, viewing. As the poem moves toward Books 11 and 12, these acts of viewing will be handed over to Adam. Yet Books 3 and 4 stage a pitched battle over the language of perspective that will not be fully resolved until the poem's end.

Words such as "prospect" and "ken" map the ownership of perspective that characterizes *Paradise Lost*. "Prospect," for example, is first used by God: "Him God beholding from his prospect high" (3.77). But the word itself, and the acts of vision associated with it, will become appropriated by Satan in Books 3 to 5. In Book 3, Satan looks down onto the Earth and is compared to a scout "Which to his eye discovers unawares / The goodly prospect of some foreign land" (3.548). Having taken over the expansive "prospect" of God "Wherein past, present, future he beholds" (3.78), Satan will literally take over the prospect made by God: "Yet higher than their tops / The verdurous wall of Paradise up sprung: / Which to our general Sire gave prospect large / Into his nether Empire neighboring round" (4.142–45). The prospect created by God—in Book 3 reduced from a timeless view to Satan's more limited view of vengeance—is once again appropriated by Satan. This process continues through Book 4 as God's own creations, as here with the Tree of Life, are transformed by Satan into his own "prospect":

Thence up he flew, and on the Tree of Life,
The middle Tree and highest there that grew,
Sat like a Cormorant; yet not true Life
Thereby regain'd, but sat devising Death
To them who liv'd; nor on the virtue thought
Of that life-giving Plant, but only us'd
For prospect. (4.194–200)

The control that Satan establishes over such prospects is confirmed by his conferring onto Eve, in her dream, possession of such a view: "Forthwith up to the Clouds / With him I flew, and underneath beheld / The Earth outstretcht immense, a prospect wide / And various: wond'ring at my flight and change / To this high exaltation" (5.86–90). Satan's appropriation of God's "prospects" becomes a form of power which Satan now has the ability to distribute to Eve.

Ultimately, by Book 11 that "prospect" will be wrested from Satan and returned to Adam by Michael: "It was a Hill / Of Paradise the highest, from whose top / The Hemisphere of Earth in clearest ken / Stretcht out to the amplest reach of prospect lay" (11.377–80). Michael's control over the final "prospects" of the poem continues into Book 12 as he instructs Adam: "each place behold / In prospect, as I point to them," a physical and spiritual mapping of biblical human history now provided to man. Satan's loss of the word "prospect" to Adam occurs as well with "ken," a word that Satan appears to own in the first two books: the only uses of the word at the poem's opening are by the fallen archangel. But as we see with "prospect," it too becomes enveloped into the perspectival view of mankind by the poem's end: "from whose top / The Hemisphere of Earth in clearest ken / Stretcht out to the amplest reach of prospect lay" (11.377–80). A perspectival battle is engaged throughout *Paradise Lost*, with Satan's initial victory ultimately negated as the words travel from God, to the fallen angels, to finally be utilized to educate Adam or to describe his now chastened perspective.

While Milton stages this battle of control through the motif of viewing, Chudleigh will appropriate this language of perspective to represent an alternative view of the character of souls and thus of the Fall: the boundlessness of the universe she represents can be accessed by inherent good souls who have visual access to this "boundless" view. She begins this reconfiguration in the opening lines of the poem, affording us the opportunity to observe this second rich set of Miltonic echoes in her verse. A focus on the ascent of the soul and the perspectival position this affords to her as speaker opens Chudleigh's poem:

Ascend my Soul, and in a speedy Flight
Haste to the Regions of eternal Light;
Look all around, each dazling Wonder view,
And thy Acquaintance with past Joys renew.
Thro' all th' Æthereal Plain extend thy Sight,
    On ev'ry pleasing Object gaze. (1–6)

In an opening entirely unlike the apocryphal Song Chudleigh claims to be paraphrasing, her poem begins with an ascent to heaven and the establishing of a perspectival position—a "prospect" if you will—from which to observe all of Creation and this boundless, infinite universe. With the ascent of the poet to "the Regions of eternal Light" and the language of "Flight," Milton's project, especially that which he undertakes in Book 3, also appears embedded within Chudleigh's opening.

Yet the seeming invocations to Book 3 are only part of what Chudleigh does with the language of visual perspective in her poem. Not only does Chudleigh emphasize the theme of sight as does Milton: she even turns to many of these images with greater frequency. Chudleigh's poem, one-sixth the length of *Paradise*

Lost, has one more use of "gaze" and only one less use of the word "survey" than Milton's epic. To Milton's four uses of "ken," Chudleigh has two. When one considers the number of lines in each poem, Chudleigh thus employs twice as many uses of the word "view" and almost twice the instances of "prospect." Thus, the theme of viewing, so central in *Paradise Lost*, is adopted by Chudleigh for her own purposes. She enters into one of the most contested sites of power in the poem, one that she will turn to her own advantage as she redeploys these motifs.

Chudleigh's use of "ken" in her poem relocates the word amid spiritual perspectives, granted to souls who are reclaiming it from Satan. Before the term is returned to Adam in Book 11, it served as Satan's perspectival position in *Paradise Lost*: casting his eye around Hell, for example, "At once as far as Angels' ken he views / The dismal Situation waste and wild" (1.59–60). In Book 3, a moment when much of the control over the visual is appropriated by Satan, we are shown Uriel through him: "the Air, / Nowhere so clear, sharpn'd his visual ray / To objects distant far, whereby he soon / Saw within ken a glorious Angel stand" (3.619–22). Chudleigh reconfigures this phrase, in which the "ken" is a product of Satan's "sharpn'd . . . visual ray," into the phrase "the sharpest Ken of Sight" (62). In fact, she appears to fuse Satan's two uses of "ken" as, now, the view is onto boundless Heavenly plains rather than onto Hell, "waste and wild":

Ye glorious Plains of pure unshaded Light,
Which far above the gloomy Verge of Night
Extended lie, beyond the sharpest Ken of Sight;
Whose Bounds exceed the utmost Stretch of Thought. (60–63)

"Ken" becomes that unbounded view open to the soul as the visual emphasis in this poem returns us to an infinite or unbounded space that allows for a focus on (hu)man's inherent goodness. At almost the very end of the poem, she returns to such a spiritualized form of viewing. As "holy Souls, who from your Bondage free, / Have reach'd th' inmost Mansions of the Skie," we are located in Heaven once again (1778–79). These "dazzling Glories . . . lie / Beyond the utmost Ken of a weak mortal Eye" (1780, 1781–82). But they are within the "ken" or "Vast . . . Prospect" (1800) of souls now distinctly separated from the sin of Satan or of mankind.

This marks Chudleigh's transformation of the "bounds" of *Paradise Lost* into the "boundless" space of her Platonic creation poem. Now, the limitations of vision, the "sharpest Ken of Sight" "beyond" which the ethereal plain "Extended lie[s]," turns "Bounds" into that which is "exceed[ed]." Turning "bounds" inside out, Chudleigh thus transforms that which was bounded into boundlessness—a fact marked by Chudleigh's use of "bound" four times in the poem, but "boundless" eight. And of those four uses of "bounds," two follow this example—where bounds are transformed into a limitless space. The other two uses of "bound" are Miltonic echoes.

This transformation of bounds into the "boundlessness" of Chudleigh's poem is also profoundly inflected by gender. We can observe this best in her negotiation of the word "gaze": amid all the perspectival language in *Paradise Lost*, only this word is not redeemed in the course of Milton's poem. "Gaze" is the only word describing visual acts accorded a purely demonic nature: only Satan, or the Fallen Angels, will "gaze." The act of gazing by Satan is explicitly voyeuristic, from his hatred-filled spying onto the Earth, to his desire-filled observation of Adam and Eve in Book 4, and finally his viewing of Eve through the course of his seduction. Chudleigh's use of "gaze" undemonizes this contested site of perspective. Chudleigh takes up, and transforms, Satan's "gazing" ability precisely because Satan introduced this term to Eve. Employed by her in the Book 5 dream, "on that Tree [one of those from Heav'n] also gaz'd," Eve has been taught by Satan how to gaze (57). And at the moment of temptation, this form of viewing is most fully associated with her fall: "Fixt on the Fruit she gaz'd, which to behold / Might tempt alone" (9.735–36). Chudleigh thus takes up the most problematic form of looking, one that both predicts the postlapsarian while linking that state to woman's action. In order to redeem Eve, Chudleigh must thus redeem the "gaze." Her very engagement with the language motifs employed by Satan exposes, on one hand, her radical acts within the poem. On the other, her engagement with Satan, as with her profoundly reworked Miltonic "source" text, allows her access to redemption for such radical acts.

The frequency with which Chudleigh uses the word "gaze" in her poem highlights the significance of this term for her project; she uses the word one more time than does Milton in her poem one-sixth the length of *Paradise Lost*. More significant, though, are the terms of her reconfiguration of the "gaze." Used, in all of its forms, almost solely by Satan in *Paradise Lost*, the word not only joins all of the language of viewing in Chudleigh's *Song*, but is used to describe the perspective accorded to her own soul (or that of the narrator), as well as that of the angels, mankind, Adam and Eve, and implicitly the reader him or herself. All, in Chudleigh's poem, are given access to the infinite space of the universe, one filled with God's goodness. The *Song* opens with the narrator's soul which "On ev'ry pleasing Object gaze[s]" (6). That soul is viewing the effects of the Flood at line 602 and the refining of the earth through the Last Judgment: "the Prodigy admire, / And on the new-form'd Glory gaze" (701–2). These may be the violent sights of the end of the world, but the viewers are transformed through this act of gazing. This comes to mark Chudleigh's sustained engagement with the word throughout her poem. "Gazing" becomes, instead, reformative. Adam and Eve "gaz'd" on "some new Wonder found" (988); angels "Gaze on, gaze on . . . And as you gaze, his Praises sing" (1062–63); "the faithful Few on their dear Saviour gaze" through the crucifixion scene embedded into the narrative; and the chosen Israelites "With Joy they gaz'd, and as they gaz'd, they sung" (1199,

1467). No longer pejorative, the "gaze" itself links one to redemption and the spiritual plane.

Most importantly, this "gaze" in Chudleigh will elide, instead of articulate, the distinction of gender. In this, Chudleigh profoundly rewrites Milton's use of Satan's view onto Adam and Eve in Book 4. It is through Satan, who "Saw undelighted" and "still in gaze" observes Adam and Eve, that we are first introduced to gender in the poem (286, 356). From Satan's perspective, Adam and Eve seem distinct: "For contemplation hee and valor form'd, / For softness shee and sweet attractive Grace" (4. 297–98). This reclaiming of visual motifs by Chudleigh's poem, in conjunction with the "boundlessness" offered to these "gazing" souls, accomplishes the goal proposed in the 1701 *Ladies Defence*: readmittance

. . . to our former State;
Where, free from the Confinement of our Clay
In glorious Bodies we shall bask in Day,
And with inlightened Minds new Scenes survey. (826–29)

Beyond gender, such "inlightened Minds" will now "survey" the universe. Women as men will be able to escape the categories of gender, now "free from the Confinement of our Clay." For, such spiritual souls, in "glorious Bodies" which are no longer material, exist outside of the physical characteristics and distinctions between men and women.

This space beyond gender will allow the narrative of the Fall—so embedded into this struggle over perspective—to be reconfigured: the terms of culpability will be rewritten. *The Ladies Defence* can both explain Chudleigh's move to compose the *Song* while exposing the powerful political component within the poem. The worldview provided by Chudleigh, shaped by strands of Platonic thought and enabled by Milton's own narrative of the Fall, transforms the Fall through the suspension of gender. The Fall becomes in Chudleigh's *Song* a simultaneous act by Adam and Eve: "Ah! thoughtless Pair! how soon were you undone!" (989); "Thrise blest that Pair, who in the Dawn of Time / Were made Possessors of that happy Clime: / But wretched they soon lost their blissful State, / Undone by their own Folly, not their Fate" (501–4). The collective sin erases gender, made irrelevant by the pre-existence of our (genderless) souls. Eve's sin is thus deemphasized as the ground upon which gendered hierarchy can be built.

In Chudleigh's negotiation of the "gaze," one demonized within *Paradise Lost* but redeemed, if you will, in the *Song*, we see an intriguing refraction of an earlier use of the gaze by a female poet, one which, as in Chudleigh's poem, allowed for an interrogation of female culpability for the Fall. As I argued in Chapter 2, Aemilia Lanyer's successful acquisition of a spiritual perspective onto Christ's Passion allows her to free women from the gendered hierarchy to which they had been condemned by the Fall. This negotiation of

acts of looking for the purposes of revising women's social and political positions recalls Regina Schwartz's interrogation of the use of the gaze within
Paradise Lost. Distributing rather than consolidating gendered power, the reading of voyeurism that Schwartz offers within the poem is instructive in considering what uses Lanyer and Chudleigh can make of the gaze, either by
refiguring it in the case of Chudleigh or allowing it to refigure women's place
within the culture. I am not suggesting here that Chudleigh maps a tri-textual
engagement of these three poems: she would have been very unlikely to know
of Lanyer's *Salve Deus*, so far away was this 1611 poem from her milieu and
her generic interests in the *Song*. I use the word "refraction" here to suggest
that—as do many of the chapters within this book—earlier seventeenth-
century problems over gender, ones that Milton engages but cannot either
fully resolve or silence, remain as traces that later writers discover and develop. The roles of gazing and its gendered associations—during the Passion,
the Fall, and visions of Creation—are two such cruxes that resonate into the
very late seventeenth century.

Chudleigh's substantively rewritten treatment of Milton's matrix of words
about visual perspective thus has profound social and political implications for
the narrative of the Fall. In response to the Parson's claim in *The Ladies Defence*
that Eve "shou'd be to a strict Subjection brought" (306), that women should
"on your Mother *Eve* alone reflect" (328), Chudleigh returns to, and reconfigures, the Fall narrative at the heart of *Paradise Lost*. In answering the Parson
through Milton's poem, Chudleigh presents us with an alternative (contemporary) interpretation of *Paradise Lost*: this poem offered to her a more radical,
even a socially disruptive, opportunity to respond to detractors of women at
the end of the century. In setting what many critics have read as an orthodox
poem against a conservative attack on women, Chudleigh was able to intervene into late seventeenth-century discourses about marriage and women's position with the institution. Through *Paradise Lost*, then, Chudleigh was able to
challenge the foundations of social and political organization in the period.
Milton's political radicalism offered Chudleigh an opportunity to engage issues
of gender hierarchy in suggestively revolutionary ways at the very end of the
seventeenth century.

In the final chapter, I turn to two women, Aphra Behn and Mary Astell,
whose politics could hardly be seen as republican or revolutionary. While my
reading of the *Song* purposely puts the stolid Tory identity of Chudleigh
under pressure, Behn's and Astell's alignment with providential monarchy and
their resistance to the contractarian arguments of late seventeenth-century
thinkers such as Algernon Sidney and John Locke is supported by their biog-
raphies and their writings. Yet they too will turn, in more and less destabilizing ways, to the figure of Satan and his role in the Fall. While neither woman
will appropriate and reform the language of and about Satan from Milton's
Paradise Lost, both writers do reconfigure a Satanic identity in their disruptive

Spaces and Traces of the Garden Story in Aphra Behn and Mary Astell: Mapping Female Subjectivit(ies) Through Patriarchialist Discourse

Mary Chudleigh's reimagination of the story of the Fall, in particular Milton's version of it, allowed her to unfetter the female "spirit" from gendered physical bodies, consequently redefining what constituted women's "selves" in the course of her philosophical poem, *The Song of the Three Children Paraphras'd*. Such unfettering was driven by Chudleigh's objections to the material conditions of marriage in the late seventeenth century and prompted her to free all, including female, spirits through her poem. Mary Astell and Aphra Behn distinctly, but in suggestively similar ways, also engage the female "self" through their engagement with the Garden space and the material(ity) of the Genesis tale. They enter the Garden in a much more physicalized manner than did Chudleigh. In fact, Astell's construction of an educative, and redemptive, seminary for women in *A Serious Proposal* returns us to the "ground" of this book: as did female defenders of Eve at the opening of the seventeenth century, Astell imagines a garden to which women are provided access. Here the social ills experienced by uneducated women can be converted from potential falls resulting from lack of knowledge into a redemptive model for regaining paradise. Alternately, Aphra Behn reveals, and revels in, an eroticized Garden space in *Love-Letters Between a Nobleman and His Sister*. While Astell offers a reconstructed prelapsarian site characterized by a redemptive vision of female knowledge, Behn engages references to Adam and Eve to explore a postlapsarian sexuality in which falls, social as well as moral, can occur again and again. What occurs within these forays into the Garden myth, though, is an engagement with issues of female interiority or subjectivity which emerge through Behn's and Astell's response to debates around marriage in the last decades of the seventeenth century.

Marriage, a culturally significant topic with fundamentally political implications, received much attention during the late seventeenth century. It becomes the vehicle through which Behn and Astell explore gender hierarchy and forms

of self-knowledge while exposing gender's association with political organization. The years 1673–1675, 1681–1686, and 1695–1700 mark significantly elevated periods of publication on the subject[1]: Behn's and Astell's interrogations
of marriage are located within certain peak moments of concern about the institution. The second of these periods marks almost the exact dates of the three
volumes of Behn's *Love-Letters Between a Nobleman and His Sister*: 1684, 1685, and
1687. Astell's *Reflections upon Marriage* occurs at the end of this third rich period
of print production, as well as in the specific year that saw the largest number
of tracts, sermons, essays, and songs on marriage: 1700. Behn's and Astell's
modes of challenging certain aspects of marriage theory—in particular the
family/state analogy that undergirded claims of governmental, and particularly
monarchical, authority—also model a female interiority disruptive of marriage's ability to stabilize theories on governmental organization.

As I have suggested, the interventions of women writers into debates in
seventeenth-century political theory layer overt, instrumental engagements of
texts with intertextual opportunities produced by that engagement. In the
course of intervening into debates about the political and marriage contract,
Behn and Astell come to reflect upon the condition and nature of the female
subject. Their texts present distinct conclusions: Behn's portrait of marriage's
instability is generated in concert with the unstable subjectivity of her female
protagonist. Astell's exploration, even promotion, of a richly developed interior for women exposes structural limitations to patriarchalist theory. Astell
produces a contingent portrait of female subjectivity, one—as with Behn—
overdetermined by motifs from the story of the Fall itself. Behn and Astell's
texts thus model what I am terming "biblical subjectivity," a form of subjectivity that recursively engages the biblical text. Whether it is Silvia in *Love-Letters*,
the female "Reflector" in *Reflections upon Marriage*, or the women Mary Astell
hopes to educate in the *Serious Proposal*, these women simultaneously occupy the
position of Eve, who is constrained by the dictates of Genesis, while they explore
subject positions distinct from conventional representation of Eve. From within
the narrative of Genesis, both Behn and Astell interrogate, even challenge, a primary component of contemporary political debate by engaging the subject of
marriage. As they do, these writers expose their own struggles to formulate a
female subject that can be distinguished from "Eve" while still echoing elements
of this Ur-narrative of "woman's" identity. Such seventeenth-century debates
around marital and political order simultaneously stage a debate about the constitution of female identity.

While the patriarchalist versus contractarian theory debate had shifted in significant ways after the events of 1688, the relationship between the family
unit and the state continued to vex theorists and theories ranging from republican to monarchist.[2] Though separated by over ten years, with Behn's *Love-
Letters* published on one side of the accession to the throne by William and

Mary and Astell's *Reflections upon Marriage* and *A Serious Proposal* on the other, these two texts were surrounded by influential patriarchalist writings such as those by Robert Filmer.[3] Filmer's *Patriarcha*, a collation of his theoretical justification for monarchical government likely written in the years before the Civil War, was published posthumously in 1680; at this point it gained the attention of, among others, John Locke. Locke then proceeds to structure his *First Treatise* around a refutation of Filmer's text: in it, "The False Principles and Foundation of Sir Robert Filmer, And His Followers, are Detected and Overthrown" (tp, *Two Treatises*, 1698).[4] While Locke's text does not appear in print until 1698, *Patriarcha*'s 1680 publication also prompted James Tyrrell to publish *Patriarch non monarcha: The patriarch unmonarch'd* the next year (1681). Its subtitle makes explicit Tyrrell's engagement with Filmer: "being observations on a late treatise . . . published under the name of Sir Robert Filmer . . . in which the falseness of those opinions that would make monarchy Jure divino are laid open."

If Behn's text is produced in an environment where Filmer was actively debated, so too was Astell's *Reflections upon Marriage*, originally published in 1700. Locke's explicit attack on Filmer—almost definitely written in the early 1680s—was first published in 1698 as the *Two Treatises of Government*.[5] That same year, Algernon Sidney's *Discourses Concerning Government* appeared; this posthumous publication, which had been used to convict Sidney of treason, declares in its first sentence a similarly active engagement with Filmer's thought: "Having lately seen a Book, intituled *Patriarcha*, written by *Sir Robert Filmer*, . . . I thought a time of leisure might be well employed in examining His doctrine" (B1r).

The "Reflections" that both Behn and Astell provide on marriage thus exist within a triangulated relationship between foundational narratives of Genesis and debates over the relationship between the family and the state. Both Filmerian patriarchal theory and Locke's response in the *First Treatise of Government* employ the originary Genesis narrative for justifying forms of government. Appropriately, then, Behn's and Astell's engagement of pre- and postlapsarian gardens, ones frequently inflected through Milton's *Paradise Lost*, speak to the family/state analogy and its political implications. Since *Paradise Lost* was the most significant poetic retelling of Genesis in the second half of the seventeenth century, their engagement with Milton is consequently not surprising.

But the implications of Milton's politics might be so: as Chapter 6 has indicated, Milton's reputation as a regicidal Republican often competed with his status as poet. Nonetheless, Milton, Behn, and Astell are all linked by their interrogation of the severability of marriage. Milton, whose prose works were republished in 1698, directly addressed the issue of divorce in his 1640s tracts. In a sensationalist and eroticized format, Behn is similarly narrating options for the severability of marriage throughout *Love-Letters Between a Nobleman and His*

Sister, a narrative in which all the central relationships are the result of de facto divorces. And Mary Astell's *Reflections upon Marriage*, "Occasion'd by the Duke & Dutchess of Mazarine's" separation, is centrally concerned with the implications of bad marriages—the very issue that drove Milton so passionately to explore the divorce issue. Divorce itself, as Rachel Weil has shown, is a profoundly political issue in the late seventeenth century.[6] Milton's own writings on divorce and the terms of Astell's famous challenge to Milton underscore this: "I suppose there's no Man but likes it very well in this; how much soever Arbitrary Power may be dislik'd on a Throne, not *Milton* himself wou'd cry up Liberty to poor *Female Slaves*, or plead for the Lawfulness of Resisting a Private Tyranny" (46–47). In her rebuke to Milton, Astell explicitly stresses the politically resonant language of "Liberty" and "Tyranny," fusing the domestic event of divorce with the language of political resistance.[7]

Thus, if one wanted to speak to issues of marriage, particularly the politically inflected first marriage at the heart of Filmer's thinking and responses by Tyrrell, Sidney, and Locke, Milton offered a canonical and culturally resonant portrait of Adam and Eve through which to engage the topic. Cultural invocations of or rewritings of *Paradise Lost* in the late seventeenth century highlight how issues of gendered hierarchy could be negotiated through *Paradise Lost*. John Dryden's 1678 publication of *The State of Innocence*, the operatic version of *Paradise Lost* that a disdainful Marvell refers to as "tagged," began a small trend; when John Hopkins undertook an "imitation" of Books 4, 6, and 9 in 1699, he justified his poetic undertaking through Dryden's earlier work. When rewriting Milton's poem in rhyme, John Dryden's, as John Hopkins's, choices highlight *Paradise Lost*'s status as a cultural repository for debates over gender in the late seventeenth century; Joseph Wittreich has even suggested that Dryden rewrites the poem to correct the representation of Eve presented in Milton's epic, transforming it from an "Eviad," in Barbara Lewalski's view, to an "Opera of Adam."[8] For both Dryden's and Hopkins's much harsher judgments delivered to Eve at the Fall present a much different image of the relationship between man and woman. In Dryden, the "curse" Eve receives after taking the forbidden fruit is much more extreme than in *Paradise Lost*: "She, by a curse, of future wives abhorr'd, / Shall pay Obedience to her lawful Lord: / And he shall rule, and she in thraldom live; / Desiring more of love than man can give" (41).[9] While Dryden's prefallen Eve illustrates a desire for knowledge and access to reason, in her transgression she is placed in more than the state of "Obedience" that marks the biblical and Miltonic punishment.[10] In addition to the "rule" that Milton gives man over woman, Dryden accords Eve, and all subsequent women, the status of "thrall"; for Wittreich, these definitive alterations are meant to "cancel Miltonic ambiguity" in the representation of Eve ("Maneuvers," 249). Hopkins also recreates the interactions of Adam and Eve in his "imitations," leaving us with an equally harsh claim about gender hierarchy in Book 9: "And the Wife blames the Man who should restrain her Will"

(56), states the narrator, recalling the "thrall"-like status assigned to women by Dryden.[11]

Because of the alternatives that Dryden and Hopkins present, Astell and Behn may have found *Paradise Lost* and Milton's portrait of Eve simpatico with their own concerns.[12] Defenders of women could certainly deploy the poem to argue against women's status as subordinate "thralls." *The Female Preacher*, published the same year as Hopkins's "imitations," employs frequent references to the Genesis story to defend women.[13] Countering the language of Dryden's "thraldom" in which women now must "live," the anonymous author defends women by arguing that a wife is "social help, not a servile one" (21). The voice of "The Great Milton, a very grave Author" appears, praising Eve as the *"fairest of Creation! last and best / Of all God's Works"* (21). Milton thus becomes the very defense against the claim that women are "thralls" to their husbands: in *The Female Preacher*, " 'Tis granted the Woman was created for the Man, but we deny that this is any pretence to use the *limited Power* which Heaven has given him to the Unhappiness and Ruin of a Creature that was made for him" (21, C3r; my emphasis).[14] Available for quotation and co-optation, Milton's poem is fully integrated into this cultural discussion about women's pre-and postlapsarian condition.

For this reason, Behn and Astell may well have turned to his account of the originary marriage and the portrait of gendered hierarchy conveyed in the poem while engaging the issues of wrongly matched marriages explored in his Divorce tracts. Milton's writing allows them, as it had allowed writers such as Dryden, Hopkins, and the author of *The Female Preacher*, to engage these issues in the last two decades of the seventeenth century. Like Dryden and Hopkins, they will produce a resistant reading of *Paradise Lost*, yet in terms that are quite different. Unlike Chudleigh, who rewrites the potential within *Paradise Lost* to free women from the "Confinement of [their] Clay" (*Defence*, 827), Behn and especially Astell rewrite aspects of Milton's Eve, exploring her position in marriage and the implications for describing an internal subjectivity for her.[15]

Aphra Behn's three-part novel, *Love-Letters Between a Nobleman and His Sister*, will refract specific elements of the Garden narrative into her account of scandalous and faux marriages. Following the exploits of Philander and Silvia, brother- and sister-in-law, as they escape her parents' manor home in order to continue their transgressive love affair, this epistolary novel builds upon the sexual scandal of Lady Henrietta Berkeley and Lord Grey.[16] Additionally, political plots encircle the narrative as Philander initially joins Cesario, a figure for the Duke of Monmouth, in plotting the overthrow of the king. By the third volume, this narrative becomes a lightly veiled account of the failed 1685 Monmouth Rebellion: staged by Charles II's illegitimate son against his uncle now on the throne, these events dominate the final pages of the novel. Because the political rebellion of the Duke of Monmouth is interwoven with the sexual substitutions of wives for sisters, then mistresses for lovers, the question of the relationship between private love affairs and monarchical legitimacy remains at the center of the novel and interpretations of it. Since political treachery is positioned alongside emotional treachery, one would expect these two spheres to comment upon each other. Yet, as many critics have noted, the novel resists a coherent reading of corollaries between the "private" or domestic world of Silvia's lovers and narratives of political rebellion. Even when critics argue for the connection between personal and political spheres in the novel, no simple Whig/Tory distinctions between these spheres are sustainable for long: Philander's possibly Whiggish exchangability of allegiance is soon reflected in Silvia's emotional and bodily circulation in the world.[17] Similarly Cesario, the figure for the rebellious Monmouth, does take on a lover whom he considers his wife. Yet the loyalty Cesario and his lover Hermione show to each other is heroic: a reading of this as an analogue for rebellion becomes impossible to sustain.

I would suggest instead that Behn is purposely interrogating modes of connecting political and sexual events in her novel. Flirting with interconnections between familial and "state" spheres, the very basis for Filmer's thinking in *Patriarcha*, Behn comes to radically different conclusions about the connection between familial, and especially marital, metaphors for describing and legitimating the state. The consequence in the *Love-Letters* is a sustained parody of marriage, shown to be unable to effect either personal or political stability. The larger consequence is an undermining of the patriarchalist analogy of the family and state. Turning, as do Filmer and Locke, to the originary story of the Garden and the Fall, Behn engages the political implications of marriage through her use of a perversely rewritten Edenic narrative. Moving beyond a single or monogamous model to the doubling, even tripling of such unions, Behn's narrative defies any image of a stable marital union. She thus undermines, even annihilates, marriage as a model for a stable state.

As a method for and a consequence of fracturing the narrative of the Garden's originary marriage, Behn exerts extreme pressure on her protagonists' identities. Multiple narratives of the originary Fall story are achieved by assigning doubled and shifting identities of Adam and Eve within Behn's narrative. Behn thus employs sliding referents and substitutions in her portraits of Silvia and Philander; the multiple identities that Silvia and others occupy thus correspond with the many second or even third marital "unions" imagined, asserted, or performed within *Love-Letters*. Silvia thus descends into a particularly contingent subjectivity, in part defined by biblical categories of femininity while simultaneously invoking the period's political instability. Partially constructed through accounts of Eve, Silvia will also be described through the language of Satan's rebellion and fall. Thus, the political and religious rebellion undertaken by Satan is reoriented within *Love-Letters*. Silvia, who will herself rebel against the grounding narrative of seventeenth-century patriarchalist thought, shows the family/state analogy to be unmoored and emptied of significance through her plurality of marriages and plurality of identities. Thus,

Silvia's identity as both Eve and as a seventeenth-century whore at the center of political events will dispute marriage's capacity to ground monarchical authority in Restoration England. Ironically, in Behn's libertine-inflected novel, the very turn to a biblically defined identity for women undermines the gendered hierarchy produced by the Genesis tale. Behn's own highly unconventional lifestyle may well have made marriage an unworkable institution for her personally. While her skepticism about marriage in this novel was unlikely to have been an intentional critique of the Stuart kings whom she repeatedly eulogized, the implications of undermining the marital union in her novel nonetheless effect the political system that rested upon a narrative of Paradisical marriage.[18]

From the opening pages of the novel, the garden space in Silvia's family's estate, Bellfont, contains repeated Edenic references. This association of the two lovers with Adam and Eve is underscored through repeated references to their love as originary: "in my Creation I was form'd for Love, and destin'd for my *Silvia*, and she for her *Philander*," a sentiment that Silvia mouths, if not fully echoes: "You say my Adorable Brother, we were destin'd from our Creation for one another" (16, 50). While the sentiment of being created for another resonates through many romances, "Heaven" is repeatedly represented as the agent here. The details thus recall Adam's successful request to have a mate created for him in the Garden. Asserting the heavenly status of their marriage, Silvia continues to validate their love by invoking language about the creation of Eve for Adam: "divine decrees at our Creation" validate their relationship (110); "Marriages are made in Heaven" (111), and thus Silvia "is thy Wife, *Philander*, He is my Husband, this is the match" (112).

These invocations of the Edenic narrative will be turned on their head by the structuring narrative of incest in the novel and Behn's playful doubling of marriage(s). The tradition of the enclosed garden now fuses with the incestuous love of a brother (in-law) and sister, a component, of course, of the originary Genesis narrative. The opening letter of the novel even offers biblical justification for incest between consanguineal relations.[19] Though initially denying that they are truly brother and sister, Philander ultimately rewrites the implications of the biblical injunction "be fruitful and multiply": "let us love like the first race of men, nearest allied to God, promiscuously they lov'd, and possess'st, Father and Daughter, Brother and Sister met, and reap'd the joys of Love without controul, and counted it Religious coupling, and 'twas encourag'd too by Heav'n it self" (12). Explicitly Adam and Eve in their configuration as "the first race of men," Philander's letter goes on to tighten this association through the incestuous pairings of "Father and Daughter, Brother and Sister," both familial relationships which Adam and Eve could be said to enact. As Ellen Pollak has pointed out, incestuous practices had some "legitimacy," since Genesis orders the siblings Adam and Eve to reproduce (61). But by doubling the incestuous relationships, "Father and Daughter" *and* "Brother and Sister," Behn highlights the distinct forms of incest that could be seen as characterizing Adam and Eve's marriage; since Adam generates Eve through his rib, they could also be viewed as father and daughter. From the very beginning, then, the method Behn employs to establish connections between Silvia and Philander and Eve and Adam are doubled, occupying the incestuous status of both a "Brother and Sister" and a "Father and Daughter."

Philander's justification of incest in the Garden in order to validate this union between himself and Silvia thus shows how destabilized an otherwise grounding narrative or identificatory story can become. While the incest of Adam and Eve may have had some biblical justification, the kinship relationship of a brother- and sister-in law was consistently condemned, as in a tract by John Turner published the same year as the first part of *Love-Letters*. The gestures to the first marriage of Adam and Eve throughout the seduction of Silvia thus serve to pervert rather than to sustain the conventions of the first marriage.

As the novel, and its invocation of the language of Eden, moves forward, the same doubling of elements from the Garden narrative extends to the portrait(s) of Eve. We continue to hear echoes of Adam and Eve in the Garden as "Eve"-like descriptions are bestowed upon the woman who will follow Silvia in Philander's affections. The narrator, in a passage that Janet Todd views as a direct reference to *Paradise Lost*, critiques Silvia's actions as follows:[20]

Love else were not to be number'd among the passions of men, and was at first ordain'd in Heaven for some divine motion of the Soul, till *Adam* with his loss of *Paradise* debaucht it, with jealousies fears, and curiosities, and mixt it with all that was afflicting; but you'l say he had reason to be jealous, whose Woman for want of other Seducers listen'd to the Serpent, and for the Love of change wou'd give way even to a Devil, this little Love of Novelty and knowledge has been intail'd upon her daughters ever since, and I have known more Women rendered unhappy and miserable from this torment of curiosity, which they bring upon themselves, than have ever been undone by less villainous Men. (191)

While this comment associates Silvia explicitly to a fallen Eve, it is surrounded by references to Philander's new object of desire, Calista, who now becomes the beneficiary of associations with Eve. This includes the very location of their meeting in an (Edenic) garden. For, Philander encounters and then begins to pursue his second postmarital conquest, Calista, in a garden space whose perfection Behn stresses: it is "so delightful a place, which art and Nature had a greed to render Charming to every sense" (233). We had previously heard about Philander's encounter with Silvia in an "Arbour" recalling the bower of Adam and Eve where Calista and Philander will now meet. Further, Calista's beauty, but also innocence, prepares the reader for the novel's explicit comparison of her to Eve: "in the very purity of her innocence," she "appear'd like the first born Maid in Paradice" (236). Throughout these scenes, Philander occupies the role of Adam discovering his beautiful Eve; he is associated with the "new-form'd man," language evocative of the first "formed" Adam (236). Calista will consequently become substituted into the position of Eve previously occupied by Silvia, a process of substitution we have previously seen: Silvia, of course, had been previously substituted in the position held by her own sister as Philander's first, and legal, "wife."

As Silvia's own position as Edenic wife is challenged by this second Eve-like figure, the doubling of "Heaven"ly generated "marriages" challenges the notion of a singular Edenic marriage. The doubledness of marital practice has been introduced from the novel's opening, of course: since Philander is married to Silvia's sister, Mertilla, Philander and Silvia's association with Adam and Eve already "doubled" the number of Eves occupying that signifying position. While this "Adam" pursued a second union, described in Edenic language, he now compounds the situation by introducing a third Eve, Calista. This multiplication of "Eves" within the text leads to the most destablizing use of the Garden story. By casting Silvia and Philander as Adam and Eve figures, but then offering that multiplication of the "first" marriage through Philander's predisposition to stray, Behn fundamentally perverts the status of the "first" marriage as the foundation for either domestic or governmental modes of organization: the biblical identity so easy for Silvia and Calista to slip into shows itself to destabilize the premises of the first, Edenic marriage.

In addition to such substitutions, mock marriages, such as Silvia's to Brillyard, continue to undermine any stabilizing narrative of marriage. "Marriages" and their perversions multiply in the texts as Silvia, married to Brillyard, whose authority she simply refuses to acknowledge, pursues a second marriage with Octavio upon her jilting by Philander. (It could be seen as a third marriage were we to grant status to her and Philander's "Edenic" marriage.) At Philander's return, the narrator describes Silvia's view on marriage to him: "She regards him as one to whom she had a peculiar Right as the first Lover: She was married to his Love, to his Heart" (344). This form of "marriage," where actual contracts are elided and emotional desire is articulated as the ultimate form of association between a man and woman, sustains the doubling of and in marital unions: though legally married to Brillyard, she is "married" to the idea of Philander. As she adds Octavio to her emotional harem, this doubling becomes a tripling of unions: "but she could not indure to think of losing either: She was for two Reasons covetous of both, and swore Fidelity to both, protesting each the only Man; and she was now contriving in her Thoughts how to play the Jilt most Artificially; a Help meet, tho' natural enough to her Sex, she had not yet much essay'd, and never to this purpose" (345). Silvia's duplicity in love, which has followed from the doubledness of the status of "marriage" that she has lived, operates as more than just an indicator of her (now) manipulative, constantly performative, character. The divine or even legal status of marriage, expressed here in the language of "Help meet," is repeatedly invoked in order to be fundamentally parodied.

Appropriately, Behn's novel continuously interweaves explicit political language into the narrative: while (faux) marital unions may not support political stability, they still are infused with political significance. When Silvia learns of Philander's "perfidy," she claims that "thou hadst better have been damn'd, or have fall'n, like an ungrateful Traytor as thou art" (218). She thus lays blame at his feet in language that interweaves Philander's political and personal traitorous actions:

> thou seest base Traytor, I do not fall on thee with treachery, as thou hast on thy King and Mistress, to which thou has broke thy Holy vows of allegiance and Eternal Love! but thou that hast broke the Laws of God and Nature! What cou'd I expect, when neither Religion, Honour, common Justice, nor Law cou'd bind thee to humanity; thou that betray'd thy Prince, abandon'd thy Wife, renounc'd thy Child, kill'd thy Mother, ravisht thy Sister, and art in open Rebellion against thy Native country, and very Kindred, and Brothers. (218)

This litany of Philander's sins aligns his domestic "perfidy" to his political rebellion against his King. Silvia's attack here appears to confirm the stability of the family/state analogy: a disloyal Whig will be a disloyal husband and lover. Such an association between political and personal weaknesses might align Silvia's remarks, and possibly Behn's views, to the body of patriarchal thought. And yet, the narrative has erased any stability in marriage, and thus disrupted any effective, or affective, analogy between individual relationships and political order.

Codified as the building blocks of all subsequent marriages as well as of all future political justification and hierarchy in patriarchalist thought, Behn's play with these Genesis motifs carries profound political implications. The union of Adam and Eve, and the unity implied by the first marriage, underlay Filmer's theories of government. At the heart of Filmerian patriarchal theory, the first and subsequent marriages become distorted by Behn into a parody of social and political stability. In seeking a replacement for Mertilla, Philander trades one "wife" for another; Silvia's position as a "wife" is thus underscored and mocked by the Eve imagery. The account of Calista and Philander repeats this very narrative, while this pattern of substitutability exposes marriage's inability to operate as a stabilizing institution.

While the family/state analogy is repeatedly undermined by the behavior of both Silvia and Philander, their doubledness in the practices of love is matched by their unmoored identities, especially in sequences that invoke Milton's poem. Silvia is the character who shows the most ability to occupy multiple subject, as well as "marital," positions.[21] This portrait of Silvia's elusive "self" is infused with specifically Miltonic imagery. Her account of this social and moral fall aligns her to Lucifer. In the earliest stage of their romance, she had been "Angel-Brightness" to Philander as he saw in her "a Heaven of solid joy . . . open'd to my view" (86). And yet, only one letter later, Philander will accuse her of being the treacherous "snake that bask'd beneath the gay, the smiling flowers" (81). That she can be Satanic one moment and a prefallen portrait of Luciferan "Angel-Brightness" the next illustrates a slippage between innocence and malevolent temptation that defines the unstable character of Silvia. Modulated through the details of *Paradise Lost*, Silvia is transformed into the fallen angel: "Oh! thou had'st raised me to the height of Heaven to make my Fall to Hell the more precipitate. Like a fallen Angel now I howl and roar, and curse that Pride that taught me first Ambition; 'tis a poor Satisfaction now, to know (if thou could'st yet tell Truth) what Motive first seduced thee to my Ruin?" (371). Philander's behavior has been more than a seduction; it has transformed her into the very identity of the "Divel": "I (destin'd thy evil genius) was born for thy tormenter, for thou hast made a very Fiend of me, and I have Hell within; all rage, all torment, fire, distraction, madness; I rave, I burn" (218–19). This internalization of "Hell" invokes for the reader Milton's portrait of a tormented Satan, who "myself am Hell" as he reflects on his condition in Book 4 (75). Characterized by revenge, Satan contains "the hot Hell that always in him burns" (9.467). A "Fiend," tormented and looking to torment because of the "Hell" within herself, Silvia becomes defined by her desire for "Revenge" as her earlier Eve-like innocence descends into Satanic internal torment.

By casting Silvia as a, in fact the, fallen angel, Behn models Silvia's identity on Milton's Satan. The effect is to paint Silvia as rebellious of moral constraint: she has fallen, through love, into a position outside of acceptable social practices. For Silvia "quintessentially embodies unrecuperated female defiance of male supremacy" in her transformation into a mistress and then a whore (Pollak, 85). Her identity as a rebel fallen angel further invokes the same political rebellion undertaken by Milton's Satan. For Silvia's rebellion—highlighted by her identity as a fallen Eve who becomes the rebellious Satan—defies patriarchalist thought. As she shows through her behavior and her many perversions of the institution of marriage, Silvia rejects the identity of a "wife" or "help meet" upon which the foundation of marital and thus political stability could be established. A rebel aligned with Satan through sliding signifying practices within the novel, she destroys the very analogy of the family and the state built upon the gender hierarchy in a stable institution of marriage. She rebels, if you will, against patriarchal theory.

What emerges in the course of Silvia's development in the novel could almost be considered the transactional cost of participating in debates around political legitimacy. The very slipperiness of her identity, where Silvia can be Eve, Lilith, and Satan, illustrates Behn's intervention into debates around political organization while exposing the implications for female subjectivity: the "faux" marriage(s) in which Silvia finds herself are as unstable as her identity. If the destabilization of the Filmerian metaphor of family and state is accomplished through fracturing marriage as an institution, it fractures Silvia's "self" as well. Behn's intervention is a significant one: though not arguing against monarchy itself, she does—playfully, ironically, erotically—narrate the fundamental problem with patriarchal theory: marriage cannot generate stability, political or otherwise. For that stability to exist, the figure of Eve needs to remain as "help meet" in the domestic sphere in order to model the political. Once Silvia rebels against this social structure as did Satan, the ideological framework collapses. Most importantly, it is Behn's invocation of the Genesis narrative, particularly aspects of Milton's Garden, that highlights the effects of constituting Silvia through the biblical subject Eve.

For, in the course of using Eve to describe aspects of this character, the novel presents a Silvia more like the rebellious Satan or a seducing prostitute than either prelapsarian wife or future mother to mankind. The narrative seeks to shatter any singular subjectivity in Silvia. *Love-Letters* turns to these biblical echoes to expose the unworkable family/state metaphor—a goal, I am suggesting, of Behn's. In order to dismantle tenets of patriarchal theory through her narrative, Behn dismantles the figure of Silvia. Transformed into a "help-meet"/whore who contracts (faux) marriages, Silvia experiences the dissolution of a "self" as a result of the interpolated Fall narrative within *Love-Letters*. Identified through this Garden narrative as a fallen Eve, then possibly as Lilith (the rejected first wife of Adam known in Gnostic traditions), Silvia cannot achieve a singular subject position. Behn's narrative thus illustrates the interesting method and consequence of woman's involvement in political theory debates in the period. By engaging this set of issues through the original Garden narrative, Silvia remains divided between identification with Eve and some form of an independent self. This form of biblical subjectivity, where the female character is assumed into an identity as Eve, becomes in Behn's hands the fracturing of female subjectivity. Silvia, through her link to Eve, is caught between the trope of the first mother and a subject with a stable internal identity. Silvia can thus only be seen as pieces of a character rather than a more singularly constituted character.

Again, the intervention into and through *Paradise Lost* both prompts and records this process. The question of Eve's interiority and the status of her subjectivity have been debated by Milton critics. Yet the genesis of such critical debates can be observed in first Aphra Behn's and then Mary Astell's engagements with *Paradise Lost*. For Behn, the very efforts to discuss aspects of political organization draw her to the figure of Milton's Eve, resulting in a portrait of decentered subjectivity. Like Behn, Astell will take up the issue of marriage, explicitly in *Reflections upon Marriage* and implicitly in *A Serious Proposal*. We can observe Astell argue for a reconsideration of marriage through the very motifs of the Garden that structure *A Serious Proposal*. She too is drawn to Milton's portrait of Eve as it defines the problems of marriage in concert with an articulation of female interiority within a reframed Garden narrative. Astell will grant to women a kind of subjectivity or interiority often effervescent or intermittent in *Paradise Lost*. The interior self becomes a force in Astell through which women can rewrite conventions of femininity, though they are still constituted by the portrait of Eve. Astell will thus deploy "biblical subjectivity" to define female identity in her writings in her efforts to describe and denigrate the institution of marriage.

Considering women's character through the narrative of the Fall would necessarily take on a social and political dimension. Framing her discussion of marriage in *Reflections* with the theory of William Whiston, whom she quotes arguing that "before the Fall there was a greater equality between the two Sexes" (11), Astell's reconstruction of the Garden narrative in both of her tracts becomes as much a political as a social "Proposal." Astell, like Behn, will thus (re)write political theory through the Garden.[22] Astell defines a female interiority that undermines the state's ability to ground itself on the marital contract by promoting the choice made by a "self" when evaluating marriage. Her engagement of writers—such as Whiston and Milton—who engage the politically and theologically charged narrative of the Fall thus results in a fundamental destabilization of the institution of marriage. As she restores women to a "greater equality" with men, her challenges to the institution of marriage—and thus to the ideological backbone of patriarchalist theory—become as profound as Behn's.

Milton's influence on Astell, or least her engagement with his thought, is recorded explicitly by Astell herself. She critiques Milton, who "himself wou'd cry up Liberty to poor *Female Slaves*" (*Reflections*, 46–47); this might explain her remark in *Moderation truly stated* that he was "a better Poet than Divine or Politician" (80). Her engagement with Milton's poetry can be further tracked within the garden imagery she utilizes in *A Serious Proposal*. J. David Macey Jr. effectively argues that Astell appropriates "the pastoral rhetoric of *Paradise Lost*" in her *Serious Proposal* (165), linking Astell's account of Eve with Milton's characterization of her as Eden's "fairest unsupported Flower" and documenting Astell's use of the geographic placement of Eden on a "steep savage Hill" (165, 166). At a more general level, of course, Astell is drawing upon, and recasting, the Edenic narrative in her proposed prelapsarian "monastery": "Happy Retreat! which will be the introducing you into such a *Paradise* as your Mother *Eve* forfeited, where you shall feast on Pleasures" (19). Yet as we will see, this space lacks the forms of temptation that produced the original Fall: "Here are no Serpents to deceive you, whilst you entertain your selves in these delicious Gardens" (19–20).[23] Deploying throughout her two texts the language of temptation and knowledge, Astell consistently invokes the story of the Garden and Fall.

Astell thus embeds the narrative of the Garden into her *Serious Proposal* about women's needed rejection of the temptations of courtship and the interwoven temptations of superficiality. Often "in view of the Enemy and the familiarity and unwearied application of the Temptation" (18), women are exposed to "A constant Scene of Temptations" (31), thus "violently tempted"

(40) to "a thousand seductions and mistakes" (21). This portrait of the world, in which the (dangerous) practices of courtship are described, can only be countered by the safety offered in the garden space: "for their greater security" women should be "willing to avoid *temptation*" there (18). They will be able to avoid such temptation now through knowledge itself, as women are provided a redemptive form of the original fruit. In the monasteries she proposes in *A Serious Proposal*, women will now be "daily regaled on those delicious Fruits of Paradice," the "Tree of Knowledge" that men have "so long unjustly *monopoliz'd*" now available to women (38, 24). No longer the tree itself or the knowledge it represents, temptation becomes redefined as the practices of the social world— courtship, sexual seduction, even marriage—that threaten our reconfigured Eves. While other critics, such as Ruth Perry and Rachael Weil, have noted Astell's portrait of courtship's danger, Astell specifically deploys Genesis language to provide a narrative of female education that redeems its members from the Fall.[24] Made explicit in her extended discussion of marriage in *Reflections*, women are presented with, and are being educated to avoid, a fall into (a bad) marriage through these two tracts. Astell instead offers women access to the very knowledge that will now prevent them from such a fall.

These broader thematic connections between the story of the original Garden and her views on marriage and on female education become explicitly linked to Milton's earlier epic as Astell centers on the development of a female "inside." As Astell critiques and attempts to reform female exteriority—the very shortcomings that allow women to be tempted—she specifically negotiates the language of *Paradise Lost* and *Samson Agonistes* to construct and encourage women's inwardness. In her efforts to promote the soul, she will stress internal, spiritual values that are highlighted through the contrast between language of the outside versus the inside.[25] Astell's intertextual interventions into Milton's account of the Fall thus allow her to engage the gender hierarchy established within this poem while highlighting the political implications of these accounts of marriage in the Garden.

The first of these intertextual echoes to Milton emerges through Astell's emphasis on developing an inner self in order to resist temptation. The Edenic narrative she inflects through her writing thus attempts to train women to avoid an irreversible "fall" into a bad marriage. Astell's goals of reforming superficial women are enacted through her promotion of the transformation of the "outside" into another kind of "ornament." In the "Introduction" to Part II of the *Serious Proposal*, Astell asks "why shou'd that which usually recommends a trifling Dress, deter us from a real Ornament?" (72–73). Rejecting a "gay outside" that makes a "splendid appearance" (73), "Ornament" and "Beauty" become redefined to that which elevates the mind and the soul. "Books are now become the finest Ornaments of your Closets" (75) as the "Beauty of your Bodies is but a secondary care" (75); "true Vertue has Beauty enough in her self t'attract our hearts and engage us" (74): "Ornament" is consequently transposed from an external to an internal trait as women will "adorn . . . their minds with useful Knowledge" (24). Women are to learn that it will not be external "Encomiums" issued by the culture that will be "so satisfactory," but instead the "calm and secret Plaudit of her own Mind" (13). Transforming the language of physical beauty into knowledge and an interior, intellectual beauty, Astell redefines the terms of these women's appeal as she transforms outsides into insides.

The very link between "ornament," the language of that which is "outward" rather than "inward," interweaves Astell's revised Garden narrative with Milton's account of Eve. Eve's status as an "ornament" in the language of both Adam and Raphael constructed Eve as only an "outside." It is into this presentation of Eve that Astell will intervene. Even during his seemingly heretical Book 8 assignment to Eve of a form of "absolute"ness as a function of her loveliness, Adam sustains the poetic party line about her association with that which is "outward" or an "outside"—even if she is nonetheless "fair." In Raphael and Adam's exchange at the end of the book, Eve is described by man and angel as having had "on her bestow'd / Too much of Ornament" (8.537–38), "so adorn[ed]" as she is "for thy delight" (576). Through this passage, Eve's beauty and her person are described in the language of an "outside" or as "outward" four times. In fact, Adam is himself instructed to transform his account of her beauty as "outward" into an "outside." When describing his quandary in comprehending Eve's "absolute" "beauty," Adam affirms that "in outward show" she is "Elaborate," though of "inward [traits] less exact" (548, 538–39). Further, she is "inferior" "in the mind / And inward Faculties" (541–42). These "most excel," but since she is associated with "outward" traits, she also "resembl[es] less" the "Image" of God (542–44). When Raphael refines Adam's language to describe Eve as "An outside . . . fair no doubt," Raphael increases the level of superficiality assigned to Eve (568). In response, Adam "repli'[s]" as he has been instructed, repeating Raphael's term for distinguishing Adam's access to the interior, "outside" of which Eve is firmly to remain: "Neither her out-side form'd so fair, nor aught / In procreation common to all kinds," he assures Raphael, "So much delights me, as those graceful acts" of hers (8.595, 596–97, 600). The addition of the hyphen dividing "out" and "side" may underscore what has been asserted throughout: Eve stands "out-side" of a claim to either "inward Faculties" or the "inward"ness that *Paradise Lost* will increasingly value as it moves to the end.

The echoes of this attack on Eve's external nature continue within the much more negative portrait of her in Book 10 as well as in description of Dalilah in *Samson Agonistes*. In Adam's anti-feminist diatribe, Eve now becomes "but a show / Rather than solid virtue" (10.883–84), her "fair" "outside" now a "fair defect / Of Nature" (10.891–92). Thus, in the moments in *Paradise Lost* and *Samson Agonistes* where the anti-feminist position is most clearly expressed, woman's evil nature is articulated through language of the "outward." In the 1671 poem, Dalilah and then all women are thus denied interior traits by the Chorus, reduced to only the "outward ornament . . . lavish't on thir Sex" (1025, 26). Women's "inward gifts / Were left for haste unfinish't, judgment scant, / Capacity not rais'd to apprehend / Or value what is best" (1026–29). The external "out-side" traits that characterize women in the judgment of the Chorus are a marker of gender difference. As we will see, the distinction between "inward" and "outward" characteristics plots a gender hierarchy in *Paradise Lost* that Astell will rewrite.

Astell's monastery, in contrast, is designed to develop in women the very "inward gifts" that these exchanges in Milton's poems deny to women. Astell's revision of women's status as an "Ornament" challenges the very assertions of gendered categories displayed by Milton's later closet drama and the final books of *Paradise Lost*. By reconfiguring her Eve-like, prelapsarian pupils as possessors of such "inward Faculties" or "gifts," Astell rewrites both the Fall narrative and Milton's explicit gendering of "inwardness." Astell's educative process of self-improvement and self-understanding that marks both *Reflections* and *A Serious Proposal* defies the female gendering of "outside" and "outward" traits, literally giving back to Eve a garden space now filled with women possessing an inwardness previously denied them. Astell's focus on the terms of women's education and her transformation of the terms of the temptation thus allow her to configure Eve as educated into and through subjectivity. The development of women's "inward" nature becomes Astell's doubled practice of invoking Milton's Eve in order to reconfigure such a portrait of femininity.

This process of redefining the mental and interior traits of and in women continues to occur through revisions of key motifs from Milton's *Paradise Lost*. Early in *A Serious Proposal*, Astell details the form of "temptation" to which women are subjected, a scene that continues to argue for women's retreat to the Garden-like space of the monastery. And yet, the same themes of developing women's interior characters are now linked to Milton through an unusual use of language about the self:

From whence it easily follows, that she who has nothing else to value her self upon, will be proud of her Beauty, or Money, and what that can purchase; and think her self mightily oblig'd to him, who tells her she has those Perfections which she naturally longs for. Her inbred *self-esteem* and desire of good, which are degenerated into Pride and mistaken *Self-love*, will easily open her Ears to whatever goes about to nourish and delight them; and when a cunning designing Enemy from without, has drawn over to his Party these Traytors within, he has the Poor unhappy Person at his Mercy, who now very glibly swallows down his Poyson. (12; my emphasis)

Maintaining the theme of temptation by superficiality that women must resist, Astell asserts that women's "inbred self-esteem and desire of good" will allow them to resist "Pride" and a fall into "mistaken Self-love."

Yet Astell deploys the terms "self-esteem" and "Self-love" to draw another connection to Milton's writing and thoughts on gender. As Matthew Jordan has argued, Milton appears to have coined the modern meaning of the word
"self-esteem": "self-respect" or sense of one's self (1). A closer look at the use of
the word "self-esteem" highlights the significance of Astell's use of the word.
Throughout the late seventeenth century, "self-esteem" and "self-love" were
equivalents.[26] Only Milton in *Paradise Lost*, John Norris in *A Sermon Preach'd*, and
Mary Astell in *A Serious Proposal* treat self-esteem as a positive trait. For Astell,
"Self-love" is degenerated "self-esteem"; "self-esteem" in its natural, unfallen state
is "inbred" and propels one toward a desire for good. Astell thus distances it from
the meaning of "Pride" or conceit to which other writers equate the notion of
"self-esteem." In this, Astell shows the influence of John Norris, who saw the love
of God as a force that would draw the mind to perfection (Springborg, 51, n. 36),
and of Pierre Nicole who made this same distinction between "appropriate self-
esteem" and "destructive self-love" (51, n. 37). Yet Astell's use of this term, which
aligns her with a particular philosophical tradition, highlights women's need to
find value in the self rather than to allow the self to devolve into vanity and pride:
these sins prevent one from understanding one's self worth. In such a context,
Milton's own use of the term appears to be both Astell's source and her explicit
target: she employs this term exactly as did Milton, for her distinction between
"self-esteem" and "Self-love" is the very one made by Milton. No contemporary
of Milton or Astell makes a similar linguistic distinction.

Further, the context in which both Astell and Milton employ this particular
definition of "self-esteem" occurs amid discussions of the gendering of inwardness, or of subjectivity—the very issue that Astell is considering here and
more generally in *A Serious Proposal* and *Reflections upon Marriage*. In this second
set of Miltonic echoes within Astell's essays, we again see her engaging the
issue of gendering subjectivity just as Milton had done. For when we turn to
Milton's use of "self-esteem" in his Book 8 exchange with Raphael, he stresses
the gendering of these interior states. Almost all other late seventeenth-century
writings consider "self-esteem" a threat all Christians must resist. But in *Paradise Lost*, the conversation between Adam and Raphael offers "self-esteem" to
Adam, allowing him to understand his "value"—in contradistinction to the
value he has mistakenly accorded to Eve.

After critiquing Adam's "attribúting overmuch to things / Less excellent" in
his account of Eve, Raphael labels her "An outside . . . fair no doubt" and calls
on Adam to

      weigh with her thyself;
Then value: Oft-times nothing profits more
Than *self-esteem*, grounded on just and right
Well manag'd; of that skill the more thou know'st,
The more she will acknowledge thee her Head,
And to realities yield all her shows. . . .   (570–75; my emphasis)

In order to counter Adam's misinterpretation of Eve's possession of "Dominion," Raphael instructs him to value what is inside of himself; Eve's "outside" traits will be offset by Adam's focus on his internal value. Further, it is his internal value that makes him superior to Eve. Astell's deployment of the word "self-esteem" will thus allow her to intervene into this conversation between Adam and Raphael. The effect? Provide women with this very form of "self-esteem," and consequently a sense of internal value, from which they have been distanced by Milton's Book 8 narrative.

In *Samson Agonistes*, we see the inverse of "self-esteem," "self-love," defined and gendered within the poem. While Astell will describe "self-esteem" as "innate" to women in *A Serious Proposal*, *Samson Agonistes* describes "self-love" as an inherently female trait. In a Chorus passage describing the weaknesses and dangers of Dalilah, the audience is asked:

Is it for that such outward ornament
Was lavish't on thir Sex, that inward gifts
Were left for haste unfinish't, judgment scant,
Capacity not rais'd to apprehend
Or value what is best
In choice, but oftest to affect the wrong?
Or was too much of *self-love* mixt,
Of constancy no root infixt,
That either they love nothing, or not long? (1025–33; my emphasis)

Not just Dalilah's character but that of women in general becomes linked to "self-love." Their "outward ornament" that has been "lavish't on thir Sex" testifies to the external nature of women, especially since their "inward gifts" were "left for haste unfinish't." A reader must be careful not to conflate Milton with the Chorus in this play, yet the passage nonetheless sustains this constellation of "self-esteem," "self-love," interiority, and gender that structures the Book 8 exchange in *Paradise Lost*. The pride or self-conceit associated with women in *Samson Agonistes* appears in *Paradise Lost* as the gendered opposite to the masculine "self-esteem" that should allow Adam to value and to understand his superior "inward gifts."

The only two writers in the late seventeenth century who treat these terms as opposed, rather than as interchangable, Milton's and Astell's treatment of "self-love" and "self-esteem" as well as their gendered use of these terms draw these three texts from 1667, 1671, and 1697 closely together.[27] Milton embedded these words into an explicit discussion of an "inward" male character versus an "outside" female character. To this, Astell responds: in an extension of her argument that women need to put away the superficial and develop that which is internal, she revisits these terms and these concepts through Milton. In other words, Astell accords to women the "self-esteem" granted to Adam alone in *Paradise Lost*. And in doing so, Astell challenges the view of women as only "outsides" as she constructs the very internal identity that will allow them to resist the "temptations" of the social world and the institution of marriage.

Astell's use of the word "self-esteem" in the final pages of *A Serious Proposal* continues to negotiate Milton's representation of women and the larger question of women's interior state. Astell's primary argument in the *Proposal* is the need for women to move away from an external focus on vanity and toward a more sustained relation with God: she remarks that woman's "Self-Esteem does not terminate in her *Self* but in GOD, and she values her self only for GOD's sake" (179). Woman's spiritual identity, then, will develop "her *Self*." The intimate relationship between a woman's "Self" and God described here also has the effect of rewriting any portrait of woman's secondary relationship to God. To this theme, Astell will return again and again: "'tis certainly no Arrogance in a Woman to conclude, that she was made for the Service of GOD, and that this is her End. Because GOD made all Things for Himself, and a Rational Mind is too noble a Being to be Made for the Sake and Service of any Creature" (*Reflections*, 11). In describing this relationship with God, one equal to that of Adam since woman could not be made for the "Sake and Service" of another (Adam), Astell again draws on William Whiston's thought to buttress her own project of elevating women's status. Since Whiston "grant[s] the Equality of Humane Souls," women cannot be "subject to such a low Condition" (272). When exploring the state of women's "self-esteem," Astell engages the status of women along these lines to reject the position for women asserted in Milton's Book 4 line, "Hee for God only, shee for God in him" (299).

This sequence thus exposes another of Astell's specific linguistic interventions into one of the most resonant and significant interpretive cruxes in *Paradise Lost*. In *Reflections upon Marriage*, Astell takes up the implications of the secondary nature of women in her tract on marriage: "The Relation between the two Sexes is mutual, and the Dependance Reciprocal, both of them Depending intirely upon GOD, *and upon Him only*; which one wou'd think is no great Argument of the natural Inferiority of either Sex" (13; my emphasis). Astell's challenge to women's "Inferiority" to men is expressed through the "mutual" and "Reciprocal" dependence upon God which she details here. Astell thus explicitly challenges the differential access to God articulated in the Book 4 line. A crux in contemporary criticism as well as point of debate in eighteenth-century editorial practices,[28] Book 4's distinction between Eve and Adam's relationship to God prompts Astell to argue explicitly against the "natural Inferiority of either Sex" (13) through the terms "mutual" and "Reciprocal." She reworks "only" to modify one's relation to God, instead of delimiting access to God for "only" Adam. Astell thus defines the relationship of man and woman to God as they both "Depend. . .intirely" "upon" God.

These intertextual moments linking Astell's texts and Milton's *Paradise Lost*, and at times *Samson Agonistes*, also speak to issues of political hierarchy and organization. The matrix that her writings establish between interiority and the language of governmental control offers another thematic and linguistic connection to Milton. For Milton's poems are fundamentally concerned with the relationship between accounts of (male-gendered) interiority and its relationship to valid governmental organization. Astell may or may not have discerned this cultural matrix as it unfolds in the last part of *Paradise Lost* and *Paradise Regained*. Yet the manner in which male inwardness is linked to political access or control, more broadly in the culture and in Milton, does appear to prompt Astell's interweaving of the language of interiority with political organization in her own writings.

Embedded in Astell's rich body of references to women's outward versus inward traits are connections between inwardness and political language. In *Reflections upon Marriage*, for example, Astell describes how "tho' the Order of the World requires an *Outward* Respect and Obedience from some others, yet the Mind is free, nothing but Reason can oblige it, 'tis out of the reach of the most absolute Tyrant" (56). The female subject is described here as able to free herself, mentally if not physically, from the tyrannical conditions of a marriage. The passage itself resonates with Satan's famous lines on mental power:

The mind is its own place, and in itself
Can make a Heav'n of Hell, a Hell of Heav'n.
What matter where, if I be still the same,
And what I should be, all but less then hee
Whom Thunder hath made greater? Here at least
We shall be free . . . (254–59)

Astell's seeming invocation of Satan's interiority speech fits more generally into her narrative of seduction and the Fall, which she has trained women to avoid through education. Yet inner control comes to be linked explicitly to the language of political authority in Astell: Women's "only endeavour shall be to be absolute Monarchs in our own Bosoms" (*Proposal*, 180).

Milton's own connections between political authority and inwardness provide an effective backdrop against which to consider Astell's textual interventions, ones that will lead us back to the same debate in which Behn appeared to participate: the political importance of marriage as an institution, used differently by theorists for republican and monarchical forms of government. We have seen Astell rewrite elements of Milton's poems in her efforts to construct female interior values and prepare women to resist the seductions of a bad marriage. Now we see her turn to the highly political implications of marriage by querying, and ultimately supplanting, the family/state analogy upon which patriarchalist theory rested. In promoting female inwardness, she establishes a link between such a state of subjectivity and governmental structure, which are equally linked in Milton's last poems. Milton's writings thus serve as an excellent backdrop against which to observe Astell's move from describing the social identity of women to positioning them within the highly-charged political institution of marriage.

As numerous commentators on Milton illustrate, by Book 12 of *Paradise Lost* accounts of government are associated with internal control acquired by the self. In *Paradise Lost*, the "outward" structure of government is determined by the "inward" state of man, a "core political principle" for Milton that also receives sustained attention in *Paradise Regained* (Lewalski, *Life*, 517). As Christ rejects Satan's offer of kingship and thus governmental control, internal control comes to be valued as the true form of government:

Yet he who reigns within himself, and rules
Passions, Desires, and Fears, is more a King;
Which every wise and virtuous man attains:
And who attains not, ill aspires to rule
Cities of men, or headstrong Multitudes,
Subject himself to Anarchy within,
Or lawless passions in him, which he serves. (2.466–72)

Not simply a metaphor for self-control, that which is genuinely "Kingly . . . Governs the inner man" (2.476–77) as only the inwardly righteous man will be capable of true rule.

What few commentators have noted is that this state of interiority becomes exclusively associated with men. The fusion of the language of "inwardness" and political language is never used by the narrator or another character to describe Eve; she only uses it herself when rationalizing her eating of the apple: "But if Death / Bind us with after-bands, what profits then / Our inward freedom?" (9.760–62). For inwardness and the political control it provides are always gendered male in Milton's poetry. *Samson Agonistes*'s Chorus explicitly declares this gendering of political power and the internal. Insisting that women's "outward ornament" are "lavish't on" her, while exposing her "unfinish't" "inward gifts," the Chorus then states the interwoven consequences for political order and a gender hierarchy: "Therefore God's universal Law / Gave to the man despotic power / Over his female in due awe, / Nor from that right to part an hour, / Smile she or lour" (1053–57). As *Paradise Lost* engages the fundamental link between interiority and governmental structure, Eve's position "out-side" of a state of inwardness becomes her simultaneous position outside of political organization.

This focus on (masculine) interiority—terms granted to Adam and Christ in Milton's later poems—highlights the stakes for Astell. As Astell constructs an inward nature for women, precisely through rewriting the story of the Fall and in order to force a reevaluation of marriage, she has granted women access to a gendered and politically inflected inwardness. Stated boldly, a gendered hierarchy is built upon variable access to this inwardness or subjectivity: because women lack the "inward gifts" that are necessary for true government, they are necessarily positioned as secondary—and as the subject to be ruled within the household. Yet if they are granted these "inward gifts," their access to this masculine prerogative is revealed.

Astell's emphasis on female interiority, in conjunction with her focus on marriage, explains why Milton, both poet and pamphleteer, features so centrally in her writings. For her replotting of the Garden narrative through specific engagements with Milton's text becomes her contribution to political thought. We know, of course, that she criticized Milton for his double standard on political and domestic tyrants, allowing a "Private Tyranny" by not "cry[ing] up Liberty to poor Female Slaves" (*Reflections*, 46–47). Astell's politically significant writing derives from her engagements with Milton's poetry and William Whiston's theories. Astell's reconfiguration of elements of *Paradise Lost*—for example rewriting "Hee for God only, Shee for God in him" into man and woman's dependence "intirely upon GOD, and upon Him only" (*Reflections*, 13)—occurs conceptually and spatially alongside her invocation of Whitson's view of Adam and Eve's "greater equality" (11); she engages these two writers on the same page of her *Reflections*.[29] Her response to aspects of Milton's poem and presentation of Eve are supported by Whitson's philosophy: she returns to narratives of the Garden in order to evaluate the pre- and postlapsarian implications of "equality." Her engagement with these two thinkers also led her to directly address the political theory of Filmer, which depended upon the originary absence of any "equality" between Adam and Eve (as well as in all subsequent gender relations). As Astell constructs an alternate vision of marriage and of women's character through her portrait of a garden space, her exploration of notions of "equality" exposes the political implications in marriage. Ultimately, as we saw with Aphra Behn, the stability of the family/state metaphor upon which Filmer depended will be profoundly undermined.[30] Both *Reflections upon Marriage* and *A Serious Proposal* thus show her engagement with the tenets of this philosophical cornerstone for Robert Filmer which—as Astell had herself pointed out—posed a conceptual problem for Milton.

Her writings thus offer a series of challenges to the patriarchal premises of monarchical organization. Prompted by her "reflections" on the politically resonant institution of marriage, Astell's process of redeeming Eves will form a series of subtle, perhaps even unconscious, acts of resistance to traditional patriarchalist theory. Again, the influence of Whiston can be felt: Astell engages the greater equality that he postulated before the Fall in a narrative imagining prelapsarian portraits of women. Astell's political "reflections" will consequently attack both Milton and Filmer for asserting either an absence of "spiritual" equality or for deriving women's enslavement through the narrative of the Fall. Immediately after critiquing Milton for positioning women as "slaves" within the family, she attacks and dismisses the "genetic" claim which buttresses patriarchalist thought. "'[T]'is true that GOD told *Eve* after the Fall that *her Husband shou'd Rule over her*" (*Reflections*, 19), comments Astell, initially appearing to support Filmer's use of the original Garden story as future justification for (monarchical) state authority. But Astell does not stop here. She proceeds to reject this central claim of patriarchalist thought, denying that "the former shou'd prove *Adam's* natural Right to Rule" (19).

Astell's many other biblically inflected narratives also dispute women's "Natural Inferiority," a status upon which patriarchal theory depended in order to assert a "natural" and organic political hierarchy. The story of Deborah, for example, illustrates how woman can be "Sovereign" over a man, if the situation is sanctified by God: "*Deborah's* Government was confer'd on her by God Himself. Consequently the Sovereignty of a Woman is not contrary to the Law of Nature" (*Reflections*, 24). By turning biblical figures against the biblical ground of Filmerian-style thought, she erodes support for his claim of gender hierarchy as monarchy's basis. Yet she has also, here, detached the family from state organization. Deborah, as a married woman, might well have to submit to her domestic governor: this concern for female sovereigns had spanned 100 years, likely preventing Queen Elizabeth from marrying in the sixteenth century while shaping the terms of William and Mary's "joint" rule until 1694. But a woman could still rule, Astell insists, when her position as "Sovereign" was appointed by God. While critics have tended to note Astell's criticisms of Locke or of Milton within her writing, here we see her actually undo, as a consequence of her considerations of female interiority and her concurrent interrogation of the question of a greater prelapsarian gender equality, the biblical premises upon which Filmerian patriarchalist theory rested.

What occurs in Astell's writings, then, is the alignment, but not analogizing, of the family and state:

Because she puts her self entirely into her Husband's Power, and if the Matrimonial Yoke be grievious, neither Law nor Custom afford her that redress which a Man obtains. He who has Sovereign Power does not value the Provocations of a Rebellious Subject, but knows how to subdue him with ease, and will make himself obey'd; but Patience and Submission are the only Comforts that are left to a poor People, who groan under Tyranny, unless they are Strong enough to break the Yoke, to Depose and Abdicate, which I doubt wou'd not be allow'd of here. (46)

In granting "Sovereign Power" to husbands over wives, Astell suggests a pattern or performance of right that both her language and her emphasis on women's evaluation of the marriage "Yoke" will undermine. Astell does imply parallels between the two when she states that "Nor will it ever be well either with those who Rule or those in Subjection, even from the Throne to every Private Family" (56). This has, I believe, prompted critics to consider her as much more aligned with Filmerian thinking than she actually is. In considering her language, which ultimately extracts the family from the state, we can discern a series of significant distinctions between her theories and those of patriarchalist theorists. Often employing sentence structures such as unanswered questions, Astell effectively undermines the basic premises of patriarchalist theory by posing, but then not answering, questions at the heart of this body of thought: "Did the bare Name of Husband confer Sense on a Man, and the mere being in Authority infallibly qualifie him for Government, much might be done" (62). Astell's construction here helps to conceal the assertion that she is actually making: "being in Authority" does not "qualifie" one for "Government" any more than does having the "bare Name of Husband confer sense on a Man" (62).

Astell thus repeatedly undermines the claim of a divine right for monarchy that was derived from the social practice of granting men "Authority" over women. On the final pages of *Reflections*, Astell appears to define men's rights and abilities as governors: "that they govern the World, they have Prescription on their side, Women are too weak to dispute it with them, therefore they, as all other Governours, are most, if not only accountable, for what's amiss, for whether other Governments in their Original, were or were not confer'd according to the Merit of the Person, yet certainly in this case, if Heaven has appointed the Man to Govern, it has qualify'd him for it" (79). Astell's sentence construction initially confutes and ultimately rejects the level of certainty accorded to patriarchalist arguments. The awarding of authority might, or might not, be linked to the "Merit of the Person." Since the claim to authority in this passage is clearly that of gender—men "govern the World, [men] have Prescription on their side"—Astell places in suspension the necessary correctness of their governorship. Additionally, Astell's use of "prescription" here exposes her assignment of male authority to "custom" or, as the OED describes, "title or right acquired by virtue of such use or possession." Filmer's claims, as those of other patriarchalist theorists, were not based on custom; they were based on authority derived from biblical precedent. Throughout, Astell's turn to the conditional tense to account for man's qualifications to "Govern" overtly side-steps the question of their God-given right to authority, the claim upon which all of Filmerian-style patriarchalist theory rests. "*If* Heaven has appointed the Man to Govern," Astell suggests (79; my emphasis); by conveying the issue of gendered authority in the conditional form, she transforms it into a question. Is "Man" "qualify'd" for governing? He is "*if*" heaven appointed him. The conditional format allows Astell a logically circular ambiguity in the very heart of male claims to govern either women or to rule the state.

In conjunction with this attack on Filmerian principles, the manner in which Astell rewrites the story of Eve, the Garden, and the institution of marriage rewrites the originary narrative upon which patriarchalist thought relies. As the final third of *Reflections upon Marriage* reveals, women's seduction and temptation into faulty relationships can be resisted through the interiority Astell develops in her reconfigured Eve-figures. They have been prepared, armed, and enabled to resist such temptations and thus to make the right choice when faced with the institution of marriage. As I have suggested through linguistic parallels to Milton's writings, Astell takes us to the figure of Eve in order to prepare all women intellectually for the one choice they will have to make:

whether to enter into the institution of marriage. While Milton explored marriage's theoretical dissolution in divorce, Astell postulates women's ability to exist outside of this institution. Her theorizing of marriage thus leads her to issues of governmental organization: If a husband is "so chosen," a woman "has made him her Head." Yet, she remains free to not accept the terms of marriage. It is through this language of choice, which Astell promotes throughout *Reflections* and *A Serious Proposal*, that she necessarily undermines the Filmerian analogy. If the basis of Filmer-style patriarchalism—the structure of women's subservience to a husband—can be rejected, the natural status of this hierarchy is denied. Astell thus turns the Filmerian dependence on marriage inside out. By articulating with detailed horror the terms of marriage and women's role in entering into it, she undermines the role marriage could play in patriarchal theory.

Filmer and Milton, political theorists who stand on the opposite side of the contractarian/patriarchalist debate, may come together in Astell's sights because both countenance, in her words, "tyranny" in marriage.[31] Her entrance into the terms of Filmerian thought and patriarchalist theory has been enabled by her engagement of Milton's own, necessarily political, Garden narrative. Like Behn, she engages the Genesis tale and Milton's *Paradise Lost* to redefine the daughters of Eve. Behn, by constructing a protean, unstable Silvia, so destabilized marriage that the Filmerian analogy could only echo parodically throughout the novel. Astell's goals were parallel, though her strategy inverted. Like Behn, she returned to the Garden narrative, her arguments about women's character and their response to marriage made from within the story of Eve. For her, the redemption tale she provides for women can occur through the rejection of marriage as a "foundational institution" for family and state. Possibly, in order to save the monarchical state, Astell needed to extract the family from it.

In the course of this meditation on contemporary political thought, Astell also re-forms the "character" of women. By portraying women as able to make reasoned choices, and providing them with the inwardness that Milton's *Paradise Lost* had made elusive for Eve and all women, Astell defines a form of female subjectivity for women who reenter, or at least reengage, the narrative of Eden. Astell thus maps for us the powerful presence of "biblical subjectivity" into the late seventeenth century, one which works inversely to Behn's invocation of Genesis and the consequent fracturing of Silvia's "self." In Astell's sustained commentary on social and political practices, women's character continues to be "plotted" by the narrative of the original Garden and the Fall itself. The general motifs of the Garden and of redemption, meant to restage the "fall" into the "tyranny" of marriage, shape Astell's story just as they shape the traits of women described in her writings. Much more so than for the men in her accounts of courtship, women are understandable through, and assimilable into, the narrative of and in the Garden. She will use this narrative to

Conclusion: Influencing Traditions of Interpretation

Engendering the Fall has attempted to alter the contexts in which we place Milton, and in doing so has tried to broaden and complicate our view of the representation of gender and its relationship to governance in *Paradise Lost*. As a result of the prism of readings of *Paradise Lost* produced in this study, we can start to answer the question: What does observing these women as they are negotiated by or negotiate a republican thinker like Milton expose to our view? In part, it exposes the innovative ways these women imagined the structure of political organization and intersected this with improvisations upon gendered categories. Lanyer offers women access to a previously denied state of "Libertie" and "Sov'raigntie," terms that engage women in a political sphere. Hutchinson re-imagines mothers' role in the formation of the state. Cavendish challenges boundaries around knowledge and the constraints placed on women's public activities implied by such limitations on knowledge. Chudleigh, Behn, and Astell all retheorize marriage as an institution, with Behn's and Astell's explicitly political engagement of Milton allowing them to reject foundational patriarchalist tenets while resisting what would become Locke's creation of the privatized sphere within liberal thought. Collectively and individually, their interactions with Milton's own foundational literary text highlight the sustained intersection between gender and political thought in the seventeenth century.

Our view of these women, accessible through the lens provided by Milton's *Paradise Lost*, also forces a reconsideration of our understanding of the development of theories on political organization. While the terms of Speght's and Sowernam's interrogation of the Garden story operate more within a patriarchal theory framework, rather than the interrogation of this theory staged by Behn and Astell, these earlier texts illustrate the profoundly foundational nature of the Adam and Eve story to political thought. As the later chapters of this study have illustrated, gestures toward and engagement with John Locke's thinking become more and more pronounced in the writings of women in the later part of the seventeenth century: Behn, Astell, and Hutchinson are engaging the set of issues that begin in the narrative of Adam and Eve and develop into models for social and political organization, such as the social contract.

It would be much harder to argue that John Locke was engaging specific texts discussed within the covers of this book than, I hope, it has been to illustrate *Paradise Lost*'s location amid texts produced by women in the seventeenth century. We can, though, position Locke in relation to Lucy Hutchinson or Aphra Behn or Mary Astell to highlight the different modes of negotiating the biblical story upon which all of these texts were grounded. As Rachel Weil has suggested, there were other alternatives to the cornerstone of Locke's *Two Treatises*, the division of the family from the state. And we can see some of that innovation occurring in the writings of many of these women: an intellectual response to patriarchal theory, which does not distinguish family from state, is outlined within Hutchinson's *Order and Disorder*. In fact, that kind of division between the sphere of the family and the political sphere was consistently resisted, whether in Speght's, Sowernam's, or Lanyer's interrogation of the *querelle des femmes* tradition, the linguistic and physical products of female prophets, or Margaret Cavendish's portrait of the Empress of *The Blazing World*. The story of the Fall served them well: in addition to rewriting the narrative of culpability, these writers imagined alternative mechanisms for engaging and designing the state apparatus. Locke's main lines of thought on governmental organization are consequently redrawn by this range of alternatives. This project is meant, then, to suggest our still partial view onto discourses of political organization, its relationship to gender, and the participation of women in this trajectory of thought. These women frequently marked out distinct positions from the theorists who have come down to us as central to the tradition of and development of liberalism. These women's texts also prompt us to reconsider the feminist critique of liberalism. Writers like Hutchinson, Behn, and Astell, theorizing the relationship of women to the state, offer an alternate picture of the formative moments of liberalism.[1] If liberalism as a political system marginalizes women—as thinkers such as Carole Pateman and Lorenne M. G. Clark would argue[2]—this is in part because the tradition of thought that constitutes liberalism has been constructed without the voices of these female political theorists.

So, what does placing these women in an indirect dialogue with Locke, Sidney, or Tyrrell do to our view of the liberal tradition? My answer is that we will see a differently constructed intellectual line once we include these women's engagement with social and political organization. I would thus disagree with the conclusion that Katherine Gillespie comes to in *Domesticity and Dissent in the Seventeenth Century: English Women's Writing and the Public Sphere*; for Gillespie, the participation by a series of female prophets in the public sphere initiates a trajectory of thought that leads to Locke's notions of the sovereign individual and the free market: "In a small group of sectarian women writers, liberalism finds its 'mothers'" (262). Yet, a teleology of modern liberal thought formulated at mid-century in women's visions and publications is not what I discovered amidst the range of women writers, poets, and polemicists featured here. I do agree with Gillespie that all of these writers illustrate how embedded gender was into any account of social and political formation; these women all engage this concept through the story of the Garden and the Fall. Their thinking through the Genesis narrative thus helps to expose the formative aspect of this origin story to "modern" political thought.[3] Further, this challenges the oft-asserted transition from a period of "premodernity" to "modernity" in Locke's thought. Questions of gender necessarily raised through the story of the Garden consequently expose that this narrative is the underpinning of Locke's *Second Treatise*. Further, the recursive use of the Garden narrative by writers from Speght and Lanyer to Chudleigh and Astell forces a reconsideration of what "modern" can mean, and how fully categories of gender difference are embedded into this definition. Their writings equally expose how these issues resonate through Locke's foundational text on state organization.

The recursivity that dominates these women's engagement of the biblical narrative, their individual and composite return to this story, offers a backdrop that brings Locke's own deployment of the Garden story in *The Two Treatises of Government* into a different focus. Locke returns twice to the garden in the *Two Treatises*. After engaging the Garden story in his detailed attack on Filmer's *Patriarcha* in the *First Treatise*, Locke appears to turn towards a more secular version of "Nature." As part of his portrait of the natural world in which man exists, Locke develops theories of the "state of nature" as well as detailing the prominent, even foundational, role of labor in the organization of the state. Yet, as many Locke scholars have remarked, theological precepts continue to frame this text, as they do many of Locke's writings.[4] I will suggest that echoes to the biblically defined "Garden" in the *First Treatise* are present in the language and structure of Locke's argument in the *Second Treatise*. But more importantly—and a point most brought into focus by the writings of Speght, Hutchinson, Cavendish, Behn and Astell—the grounding relationship of man and woman is modeled on Genesis aspects of Locke's thought. Simultaneously, Locke is reconfiguring certain aspects of the Garden narrative, yet these aspects open up a distinction between the treatment of men and women in the *Treatises*. Like feminist critics of Locke, I am interested in how the foundational narrative that Locke produces is making fundamental distinctions about gender. But I want to emphasize, as does Hans Blumenberg in his discussion of the recursive character of major cultural transformations, that Locke's foundational political text is still plotted onto the foundational Genesis narrative—with some fascinating consequences for any concept of "modern" subjectivity.

The Garden, made material as well as acted upon by Locke's vision of mankind, is reconfigured, but not displaced, in the *Second Treatise*. In the fifth chapter of the *Second Treatise*, in which Locke's foundational theory of "property" is introduced, we hear how men who labor will acquire property: "The *Labour* of his Body, and the *Work* of his Hands, we may say, are properly his" (para. 27). This acquisition of property is described through, and justified by, the need to acquire food through labor: "He that is nourished by the Acorns he pickt up under an Oak, or the Apples he gathered from the Trees in the Wood, has certainly appropriated them to himself" (28). By linking labor in its originary moment to the gathering of food, we seem theologically positioned in a postlapsarian space: as Adam after the Fall, and as a result of our sin, we will need to labor or "toil" in order to eat. As in Genesis, the language of postlapsarian judgment, labor, and the acquisition of food is linked: "Cursed is the ground for your sake; in toil you shall eat of it all the days of your life" (Genesis 3:17); "In the sweat of your face you shall eat bread till you return to the ground" (Genesis 3:19). Further, the link to an ever resonant "Apple" gathered for food suggests the deep structures of the biblical story still encircling Locke's narrative.

Labor serves Locke differently, of course: it is practically redemptive as it allows the reclamation of the land around us. Nor does labor need be characterized as marking the postlapsarian: it could be (as in Milton) an activity fully celebrated within the Garden. I want to suggest that the secularized garden space is introduced to us here, one that intersects labor and food collection in order to recall the place in which Adam and Eve—the "first society"—resided. Locke's terms also continue to dispute Filmer's arguments. For Filmer, Adam's "dominion" comes through the grant of God. For Locke, this "dominion" is reconfigured into an act, labor, that results in Locke's alternate definition of dominion, the "*Right of Property*": "Thus *Labour*, in the Beginning, *gave a Right of Property*" (para. 45).

It is here that the gestures back to the *First Treatise* intersect with questions of gender, and of gendered distinctions. In Locke's attack on Filmer, he engages an alternative narrative of "Adam"'s creation and the forms of authority that this authorizes. Yet as Locke moves into the *Second Treatise*, he seems almost as interested in putting Adam behind him as he is about putting Filmer's theories to rest. Thus, the very hierarchy, and the consequent justification for monarchy, that positions Adam above all men becomes replaced by a more generic "Man" at the center of Locke's discussion of state formation. If Chapter 1 of the *Second Treatise* dismisses Filmer's claims about Adam's receipt of "dominion" because it validates monarchy, Chapter 2 announces a set of general propositions true of all men, regardless of their descent from Adam: "To understand Political Power right, and derive it from its Original, we must consider what State all Men are naturally in" (para. 4). In part, Locke needs to do this to maintain his argument with, and his rejection of, Filmer: "Man" needs to become distinct from "Adam." Were they fully reassimilable, Filmer's originary narrative might retain more power.

Narratively, after introducing to us how "man" can enact this very idea of "dominion" over the land—through acts of labor and *not* through a Filmerian inheritance of such power—woman now will be reintroduced. But while Locke appears to open up a space between the original man and the men who will now labor for their own dominion, he does not do so with women: they remain figures of Eve in Locke's narrative. Structurally, women appear in the narrative at an analogous point to that of Eve in Genesis 2. Following Locke's adaptation of the form of acquiring "dominion" in the chapter on property, women emerge in the next chapter, "Of Paternal Power"; woman, produced second in the more detailed Genesis 2 account, now emerges in this second account of social formation in the *Second Treatise*.

Feminist Locke scholars have debated the implications of Locke's awarding "equal Title" to women in this chapter; their focus is on whether women experience an improved or denigrated position after or under liberalism. Yet if we consider Locke in a tradition of debates about governmental organization occurring through the narrative of Genesis, our lens of interpretation will perceive women differently at their moment of introduction into Locke's text. The terms of this "equal Title" sustain the connection between the figure of Eve in the *First Treatise* and the portrait of women in the *Second*. For as "women" are returned to this account of social (and implicitly political) organization, they are interpolated into an identity as mothers. In commenting on the term "Paternal Power," Locke remarks that the term "seems so to place the Power of Parents over their Children wholly in the *Father*, as if the *Mother* had no share in it, whereas if we consult Reason or Revelation, we shall find she hath an equal Title" (para. 52). While other critics of Locke's liberalism will object to the "natural inferiority of women due to their naturally disadvantaged position with respect to reproduction" (Clark, 37), the constitution of women as mothers maintains their connection, above all, to the Genesis tale. In contrast, "Man" has been provided with an alternative narrative for the acquisition of his dominion: their traditionally postlapsarian use of labor is now reformed to allow the acquisition of property and begin the very development of state organization.

In contrast, when women return to Locke's narrative, they do so only through the mechanism of motherhood. In sharp contrast to "Man," who becomes distinguished from "Adam" throughout Locke's *Two Treatises* in order to underscore his argument against Filmer, the process by which "Woman" is introduced continues to align her with Eve. When the premises of the emerging "domestic" sphere are detailed in the *Second Treatise*, it is through an emphasis on, as Clark indicates, woman's maternal identity; "the Female" becomes "Mother" even though not initially introduced in those terms: "because the Female is capable of conceiving, and *de facto* is commonly with Child again, and Brings forth too a new Birth long before the former is out of a dependancy," there exists "an Obligation to continue in Conjugal Society with the same Woman longer than other Creatures" (para. 80). For woman to be collapsed into mother throughout Locke's *Second Treatise* further underscores the domestic sphere in which women operate—and thus illustrates the process by which Locke divides the domestic/private and public spheres.[5] But Locke's mode of characterizing women in the *Second Treatise* also recalls the very name of Eve: she is "the mother of all living" (Genesis 3:20). This location of women as the site of reproduction does pave the way for the distinction between reproductive roles and public ones. And yet it accomplishes that distinction through a biblical identity for women, linking them to Eve since the "Female" (read mother) "is capable of conceiving, and *de facto* is commonly with Child" (80).

It is this differential between the manner of interpolating men and women through the biblical story, one repeated in Locke, that illustrates the contributions made possible by viewing the writers in this study within a tradition of political theory. The final chapter made explicit the recursive use of the Bible by Aphra Behn and Mary Astell; their return to the Genesis narrative offered two different portraits of how the identity of (a gendered) self illuminates a "biblical subjectivity" for women. The centrality of their engagement with the Garden story suggests its usefulness as a position from which to theorize the formation of the state. Their writings expose a distinctly gendered self, in the case of Behn an unstable portrait of the female self, while in the case of Astell one provided interiority. Culturally, these women were allowed a certain latitude to produce distinct types of texts by entering through the biblical story: the protection offered by speaking through biblical motifs or on biblical topics has been well covered by early modern critics.[6] That latitude was simultaneously self-containing: what I have called a "biblical subjectivity" made a certain kind of female speech possible while aligning women to a story within which existed a powerful, and powerfully gendered, condemnatory impulse.

Yet within the narrative of the Garden and the Fall, there exists both a postlapsarian gender hierarchy as well as the interpretive possibility of an alternate, prelapsarian vision: Chudleigh reenvisions a spiritual condition without gender; Speght and Hutchinson imagine it lost by a more mutual sin; Lanyer and Cavendish imagine the ultimate utopic return to the beginning. It is that doubleness within the potential of the Genesis narrative that allows us to reconsider the interpretive pressure exerted by this "conversation" between women writers, Milton, and even Locke. Critical discourses around both Milton and Locke are necessarily reformed by these views onto and uses of the biblical narrative, the gender hierarchy implicit in this story, and the implications for political organization. By reimagining the terms of a tradition of influence and the new voices drawn in through this process, an alternative critical heritage for *Paradise Lost* emerges at the same moment that we observe "the" narrative of the formation of liberalism and its associations with "modernity" redrawn.

Notes

Introduction. Rethinking the Practices of Influence, Intertextuality, and (Modern) Subjectivities

1. Victoria Kahn's *Wayward Contracts* gives a helpful overview of the political theorists who have located the "emergence of a distinctively modern conception of political obligation" in the seventeenth century (1).

2. See Shanley's "Marriage Contract and Social Contract, Pateman's *Sexual Contract*, and Kahn's *Wayward Contracts* on the relation between these two forms of contract.

3. For the most extensive treatment of patriarchalist theory in the seventeenth century, see Gordon Schochet's *Patriarchalism in Political Thought*.

4. One exception would be Mary Beth Rose's "Gender and the Heroics of Endurance." David Norbrook and Kathryn Schwarz have also noted suggestive connections between Milton and women writing in the seventeenth century.

5. Louise Schleiner's *Tudor and Stuart Women Writers* does consider women and male writers in concert.

6. More recent work that has considered the influence of male writers on these newly canonized of women writers. See *Cavendish and Shakespeare: Interconnections* and Susanne Woods's and Shannon Miller's articles in *Worldmaking Spenser*.

7. See Thomas Edwards, *Gangreana*, Second Part, 10–11.

8. There are female writers who engage Milton's texts that are not included in this study, such as Jane Lead and Judith Drake. Their writings do not explore the political implications of the story of the Garden and the Fall as explicitly as Locke and Filmer and the women featured in this study.

9. Patrick Cheney's and Lars Engle's recent work counters this trend.

10. This approach also can challenge the bifurcated practice of granting the language of agency to women writers while generally describing male authors as shaped by cultural forces.

11. See the introduction to Peter Herman's *Destabilizing Milton*.

12. I would thus agree that Milton s text is "an arena for conflict" (Wittreich, "Milton's Transgressive Maneuvers," 244) in which a range of engagements with and responses by seventeenth-century women writers expose the multiplicity of readings about gender—both for twenty-first-century critics and for Milton's contemporary readers. The greatest different between my study and Wittreich's range of work on this topic is his conclusion that seventeenth-century women consistently view Milton's text as more liberating, while I see women exhibiting a range of responses to Milton's poem.

13. Blumenburg is in large part revising the observation of Carl Schmitt in *Political*

Theology that "all significant concepts of the modern theory of the state are secularized theological concepts" (36). For a discussion of the concept of the secular, particularly in the context of contemporary events and conflicts between the "West" and the Muslim world, see Talal Asad's *Formations of the Secular*.

14. Blumenberg's describes the "reoccupation" of "answer positions" that "become vacant" in the course of shifts in thinking over time (65–78).

15. Kristie M. McClure's *Judging Rights* frames Locke's political theory within a seventeenth-century, theologically inflected map of the divine architecture of the world. John Dunn's *The Political Thought of John Locke* makes a sustained claim about the theological structures framing Locke's thought.

16. Lorenne Clark in "Women and Locke" criticizes Locke for his essentialist treatment of women, while Chris Nyland describes Locke as "an early supporter of the right of women to be treated as equals with men" (59).

Chapter 1. Serpentine Eve: Plotting Gender in the Seventeenth-Century Garden

1. For the purposes of uriderscoring the role of this tradition and the conventions that shape it, I will maintain the phrase "anti-feminist" throughout the essay to distinguish it from a more general misogynist tradition.

2. For a collection that contains a range of cultural documents in the Jacobean Pamphlet debate, see Susan Gushee O'Malley's *"Custome Is an Idiot"*.

3. The 1634 edition reads: "Printed at London by T.C. and are to be sold by F. Grove, at his Shop, at upper-end of Snow-hill, neere the Sarazens head without New=gate 1634," the very same inscription as in 1637. In order to locate these sites, I have relied on the Map of Early Modern England, which shows a "Smowhill" adjacent to the "Saracen's Head." See the Web site maintained by Janelle Jenstad at mapoflon don.uvic.ca.

4. See Dobranski's *Milton, Authorship, and the Book Trade*, especially chap. 3, on Milton's involvement with booksellers and printers.

5. The question of the gender of Sowernam and Munda continues to be debated. See Ann Rosalind Jones and Simon Shepherd on the sex of Munda. See Purkiss, "Material Girls," on the rhetorical implications of a female pseudonym. For clarity of argument, I will assume throughout this essay that Sowernam, as Speght, is a woman: I base this on Sowernam's specific moves that accord so closely to those of Speght.

6. Peter Herman also sees *Paradise Lost* as producing its own critical reading of misogyny in "The More to Draw His Love" in *Destabilizing Milton*.

7. Alternately, many defenses previous to Speght's and Sowernam's attacked women while claiming to defend them, as in Nicholas Breton's "The Praise of vertuous Ladies, and Gentlemen" (1597). For the dispute over Gosynhill's authorship, see Henderson and McManus, *Half Humankind*, 137 n. 4.

8. See Lewalski's "Female Text, Male Reader Response" for an account of heavily annotated marginalia in a copy of Speght's *A Mouzell for Melastomus*. The author of this response has been suggested to be Joseph Swetnam, whose reactions/responses might well have been the beginnings of a published attack, and thus a continuation of the "debate."

9. In the sixteenth century, scattered references to the Fall in the majority of attacks on women are countered by defenses of which 10 to 25 percent are engaging the narrative of the Fall. In the seventeenth century, this percentage rises: the proportion of Eve-based attacks in Swetnam's text to the Eve-based defenses in Speght is about 1 to 20.

10. See Patricia Phillippy's discussion of *Mortalities Memorandum* in "The Mat(t)er of Death," which considers Eve as a figure of both life and of death in the *ars moriendi* tradition.

11. Wittreich in "'Inspir'd with Contradiction'" notes that the poem is "mapped by—and a mapping of—debates between the sexes in the seventeenth century" (136).

12. For work on women prophets at mid-century, see Marcus Nevitt's *Women and the Pamphlet Culture* and Gillespie's *Domesticity and Dissent*. For work on women petitioners, see especially chap. 4 in Suzuki's *Subordinate Subjects*.

13. Critics view the terms of Agrippa's defense of women in somewhat different ways. McBride and Ulreich view it as a "playful . . . trope" (105), while James Turner considers that Agrippa's arguments are a rhetorical game. Linda Woodbridge considers Agrippa's argument overall as a "rhetorical paradox,' and concludes that "Agrippa's hyperbolic praise of women is not an ironic vehicle for laying bare the sex's unworthiness but a graphic demonstration of the absurdities one must resort to if one claims superiority for either sex" (42). All agree, though, that these female defenders take up Agrippa's defenses in serious ways.

14. Adam thus articulates the lesson provided by Raphael: "of that skill the more thou know'st, The more she will acknowledge thee her Head, / And to realities yield all her shows" (8.573–75).

15. See McColley's argument in *Milton's Eve* that Milton "assigns more dignity to Eve than was usual" in the analogs (35).

16. McBride and Ulreich cite this line in "Eve's Apology" and suggest that Milton does "occasionally seem to be responding to other voices in the *querelle* that did argue for Eve's essential superiority" (107).

17. Thomas Luxon in *Single Imperfection* comments on the experience of loneliness in the first couple (120).

18. Such inclinations of Eve also establish another richly intertextual set of echoes between Milton's portrait of Eve in the Book 5 dream and the Book 9 Fall and the Eve-like figure in Speght's "A Dreame." Drawing upon a series of parallel motives—the night-time situation of a dream, the focus on visual access to the fruit—Milton's evocative dream sequence appears to revise, even correct, the possibilities offered by Speght's "A Dreame." See also Josephine Roberts's "Diabolic Dreamscape in Lanyer and Milton" for a discussion of these two "dreams."

19. For two studies that consider a wide range of classical and biblical traditions deployed within Milton's representation of the Garden, Adam, and Eve, see James Turner's *One Flesh* and Diane McColley's *Milton's Eve*.

20. For a discussion of the supplementarity of Eve from a Derridean perspective, see Mary Nyquist's "The Genesis of Gendered Subjectivity."

21. Wittreich, in "He Ever was a Dissenter," argues that the debate over the sexes, as expressed in Swetnam's text, "is making an incursion" into the biblical commentary of theologians like Andrew Willet, Henry Ainsworth, and John Salkeld, which will later make its presence known in *Paradise Lost*. Thomas Luxon also asserts an agonistic connection, describing Milton's "frontal attack on . . . protofeminist tracts" by writers like Speght and Sowernam (147).

22. In this, Hughes follows Richard Bentley's suggested emendation in his 1732 edition, which Hughes characterizes as "inevitable" (Book 9, n. 1183). In other modern editions, such as the Norton (edited by Scott Elledge) and the Longman (edited by Alastair Fowler), these editions make the "W" in "women" lower case. Only Flannagan's edition replicates the upper case "W" in "Women"; utilized in the 1667 and 1674 edition, this original capitalization by Milton stresses the category of all women.

23. The other two are in Book 4.408–9 and 11.582.

24. Various critics have attempted to challenge the status of this line by attributing to Satan this perspective onto Adam and Eve. James Grantham Turner in *One Flesh* and Michael Wilding in "'Their Sex Not Equal Seemed'" argue that the line is not from the narrator's perspective, while Neil Forsyth in *The Satanic Epic* concludes that we see here through Satan's perspectival view.

25. Christine Froula's formative essay, "When Eve Reads Milton," which argues that Eve is successfully contained within patriarchal discourse following the Book 4 account of her creation, has been very influential on my reading of Eve.

26. McColley describes this sequence as blatantly misogynistic (30), while Kristin Pruitt describes his attack as "brutal" (68).

27. See S. Ernest Sprott's discussion of "extrametrical supernumerary syllables" in *Milton's Art of Prosody*. André Verbart then builds upon this argument in "Measured Hypermetricality in *Paradise Lost*" to show the range of meanings Milton was able to convey through his use of extra syllables, especially after the Fall.

28. For an overview of the family/state analogy at the heart of seventeenth-century patriarchalist theory, see Gordon Schochet's *Patriarchalism in Political Thought.*

29. See David Norbrook's *Writing the English Republic*, a study of the tradition of republicanism in the seventeenth century. On the marriage and political contract, see Shanley's "Marriage Contract and Social Contract" and Kahn's *Wayward Contracts.*

30. Milton's engagement with the family/state analogy may seem odd given his rejection of the monarchical claims supported by patriarchalist theorists such as Sir Robert Filmer. On Milton and Filmer, see Norbrook, *Writing the English Republic*, 483.

31. Milton scholars and political theorists alike have struggled with whether republican thought was more or less inviting for women. See Norbrook on gendered hierarchy and republican thought, *Writing the English Republic*, 483.

Chapter 2. Gazing, Gender, and the Construction of Governance in Aemilia Lanyer's Salve Deus Rex Judaeorum *and Milton's* Paradise Lost

1. See particularly Elaine Beilin's *Redeeming Eve* and Barbara Lewalski's *Writing Women in Jacobean England*. Mihoko Suzuki in *Subordinate Subjects* establishes Lanyer's connection to the anti-feminist tradition.

2. See Susanne Woods's introduction to *The Poems of Aemilia Lanyer* for information on the volume's publishing history and the composition of extant copies of the poem.

3. Following her marriage to a court musician, Alfonso Lanier, Aemilia's relationship to the court occurred through her husband, employed by Elizabeth and then by James. Prince Henry received a presentation copy, possibly from Margaret, Countess of Cumberland, or from Henry's master of music, Nicholas Lanier (Aemilia's Lanyer's brother-in-law). As to the Skipton performance of a masque including the character of Comus in 1636, see Martin Butler's suggestion that the performance might have been *Pleasure Reconciled to Virtue* in "The Provincial Masque of *Comus*, 1636."

4. "The Passion" might well have been part of a projected set of poems on important church calendar events, such as had been produced by Herbert and Donne (Hanford, 144).

5. Most critics agree, stressing the problems a Puritan poet would face turning to the Crucifixion, a topic critics have ruled "uncongenial" for Milton. Alternately, Erin Henriksen, in "The Passion in *Poems of Mr. John Milton*" argues that Milton employs a strategy of "omission and supplement" to engage the "Passion" in this and other poems.

6. My number comes from searches conducted through the English Short Title Cat-

alog. I have not included Donne's and Herbert's poems. Donne's, published in 1633, would have circulated extensively in manuscript and thus probably would have been known by Milton.

7. Martz is considering the challenges of mediation poems for Christian writers, while other critics have noted the particular challenges that the Passion poem genre posed for Protestants. The religious background or identity of Aemilia Lanyer, which has been clearly established, has interesting implications for her ability to operate effectively within the Passion poem genre: her possible Catholicism through her Venetian father might explain Lanyer's ability to engage the heavily visual traditions of the Passion poem.

8. This suggestively parallels the flight imagery that Milton will master in Book 1 of *Paradise Lost.*

9. Few critics have considered Lanyer's poetry in the context of other poets writing Passion poems, though Janel Mueller in "The Feminist Poetics of 'Salve Deus Rex Judaeorum'" compares Lanyer's treatment of the Passion poem to Giles Fletcher's *Christs Victory, and Triumph.*

10. Even the most "traditional" of these early Passion poems, John Davies's *The Holy Roode, or Christs crosse: Containing Christ Crucified, described in Speaking-picture* begins with an account of "that blest Body . . . Hung on the Cross," requiring no complicated framework to gaze upon the body of Christ and thus begin his Passion poem.

11. Gervase Markham's 1600 *The Tears of the Beloved: or, The Lamentation of Saint John, Concerning the death and passion of Christ Iesus our sauiour* joins an anonymous 1602 *Saint Peters Tears* and Robert Southwell's 1616 *S. Peters Complaint* in such a use of the apostle.

12. Biernoff is useful for her consideration of what "redemptive vision" can do for female religious figures in the Middle Ages who contemplate the Passion, a practice employed equally by Lanyer.

13. See Patrick Cook for a discussion of the connection between "The Description of Cooke-ham" and the meditative, Loyola tradition of the Passion poem.

14. Stephen Orgel's *The Jonsonian Masque* details the effect of visual perspective and royal power within early seventeenth-century masques. See also Richard Helgerson's discussion of mapping and national identity in *Forms of Nationhood.*

15. See Kari Boyd McBride's *Country House Discourse* for her discussion of the treatment of the house in Lanyer's poem.

16. See Esther Richey's *The Politics of Revelation*, which locates Lanyer's poem among the politically contested acts of revelation in the period.

17. Critics have debated the implications of our view provided along the line of site of Satan. See both Michael Wilding and Neil Forsyth on this issue.

18. For an insightful analysis of the traded gazes throughout the poem and a challenge to Lacanian readings of the gaze, see Regina Schwartz's "Rethinking Voyeurism and Patriarchy."

19. An alternate meaning of "simply" as "Poorly, badly, indifferently; meanly, inadequately; weakly, feebly" (OED, definition 4) could inflect Lanyer's use of the word for Eve at the moment of the Fall. Yet Lanyer's defense of Eve seems to stress her absence of guile and of craft rather than her weakness.

20. Within Milton's other English poems, there are no phrases resembling "stupidly good" that undermine or limit the notion of goodness. A few phrases function in a similar fashion to "household good"; *Samson Agonistes* uses "domestic good" (1048). The phrase "public good" is employed in *Samson Agonistes* (867) as well as *Paradise Regained.*

21. For an overview of the modifications Milton makes to the tradition of Eve, see Diane McColley, *Milton's Eve* and James Turner, *One Flesh.*

22. There is a critical disagreement about the voice that speaks these lines. Hutson

and Lewalski see the voice as Lanyer's or the narrator's, while many more recent interpretations of the poem have read the "Apologie" as the voice of Pilate's wife, only shifting to the narrator at the line 833.

23. Guibbory argues that Lanyer is rejecting the institution of marriage in this passage (204, 202).

24. Constance Jordan argues that seventeenth-century domestic tracts "qualified . . . the extent to which the family constitutes a little government or state; and . . . the kinds of power and authority husbands and fathers can exercise within it" (*Renaissance Feminism*, 287). These tracts, then, did break down the analogy, though they do not utterly dispense with it.

25. Because of the complicated timing of the emergence of what we would call a "public" versus a "private" sphere, I will be employing the terms "household" versus "political" or "social" realms.

26. The one significant exception to this primarily domestic character of the "household" is the use of the word to describe the royal or imperial household. Milton's strong republican leanings suggest that he would not be invoking the royal connotation.

27. Maria Magro similarly argues that "Milton takes a preexisting discourse of antifeminism and from this creates a model of sexualized domesticity on which he basis [sic] man's public role" ("Sexualized Woman," 109).

28. Katherine Gillespie positions mid-century women writers as predicting, rather than offering a distinct set of alternatives to, Locke's division of the public and private spheres at the end of the century. *Engendering the Fall* takes issue with this argument.

Chapter 3. Milton Among the Prophets: Inspiration and Gendered Discourse in the Mid-Seventeenth Century

1. Milton would have disagreed with many elements of Poole's argument, though her reliance on the family/state analogy does appear within traces of Milton's writing on divorce. Milton himself makes this connection explicitly in *The Doctrine and Discipline of Divorce* when he says it is "unprofitable and dangerous to the Common-wealth, when the household estate, out of which must flourish forth the vigor and the spirit of all public enterprizes, is so ill contented and procu'd at home, and cannot be supported" (247).

2. See Katharine Gillespie's discussion of Elizabeth Poole in *Domesticity and Dissent*.

3. See Teresa Feroli's view of Poole's negotiation of the "hierarchical chain of command" to "embrace political roles for women" (71). Feroli and I differ on Poole's deployment of the language of weakness. More generally, I would distance this prophet from C. B. Macpherson's traits of "possessive individualism," while Feroli sees her as embodying this trait.

4. See Rachel Trubowitz, "Feminizing Vision," for a discussion of how divine inspiration was used by "those outside of and excluded from traditional arenas of political power and religious authority" (15).

5. For a discussion of Milton amid a classical tradition of visionary poetry, see Joseph Wittreich's *Visionary Milton*. See William Kerrigan's *Prophetic Milton* for the most detailed exploration of the Christian tradition of prophecy in Milton's poetry.

6. In her chapter on Lanyer, Esther Richey gestures at some similarities between Milton and women prophets that she sees resonating from one source: Thomas Brightman's apocalyptic commentary (37).

7. See Joseph Wittreich's *Visionary Poetics*, a study of the language of prophecy from sources such as the Book of Revelation, which traces the use epic poets make of this convention.

8. For example, Kerrigan compares Milton's account of his method of composition with biblical prophets and authors of scripture.

9. While not suggesting an explicit connection between Abiezer Coppe and Milton, David Loewenstein does compare Coppe to the "polemical and prophetic Milton" (100) while noting the proximity of the publication dates of *A fiery flying roll* and *Eikonoclastes*.

10. If you add phrases that invoke aspects of or figures for God, such as *Voice of a Shepherd*, *Voice of the Iron Rod*, *Voice of the Temple*, and *Voice of Thunder . . . from the Throne of God*, the number goes to 38.

11. For discussions of apocalyptic thought in the seventeenth century, see Paul Christianson's *Reformers and Babylon* and Margarita Stacker's *Apocalyptic Marvell*. Leland Ryken in *The Apocalyptic Vision in Paradise Lost* focuses on Milton's contribution to the tradition. Esther Gilman Richey's *The Politics of Revelation in the English Renaissance* considers the apocalyptic influence of the final book of the New Testament on a range of sixteenth- and seventeenth-century writers.

12. Elizabeth Sauer provides an alternate reading in "Maternity, Prophesy, and the Cultivation of the Private Sphere," distinguishing male and female forms of creativity instead of seeing the form of androgyny Mollenkott identifies in Book 1.

13. Virginia Mollenkott also highlights the passive nature of receiving spiritual inspiration in the Book 1 invocation.

14. See Rachel Trubowitz's "Feminizing Vision," where she compares Marvell's and Milton's negotiation of female prophetic speech.

15. These citations are from *A Collection of Ranter Writings from the 17th Century*, ed. Nigel Smith. In "Female Preachers and Male Wives," Rachel Trubowitz discusses the gender fluidity that could mark many expressions of prophetic experience, though she discusses the simultaneous solidification of such categories and the "increasing polarization" between the sexes during the Civil War period (126).

16. Katharine Gillespie and I interpret Mary Cary's language quite differently. Unlike Gillespie, who discerns a "possessive individualism" in Cary, I see the language of the "self" as much more difficult for Cary and other female prophets to articulate within their writings. Gillespie and I thus diverge significantly over the issue of the agency of these women.

17. This poem comes from a 1000-page folio-size publication in the Bodleian Library.

18. Even when feminist critics have worked to draw agency back into these motifs of helplessness and passivity, the resulting accounts of female sectarian prophets sound exactly like William Kerrigan's description of Milton's narrator in the Book 9 invocation. Hinds argues for the female "instrument" as a "paradox," "both active and passive, both in control and controlled" (99). Kerrigan uses the same word, "paradox," to describe Milton's narrator who, as "both author and amanuensis . . . has both everything and nothing to do with *Paradise Lost*" (138).

19. In "Unsilent Instruments," Sue Wiseman comments that "to represent oneself as speaking God's work is theoretically to dissolve the unified subject-position of the speaker—for when is the speaker an 'I' and when God's agent?" (189). Hilary Hinds in *God's Englishwomen* considers this issue through a poststructuralist, French feminist approach.

20. See Nigel Smith's chapter "Prophecy, Experience, and the Self" in *Perfection Proclaimed* for a discussion of the various forms of the "self" employed by sectarians; distinguishing between the language of male and female prophets is not Smith's project.

21. See Smith on the character of this dream (*Perfection Proclaimed*, 84).

22. See Sara Van Den Berg, "Eve, Sin, and Witchcraft" on the dream.

23. I am indebted to David Loewenstein for suggesting these two tracts to me.

24. See Gillespie for a rethinking of the Habermasian terms of the "public sphere" in mid-seventeenth-century England.

25. See Crawford, *Marvelous Protestantism*, 156–57, where she also discusses Jane Lead, whose tract includes accounts of a "ghostly birth" and a "traveling hour" (157).

26. Crawford's *Marvelous Protestantism* argues the similarity between prophecy and prodigious births, though such births are the center of her book. I wrote this chapter before the appearance of Crawford's book, but nonetheless have tried to engage her argument as fully as possible.

27. Elizabeth Sauer sees the "allegory of monstrous birth" as distinguishing between male and female reproductive functions ("Maternity," 140), though Milton's own Book 1 invocation seems to confuse stable gendered categories in accounts of birth. Also see Mollenkott.

28. See Louis Schwartz, "'Conscious Terrors' and 'the Promised Seed.'"

29. While I would agree with Crawford that the majority of the texts supported parliamentarian politics, this was by no means universally true. Prodigious births were used as ideological weapons by Presbyterians (Thomas Edwards), Royalists, and Parliamentary supporters. Thus, it operates as a more heterodox discourse, its heterodoxy an attraction for Milton after the Restoration.

30. After the large number of monstrous births recorded in the 1640s and early 1650s, only two appear to have been recorded in the 1660s. See Crawford for a reading of monstrous and prodigious births as redrawn by the rise of Baconian science and the formation and growing influence of the Royal Society (181).

31. See Katherine Romack, "Monstrous Births and the Body Politic."

32. Rachel Trubowitz has suggested that this scene, particularly the representation—through rape and incest—of the establishment of a monarchical line, counters earthly narratives of the production of dynasty ("Single State").

33. The dominant meaning of "member" in this phrase seems to be of body parts—a limb or other part attached to the trunk. And yet a somewhat more obscure use of "member" maintains the political implications embedded in the body politic motif within this episode. Also a "component part or branch of apolitical or commercial body" (OED), the physical (if monstrous) appearance of Death argues for the indistinguishable nature of his political identity.

34. My reading in this chapter, as throughout this study, forces a reconsideration of Christine Berg and Philippa Berry's claim in "Spiritual Whoredom" that Milton was "unable to admit women to possession of the logos" (51).

Chapter 4. Maternity, Marriage, and Contract: Lucy Hutchinson's Response to Patriarchal Theory in Order and Disorder

1. Joseph Wittreich discusses the poem in "Milton's Transgressive Maneuvers," but assigned authorship to Sir Allen Apsley, Lucy Hutchinson's brother.

2. Norbrook makes his attribution argument in "'A devine Originall': Lucy Hutchinson and the 'Woman's Version'" and his introduction to Lucy Hutchinson's *Order and Disorder*.

3. Moore assumed male authorship of the first five cantos of the poem.

4. Kowaleski-Wallace's argument in part extends the claims made by Susan Gubar and Sandra Gilbert in *Madwoman in the Attic*.

5. See also Wittreich's recent work that makes a similar claim, including "'John, John, I blush for thee,'" and "Milton's Transgressive Maneuvers."

6. This is not to deny the rich circulation life open to a manuscript. Hutchinson was

part of a circle of active readers and writers, and the text of *Order and Disorder* could well have circulated among them. See Arthur Marotti's work on Donne and the essay collection edited by Crick and Waltham, *The Uses of Script and Print, 1300-1700*, on the circulation of manuscripts.

7. For a detailed distinction between the Restoration politics of Milton and Lucy Hutchinson, see David Norbrook's "Milton, Hutchinson, and the Republican Biblical Epic," 52–53.

8. In "Transgressive Maneuvers," an essay published before Norbrook's attribution of *Order and Disorder* to Lucy Hutchinson, Wittreich views the poem as providing "a series of predictable answers" to the questions posed by Milton's biblical epic.

9. See Christine Froula's essay, "When Eve Reads Milton," on the repressed figure of the mother in *Paradise Lost*. Other critics to discuss the figure of reproduction in *Paradise Lost* include Regina Schwartz in *Remembering and Repeating: Biblical Creation in* Paradise Lost and Michael Lieb in *The Dialectics of Creation: Patterns of Birth and Regeneration in* Paradise Lost. See Erin Murphy, "Milton's 'Birth Abortive,'" for a reading of Milton's response to Robert Filmer's patriarchialist theories through the representation of the family in *Paradise Lost*.

11. See Michael Lieb's *The Dialectics of Creation* on the interconnection of birth and death images in *Paradise Lost*. Lieb's book does not, though, speak to the gendered implications of such motifs.

12. For a biographically inflected, historicist reading of the birth imagery in the Sin sequence, see Louis Schwartz, "'Conscious Terrors' and 'The Promised Seed.'"

13. See Wittreich's *Feminist Milton* on how women thinkers and writers reworked Books 11 and 12.

14. See David Norbrook's detailed comparison of the two poems' politics in "Milton, Hutchinson, and the Republican Biblical Epic."

15. David Norbrook interestingly suggests that Lucretius's own political identity might have appealed to Hutchinson ("Republican Epic," 45).

16. Lucretius's poem does not, though, become some paean to women, despite the poem's focus on the maternal generative body. As Nugent has shown in "Mater Matters: The Female in Lucretius' De Rerum Natura," women are exposed in the text as "malodorous or dangerous," and as linked to the natural sphere while simultaneously distanced from any power in the cultural realm (203).

17. Maureen Quilligan argues that Milton offers a "cosmic femaleness" here, with a female earth, a female light, the water being described as a womb, and, of course, this image of all creatures coming from the earth's womb. I would counter that four references to Creation in the book, even those which actually use language such as "womb" or "birth," explicitly do not assign a female gender to these metaphors. Here, of course, the "fertile womb" is gendered female with the pronoun "her."

18. For a discussion of how various pamphlet writers negotiate the P and J accounts, see Mary Nyquist, "The Genesis of Gendered Subjectivity in the Divorce Tracts and in *Paradise Lost*"

19. Hutchinson s profound revision of traditional marriage commentaries within this scene is highlighted by a comparison with Milton's analogous scene. In Nyquist's view, Milton's attribution of Genesis 2:24 illustrates his promotion of a "contracted view" of marriage rather than a sacramental one (113–14). In attributing to Adam chapter 2:24 of Genesis, "Therefore shall a man leave his father and his mother, and shall cleave unto his wife: and they shall be one flesh," the union between Adam and Eve lacks the statement by God, or Moses, which had been interpreted in divorce commentaries as its indissoluble nature. As Nyquist explains, Calvin had recognized the interpretive choices for the speaker of this verse: Adam, God, and Moses are all eligible (113).

Calvin will ultimately assign to Moses Genesis 2:24, a decision that Milton rejects (Nyquist, 113–14). Milton transforms the practice surrounding the first marriage into an explicitly contractual representation of marriage, a position consistent with his position in the divorce tracts. God's lack of appearance within Book 8 of *Paradise Lost* means that only Adam speaks about marriage; Milton thus quite explicitly rejects God's sanctification of marriage, a process that Hutchinson chooses to highlight.

20. For a discussion of legislative changes to the marriage ceremony in the Interregnum, see Chris Durston's "'Unhallowed Wedlocks': The Regulation of Marriage During the English Revolution." The 1653 Act voted in by the Barebones Parliament barred any marriages but those performed by a justice of the peace; the act transformed marriage into a civil act, one requiring a representative of the state to perform it, as well as witnesses and a recording of this civil union. Church marriages were consequently banned, though many couples, entirely confused by the terms of the marriage act, would marry twice, once under the auspices of the civil practice and then marry within the church. See Durston, and Lawrence Stone in *Uncertain Unions: Marriage in England 1660–1753* on marriage practices during the mid-seventeenth century that the 1653 and 1657 marriage acts were attempting to standardize.

21. For a reading of the limited space for consent offered to Eve in Milton's marriage sequence, see Lynne Greenberg's "A Preliminary Study of Informed Consent and Free Will in the Garden of Eden: John Milton's Social Contract."

22. I am emphasizing the language associating marriage with contract here, though the spiritual component of marriage is made explicit by Hutchinson in both the subsequent solemnization by God and, 60 lines later, language from the Song of Songs.

23. For an illustration of how consistently these discourses were woven together, see Margaret Sommerville's *Sex and Subjection: Attitudes to Women in Early-Modern Society*.

24. See Mary Lyndon Shanley's "Marriage Contract and Social Contract" and Lynne Greenberg's, "A Preliminary Study of Informed Consent" for a general discussion of the interrelationship between the marriage contract and contract theory. For a more general study about the emerging culture of contract in the seventeenth century, see Craig Muldrew's *The Economy of Obligation: The Culture of Credit and Social Relations in Early Modern England*. Also see Victoria Kahn's *Wayward Contracts*.

25. For precursors to and contemporaries of Filmer, see Chapters 5 and 6 of Gordon Schochet's *Patriarchalism in Political Thought*. Despite the late publication date of *Patriarcha*, his theories would have been known from a series of other publications in the 1640s, including *The Freeholders Grand Inquest, The Anarchy of a Limited or Mixed Monarchy*, and *Observations Concerning the Originall of Government*. For a summary of the arguments about the date of the manuscript of *Patriarcha*, see Johann Sommerville's introduction to *Filmer: Patriarcha and Other Writings*; Sommerville's edition also includes *Free-holders Grand Inquest, Anarchy*, and *Observations*.

26. The opposition between Milton's and Filmer's ideas can be traced through publication and through events. Filmer's 1652 *Observations Concerning the Originall of Government* was a critical examination of, among other texts, Milton's *Defensio pro Populo Anglicani* and Hobbes's *Leviathan* (Schochet, 120). Milton's poetic works are viewed in the period as engaging Filmer as well. In 1683, James Parkinson was expelled from Lincoln College at Oxford because he had prompted students to read Milton as a rebuttal to Filmer (Schochet, 207).

27. Other scholars of the early modern period have commented on the effect of employing only the male portion of the fifth commandment in seventeenth-century discussions of political theory, including Catherine Belsey, *The Subject of Tragedy*.

28. The 1679 publication of only the first five cantos of *Order and Disorder* suggests how explicitly Hutchinson wished to place her poem in conversation with Milton:

Canto 6 on moves beyond the scope of Milton's poem set largely in the Garden of Eden. Perhaps the more politically unorthodox views that Hutchinson expresses seemed acceptable in manuscript, but not in print.

29. To suggest that Hutchinson, a devout Parliamentarian, could have been influenced by the thought of Hobbes, whose political allegiance bound him to the exiled court of Charles II, might seem problematic. Yet, although Hobbes's leanings may have been royalist, his conclusions provided a clear argument against patriarchalism. Further, his *Leviathan* was seen by many royalists as undercutting a God-sanctioned right of monarchical rule. Politically Hutchinson might have considered Hobbes because of the fusion of consent theory and the acknowledgment of the erasure of parental authority in the work of Filmer. She would also have been familiar with Hobbes's mechanistic philosophy: his *Leviathan* draws extensively from the Epicurean philosophy that Lucretius versifies in *De rerum natura*.

30. See Introduction to *Order and Disorder*.

31. See the Introduction to Weil's *Political Passions*.

Chapter 5. The Two Faces of Eve: Gendering Knowledge and the "New" Science in Paradise Lost *and Margaret Cavendish's* Blazing World

1. For the best exploration of the battle between "natural" and "experimental" science, rather than a positivistic reading of the winners, see Shapin and Schaffer's *Leviathan and the Air-Pump*.

2. While Hobbes offers a much more systematic method promoting philosophical bases for comprehending the world around us, Cavendish's method, if not her systemization, shares much with Hobbes's thought. Among the many disputes that mark Cavendish criticism is the widely divergent characterization of her work as either "systematic" or "chaotic" (see Susan James's versus Sarah Hutton's views of Cavendish). See Eve Keller's "Producing Petty Gods," which argues that Cavendish is specifically responding to Hooke in her *Observations* and *The Blazing World*.

3. Kester Svendsen's *Milton and Science* links Milton to a Medieval view of scientific practice and suggests that he is as unaware as uninterested in the new science. Many recent studies have worked to counter this traditional assessment of Milton and his writings, especially Harinder Singh Marjara's *Contemplation of Created Things*, Karen Edwards's *Milton and the Natural World*, and Nicholas van Maltzahn's work on Milton and the Royal Society.

4. All critics of Cavendish agree that she is a committed monist, though the movement of souls and animation of bodies in the *Blazing World* does raise some interesting questions. See Susan James's "The Philosophical Innovations of Margaret Cavendish" for details about this transformation in Cavendish's thought. In *The Matter of Revolution*, John Rogers argues that vitalism allowed Milton to retain a theory of individual free will that the mechanism of Hobbes, focused entirely on the physical force that provides that one object will propel another, disallowed.

5. See Stephen Fallon's *Milton Among the Philosophers* for an account of Milton's move from a dualist to a monist position

6. My assertion about the similarity in philosophical thought between Milton and Cavendish is derived from the work of Steven Fallon, John Rogers, Susan James, Sara Hutton, and Eileen O'Neill.

7. While the mechanisms, even the physical equipment, necessary to practice the "new science" were denied to her, the process of reflection that she saw as leading to truth was not. Margaret Cavendish partly parodies and partly re-imagines this

alternative for women philosophers when she produces her *Philosophical Letters, Or Modest Reflections.*

8. See Eve Keller's "Producing Petty Gods: Margaret Cavendish's Critique of Experimental Science," which argues that "*The Blazing World* responds to the routine promises of Edenic return made possible by science" (463).

9. See Keller, 465.

10. I'm indebted to Achsah Guibbory for the Hooke and Cowley references; Keller also cites the Hooke.

11. Eve Keller considers the "*redemptive* powers of the new science" (455) more generally, while I am suggesting that the motif of the Garden is explained in a much more sustained fashion throughout Royal Society rhetoric and in Cavendish's response to the highly gendered implications of that rhetoric.

12. For more information on the physical conditions under which the Society operated, see Michael Hunter's *Science and Society in Restoration England* and "The social basis and changing fortunes of an early scientific institution."

13. See especially the final chapter of *Leviathan and the Air-Pump*, "Natural Philosophy and the Restoration: Interests in Dispute."

14. See Shapin and Schaffer, Chapter 4 of *Leviathan and the Air-Pump*.

15. For Cavendish's use of Power, see Eileen O'Neill's well-footnoted edition of *Observations upon Experimental Philosophy.*

16. I thus disagree with Richard Nate's argument that Cavendish attempts to align her style to that of (male) writers within the Royal Society in order to acquire authority for her philosophy.

17. See especially Rachel Trubowitz on Elizabeth and the Empress in "Reenchantment of Utopia," 234.

18. My location of Cavendish within the Filmerian discourses of marital hierarchy differentiates my argument from Catherine Gallagher's "Embracing the Absolute." Her focus on Cavendish's use of the "absolute monarch" within her writings is a very compelling argument about "Margaret the First," yet her description of Cavendish's "political and social isolation" doesn't account for the interventions that Cavendish, admittedly through fiction, makes into issues of political and marital organization (33). For a focus on Cavendish as a "political thinker" within her plays, see Mihoko Suzuki's *Subordinate Subjects.*

19. Michael Hunter in *Science and Society* details the distinctions between the scientists and the virtuosi within the Royal Society.

20. See Elizabeth Spiller's "Reading through Galileo's Telescope: Margaret Cavendish and the Experience of Reading" for a reading of Cavendish's response to Galileo's *The Starry Messenger.*

21. Maura Brady's "Galileo in Action" will consider the distance, and the difference, between Raphael's view onto the universe and the view provided through the telescope. Brady's larger argument is that the reader of *Paradise Lost* should embrace the difficult work of seeing and knowing outlined in the poem. For an excellent article that explores how perspective is reconfigured by the "new space of telescopic astronomy" (22), see Marjorie Nicolson's "Milton and the Telescope."

22. See Dava Sobel's *Galileo's Daughter*, 286.

23. For an exploration of how this Book 4 question of Eve's poses epistemological problems that resonate throughout Adam's exchange with Raphael and the entire poem, see Judith Scherer Herz's article "For whom this glorious sight."

24. John Guillory, in "From the Superfluous to the Supernumerary," discusses the intersection between this discourse of astronomy and sexual hierarchy in Book 8. See especially pages 81–84.

25. The structure of Book 7 in the 1667 first edition would underscore Adam's increasingly unbounded questions or assertions. The Book, which would be divided into Books 7 and 8 in 1674, begins with a question that does not exceed appropriate human understanding: God's creation of the world. The next question by Adam—about the universe and the stars—does violate the boundaries. He then continues this act of violating boundaries in his assertions about Eve.

26. Articulated most clearly by Stephen Fallon, but supported as well by the scholarship of John Rogers, the underpinnings of Milton's thought philosophically distinguish him from members of the Royal Society. Nonetheless, biographical connections between Milton and members of the Society are plentiful. His own circle of acquaintances, such as Lady Katherine Ranelagh, Robert Boyle's sister, drew him close to certain key members. Such connections to the Hartlib circle suggest the same points of intellectual contact.

27. Edwards claims that as terms and concepts, "*experience* and *experiment* were almost, but not entirely, interchangeable" (21).

28. For Edwards's reading of the use of "experience" versus "experiment" in the poem, see *Milton and the Natural World*, 17–21.

29. "Experiments" is used 45 times in the 1660s, "experimental" 19 times, and "experiment" three times. The overwhelming majority of the titles relate to the more contemporary meaning of scientific experimentation. Generally, about 20 percent of the titles draw on the word in a religious or theological context, such as a tract in which "true wisedom described the excellency of spiritual, experimental, and saving knowledge."

30. Sarah Hutton's "In Dialogue with Thomas Hobbes: Margaret Cavendish's Natural Philosophy" establishes much more of a link between Cavendish's and Hobbes's thought than have other Cavendish critics. As she shows, both viewed "Experimentation [as] secondary to rational enquiry, as sense perception is subordinate to reason" (424).

31. In Edwards's reading, designed to illustrate that Milton was positively engaging Boyle's experimental approach, Eve begins to read evidence correctly. Yet she is waylaid by Satan's manipulation. For her full argument, see *Milton and the Natural World*, 15–39.

32. Edwards suggests that there is no necessary contradiction between God's injunction not to eat of the Tree of Knowledge and the practices of experimental philosophy: Eve could have utilized these practices and come to the proper conclusion not to eat from the tree of knowledge: "Experimentalism does not conflict with and indeed would have complemented the theological injunction not to eat the fruit" (37). Yet Edwards's claim that experimentalism and the theological injunction to Adam and Eve are not inconsistent suggests that querying the injunction itself would be acceptable. Even if Eve had maintained, in Edwards's terms, all the practices of a true experimental philosopher, she would have erred by pursuing the question.

33. Quoted in *Leviathan and the Air-Pump*, 36.

34. See Laura Favero Carraro's "Women's Discourse on Science and Learning and the Image of the Learned Lady."

35. See Stanley Fish's *Surprised by Sin* on the implication of "experiment" and modern science in the Fall scene.

36. Guillory disputes that Adam's question derives from Eve's Book 4 query (80).

Part III Introduction

1. See Mark Goldie's second volume on the reception of Locke's politics between 1705 and 1760, which follows the reactions of patriarchalist theorists to the social contract.

2. See Maria Magro's "Milton's Sexualized Woman," and Beth Kowaleski-Wallace's "Milton's Daughters: The Education of Eighteenth-Century Women," which argue that female authorship was reconfigured in the later seventeenth century.

Chapter 6. Rewriting Creation: Mary Chudleigh's The Song of the Three Children Paraphras'd *and* Paradise Lost

1. One of these shifts is the focus of Royalists onto the "urban prostitute," explored by Melissa Mowry in *The Bawdy Politic in Stuart England*.

2. For a summary of the critical debate over the composition dates for Locke's *Two Treatises*, see the introduction to Peter Laslett's Cambridge edition.

3. Though she does not discuss Chudleigh, Rachel Weil's *Political Passions* illustrates how central family structure was to political thought through the 1680s and 1690s.

4. Mary Astell queries, in *Reflections upon Marriage*, "to whom [do] we poor Fatherless Maids, and Widows who have lost their Masters, owe Subjection? It can't be to all Men in general" (29).

5. Lady Mary Chudleigh publishes the versified *The Ladies Defence* in 1701. Some critics have attributed to her the prose *Female Advocate*, which initially appeared under the title *The Female Preacher* in 1699.

6. Margaret Ezell has edited all of Chudleigh's published writings in the Oxford Women Writers in English series. The Dictionary of National Biography entry, also by Margaret Ezell, refers to a number of manuscripts mentioned in family memoirs, including two tragedies, operas, a masque, and poetic translations. Yet none of these have been found.

7. Joseph Wittreich briefly discusses Mary Chudleigh's response to *Paradise Lost*, especially in *The Female Advocate* which Wittreich attributes to her (*Feminist Milton*, 51–52).

8. For a historical overview of the settlement, see Lois Schwoerer's *The Declaration of Rights, 1689*. Rachel Weil's *Political Passions* provides an interpretative overview of the settlement of 1688.

9. See Weil, *Political Passions*.

10. See Lois Schwoerer's "Images of Queen Mary II" for an analogous discussion of how laws about the family, in particularly those covering a "femme covert," were applied to the issue of marital authority in the royal couple (728).

11. While Wittreich argues for Chudleigh's authorship of this earlier defense in *Feminist Milton*, Margaret Ezell explicitly rejects this authorial attribution.

12. Wittreich briefly comments on Chudleigh's praise of Milton within the poem to Dryden (*Feminist Milton*, xxv).

13. The form, which Milton did use in a few poems, was made popular in the Restoration by Abraham Cowley, who published a collection of odes in 1656.

14. I am indebted to Shil Sen for pointing out the pregnancy imagery in the verb "dilate."

15. Though by no means an exact measure, the Chadwick-Healy Literary Theory database offers an intriguing way of measuring references to poets in the period, an approximate form of our more exact humanities citation index. Dryden receives twice the attention of Milton from 1667 to 1703, though these numbers will be reversed by 1750. While Milton was either half or a third as significant as Dryden in this time period, he is arguably twice as significant as Cowley, who gets slightly more than half of line 33, while Milton receives only the place-keeping line "Then Milton came" (33).

16. See Richard Helgerson, "Barbarous Tongues," in *Forms of Nationhood* for a con-

sideration of the role that such sixteenth-century discussions of rhyme had on national identity as well as on poetic innovation.

17. The approximately 45 verses occur on signatures Blv-B2r in the 1629 Book of Common Prayer.

18. See Barbara Olive's "The Fabric of Restoration Puritanism": the story of the persecution of the "three children" was used frequently by Puritans (124).

19. The apocryphal section of Daniel, inserted in 3:23–24, provides a tribute to God for all of the things in this world; the structure of the "Song" that appears in the Book of Common Prayer is a list of these created elements of and in the world. Narratively, the poem is understood as the tributes sung to God who saves the three children from the furnace into which they had been thrown by Nebuchadnezzar.

20. The Cambridge Platonists, a "school" of thought actually named in the nineteenth century, countered in their philosophy the mechanistic, dualist world presented by Descartes and Hobbes while stressing the presence of God within nature as well as the infinite goodness of God. Opposing what they saw as philosophical ideas that could lead individuals to reject God, they emphasized deification, or the access to the divinity of God through our own spiritual ascension. For an excellent overview of the main figures within the Cambridge Platonist school, see Sarah Hutton's chapter in *A Companion to Early Modern Philosophy* and Tod E. Jones's introduction to *The Cambridge Platonists*.

21. Certainly Du Bartas's *Devine Weekes* would still have been an important poem at the end of the seventeenth century. But Chudleigh's nationalist focus in her poem on Dryden, combined with her references to Milton within her poems and prefacing her essays, argues for the significance of his poem for her.

22. See John Smith's and Ralph Cudworth's deemphasis of the physicality of damnation and of Hell; both considered Heaven and Hell as only "spiritual," even internal, conditions (Tod Jones, 32).

23. See Merritt Hughes on the link to Plato's *Timaeus* in 5.469–71. Alternately, Steven Fallon argues that Milton no longer held his earlier neo-Platonic philosophy by the time of the composition of *Paradise Lost*.

Chapter 7. Spaces and Traces of the Garden Story in Aphra Behn and Mary Astell: Mapping Female Subjectivit(ies) Through Patriarchialist Discourse

1. Utilizing the EEBO search term of "marriage," these three periods of time show groupings of texts with four and usually five texts produced in each of these years: the years around them generally had one to three, averaging closer to two.

2. The metaphor of the family as a model for the state still featured centrally in many texts produced after the Settlement of the throne onto William and Mary. Specifically, many tracts that debated taking the Oath of Allegiance to the new monarchs had to negotiate the family and/or marital metaphor in evaluating whether to shift allegiance from James II to William and Mary. See Sherlock's *The Case of the Allegiance due to Soveraign Powers* (1691), *An Examination of the Scruples of Those who Refuse to Take the Oath of Allegiance* (1689), and *Reflections upon the Opinions of Some Modern Divines, concerning the Nature of Government in General, and that of England in particular* (1689).

3. The representational nature of Filmer's thinking for patriarchalist thought has been debated by political theorists. Gordon Schochet in *Patriarchalism in Political Thought* and Mark Goldie in "John Locke and Anglican Royalism" argue for Filmer's ideas as a summary of patriarchal thinking (Schohet) and for Filmer's importance through the century. See James Daly in *Sir Robert Filmer and English Political Thought* for an alternate view of Filmer's importance to other patriarchalist theorists.

4. For debates over the order of composition of the *Two Treatises*, see John Ashcroft's edition of Locke and John Marshall's *John Locke*.

5. Though it appeared anonymously, Locke's authorship was considered an open secret.

6. See Weil's chapter on "The Politics of Divorce" in *Political Passions*.

7. See Mary Nyquist on Astell's reaction to the "contractual relations" Milton develops in both *Paradise Lost* and the Divorce tracts ("Gendered Subjectivity," 124).

8. Barbara Lewalski describes the poem in these terms in "Milton on Women—Yet Again" (58). The "Opera of Adam" comes from Thomas Brown (1688), cited in Wittreich ("Maneuvers," 248).

9. Eve's language about women's position after the Fall, "Curst with that reason she must never use," Louis Martz calls "the most powerful speech in the play" ("Dryden's Poem," 195).

10. There is much critical debate over Dryden's representation of Eve. Anne Ferry terms her a "coquette" (21), while Bernard Harris terms her "a romantic heroine" (135). Jean Gagen sees Eve as having a much more "active role" in the play than does Milton's Eve, "and clearly surpasses [Milton's Eve] in intelligence" (137). Many of these readings of Eve are drawn together in Melissa Cowan Sage's view of her as symbolizing "both the self-assertiveness and sensuality of the libertine hero," who embodies both "heroic desire" and "heroic valor" (40).

11. Dryden's and Hopkin's own negotiations of Milton's representation of Adam and Eve thus complement John Dunton's well-known conclusion on *Samson Agonistes*: that after the unorthodox representation of Eve in *Paradise Lost*, Milton returned to appropriate images of women and man's "despotick Power / *Over his female*" (quoted in Wittreich, *Feminist Milton*, 26).

12. As Joseph Wittreich first illustrates in *Feminist Milton*, women in the eighteenth century explicitly engaged Milton's epic to defend women's role in the family; as the book shows, some women readers who interrogated this text drew upon it to support or elevate women's cultural status, such as Jane Lead (see esp. Wittreich's " 'John, John, I Blush' "). Astell and Behn, though, contest aspects of the poem as they negotiate the gender ideolog(ies) within *Paradise Lost*.

13. As I note in Chapter 6, Wittreich and Ezell disagree on Chudleigh's authorship of this tract.

14. Wittreich discusses this text in *Feminist Milton* (52).

15. Jane Lead's invocation of Milton in works such as *A Fountain of Gardens*, as Wittreich has shown, also engage Milton in terms that suggest she found it a more liberating text for women to engage as writers (see "Transgressive Maneuvers"). Lead, whose use of Milton is closer to Chudleigh's engagement of the mystical imagery in the poem, does not engage the explicitly political issue of governmental organization as do Behn and Astell, and for that reason I do not treat her in this study.

16. The epistolary form of the novel and its connection to the rise of the novel has received attention from Judith Gardiner in "The First English Novel: Aphra Behn's *Love Letters*. The Canon," John Richetti in *"Love-Letters Between a Nobleman and His Sister*. Aphra Behn and Amatory Fiction," and Warren Chernaik, "Unguarded Hearts: Transgression and Epistolary Form in Aphra Behn's *Love-Letters* and the Portuguese Letters."

17. Toni Bowers explicitly engages the relationship between political events of the period and character interactions in her article on "Seduction Narratives and Tory Experience in Augustan England." See Mona Narain, "Body and Politics in Aphra Behn's *Love Letters Between a Nobleman and His Sister*, Alison Conway in "The Protestant Cause and a Protestant Whore: Aphra Behn's *Love Letters*" and Julie Schutzman, "Ruling Pas-

sions: Sovereignty, Femininity and Fiction, 1680–1742," for differing readings of the relationship between the personal and political events in the novel.

18. Despite a tradition of reading Behn as a staunch Royalist, recent critics including Margaret Ferguson and me have begun to question how strong her support for the crown is during the last few years of James II. See Ferguson, "Conning the 'Overseers,'" and Miller, "Executing the Body Politic."

19. As Todd notes, a number of works, produced right around the time of the first part of *Love- Letters*, take up the status of consanguinity. See for example John Turner's 1684 *A Resolution of Three Matrimonial Cases*, which considers issues like "Whether it be lawful for a man to marry his deceased wife's sister's daughter."

20. Her footnote reads: "Milton's *Paradise Lost* was published in 1667 and it inspired a constant stream of poems discussing the Genesis myth and assessing the relationship between men and women in this period" (191). Carol Barash makes an even stronger assertion about Behn's engagement with *Paradise Lost*, remarking that lines from "To Mr. Creech (under the Name of *Daphnis*)" on his Excellent Translation of *Lucretius*" form a "deft echo of both *Paradise Lost* and Dryden's *State of Innocence*" (105).

21. See Janet Todd's article, "Who Is Silvia? What Is She?" on Silvia's shifting identity in the novel. In "A Protestant Cause and a Protestant Whore," Alison Conway considers the unstable identity of Silvia amid the ever-shifting political events of the period.

22. My positioning of Astell as engaged in political theory owes much to critics like Ruth Perry, Hilda Smith, and more recently Rachel Weil.

23. Macey also details a number of linguistic similarities that draw this otherwise conventional invocation of Eden toward specific Miltonic imagery.

24. For Weil, Astell's representation of seduction becomes "a kind of political allegory" (154).

25. Ruth Perry in *The Celebrated Mary Astell* comments on Astell's "insistence on women's right to a life of the mind" (99). Hilda Smith, in *Reason's Disciples*, also stresses the role of reason and the development of women's minds within Astell's writings.

26. I have employed the keyword search of full-text documents from the Early English Books database. Of 53 references in 38 texts from 1650–1715, only two, Milton's *Paradise Lost* and John Norris's 1685 *A Sermon Preach'd*, detach the negative meaning of "self-love" from "self-esteem": Norris remarks that "Neither is this *Self-esteem* only the *Reward* of Vertue but also the *Cause* of it too, and consequently 'tis not only *allowable*, but also highly *needful* that we should think *Honorably* of our selves" (20). This is obviously not a full portrait of the use of the word: full-text versions of documents account for about 9 percent of all EEBO documents. Yet the consistency of the references points to the unique manner in which Milton, Norris, and Astell are employing this term.

27. Only John Norris uses the word "self-esteem" in this way in the period. A close friend and correspondent of Mary Astell, he develops a non-pejorative theory around the concept of "self-love." See his 1688 *Theory and Regulation of Love: A Moral Essay in Two Parts*.

28. As Wittreich details, Bentley thinks Milton "*must have meant* to champion the quality of the sexes"; thus Bentley amends the Book 4 line by adding this note: "A shameful error to have pass'd through all the Editions. The author give it, *He for God only, She for God AND Him*" (quoted in *Feminist Milton*, 55).

29. Patricia Springborg's edition identifies a reference to William Whiston's *New Theory* on the same page as Astell's reconfigured "Miltonic" line on women's relationship to God.

30. Rachel Weil argues for Astell's support for the analogy in *Political Passions*, while Hilda Smith sees Astell as tolerating, if not "appreciat[ing]," the analogy (*Reason's*

Disciples, 132). I am suggesting a much more radical undermining of the analogy than other critics.

31. See Perry's claim that Astell is demanding a "single standard" from Milton and perhaps other republican thinkers.

Conclusion. *Influencing Traditions of Interpretation*

1. Sharon Achinstein's essay on Elizabeth Singer Rowe, "'Pleasure by Description,'" suggests how this eighteenth-century poet "disrupts the story told by feminist historians of political thought" by showing Rowe embracing, rather than being marginalized by, the liberal tradition (65).

2. See Lorenne M. G. Clark's assessment of Locke's view of women in "Women and Locke."

3. For an alternate approach to the use of the Genesis myth in political thought, see Margaret Canovan's "On Being Economical with the Truth: Some Liberal Reflections."

4. See John Dunn's *The Political Thought of John Locke*, which argues a theological underpinning to Locke's text, and Kirstie M. McClure's *Judging Rights*, which argues for a theologically inflected conceptual architecture pervading Locke's thought.

5. While Locke prepares for this division within the logic of his tract earlier, that division is firmly and clearly made at paragraph 71 in the *Second Treatise*: "But these two *Powers, Political* and *Paternal, are so perfectly distinct* and separate; are built upon so different Foundations, and given to so different Ends, that every Subject that is a Father, has as much a *Paternal Power* over his Children, as the Prince has over his; And every Prince that has Parents owes them as much filial Duty and Obedience as the meanest of his Subjects do to theirs; and can therefore contain not any part of degree of that kind of Dominion, which a Prince, or Magistrate has over his Subject" (314).

6. See in particular Elaine Beilin's *Redeeming Eve*.

Works Cited

Book of Common Prayer. London, 1629.
A Declaration of a strange and Wonderfull Monster: Born in Kirkham Parish in Lancashire. . . . London, 1646.
An Examination of the Scruples of Those who Refuse to Take the Oath of Allegiance. London, 1689.
The Famous Tragedie of the Life and Death of Mris. Rump. . . . London, 1660.
The Female Preacher. London, 1699.
"Festa Georgiana, or the Gentries & Countries Joy for the Coronation of the King on St. Georges Day." London, 1661.
Haec-Vir: Or The Womanish-Man: Being an Answere to a late Booke intituled Hic-Mulier. London, 1620.
Hic Mulier: Or, The Man-Woman: Being a Medicine to cure . . . the Masculine-Feminines of our Times. London, 1620.
The Life and Death of Mris Rump. And the Fatal end of her Base-born brat of destruction. . . . London, 1660.
The manner of the Solemnity of the Coronation of His most Sacred Majesty King Charles. London, 1660.
The most strange and wounderful apperation of blood in a poole. . . . London, 1645.
Mrs. Rump brought to Bed of a Monster, with her terrible pangs, bitter Teming, hard Labour, and lamentable travel from Portsmouth. . . . London, 1660.
The Ranters Monster: Being a true Relation of one Mary Adams. . . . London, 1652.
Reflections upon the Opinions of Some Modern Divines, concerning the Nature of Government. London, 1689.
Saint Peters Tears. Supposedly written vpon his weeping sorrowes for denying his Maister Christ. London, 1602.
Signs and wonders from Heaven. With a true Relation of a Monster borne. . . . London, 1645.
A Strange and True relation of a Wonderful and Terrible Earth-quake. . . . London, 1661.
The Strange Monster, or, True News from Nottingham-shire of a Strange Monster born at Grasly. . . . London, 1668.
Strange newes from Scotland, or, A Strange relation of a terrible and prodigious monster. . . . London, 1647.
Vox Infantis: Or, The propheticall child. London, 1649.

Achinstein, Sharon. "'Pleasure by Description': Elizabeth Singer Rowe's Enlightened Milton." In *Milton and the Grounds of Contention*, ed. Mark R. Kelley, Michael Lieb, and John T. Shawcross. Pittsburgh: Duquesne University Press, 2003.

Amussen, Susan. "Gender, Family, and the Social Order, 1560–1725." In *Order and Disorder in Early Modern England*, ed. Anthony Fletcher and John Stevenson. Cambridge: Cambridge University Press, 1985.

Andreini, Giambattista. *L'Adamo. The Celestial Cycle: The Theme of Paradise Lost in World Literature, with Translations of the Major Analogues*. Toronto: University of Toronto, 1952.

Anger, Jane. "Her Protection for Women . . ." In *Half Humankind: Contexts and Texts of the Controversy About Women in England, 1540–1640*. Urbana: University of Illinois Press, 1985.

Armstrong, Nancy, and Leonard Tennenhouse. *The Imaginary Puritan: Literature, Intellectual Labor, and the Origins of Personal Life*. Berkeley: University of California Press, 1992.

Asad, Talal. *Formations of the Secular: Christianity, Islam, Modernity*. Stanford, Calif.: Stanford University Press, 2003.

Ashcraft, Richard. *Locke's Two Treatises of Government*. Boston: Allen & Unwin, 1987.

Astell, Mary. *A Serious Proposal to the Ladies, Parts I & II*. Ed. Patricia Springborg. London: Pickering and Chatto, 1997.

———. *Astell: Political Writings*. ed. Patricia Springborg. Cambridge Texts in the History of Political Thought. Cambridge: Cambridge University Press, 1996.

———. *Moderation truly stated: or, a Review of a Late Pamphlet*. London, 1704.

———. *Reflections upon Marriage*. Ed. Patricia Springborg. Cambridge Texts in the History of Political Thought. Cambridge: Cambridge University Press, 1996.

Bal, Mieke. *Lethal Love: Feminist Literary Readings of Biblical Love Stories*. Bloomington: Indiana University Press, 1987.

Barash, Carol. *English Women's Poetry, 1649–1714: Politics, Community, and Linguistic Authority*. Oxford: Clarendon Press, 1996.

Baron, Sabrina. "Licensing Readers, Licensing Authorities in Seventeenth-Century England." In *Books and Readers in Early Modern England: Material Studies*, ed. Jennifer Anderson and Elizabeth Sauer. Philadelphia: University of Pennsylvania Press, 2002.

Behn, Aphra. *Love-Letters Between a Nobleman and His Sister*. Ed. Janet Todd. Harmondsworth: Penguin, 1996.

Beilin, Elaine V. *Redeeming Eve: Women Writers of the English Renaissance*. Princeton, N.J.: Princeton University Press, 1987.

Belsey, Catherine. *John Milton: Language, Gender, Power*. New York: Blackwell, 1988.

———. *The Subject of Tragedy*. London: Methuen, 1985.

Benedict, Barbara M. *Curiosity: A Cultural History of Early Modern Inquiry*. Chicago: University of Chicago Press, 2001.

Berg, Christina and Philippa Berry. "'Spiritual Whoredom': An Essay on Female Prophets in the Seventeenth Century." In *1642: Literature and Power in the Seventeenth Century: Proceedings of the Essex Conference on the Sociology of Literature*, ed. Francis Barker et al. Colchester: Department of Literature, University of Essex, 1981.

Berger, Harry. *Fictions of the Pose: Rembrandt Against the Italian Renaissance*. Stanford, Calif.: Stanford University Press, 2000.

Biernoff, Suzanne. *Sight and Embodiment in the Middle Ages: Ocular Desires*. Houndsmills: Palgrave Macmillan, 2002.

Blumenberg, Hans. *The Legitimacy of the Modern Age*. Cambridge, Mass.: MIT Press, 1983.

Boesky, Amy. "Milton, Galileo, and Sunspots: Optics and Certainty in *Paradise Lost*." *Milton Studies* 34 (1996): 23–43.

Bowers, Toni. "Seduction Narratives and Tory Experience in Augustan England." *Eighteenth Century: Theory and Interpretation* 40 (1999): 128–54.

Boyle, Robert. *Experiments and Considerations Touching Colours*. London, 1663.

———. *New Experiments Physico-Mechanicall, Touching the Air*. London, 1660.

———. *New Experiments and Observations Touching Cold, or an Experimental History of Cold, Begun. To which are added . . . An Examen of Mr. Hobs's Doctrine about Cold.* London, 1665.

———. "A Physico-Chymical Essay, containing an Experiment." *Certain Physiological Essays.* London, 1661.

———. "A Proëmial Essay . . . with some considerations touching Experimental Essays in General." *Certain Physiological Essays.* London, 1661.

———. *Some Considerations touching the Usefulnesse of Experimental Natural Philosophy.* London, 1663.

Brady, Maura. "Galileo in Action: The 'Telescope' in *Paradise Lost.*" *Milton Studies* 44 (2005): 129–52.

Breton, Nicholas. "The Praise of vertuous Ladies, and Gentlemen." *The Wil of Wit.* London, 1597.

Bullokar, John. *A true description of the passion of our Sauior Iesus Christ.* London, 1622.

Butler, Martin. "A Provincial Masque of *Comus*, 1636." *Renaissance Drama* 17 (1986): 149–74.

Canovan, Margaret. "On Being Economical with the Truth: Some Liberal Reflections." *Political Studies* 38 (1990): 5–19.

Carraro, Laura Favero and Antonella Rigamonti. "Women's Discourse on Science and Learning and the Image of the Learned Lady." *In-Between: Essays and Studies in Literary Criticism* 9 (2000): 137–46.

Cary, Mary. *The Little Horns Doom & Downfall: or a Scripture-Prophesie of King James, and King Charles, and of this present Parliament, unfolded.* London, 1651.

———. *A new and more exact mappe or, Description of New Jerusalems Glory. . . .* London, 1651.

Cavendish, Margaret. *The Description of A New World, Called The Blazing World.* London, 1688.

———. *Observations upon Experimental Philosophy.* Ed. Eileen O'Neill. Cambridge Texts in the History of Philosophy. Cambridge: Cambridge University Press, 2001.

———. *Philosophical Letters: or Modest Reflections Upon some Opinions in Natural Philosophy, maintained By several Famous and Learned Authors of this Age, Expressed by way of Letters. . . .* London, 1664.

Channel, Elinor. *A Message from God, [By a Dumb woman].* London, 1654.

Cheney, Patrick. *Shakespeare, National Poet-Playwright.* New York: Cambridge University Press, 2004.

Chernaik, Warren. "Unguarded Hearts: Transgression and Epistolary Form in Aphra Behn's *Love-Letters* and the Portuguese Letters." *Journal of English and Germanic Philology* 97, 1 (1998): 13–33.

Chidley, Katherine. *Good Counsell, to the Petitioners for Presbyterian Government.* [London], 1645.

Christianson, Paul. *Reformers and Babylon: English Apocalyptic Visions from the Reformation to the Eve of the Civil War.* Toronto: University of Toronto Press, 1978.

Chudleigh, Mary. *Essays upon Several Subjects in Prose and Verse. The Poems and Prose of Mary, Lady Chudleigh.* Ed. Margaret J. M. Ezell. Women Writers in English, 1350–1850. New York: Oxford University Press, 1993.

Chudleigh, Mary. *The Ladies Defence. The Poems and Prose of Mary, Lady Chudleigh.* Ed. Margaret J. M. Ezell. Women Writers in English, 1350–1850. New York: Oxford University Press, 1993.

Chudleigh, Mary. *The Poems and Prose of Mary, Lady Chudleigh.* Ed. Margaret J. M. Ezell. Women Writers in English, 1350–1850. New York: Oxford University Press, 1993.

Chudleigh, Mary. *The Song of the Three Children Paraphras'd. The Poems and Prose of Mary,*

Lady Chudleigh. Ed. Margaret J. M. Ezell. Women Writers in English, 1350–1850. New York: Oxford University Press, 1993.

Chudleigh, Mary. "To the Ladies." *The Poems and Prose of Mary, Lady Chudleigh.* Ed. Margaret J. M. Ezell. Women Writers in English, 1350–1850. New York: Oxford University Press, 1993.

Clark, Lorenne M. G. "Women and Locke: Who Owns the Apples in the Garden of Eden." In *The Sexism of Social and Political Theory: Women and Reproduction from Plato to Nietzsche.* ed. Lorenne M. G. Clark and Lynda Lange. Toronto: University of Toronto Press, 1979.

Conway, Alison. "The Protestant Cause and a Protestant Whore: Aphra Behn's *Love Letters.*" *Eighteenth-Century Life* 25 (Fall 2001): 1–19.

Cook, Patrick. "Aemilia Lanyer's 'Description of Cooke-ham' as Devotional Lyric." In *Discovering and (Re)covering the Seventeenth-Century Religious Lyric,* ed. Eugene R. Cunnar and Jeffrey Johnson. Pittsburgh: Duquesne University Press, 2001.

Coppe, Abiezer. *A fiery flying roll.* London, 1650.

Cowley, Abraham. *A Proposition for the Advancement of Experimental Philosophy.* London, 1661.

———. "To the Royal Society." *The History of the Royal Society.* London, 1667.

Crawford, Julie. *Marvelous Protestantism: Monstrous Births in Post-Reformation England.* Baltimore: Johns Hopkins University Press, 2005.

Crick, Julia and Alexandra Walsham, eds. *The Uses of Script and Print, 1300–1700.* Cambridge, Cambridge University Press, 2004.

Daly, James. *Sir Robert Filmer and English Political Thought.* Toronto: University of Toronto Press, 1979.

Darnton, Robert. *The Literary Underground of the Old Regime.* Cambridge, Mass.: Harvard University Press, 1982.

Davies, Eleanor. *Prophetic Writings of Lady Eleanor Davies.* Ed. Esther S. Cope. Women Writers in English, 1350–1850. New York: Oxford University Press, 1995.

Davis, John. *The Holy Roode, or Christs crosse: Containing Christ Crucified, described in Speaking-picture.* London, 1609.

Dennis, John. *The Advancement and Reformation of Modern Poetry.* London, 1701.

———. "Of Prosody." In James Greenwood, *An Essay Towards a Practical English Grammar.* London, 1722.

Dobranski, Stephen B. *Milton, Authorship, and the Book Trade.* Cambridge: Cambridge University Press, 1999.

Dryden, John. *The State of Innocence, and Fall of Man.* London, 1677.

Du Bartas, Guillaume. *His Devine Weekes and Workes.* Trans. Josuah Syluester. London, 1613.

Dunn, John. *The Political Thought of John Locke: An Historical Account of the Argument of the Two Treatises of Government.* London: Cambridge University Press, 1969.

Dunton, John. "The Challenge Sent by a Lady to Sir Thomas. . . . " London, 1697.

Durston, Chris. " 'Unhallowed Wedlocks': The Regulation of Marriage During the English Revolution." *Historical Journal* 31 (1988): 45–59.

Edwards, Karen. *Milton and the Natural World: Science and Poetry in Paradise Lost.* Cambridge: Cambridge University Press, 1999.

Edwards, Thomas. *The Second part of Gangraena.* London, 1646.

Engle, Lars. *Shakespearean Pragmatism: Market of his Time.* Chicago: University of Chicago Press, 1993.

Evans, Arise. *An Echoo to the Voice from Heaven.* London, 1652.

———. *A Voice from Heaven, to the Commonwealth of England.* London, 1652.

Ezell, Margaret J. M. "Introduction." Chudleigh, *The Poems and Prose of Mary, Lady*

Chudleigh. Women Writers in English, 1350–1850. New York: Oxford University Press, 1993.

———. *The Patriarch's Wife: Literary Evidence and the History of the Family*. Chapel Hill: University of North Carolina Press, 1987.

———. *Writing Women's Literary History*. Baltimore: Johns Hopkins University Press, 1993.

Fallon, Stephen. *Milton Among the Philosophers: Poetry and Materialism in Seventeenth-Century England*. Ithaca, N.Y.: Cornell University Press, 1991.

Ferguson, Margaret. "Conning the 'Overseers': Women's Illicit Work in Behn's 'The Adventure of the Black Lady.'" *Early Modern Culture: An Electronic Seminar*. http://emc.eserver.org/1-5/issue5.html, Issue 5.

Feroli, Teresa. *Political Speaking Justified: Women Prophets and the English Revolution*. Newark: University of Delaware Press, 2006.

Ferry, Anne Davidson. *Milton and the Miltonic Dryden*. Cambridge, Mass: Harvard University Press, 1968.

Filmer, Sir Robert. *Anarchy of a Limited or Mixed Monarchy*. Ed. Johann P. Sommerville. Cambridge Texts in the History of Political Thought. Cambridge: Cambridge University Press, 1991.

———. *Patriarcha and Other Writings*. Ed. Johann Sommerville. Cambridge: Cambridge University Press, 1991.

Fish, Stanley Eugene. *How Milton Works*. Cambridge, Mass.: Belknap Press of Harvard University Press, 2001.

———. *Surprised by Sin: The Reader in Paradise Lost*. 2nd ed. Cambridge, Mass.: Harvard University Press, 2003.

Fletcher, Anthony. "The Protestant Idea of Marriage." In *Religion, Culture, and Society in Early Modern Britain: Essays in Honour of Patrick Collinson*, ed. Anthony Fletcher and Peter Roberts. Cambridge: Cambridge University Press, 1994.

Fletcher, Giles. *Christs Victorie, and Triumph in Heaven*. London, 1610.

Forsyth, Neil. *The Satanic Epic*. Princeton, N.J.: Princeton University Press, 2003.

Fraunce, Abraham. *The Countesse of Pembrokes Emanuel. Conteining the Natiuity, Passion, Buriall, and Resurrection of Christ*. . . . London, 1591.

Friedman, Donald. "The Lady in the Garden: On the Literary Genetics of Milton's Eve." *Milton Studies* 35 (1997): 114–33.

Froula, Christine. "When Eve Reads Milton: Undoing the Canonical Economy." *Critical Inquiry* 10, 2 (1983): 321–47.

Gadbury, John. *Natura Prodigiorum: or, A Discourse Touching the Nature of Prodigies*. London, 1660.

Gagen, Jean. "Anomalies in Eden: Adam and Eve in Dryden's *The State of Innocence*." In *Milton's Legacy in the Arts*, ed. Albert C. Labriola and Edward Sichi, Jr. University Park: Pennsylvania State University Press, 1988.

Gallagher, Catherine. "Embracing the Absolute: The Politics of the Female Subject in Seventeenth Century England." *Genders* 1 (March 1988): 24–29.

Gardiner, Judith Kegan. "The First English Novel: Aphra Behn's Love Letters. The Canon." *Tulsa Studies in Women's Literature* 8, 2 (1989): 201–22.

Gillespie, Katharine. *Domesticity and Dissent in the Seventeenth Century: English Women Writers and the Public Sphere*. Cambridge: Cambridge University Press, 2004.

Goldie, Mark. "John Locke and Anglican Royalism." *Political Studies* 31 (1983): 61–85.

———, ed. *The Reception of Locke's Politics*. Vol. 2, *Patriarchalism, the Social Contract and Civic Virtue, 1705–1760*. London: Pickering and Chatto, 1999.

Gosynhill, Edward. *Here begynneth a lytle boke named the Scholehouse of women*. London, 1541.

———. *Mulierum Paean*. London, 1542.

Greenberg, Lynne. "A Preliminary Study of Informed Consent and Free Will in the

Garden of Eden: John Milton's Social Contract." In *Living Texts: Interpreting Milton*, ed. Kristin Pruitt and Charles Durham. Selinsgrove, Pa.: Susquehanna University Press, 2000.

Grey, Anchitell, ed. *Debates in the House of Commons, from the year 1667 to the year 1694*. 10 vols. London, 1763.

Grotius, Hugo. *Adamus Exul. The Celestial Cycle: The Theme of Paradise Lost in world literature, with translations of the major analogues*. Toronto: University of Toronto Press, 1952.

Gubar, Susan and Sandra Gilbert, *Madwoman in the Attic: the Woman Writer and the Nineteenth-Century Literary Imagination*. New Haven: Yale University Press, 1979.

Guibbory, Achsah. "The Gospel According to Aemilia: Women and the Sacred." In *Aemilia Lanyer: Gender, Genre, and the Canon*, ed. Marshall Grossman. Lexington: University Press of Kentucky, 1998.

Guillory, John. "From the Superfluous to the Supernumerary: Reading Gender into *Paradise Lost*." In *Soliciting Interpretation: Literary Theory and Seventeenth-Century English Poetry*, ed. Elizabeth D. Harvey and Katharine Eisaman Maus. Chicago: University of Chicago Press, 1990.

Hardison, O. B. "Written Records and Truths of Spirit in *Paradise Lost*." *Milton Studies* 1 (1969): 147–65.

Harris, Bernard. "'That Soft Seducer, Love': Dryden's *The State of Innocence and Fall of Man*." In *Approaches to Paradise Lost: The York Tercentenary Lectures*, ed. C. A. Patrides. London, Edward Arnold, 1968.

Hawes, Clement. "'Man is the Woman': Leveling and the Gendered Body Politic in Enthusiastic Rhetoric." *Prose Studies* 18, 1 (1995): 36–58.

———. *Mania and Literary Style: The Rhetoric of Enthusiasm from the Ranters to Christopher Smart*. Cambridge: Cambridge University Press, 1996.

Helgerson, Richard. *Forms of Nationhood: The Elizabethan Writing of England*. Chicago: University of Chicago Press, 1992.

Henderson, Katherine Usher, and Barbara McManus, eds. *Half Humankind: Contexts and Texts of the Controversy About Women in England, 1540–1640*. Urbana: University of Illinois Press, 1985.

Henriksen, Erin. "The Passion in *Poems of Mr. John Milton*: Milton's Poetics of Omission and Supplement." In *Milton's Legacy*, ed. Kristin Pruitt and Charles Durham. Selinsgrove, Pa.: Susquehanna University Press, 2005.

Herman, Peter C. *Destabilizing Milton: "Paradise Lost" and the Poetics of Incertitude*. New York: Palgrave Macmillan, 2005.

Herz, Judith Scherer. "'For Whom this Glorious Sight?' Dante, Milton, and the Galileo Question." In *Milton in Italy: Contexts, Images, Contradictions*, ed. Mario Di Cesare. Binghamton, N.Y.: Medieval and Renaissance Texts and Studies, 1991.

Heschel, Abraham J. *The Prophets*. New York: Harper & Row, 1962.

Hill, John Spencer. *John Milton, Poet, Priest, and Prophet: A Study of Divine Vocation in Milton's Poetry and Prose*. Totowa, N.J.: Rowman and Littlefield, 1979.

Hinds, Hilary. *God's Englishwomen: Seventeenth-Century Radical Sectarian Writing and Feminist Criticism*. Manchester: Manchester University Press, 1996.

Hobbes, Thomas. *Dialogus Physicus. Leviathan and the Air-Pump: Hobbes, Boyle, and the Experimental Life: including a translation of Thomas Hobbes, Dialogus physicus de natura aeris*. Trans. Simon Schaffer. Princeton, N.J.: Princeton University Press, 1985.

———. *Elements of Philosophy, the First Section, concerning Body*. London, 1656.

———. *Leviathan*. Ed. and Trans. Robert Tuck. Revised Student Edition. Cambridge Texts in the History of Political Thought. New York: Cambridge University Press, 1996.

———. *On the Citizen*. Ed. and Trans. Richard Tuck and Michael Silverthorne. Cambridge Texts in the History of Political Thought. New York: Cambridge University Press, 1998.

————. *Philosophical Rudiments concerning Government and Society*. London, 1651.

Holland, Robert. *The Holie History of Our Lord and Savior Iesus Christs natiuitie, life, acts, miracles, doctrine, death, passion. . . .* London, 1594.

Homer. *The Iliad of Homer*. Trans. Richmond Lattimore. Chicago: University of Chicago Press, 1966.

————. *The Odyssey*. Trans. Richmond Lattimore. New York: Harper & Row, 1965.

Hooke, Robert. "Preface." *Micrographia*. London, 1665.

Hopkins, John. *Milton's Paradise Lost Imitated in Rhyme In the Fourth, Sixth and Ninth Books; Containing the Primitive Loves. The Battle of the Angels. The Fall of Man.* London, 1699.

Hughes, Merritt Y. *John Milton: Complete Poetry and Major Prose*. Indianapolis: Bobbs-Merrill, 1984.

Hunter, Michael. *Science and Society in Restoration England*. Cambridge: Cambridge University Press, 1981.

————. "The Social Basis and Changing Fortunes of an Early Scientific Institution: An Analysis of the Membership of the Royal Society, 1660–1685." *Notes and Records of the Royal Society* 31 (1976): 9–114.

Hutchinson, Lucy. *Order and Disorder*. Ed. David Norbrook. Malden, Mass.: Blackwell, 2001.

Hutson, Lorna. "Why the Lady's Eyes Are Nothing like the Sun." In *Women, Texts & Histories, 1575–1760*, ed. Clare Brant and Diane Purkiss. London: Routledge, 1992.

Hutton, Sarah. "The Cambridge Platonists." In *A Companion to Early Modern Philosophy*, ed. Steven Nadler. Oxford: Blackwell, 2002.

————. "In Dialogue with Thomas Hobbes: Margaret Cavendish's Natural Philosophy." *Women's Writing* 14, 3 (1997): 421–32.

James, Susan. "The Philosophical Innovations of Margaret Cavendish." *British Journal for the History of Philosophy* 7, 2 (1999): 219–44.

Jane, Joseph. *Salmasius his Dissection and Confutation of the Diabolical Rebel Milton . . .* London, 1660.

Jones, Ann Rosalind, "Counterattacks on 'the Bayter of Women': Three Pamphleteers of the Early Seventeenth Century." In *The Renaissance Englishwoman in Print: Counterbalancing the Canon*, ed. Anne M. Haselkorn and Betty S. Travitsky. Amherst: University of Massachusetts Press, 1990.

Jones, Tod E. *The Cambridge Platonists: A Brief Introduction*. Dallas: University Press of America, 2005.

Jordan, Constance. *Renaissance Feminism: Literary Texts and Political Models*. Ithaca, N.Y.: Cornell University Press, 1990.

Jordan, Matthew. *Milton and Modernity: Politics, Masculinity, and Paradise Lost*. New York: Palgrave, 2001.

Kahn, Victoria Ann. *Wayward Contracts: The Crisis of Political Obligation in England, 1640–1674*. Princeton, N.J.: Princeton University Press, 2004.

Keller, Eve. "Producing Petty Gods: Margaret Cavendish's Critique of Experimental Science." *ELH* 64, 2 (1997): 447–71.

Kerrigan, William. *The Prophetic Milton*. Charlottesville: University Press of Virginia, 1974.

King, John N. *Milton and Religious Controversy: Satire and Polemic in Paradise Lost*. Cambridge: Cambridge University Press, 2000.

Kowaleski-Wallace, Beth. "Milton's Daughters: The Education of Eighteenth-Century Women." *Feminist Studies* 12, 2 (Summer 1986): 275–93.

Lanyer, Aemilia. *Salve Deus Rex Judaeorum. Poems of Aemilia Lanyer.* Ed. Susanne Woods. Women Writers in English, 1350–1850. Oxford: Oxford University Press, 1993.

Lanyer, Aemilia, *Poems of Aemilia Lanyer.* Intro. Susanne Woods. Women Writers in English, 1350–1850. Oxford: Oxford University Press, 1993.

Laslett, Peter. Introduction. *Locke: Two Treatises of Government.* Cambridge: Cambridge University Press, 1988.

Lead, Jane. *A Fountain of Gardens: Watered by the Rivers of Divine Pleasure.* London, 1697.

Lee, Nathaniel. "To Mr. Dryden, on his Poem of Paradise." *The State of Innocence, and Fall of Man.* London, 1677.

Lever, Christopher. *A Crucifixe: or, A Meditation vpon Repentance, and, the holie Passion.* London, 1607.

Lewalski, Barbara Kiefer. "Female Text, Male Reader Response: Contemporary Marginalia in Rachel Speght's *A Mouzell for Melastomus.*" In *Representing Women in Renaissance England,* ed. Claude Summers and Ted-Larry Pebworth. Columbia: University of Missouri Press, 1997.

———. *The Life of John Milton: A Critical Biography.* Rev. ed. Malden, Mass.: Blackwell, 2003.

———. "Milton on Women—Yet Again." *Milton Studies* 6 (1974): 3–20.

———. *Writing Women in Jacobean England.* Cambridge, Mass.: Harvard University Press, 1993.

Lieb, Michael. *The Dialectics of Creation: Patterns of Birth and Regeneration in Paradise Lost.* Amherst: University of Massachusetts Press, 1970.

Locke, John. *Two Treatises on Government.* Ed. Peter Laslett. Cambridge Texts in the History of Political Thought. Cambridge: Cambridge University Press, 1988.

Loewenstein, David. *Representing Revolution in Milton and his Contemporaries: Religion, Politics, and Polemics in Radical Puritanism.* Cambridge: Cambridge University Press, 2001.

Lucretius. *Lucy Hutchinson's translation of Lucretius: De rerum natura.* Ed. Hugh de Quehen. Ann Arbor: University of Michigan Press, 1996.

Lupton, Julia Reinhard. *Citizen-Saints: Shakespeare and Political Theology.* Chicago: University of Chicago Press, 2005.

Luxon, Thomas. *Single Imperfection: Milton, Marriage, and Friendship.* Pittsburgh: Duquesne University Press, 2005.

Macey, David. "Eden Revisited: Re-Visions of the Garden in Astell's *Serious Proposal,* Scott's *Millenium Hall,* and Graffigny's *Lettres d'une péruvienne.*" *Eighteenth-Century Fiction* 9, 2 (1997): 161–82.

Mack, Phyllis. *Visionary Women: Ecstatic Prophesy in Seventeenth-Century England.* Berkeley: University of California Press, 1992.

Magro, Maria. "Milton's Sexualized Woman and the Creation of a Gendered Public Sphere." *Milton Quarterly* 35, 2 (2001): 98–112.

Maltzahn, Nicholas van. "The Royal Society and the Provenance of Milton's *History of Britain.*" *Milton Quarterly* 32, 3 (1998): 90–95.

Marjara, Harinder Singh. *Contemplation of Created Things: Science in Paradise Lost.* Toronto: University of Toronto Press, 1992.

Markham, Gervase. *The Tears of the Beloved: or, The Lamentation of Saint John, Concerning the death and passion of Christ Iesus our sauiour.* London, 1600.

Marotti, Arthur. *John Donne, Coterie Poet.* Madison: University of Wisconson Press, 1986.

Marshall, John. *John Locke: Resistance, Religion, and Responsibility.* Cambridge: Cambridge University Press, 1994.

Martz, Louis L. "Dryden's Poem of Paradise: *The State of Innocence and Fall of Man.*" In *John Dryden (1631–1700): His Politics, His Plays, and His Poets,* ed. Claude Rawson and Aaron Santesso. Newark: University of Delaware Press, 2004.

———. *The Poetry of Meditation; a Study in English Religious Literature of the Seventeenth Century*. New Haven, Conn.: Yale University Press, 1954.

Marvell, Andrew. *The Complete Poems*. Ed. Elizabeth Story Donno. Harmondsworth, Middlesex: Penguin, 1972.

McBride, Kari Boyd. *Country House Discourse in Early Modern Europe: A Cultural Study of Landscape and Legitimacy*. Aldershot: Ashgate, 2001.

McBride, Kari Boyd and John C. Ulreich. "Answerable Styles: Biblical Poetics and Biblical Politics in the Poetry of Lanyer and Milton." *Journal of English and Germanic Philology* 100.3 (2001): 333–54.

———. "'Eves Apologie': Agrippa, Lanyer, and Milton." In *"All in All': Unity, Diversity, and the Miltonic Perspective*, ed. Charles W. Durham and Kristen A. Pruitt. Selingsgrove, Pa.: Susquehanna University Press; London: Associated University Presses, 1999.

McClure, Kirstie Morna. *Judging Rights: Lockean Politics and the Limits of Consent*. Ithaca: Cornell University Press, 1996.

McColley, Diane Kelsey. *Milton's Eve*. Urbana: University of Illinois Press, 1983.

Miller, Shannon. "Executing the Body Politic: Inscribing State Violence onto Aphra Behn's Oroonoko." In *Violence, Politics, and Gender in Early Modern England*, ed. Joseph P. Ward. New York: Palgrave Macmillan, 2008.

———. "'Mirrours More Then One': Edmund Spenser and Female Authority in the Seventeenth Century." In *Worldmaking Spenser: Explorations in the Early Modern Age*. ed. Patrick G. Cheney and Lauren Silberman. Lexington: University Press of Kentucky, 2000.

Milton, John. *Complete Poetry and Major Prose*. Ed. Merritt Y. Hugues. Indianapolis: Bobbs-Merrill, 1984.

———. *Doctrine and Discipline of Divorce*. Vol. 4. *Complete Prose Works*. Ed. Don M. Wolfe. New Haven, Conn.: Yale University Press, 1953.

———. *Milton's Familiar Letters*. Trans. John Hall. Philadelphia: E. Littel, 1892.

———. *The Riverside Milton*. Ed. Roy Flannagan. Boston: Houghton Mifflin, 1998.

Mollenkott, Virginia R. "Some Implications of Milton's Androgynous Muse." *Bucknell Review* 24 (1978): 27–36. Special Issue of *Women, Literature, Criticism*, ed. Harry R. Garvin.

Moore, Judith. "Twentieth-Century Feminism and Seventeenth-Century Science: Margaret Cavendish in Opposing Contexts." *Reformation* 26, 1 (Spring 2002): 1–14.

Moore. C. A. "Miltoniana (1679–1741)." *Studies in Philology* 24 (1927).

Mowry, Melissa. *The Bawdy Politic in Stuart England, 1660–1714: Political Pornography and Prostitution*. Aldershot: Ashgate, 2004.

Mueller, Janel. "The Feminist Poetics of 'Salve Deus Rex Judaeorum'." In *Aemilia Lanyer: Gender, Genre, and the Canon*, ed. Marshall Grossman. Lexington: University Press of Kentucky, 1998. 99–127.

Muldrew, Craig. *The Economy of Obligation: The Culture of Credit and Social Relations in Early Modern England*. Early Modern History: Society and Culture. New York: St. Martin's Press, 1988.

Munda, Constantia, *The Worming of a mad Dogge . . .* London, 1617.

Murphy, Erin. "Milton's 'Birth Abortive': Remaking Family at the End of *Paradise Lost*." *Milton Studies* 43 (2004): 145–70.

Narain, Mona. "Body and Politics in Aphra Behn's *Love Letters Between a Nobleman and his Sister*." In *Women Writing, 1550–1750*, ed. Jo Wallwork and Paul Salzman. Special Book Issue of *Meridian* 18, 1 (2001): 151–62.

Nate, Richard. "'Plain and Vulgarly Express'd': Margaret Cavendish and the Discourse of the New Science." *Rhetorica* 19, 4 (2001): 403–17.

Nedman, Marchamont. *Mercurius Politicus*. London, 1650–1660.

Nevitt, Marcus. *Women and the Pamphlet Culture of Revolutionary England, 1640–1660.* Aldershot: Ashgate, 2006.

Nicolson, Marjorie. "Milton and the Telescope." *ELH* 2 (1935): 1–32.

Norbrook, David, "'A devine Originall': Lucy Hutchinson and the 'Woman's Version.'" *Times Literary Supplement,* 19 March 1999, 13–15.

———. Introduction. Lucy Hutchinson, *Order and Disorder,* ed. David Norbrook. London: Blackwell, 2001.

———. "John Milton, Lucy Hutchinson and the Republican Biblical Epic." In *Milton and the Grounds of Contention,* ed. Mark Kelley, Michael Lieb, and John T. Shawcross. Pittsburgh: Duquesne University Press, 2003.

———. *Writing the English Republic: Poetry, Rhetoric and Politics, 1627–1660.* Cambridge: Cambridge University Press, 1998.

Norris, John. *A Sermon Preach'd.* Oxford, 1685.

———. *Theory and Regulation of Love: A Moral Essay in Two Parts.* Oxford, 1688.

Nugent, S. Georgia. "Mater Matters: The Female in Lucretius' De Rerum Natura." *Colby Quarterly* 30 (1994): 179–206.

Nyland, Chris. "John Locke and the Social Position of Women." *History of Political Economy* 21, 1 (1993): 39–63.

Nyquist, Mary. "The Genesis of Gendered Subjectivity in the Divorce Tracts and in *Paradise Lost.*" In *Re-Membering Milton: Essays on the Texts and Traditions,* ed. Mary Nyquist and Margaret W. Ferguson. New York: Methuen, 1988.

Ogilby, John. *The Entertainment of His Most Excellent Majestie Charles II, in His Passage through the City of London to his coronation.* London, 1662.

Oldys, Alexander. "An Ode by way of Elegy on . . . Mr. Dryden." London, 1700.

Olive, Barbara. "The Fabric of Restoration Puritanism: Mary Chudleigh's The Song of the Three Children Paraphras'd." In *Puritanism and Its Discontents,* ed. Laura Lunger Knoppers. Newark: University of Delaware Press, 2003.

O'Malley, Susan Gushee, ed. *"Custome Is an Idiot": Jacobean Pamphlet Literature on Women.* Urbana: University of Illinois Press, 2004.

O'Neill, Eileen. Introduction to *Observations upon Experimental Philosophy.* Cambridge Texts in the History of Philosophy. Cambridge: Cambridge University Press, 2001.

Orgel, Stephen. *The Jonsonian Masque.* Cambridge, Mass.: Harvard University Press, 1965.

Pateman, Carole. *The Sexual Contract.* Stanford, Calif.: Stanford University Press, 1988.

Perry, Ruth. "Mary Astell and the Feminist Critique of Possessive Individualism." *Eighteenth-Century Studies* 23 (1990): 444–57.

———. *The Celebrated Mary Astell: An Early English Feminist.* Chicago: University of Chicago Press, 1986.

Phillippy, Patricia. "The Mat(t)er of Death: The Defense of Eve and the Female *Ars Moriendi.*" In *Debating Gender in Early Modern England, 1500–1700,* ed. Cristina Malcolmson and Mihoko Suzuki. New York; Houndsmills: Palgrave Macmillan, 2002.

Pollak, Ellen. *Incest and the English Novel, 1684–1814.* Baltimore: Johns Hopkins University Press, 2003.

Polydorou, Desma. "Gender and Spiritual Equality in Marriage: A Dialogic Reading of Rachel Speght and John Milton." *Milton Quarterly* 35, 1 (2001): 22–32.

Poole, Elizabeth. *A Vision: Wherein is manifested the disease and cure of the Kingdome. Being the summe of what was delivered to the Generall Councel of the Army.* London, 1648.

———. *An Alarum of War, Given to the Army.* London, 1649.

Poole, Kristen. *Radical Religion from Shakespeare to Milton: Figures of Nonconformity in Early Modern England.* Cambridge: Cambridge University Press, 2000.

Poole, William. *Milton and the Idea of the Fall.* Cambridge: Cambridge University Press, 2005.

Pope, Mary. *Behold, here is a word or, an Answer to the late Remonstrance of the Army.* London, 1649.

Pordage, Samuel. "Heroick Stanzas on his Maiesties Coronation." London, 1661.

Powell, Chilton Latham. *English Domestic Relations, 1487–1653.* New York: Columbia University Press, 1917. *Rpt.* New York: Russell & Russell, 1972.

Power, Henry. *Experimental Philosophy, in Three books: containing New Experiments Microscopical, Mercurial, Magnetical. . . .* London, 1664.

Pruitt, Kristin. *Gender and the Power of Relationship: "United as one individual Soul" in Paradise Lost.* Pittsburgh: Duquesne University Press, 2003.

Purkiss, Diane. "Material Girls: The Seventeenth-Century Woman Debate." In *Women, Texts & Histories, 1575–1760,* ed. Clare Brant and Diane Purkiss. London: Routledge, 1992.

Quilligan, Maureen. *Milton's Spenser: The Politics of Reading.* Ithaca, N.Y.: Cornell University Press, 1983.

Radzinowicz, Mary Ann. "The Politics of *Paradise Lost.*" In *Politics of Discourse: The Literature and History of Seventeenth-Century England,* ed. Kevin Sharpe and Steven Zwicker. Berkeley: University of California Press, 1987.

Richey, Esther Gilman. *The Politics of Revelation in the English Renaissance.* Columbia: University of Missouri Press, 1998.

Richetti, John. *"Love Letters Between a Nobleman and His Sister:* Aphra Behn and Amatory Fiction." In *Augustan Subjects: Essays in Honor of Martin C. Battestin,* ed. Albert Rivero. Newark: University of Delaware Press, 1997.

Roberts, Josephine A. "Diabolic Dreamscape in Lanyer and Milton." In *Teaching Tudor and Stuart Women Writers,* ed. Susanne Woods and Margaret P. Hannay. New York: Modern Language Association of America, 2000.

Rogers, John. *The Matter of Revolution: Science, Poetry, and Politics in the Age of Milton.* Ithaca, N.Y.: Cornell University Press, 1996.

Romack, Katherine, "Monstrous Births and the Body Politic: Women's Political Writings and the Strange and Wonderful Travails of Mistres Parliament and Mris. Rump." In *Debating Gender in Early Modern England, 1500–1700,* ed. Cristina Malcolmson and Mihoko Suzuki. New York; Houndsmills: Palgrave Macmillan, 2002.

Romack, Katherine and James Fitzmaurice, eds. *Cavendish and Shakespeare: Interconnections.* Aldershot: Ashgate, 2006.

Rose, Mary Beth. " 'Vigorous Most/When Most Unactive Deem'd': Gender and the Heroics of Endurance in Milton's *Samson Agonistes,* Aphra Behn's *Oroonoko,* and Mary Astell's *Some Reflections upon Marriage.*" *Milton Studies* 33 (1997): 83–100.

Rowlands, Samuel. *The betraying of Christ. Iudas in despaire. The seuen Words of our Savior on the Crosse. With Other Poems on the Passion.* London, 1598.

Ryken, Leland. *The Apocalyptic Vision in Paradise Lost.* Ithaca, N.Y.: Cornell University Press, 1970.

Sage, Melissa Cowan. "The Libertine-Libertarian Dichotomy in Dryden's *The State of Innocence.*" *English Language Notes* 21, 3 (March 1984): 38–44.

Salandra, Serafino Della. *Adamo Caduto. The Celestial Cycle: The theme of Paradise Lost in world literature, with translations of the major analogues.* Toronto: University of Toronto Press, 1952.

Sauer, Elizabeth M. "The Experience of Defeat: Milton and some Female Contemporaries." In *Milton and Gender,* ed. Catherine Gimelli Martin. Cambridge: Cambridge University Press, 2004. 133–52.

———. "Maternity, Prophesy, and the Cultivation of the Private Sphere in Seventeenth-Century England." *Explorations in Renaissance Culture* 24 (1998): 119–48.

Schleiner, Louise. *Tudor and Stuart Women Writers.* Bloomington: Indiana University Press, 1994.

Schmitt, Carl. *Political Theology: Four Chapters on the Concept of Sovereignty.* Cambridge, Mass.: MIT Press, 1985.

Schochet, Gordon J. *Patriarchalism in Political Thought: The Authoritarian Family and Political Speculation and Attitudes, especially in Seventeenth-Century England.* New York: Basic Books, 1975.

Schoenfeldt, Michael. "'That spectacle of too much weight': The Poetics of Sacrifice in Donne, Herbert, and Milton." *Journal of Medieval and Early Modern Studies* 31, 3 (Fall 2001): 561–84.

Schutte, Anne. "'Such Monstrous Births': A Neglected Aspect of the Antinomian Controversy." *Renaissance Quarterly* 38, 1 (Spring 1985): 85–106.

Schutzman, Julie. "Ruling Passions: Sovereignty, Femininity and Fiction, 1680–1742." PhD Dissertation, University of Pennsylvania, 1999.

Schwartz, Louis. "'Conscious Terrors' and 'The Promised Seed': Seventeenth-Century Obstetrics and the Allegory of Sin and Death in *Paradise Lost.*" *Milton Studies* 32 (1995): 63–89.

———. "'Spot of Child-Bed Taint': Seventeenth-Century Obstetrics in Milton's Sonnet 23 and PL 8 462–78." *Milton Quarterly* 27, 3 (1993): 94–106.

Schwartz, Regina M. *Remembering and Repeating: Biblical Creation in Paradise Lost.* Cambridge: Cambridge University Press, 1988.

———. "Rethinking Voyeurism and Patriarchy: The Case of *Paradise Lost.*" *Representations* 34 (Spring 1991): 85–103.

Schwarz, Kathryn. "Chastity, Militant and Married: Cavendish's Romance, Milton's Masque." *PMLA* 118, 2 (2003): 270–85.

Schwoerer, Lois G. *The Declaration of Rights, 1689.* Baltimore: Johns Hopkins University Press, 1981.

———. "Images of Queen Mary II, 1689–95." *Renaissance Quarterly* 42, 4 (1989): 717–48.

Shaftesbury, Anthony Ashley Cooper, Earl of. *Characteristics of men, manners, opinions, times.* Vol 1. London, 1711.

Shanley, Mary Lyndon. "Marriage Contract and Social Contract in Seventeenth Century English Political Thought." *Western Political Quarterly* 32, 1 (1979): 79–91.

Shapin, Steven and Simon Schaffer. *Leviathan and the Air-Pump: Hobbes, Boyle, and the Experimental Life.* Princeton, N.J.: Princeton University Press, 1985.

Shawcross, John, ed. *Milton: The Critical Heritage.* New York: Barnes & Noble, 1970.

———. *Rethinking Milton Studies: Time Present and Time Past.* Newark: University of Delaware Press, 2005.

Shepherd, Simon. *The Women's Sharp Revenge: Five Women's Pamphlets from the Renaissance.* London: Fourth Estate, 1985.

Sherlock, William. *The Case of the Allegiance due to Soveraign Powers.* London, 1691.

Sidney, Algernon. *Discourses Concerning Government.* London, 1698.

Simons, Patricia. "Women in Frames: The Gaze, the Eye, the Profile in Renaissance Portraiture." *History Workshop* 25 (1988): 4–30.

Smith, Hilda. *Reason's Disciples: Seventeenth-Century English Feminists.* Urbana: University of Illinois Press, 1982.

———, ed. *Women Writers and the Early Modern British Political Tradition.* Folger Institute. Cambridge: Cambridge University Press, 1998.

Smith, Nigel. *A Collection of Ranter Writings from the 17th Century.* London: Junction Books, 1983.

———. *Perfection Proclaimed: Language and Literature in English Radical Religion, 1640–1660.* Oxford: Clarendon Press; New York: Oxford University Press, 1989.

Sobel, Dana. *Galileo's Daughter: A Historical Memior of Science, Faith, and Love*. Harmondsworth: Penguin, 2000.

Sommerville, Johann. Introduction to Robert Filmer, *Patriarcha and Other Writings*. Cambridge: Cambridge University Press, 1991.

Sommerville, Margaret. *Sex and Subjection: Attitudes to Women in Early-Modern Society*. London: Arnold, 1995.

Southwell, Robert. *S. Peters Complaint. And Saint Mary Magdelens funerall teares*. London, 1616.

Sowernam, Ester. *Ester hath hang'd Haman: or An Answer to a lewd Pamphlet*. London, 1617.

Speght, Rachel. "A Dreame." *The Polemics and Poems of Rachel Speght*. Ed. Barbara Kiefer Lewalski. Women Writers in English, 1350–1850. New York: Oxford University Press, 1996.

———. "Mortalities Memorandum." *The Polemics and Poems of Rachel Speght*. Ed. Barbara Kiefer Lewalski. Women Writers in English, 1350–1850. New York: Oxford University Press, 1996.

———. *A Mouzell for Melastomus. The Polemics and Poems of Rachel Speght*. Ed. Barbara Kiefer Lewalski. Women Writers in English, 1350–1850. New York: Oxford University Press, 1996.

Spencer, John. *A Discourse Concerning Prodigies*. London, 1663.

Spenser, Edmund. *The Faerie Queene*. Ed. Thomas Roche, Jr. Harmondsworth: Penguin, 1978, 1984.

Spiller, Elizabeth. "Reading Through Galileo's Telescope: Margaret Cavendish and the Experience of Reading." *Renaissance Quarterly* 53, 1 (2000): 192–221.

Springborg, Patricia. Introduction and Notes to Astell, *A Serious Proposal, Parts I & II*. London: Pickering and Chatto, 1997.

Sprott, S. Ernest. *Milton's Art of Prosody*. Oxford: Basil Blackwell, 1953.

Stocker, Margarita. *Apocalyptic Marvell: The Second Coming in Seventeenth Century Poetry*. Athens: Ohio University Press, 1986.

Stone, Lawrence. *Uncertain Unions: Marriage in England 1660–1753*. Oxford: Oxford University Press, 1992.

Suzuki, Mihoko. *Subordinate Subjects: Gender, the Political Nation, and Literary Form in England, 1588–1688*. Aldershot: Ashgate, 2003.

Svendsen, Kester. *Milton and Science*. New York: Greenwood Press, 1965.

Swetnam, John. *The Arraignment of Lewd, Idle, Froward, and unconstant women*. London, 1615.

Tattle-well, Mary and Joan Hit-him-home. *The womens sharp revenge*. London, 1640.

Taylor, John. *The Juniper Lecture. With the description of all sorts of women, good, and bad. . . .* London, 1639.

Todd, Janet. "Who Is Silvia? What Is She? Feminine Identity in Aphra Behn's *Love Letters between a Nobleman and His Sister*." In *Aphra Behn Studies*, ed. Janet Todd. Cambridge: Cambridge University Press, 1996.

Trapnel, Anna. *The Cry of the Stone*. Ed. Hilary Hind. Tempe, Ariz.: ACMRS, 2000.

———. *Strange and Wonderful Newes from White-hall: Or, The Mighty Visions*. London, 1654.

Trubowitz, Rachel. "'The Single State of Man': Androgyny in *Macbeth* and *Paradise Lost*." *Papers on Language and Literature* 26, 3 (Summer 1990): 305–33.

———. "Female Preachers and Male Wives: Gender and Authority in Civil War England." In *Pamphlet Wars: Prose in the English Revolution*, ed. James Holstun. London: Frank Cass, 1992.

———. "Feminizing Vision: Andrew Marvell and Female Prophesy." *Women's Studies* 24 (1994): 15–29.

———. "The Reenchantment of Utopia and the Female Monarchical Self: Margaret Cavendish's *Blazing World*." *Tulsa Studies in Women's Literature* 11, 2 (1992): 229–45.

Turner, James Grantham. *One Flesh: Paradisal Marriage and Sexual Relations in the Age of Milton.* Oxford: Clarendon Press; New York: Oxford University Press, 1987.

Turner, John. *A Resolution of Three Matrimonial Cases.* . . . London, 1684.

Tyrrell, James. *Patriarch non monarcha: The patriarch unmonarch'd.* London, 1681.

Van Den Berg, Sara. "Eve, Sin, and Witchcraft in *Paradise Lost.*" *Modern Language Quarterly* 47 (1986): 347–65.

Verbart, André. "Measure and Hypermetricality in *Paradise Lost.*" *English Studies* 80.5 (1999): 428–48.

Virgil. *The Aeneid of Virgil.* Trans. Allen Mandelbaum. Berkeley: University of California Press, 1981.

Watts, Isaac. "The Adventurous Muse." *Horae Lyrica.* London, 1748.

Wehrs, Donald. "*Eros,* Ethics, Identity: Royalist Feminism and the Politics of Desire in Aphra Behn's *Love Letters.*" *SEL* 32 (1992): 461–78.

Weil, Rachel. *Political Passions: Gender, the Family, and Political Argument in England, 1680–1714.* Manchester: Manchester University Press, 1999.

Whiston, William. *A New Theory of the Earth.* . . . London, 1696.

Wight, Sarah. *A Wonderful Pleasant and Profitable Letter Written by Sarah Wight.* London, 1656.

Wilding, Michael. "'Their Sex Not Equal Seemed': Equality and Hierarchy in John Milton's *Paradise Lost.*" In *The Epic in History.* ed. Lola Davidson, et al. Sydney Aus.: Sydney Assn. for Studies in Soc. & Culture, 1994.

Winstanley, Gerrard. *Fire in the Bush.* . . . London, 1650.

Winstanley, William. *The Lives of the Most Famous English Poets.* London, 1687.

Winthrop, John. *A Short Story of the Rise, reign, and ruin of the Antinomians, Familists, & Libertines, that infected the Churches of New-England: . . . And the lamentable death of Ms. Hutchison.* . . . London, 1644.

Wiseman, Sue. "Unsilent Instruments and the Devil's Cushions: Authority in Seventeenth-Century Women's Prophetic Discourse." In *New Feminist Discourses: Critical Essays on Theories and Texts,* ed. Isobel Armstrong. London: Routledge, 1992.

Wittreich, Joseph Anthony. *Feminist Milton.* Ithaca, N.Y.: Cornell University Press, 1987.

———. "'He Ever Was a Dissenter': Milton's Transgressive Maneuvers in *Paradise Lost.*" In *Arenas of Conflict: Milton and the Unfettered Mind,* ed. Kristin Pruitt McColgan and Charles W. Pruitt. Selinsgrove, Pa.: Susquehanna University Press, 1997.

———. "'Inspir'd with Contradiction': Mapping Gender Discourses in *Paradise Lost.*" In *Literary Milton: Text, Pretext, Context,* ed. Diana Treviño Benet and Michael Lieb. Pittsburgh: Duquesne University Press, 1994.

———. "'John, John, I blush for thee!': Mapping Gender Discourses in *Paradise Lost.*" *Out of Bounds: Male Writers and Gender(ed) Criticism,* ed. Laura Claridge and Elizabeth Langland. Amherst: University of Massachusetts Press, 1990.

———. "Milton's Transgressive Maneuvers: Receptions (then and now) and the Sexual Politics of *Paradise Lost.*" In *Milton and Heresy,* ed. Stephen Dobranski and John Rumrich. Cambridge: Cambridge University Press, 1998.

———. *Visionary Poetics: Milton's Tradition and His Legacy.* San Marino, Calif.: Huntington Library, 1979.

Woodbridge, Linda. *Women and the English Renaissance: Literature and the Nature of Womankind, 1540–1620.* Urbana: University of Illinois Press, 1984.

Woods, Susanne. Introduction to *The Poems of Aemilia Lanyer.* Women Writers in English, 1350–1850. Oxford: Oxford University Press, 1993.

———. "Women at the Margins in Spenser and Lanyer." In *Worldmaking Spenser: Explorations in the Early Modern Age,* ed. Patrick G. Cheney and Lauren Silberman. Lexington: University of Kentucky Press, 2000.

Index

Abbadie, James, 177

Abel, 126; birth of, 124

Adam: and anti-feminist tracts, 33; birthplace, 28; character, 42–43; on Eve, 34, 38; as father, 124; helpmate search, 35; and monarchical authority, 124; and self-esteem, 221, 222; and structure of universe, 156; views world through sense, 1606; on women, 39. *See also* Adam and Eve; *Paradise Lost*

Adam and Eve: and dominion over children, 129; gazing and political power, 60; and God, 223; and knowledge, 155; and marriage contract, 2, 119, 124, 133; and nature of world, 165; and political theory, 16, 46; relationship of and government authority, 2; and Royal Society, 143; and subjectivity, 13; used to respond to anti-feminist tracts, 24

Adamo Caduto (Salandra), 41, 44

Adamo, L' (Andrieni), 41, 44

Adams, Mary, 97

Adamus Exul (Grotius), 35, 41

"Adventurous Muse, The" (Watts), 187

Aeneid (Virgil), 184

Agrippa, 33, 239n13

Alarum of War, An (Poole): image of physical weakness, 80; language of pregnancy, 96

Amussen, Susan, 45

Andreini, Giambattista, 41, 44, 71

Androgyny, 87

Anger, Jane, 19, 67; and priorities, 34

"Apology for Womankind," 41

Areopagitica (Milton), 155

Armstrong, Nancy: on Locke, 11; Milton as modern author, 10. See also *Imaginary Puritan*

Army General Council, 79, 80

Arraignment of Lewd, Idle, Froward, and unconstant women, The (Swetnam), 19, 21–23; and anti-feminist tropes, 33; Speght on, 29; written to silence women, 38, 39

Astell, Mary, 5, 175, 207; and divine right, 228; Eve's image, 5, 219; and female identity, 14; and female inferiority, 227; freedom of, 174; Garden reconstruction, 204, 217, 228, 233; Genesis language, 218, 229–30, 236; language of choice, 229; and Locke, 232; and marriage, 171–72, 205–7, 216, 231; and Milton, 3, 217; monastery idea, 220; and *Paradise Lost*, 4, 107, 167, 216; and political theory, 11; and Satan, 224; and self-esteem, 221–22; and self-knowledge, 206, 221; and temptation, 220; a Tory, 190, 203; women's appeal, 219; on women's interior self, 217; and women's subjectivity, 14, 205–30

Attaway, Mistress, role of Milton's divorce tracts, 3, 9

Bacon, Francis, 138, 141

Bal, Mieke, 13

Barebones Parliament, 121

Baron, Sabrina, 22

Behn, Aphra, 14, 203, 232, 236, 252n16; family/state analogy, 210, 226; and female subjectivity, 16, 205–30; Garden motif, 204; Genesis motif, 214, 216, 229–30, 233; on incest, 212; lifestyle, 211; and marriage, 171–72, 205–7, 211, 231; and Milton, 3, 5, 171; and *Paradise Lost*, 4, 107, 167, 203; on patriarchal theory, 216; and Satan, 215

Behold, here is a word or, An Answer to the late Remonstrance of the Army (Pope), 103

Belsey, Catherine: on gendering subjectivity, 12; Milton as modern author, 10

Acknowledgments

A book on a "conversation" that I trace between women writers and Milton appropriately had its genesis in many conversations. My graduate students in a 1996 seminar on seventeenth-century writers and *Paradise Lost* were inquisitive, challenging, and innovative, and they allowed me to first perceive the outlines of *Engendering the Fall*. That exchange continued in a 2001 Folger Institute Seminar on Seventeenth Century Women Intellectuals, beautifully organized and orchestrated by David Norbrook. The seminar was also made a particular pleasure by Erin Murphy, Lynn Greenberg, and Kathy Romack, all of whom encouraged this project at a very early stage and have continued to do so. I'm extremely thankful to the Folger Library and the American Society for Eighteenth Century Studies, which funded my participation in that seminar. This productive conversation continued at the Tanner Humanities Center at the University of Utah: they provided me with financial support at the Center and fellowship in every sense of the word during 2001–2002. My special thanks to Shawn Smith, Gene Fitzgerald, Megan Armstrong, Janet Theiss, and particularly Colleen McDannell for making that such a productive and pleasurable year. The UC Davis Renaissance Colloquium, and especially Frances Dolan and Margaret Ferguson, gave wonderful feedback to an early version of Chapter 3 and to the larger project. In the final stages of the book, the Folger Institute and the American Society for Eighteenth Century Studies again made possible my participation in a wonderful seminar on John Locke and his intellectual milieu: I am indebted to John Marshall for bringing Locke's political theory and philosophy into focus for me.

My home institution, Temple University, has also provided generous support for this project, including a Grant-in-Aid in 2002, a Study Leave in 2003–2004, and a Mid-Career Fellowship in Fall 2005. The Center for Humanities at Temple University also provided a supportive intellectual environment for the completion of this project in 2006. Shil Sen, Jed Palmer, Michael Martin, Anna Peak, and Christopher Mote were excellent research assistants during the final stages of completing the book. And the two anonymous readers for the press provided me with extraordinarily detailed and helpful suggestions for improvement.

Yet it is the less formal conversations with scholars that imprint and improve one's work the most. Our Philadelphia WIP (Works-in-Progress) group has been a God-send for this project; thanks to Kathy Rowe, Lauren Shohet, Nora Johnson, Claire Busse, Matt Kuzusko, and Steve Newman for modeling an ideal form of supportive intellectual exchange. Melissa Mowry and Toni Bowers generously welcomed me into a community of late seventeenth-century scholars as I began working with Behn and Astell. Adam Lutzker and Christopher Georges patiently let me reiterate how "It's all in Book 9" while they helped me to see the larger stakes in this project. Heather James turned the gardens of the Huntington Library into the perfect place to think about Milton. And Evelyn Tribble, Michael Gamer, Alan Singer, and Matthew Greenfield have remained supportive colleagues, whether near or far.

My family has always provided wonderful and multifaceted support, whether providing me a place to stay in the Edenic space that is California, paying for long lunches to recover from drafting, or offering proofreading help on the way to the wine country. Finally, thanks to John Roskelley, my partner in all things, whether in the garden, in our own domestic space, or just in conversation.